THE
MASTERFUL
WAY

THE MASTERFUL WAY

THE 5-STEPS OF BEING THE WELL-MANIFESTED LIFE

DANIEL WINGATE

Matador
9 Priory Business Park,
Wistow Road, Kibworth Beauchamp,
Leicestershire. LE8 0RX
Tel: 0116 279 2299
Email: books@troubador.co.uk
Web: www.troubador.co.uk/matador
Twitter: @matadorbooks

ISBN 978 183859 186 1

British Library Cataloguing in Publication Data.
A catalogue record for this book is available from the British Library.

Printed and bound in the UK by CPI Group (UK) Ltd, Croydon, CR0 4YY
Typeset in 11pt Adobe Garamond Pro by Troubador Publishing Ltd, Leicester, UK

Matador is an imprint of Troubador Publishing Ltd

*To expanding the Cause of the Universe
whose only desire is to grow and evolve more Life.
And, to my family and our four-legged fur balls.*

CONTENTS

Introduction

The Masterful Way is intentional, it is deliberate and it is powerful. It is a life of joy and happiness, which is ultimately all any of us seeks. This book is about Mastering this kind of life and you will find this book to be different. What it contains is not new, necessarily, but it is different. It is not another book on the Law of Attraction. Nor is it a treatise on the next generation of New Thought. This is a book about Mastery; the Tool-Set, the Skill-Set and the Mind-Set. It is an in-depth perspective on Universal truths and the Laws governing all energy, which is all and through all. This is a book about the journey of living your highest Self and taking full charge of your Co-Creative power.

I believe most of us have either intentionally, or perhaps unintentionally, given up control over our innate power, over our divinity, in deference to circumstances and forces outside of ourselves. Over time, bit by bit, we have incrementally covered over our divine nature with layer upon layer of junk; the stuff that gets in our way and slows us down. Furthermore, most of us are completely unaware of what this junk is. We know it is there; we feel its weight upon us. We just can't seem to define it, let alone get rid of it.

If all of this stuff is slowing us down, the question becomes, "slowing us down from what?" All of us instinctively know we are on some sort of journey through life, even if our only thought of it is as a journey from birth to death. Regardless, I propose we have got this wrong. We are not on a journey *through* life. Rather, we are on a journey OF Life. Of Being the life we are born to Be. However, all the junk we have accumulated keeps us from manifesting our desires and living our intentions. It shackles us to a millstone of circumstance we try to push up a hill. It stops us from the very thing we all desire; happiness, love, peace and joy, and places it all in a realm just beyond our reach. It is the stuff of doubt, fear, insecurity, complacency and of not taking personal responsibility.

What you will find in this book is the toolset, skillset and mindset of Mastery. In it you will find an unfolding of truths to help you understand the suite of Universal Laws that define all that Is. You will find perspectives on what is actually real and what is not. You will be given tools to help you work with the Universal Laws and how to get out of your own way. Most importantly, this book will help you define your desires and help put you on the road of Mastery. It will help you find your intention and help you remove obstacles, mostly of your own making, and define what it is you uniquely have to say, which benefits us all.

WHAT TO EXPECT

This book is divided into three parts. Part one, The Toolset, presents the groundwork of Mastery. In it I discuss Being, desire, manifestation tools and the constructs of time and truth. In the first two chapters, I present the foundational concepts of Being and the 12 Universal Laws that govern all energy. Chapter 1 introduces Being as the very essence of who we are and what we are all here to say on our journey of life. Being is our power, our uniqueness and our exclusive expression of God, or the Universe, hungry to expand through us. Being is unique to all of us because it defines what we have to say as individualised points within the energy that is the Universe, or the Mind that is God. This introductory chapter explains the many ways we may be inclined to say whatever it is we have to say through what we will come to understand as the Process of desire.

The power of intention and conscious awareness provides the fuel that feeds the Well-Manifested Life. We are all enabled if not encouraged to utilise this power, or we may choose to give it up through unconsciousness. There are consequences for both actions. Intentional use produces intended results. Unintentional use most often produces less than desirable results, or the results we actively do not want in our lives.

In Chapter 1, I begin to discuss fear and the insidious power it can wield over us, if we let it do so. I also begin the discussion on the one true desire all of us are seeking regardless of conscious intention. I further introduce one of the basic manifestation "formulas", and also the most profound. The power of I AM; the power of your word. I AM is your statement to the Universe; the statement of your desires. I AM is the power of intention and the declaration of Truth. It is the structure of Being.

I further provide the framework around which the following chapters are placed and provide the context for what is to follow. I situate the book within this context and provide an explanation of how words, ideas and Processes such as God and the Universe are to be used throughout. I further offer a challenge to those who may struggle with the way in which the ideas and observations are connected together, which definitely flies in the face of traditional views of the sacred as well as the profane. Finally, I set the intent of the entire book itself and offer my desire for its contents to be of use and of help to those of us who are awakening to the possibilities of their own unique Mastery of Being and how to manifest more of it intentionally.

In Chapter 2, Being is defined by what it is and what it is not. All we hope for, believe and want for our lives is true happiness and in this chapter I begin to walk you through the process of helping re-identify the placement of the object of happiness along the journey on which we are all placed. I provide an overview of the suite of 12 Universal Laws that govern all that is energy, which is essentially everything there is. I further categorise these Laws into three distinct groupings, which helps deepen the understanding and use of them. These three groupings are the Primary Laws, the Static Laws and non-static laws, or Laws of Action. The intention of this is to understand how all 12 Universal Laws fit together and why it is important to recognise the necessity of gaining wisdom in all 12 Laws, not simply one in isolation of all the others. These Laws are interdependent and cannot be effectively used or understood outside the Wholeness of them all.

Next I offer what is perhaps the key idea presented throughout this work. *The Process that is God.* I distinguish the Process of God, or the Universe, from any entity outside of ourselves, to that which is a constantly growing, evolving and desiring flow of energy. The Process is the mastermind of all that is, ever was and ever will be. This Process defines the Oneness of the Universe and everything in it, including us. Further I explain our role in this Process of evolution and growth as one of Co-Creation.

Non-resistance is the work of getting out of our own way. It allows the Universe to evolve through us. In this grounding chapter I begin to explain the importance of understanding how working with the 12 Universal Laws is the key to breaking the resistance most of us have spent a lifetime building up and provide the context around why this resistance breaking is hard work. While many manifesting gurus out there profess Mastery is the easiest thing in the world to achieve, a more complete understanding of what is involved in getting to that place of Mastery and ease is provided.

Lastly, the ideas I present to this point are given definitions; definitions about Being and the ultimate goal of happiness. Introduced is the truth about what it means to be what the Bible calls "The Light of the World" and I end this chapter with a set-up for the rest of the chapters to follow, beginning with what it means to desire.

In Chapter 3, I offer a deep dive into the power of desire. Desire is not a hope. It is not a wish, a need or a want. Desire is a passion; a deep, abiding urge. Each desire defines what we have to say and it shapes our experiences, which in turn shapes our Being. I offer a more complete picture of both desire and the manifestation of said desire in our lives, and how we tend to separate desire from its physical manifestation. This does not serve us well. I explain the power of our words and how the use of certain words such as "desire" works with the Universal Laws vibrationally. I pick apart words that are often used as synonyms for desire, such as want, need and wish, then begin the discussion of how the energies of the masculine and feminine play themselves out in the Co-Creative Process of manifestation.

Next, I explain what I believe to be the greatest truth regarding what desire is, where it comes from and its purpose and place in the Process of the evolution and expansion of the Universe. I further develop the idea of emotions, the role they play in the manifestation Process, and how important they are, vibrationally speaking, to either the manifestation of our desires, or the resistance we have to their manifestation in the physical world.

Explained next is one of the most basic manifestation formulas, "ask and receive". It is the second formula presented in the book and the most fundamental of all the methods to be found in the lexicon of manifestation works out there. I further explain how this formula is understood through the Universal Laws, particularly the Law of Gender, and how the energies of the masculine and feminine play within the context of the ask-receive Process which, if not understood properly, curtails the manifestation of our desires or blocks them entirely.

Next I explain the mechanics of the *Process that is God* as It moves through the 12 Universal Laws. I explain the necessity of clarity as it concerns our manifestation efforts and the truth about physically embodying our desires through our Being in the space of the Present/Now. I begin to distinguish the realities of perception, where our Being lies within these realities, and where in the journey all of this belongs.

In Chapter 4, I share the importance of the use of tools as regards the manifestation of our desires. We all use them and we all need them from time to time. Affirmations, vision boards, mind movies, etc. are all tools of the trade, if you will. However, there is a distinguishing feature to all of these tools that is never discussed, in my experience.

While the Universal Laws are scientific, in that they work for everyone the same regardless of how we use them to our advantage, the tools of manifesting, such as those described above, are not scientific. The use of them is a creative art and this, I believe, explains why certain tools work for some and do not work for others.

There are some untold truths about manifestation tools that I go into in some detail in this chapter. I further explain how tools evolve along with us and how they could and should change as we evolve along with the Universe. As we become more proficient at the use of a tool for a particular purpose, we must understand at some point we may evolve past the need for it, much like training wheels on a bicycle. I examine how we must evolve to a point of Being interdependent with not only our tools but with the Universe in the Co-Creative Process.

Next I explain the death knell of all manifestation efforts; doubt. Doubt is the Devil incarnate and in Chapter 4, I detail how doubt should be understood and how its opposite, belief, pushes it out of the way. I discuss the proper use of tools and explore how some tools are not worth the time expended in their use. Certain manifestation tools are little more than energy suckers and do not necessarily do anything to advance our efforts at Mastering Being. I realise this is certainly contrary to what many manifestation leaders out there say, however, there is a very good reason why I believe this to be true and it is in this chapter I explain why.

Finally, I present the first of my own tools provided within this book. In this case, the tool I offer can replace ineffective tools and I encourage you to use it, and the other tools presented, until such time as they no longer serve you.

Chapters 5 and 6 are about time, truth and what is actually real. If it is true that the use of our tools is to help us reduce the resistance we have to manifesting our desires, and if it is true our desires and their manifestation are the happiness we all seek, why do we resist? More importantly, who or what is actually doing the resisting? In Chapter 5, I propose an explanation as to where resistance comes from through an understanding of the three entities involved in our side of the

Co-Creative Process. In order to understand resistance, we have to understand which of these three entities within us is pushing back and how to counter the friction caused.

I explain this cast of characters as your Being, your You and Your Truth. Your Being is the highest Self. Your You is that which was; the sum total of all that has gone before. Your Truth is the entity which, on the surface, seems to be the one causing the friction. All three entities are seeking one thing. Integration into your highest Self; your Being. There is something that often gets in the way, however.

Being is a state of pure non-resistance. In most cases the space between Being and desiring is met with a bit of an argument. This is your Being and Your Truth bumping heads. I explain how all of this works, or how it doesn't work, by a thorough understanding of what is happening within the context of this friction.

Next, I explain the difficulties with understanding another trinity; that of time. I draw a distinction between the past, the present and the future, only one of which exists; the Present/Now. It is this space that encompasses not only our Being, but God or the Universe and all of our desires manifested. It is the only space that is real and it is in this space that the work of Mastery takes place. The past does not exist here and neither does the future. The difficulty in manifesting our desires is most often a case of misplacing our focus on which space our desires occupy. I further explain why it is that the Universal Laws, such as the Law of Attraction, cannot draw anything to you in the two false spaces of past and future.

I further offer the second tool in this book, the tool of clarity. I help run you through an exercise in gaining clarity with whatever it may be that you are desiring and provide an insight as to how the cast of three, your You, your Being, and Your Truth, are operating through this dialogue. I conclude Chapter 5 with a few more exercises and tools that may help you on your journey of Mastery and raise your general vibrational level.

Chapter 6 exposes the truth about Your Truth. In spite of the apparent grief and argument Your Truth is giving your Being as you work through your desires and their manifestation, Your Truth is actually doing you a really big favour. The argument serves a vital purpose and it is in this chapter the purpose is revealed. I also explain a mask Your Truth is wearing, what that mask is made of and how it may be removed in order for you to get clear with your energy. This chapter explains in detail why it is so vital to tune into and engage with the dialogue, or the friction, so clarity may be achieved.

The first six chapters are mainly about a foundational understanding of your Being, what forms it and how it situates within time. With this work in place, Part Two is the skillset. In Part Two I introduce the 5-Step Process of Manifesting a Masterful Life. This section gives us a detailed understanding of how to use these steps and, more importantly, how to identify and rid ourselves of that which gets in our way.

Chapter 7 begins the conversation on providing the space in which to manifest Mastery. It is one thing to have spectacular desires and to manifest Being the one with the objects of those desires. It is another thing entirely to have a space into which these desires may take shape. This can only happen in a clean space; the clean house of your Being.

We all have dirt, junk, dust in the corners of our lives. A large part of our role as Co-Creators is to clean it up if we expect anything deeply and profoundly desirable to manifest through us. Chapter 7 details exactly the need for the clean-up job and begins to explain how to accomplish this task. It is in this chapter I introduce the 5-Step Process of both manifesting and un-manifesting anything we desire. This is the Process of Co-Creation that runs throughout the rest of this book. It is the same Process for those things we are intentionally manifesting and for ridding ourselves of those things that are no longer serving us. Chapter 7 is the key chapter as it relates to The Masterful Way.

In Chapter 8, I detail the importance of being clear on your intentions. Part of achieving a Masterful level of clarity is understanding *why* you desire anything at all. Most of us know what we want, but why do we want it? The why goes deeper than any superficiality surrounding some egoic wanting of something shiny and new. The why is the essence of desire and getting to the why of it is the foundation of true clarity. Without clarity, the Universe cannot Co-Create effectively with us.

I provide an exercise on gaining the clarity of why in this chapter. I expose what happens when we are not clear enough on our desires to the level of a behavioural change that naturally occurs as a result of Being the object of our desires manifested in the Present/Now. I provide an illustration through one of my feel-good movie favourites, *A Field of Dreams* and we take a journey through this film and how it relates to the Universal Laws and the 5-Step manifesting Process.

The themes of the next three chapters are about Maps, Phantoms, and Monsters. These are the Big Three of understanding what gets in the way of manifesting our desires. They are those things which, consciously or not, take our energy away from our intentional manifestation efforts. They are also putting vibrational energy into the Universe, which, according to Law, must bring more of them into our lives even if we are not aware they are there. There are powerful energies attached to our Maps, Phantoms and Monsters, which need to be understood and dealt with if we are to be Masters of Being.

Maps inform the zeitgeist of our Being. Most Maps are sub- or unconscious. Even so, they attract to us that which is on them, whether or not what is on them is benefiting us. Maps are sometimes called our habitual ways of thinking, believing and subsequently behaving. I offer they may be habitual, but they are not ways of thinking. They are mostly ways of not thinking and these ways are examined in Chapter 9.

This chapter scrutinises the mind and the brain. There is only One Mind of which we are all a part; separate entities within It but sharing in the Oneness of It. It is the Mind of God. The mind is emotional; the mind is perceptive; the mind is imaginative and creative; the mind understands. Because it is all of these things, the mind must be consciously controlled; to be consciously focused. We must Master the mind, which is not to say we must Master God. Rather, we must

Master our divine, creative power, the force of which is the mind. In this way we Master the life of intention.

Phantom energy is a Universal principle. It shows up after we un-manifest a monster or update a Map that no longer serves us. Just because we have done the proper work of cleaning up and clearing out our space, ridding ourselves of toxic Maps and monsters, does not mean they go away forever in an instant. They all want to be resurrected and they show up for us as phantoms of their former selves. It can't be helped. Any space we clean out has a potential to be haunted by the phantom energy of the previous occupant of that space and in Chapter 10, I discuss how this whole process works against us and what to do about it.

From the time we were children, we have all been adept at one thing almost universally. We create monsters. Monsters in the closet, under the bed, in the attic and under the stairs. When we were children, they showed up as big, scary, audacious beasts ready to devour us alive, or some other unspeakable horror. All of which we made up: mostly in the dark, mostly with a great deal of imagination and creativity, and always out of fear.

As adults, we have not lost our ability to create monsters. They are no less scary and real to us as those we made up as children. Our adult monsters are scary conversations we are afraid of having. They are those things we make up about people who have wronged us. They are about the perceptions we have of others, of ourselves and what we make up about anything that causes us to fear in some way. They are different from Maps in that they are things we are usually making up in the moment, then pick up and run with. However, like Maps, the energy of a monster is also subject to the same rules of the Universe as anything else. Whatever monster we are making up causes the Universal Laws to kick in, attracting to us whatever the monster is made of, most of which is fear. Chapter 11 explains our propensity for monster making, what it does to our Being and what to do about it. This is further illustrated through the synopsis of another film, *When A Stranger Calls*.

In the three chapters which follow, Chapters 12, 13 and 14, I get into the minutia of cleaning up your house. Even after a good clean, if we do the white glove test, most of us find a finger full of dust on the picture frames. Once the work has begun with our Maps, our monsters and with dealing with our phantoms, these chapters go in for the deep clean. In Chapter 12, I discuss that which is *too small for us*. Those bits and pieces of stuff we push to the back of the closet in the spare room of our house. Those things that no longer fit, are out of style and which accumulate over time slowing down our progress of Mastery. Getting rid of this stuff may not be as involved as un-manifesting a monster, but it does require a large dose of noticing it cluttering up the atmosphere of our Being. Here again, I apply the 5-Step Process to the idea of getting rid of that which is too small.

In the chapter which follows, I walk us through a course with which we are all hard-wired to engage; Judgment. We are in a constant state of judgment and most of it is happening sub- or unconsciously. While we are naturally inclined towards judgment, both positively and negatively, it is like everything discussed in this book. It is about noticing what is going on, when it's going on and how to slow down the unintentional use of our energies so we may place it in the intentional space of Being. This is Mastery.

Any judgment, good or bad, encourages a violation of a Universal Law, a Primary Law at that; The Law of Oneness. Any judgment causes separation. Judgment and separation of any kind puts the breaks on our intentional manifestations. I also expound upon another piece of the manifestation formula. That is the principle of measure. The amount of energy put into judging someone is returned to us in equal measure by the Law of Compensation. This is because by the Law of Oneness, when we judge someone else, we are in fact judging ourselves. It is also true by the same Law that in the measure of goodness and blessing we bestow upon another, it too is returned to us in kind. It is the Law and this chapter goes into the details of how all of this works and how to shift our judgmental thoughts and feelings.

Chapter 14 exposes a hidden piece of the manifestation formula that is often left out of the mix. While most of us are familiar with the bulk of the formula of believe and receive, which is vital to Being the physical manifestation of our desires, there is something often overlooked. This chapter is about the power of forgiveness. The idea of forgiveness carries a lot of energy associated with religion, which many of us shy away from, yet it is a vital piece of the manifestation process and cannot be ignored. In this chapter I work us through some other emotionally charged words such as sin, transgression and atonement, the understanding of which is deeply profound as it relates to Mastery and the Universal Laws.

Forgiveness is a vital component in the cleaning up of our house. In this chapter I share a very personal story of forgiveness and how participating in the actions associated with it ratcheted up my manifestation powers exponentially. My intention is that by using the 5-Step Process as it relates to forgiveness, it can do the same for you. I further discuss the three entities in the construct of forgiveness. These are the person who needs to forgive, the person who needs to be forgiven and the person who needs to forgive themselves.

Part Three details the mindset of Mastery. While the other two parts are mostly about defining, situating and cleaning up unwanted junk, the chapters that make up Part Three are about Being a Masterful Manifestor. By using the 5-Step Process and ridding ourselves of the stuff that gets in our way, we are in a much more powerful state of Being the physical manifestation of that which we Desire. This becomes our mindset.

Chapter 15 explores another big piece of the Universal Laws of manifestation. Blooming where you are planted. All desires can be thought of as seeds and for the most part, all seeds are the same. They work in the same way regardless of what kind of seed they are. Given the right conditions, they sprout, grow and produce a harvest. Said in our manifestation language, we plant a desire with the Universe, we nurture it through our Being and it produces a harvest of its physical manifestation. This begs the question, why don't all seeds of desire produce equally?

In this chapter I explain the power of the soil. While all seeds are theoretically equal, all soils are not. This is where Co-Creating through the Mastery of our Being is engaged. If we do not do the work of cleaning up that soil, getting rid of the junk, weeds and stones, the Universe can only do so much. We are *Co-Creators*, after all. We need to work with the Process and this chapter explains how.

The last two chapters detail the most important elements of Mastery. Chapter 16 is about another Universal principle with which so many of us struggle. I felt it impossible to put a book like this together without discussing it. This is *patience* and without it, we blow through a lot of unnecessary energy chasing our desires around when in fact the Universe is trying to tell us to let It do Its job. In this chapter I discuss letting go of the manifestation of our desires in the exact way we may have in mind for them to manifest. This is not counterintuitive. It is not passive. It is actually a very powerful and active practice and one that requires conscious exercise.

Patience is an Activity of trust and belief. Without trust and belief, our Being is without power. We must trust and have absolute faith in our Being the manifestation of our desires in the Present/Now if we expect to manifest our desires physically. In this chapter I share another of my tools towards this end. It is a tool in noticing just how the Universe, or God, is working towards Co-Creating our desires. We have to understand our limited thinking about the actual object of our desires. The way we perceive them may not be the most efficacious for us. The Universe may manifest something far better and in a much better way than how we think of them manifesting. The exercise provided will help build those patience and noticing muscles.

Finally, I conclude this book with a chapter devoted to gratitude. It is the final piece of The Masterful Way. Gratitude is the lubricant to our Being. It is a powerful tool and a powerful force not to be ignored. There is a physiological response to deep gratitude, which produces a chemical bonding to the object of our desires. It also feels good, which is another strong emotion the Universe responds to very favourably.

In this final chapter, I discuss the relationship between fear and gratitude, again, both of which are powerfully charged. Gratitude is a form of love and true gratitude produces the same feel-good chemicals in our brain as love and sex. It is in the space of love our intentional desires are made manifest. It is also in this space that fear, doubt and disbelief cannot enter. By keeping ourselves in the space of gratitude, we are immune to any of these negative emotions for as long as we remain in it. It is also a part of the Process that is God operating through us as It evolves and expands through our unique expression. It is gratitude that keeps us in the space of receiving the manifestation of our Being. Gratitude is the language of the Universe and without it, Mastery is impossible.

It is my most sincere desire that by reading and taking into your own Being some of what is taught in this book, you become better equipped for Mastery. By so doing, you raise the vibrational level of us all and, by implication, the vibrational level of the Universe; of God. This is the greatest joy there is.

So, turn the page and get going on building your Mastery. Begin the journey of Being a life of intention. Do it for yourself and no one else. Do it through yourself and no one else. Believe me, we will all benefit. We are all One energy. Now get busy, get out of your own way and Master the Co-Creative Process of Being. What are you stumbling over? What is slowing you down and keeping you from Being? More importantly, what do you truly desire? Turn on the lights and ask yourself, "What do I have to say?"

PART ONE: THE TOOLSET

THE MASTERFUL WAY

THE MASTERY OF BEING

THE MASTERY OF DESIRE

THE MASTERY OF YOUR TOOLS

THE MASTERY OF TIME

THE MASTERY OF TRUTH

In Part One we explore the toolset of Mastery; the very basics of Desire. We uncover core truths about fundamental elements of Being the Well-Manifested Life and lay the foundation for understanding and applying the 5-Step Process of Mastery which follows.

Chapter One

The Masterful Way

If you read the introduction, then let's continue with a few questions. If you did not, you can either go back and read it, or start here by asking…

What is it you desire to be more than anything else? Without any restrictions, what is it you have to say with your life? What gives you joy? What do you absolutely have to do, have to be, and have to accomplish in this lifetime?

Not clear? Let's try it from a different perspective. How about these questions…

What is getting in your way? What is slowing you down? What are you afraid of or what are you hiding behind? What are you faking? What are you making up? How are you contributing to the very thing you are complaining about? What is too small for you and why do you hold on to it? Isn't it time to turn on the lights and have a good look around? What do you need to clean up?

These questions and more like them define what this book is all about. This Masterful Way is a journey of intention, of purpose, of meaning and of passion. It is through the Mastery of this journey that each and every one of us unfolds that inimitable *something we have to say,* something we have to Be, to manifest, to deliver to the Universe or, more aptly, something for the Universe to deliver through us. What this something is lies at the very core of who we are. It is the music born within us. It is that great potential inside all of us. It is our reason for, what we will come to understand as, our Being. It is what gives the human side of our existence its divinity. By truly living our Being-ness, we manifest through our lives that which is *what we have to say.*

Therefore, Being is our meaning. It is our calling; our passion; our bliss; our truth. It is our true desire. It is that feeling we are here to be more than the way we are currently showing up. Because if we were truly Being that, we wouldn't be manifesting that feeling. Being is expressing our desires. This expression is sometimes called talent, or natural inclination, aptitude or gift. It has been called our mission, our dream. Whatever it may be called, that *whatever-it-is* is our own, individualised expression of the Universe, unique to each one of us and all of It is hungry to be articulated. The music needs to be played and you are the instrument to play it.

We intrinsically know we are this individualised expression. It is what Robert Browning called "the spark". We know we have it. We all have experienced the clarity of its presence at some point in our lives; its tug; its calling. Some of us, too few perhaps, heed this calling and those who do, take it up and run with it. Some of us may have felt its calling once then forgot about it, put it away or buried it deep inside. It's still there. It never goes away. But the question is, exactly what is behind that which is yearning to be expressed through us? What is it behind that which wells up from within and calls to us? Where did it come from? More importantly, where is it going?

The Universe and everything in It is in a constant state of expression; of growth and evolution. Just look around and see in how many ways It is doing just that. The Universe is everywhere and is everything within and without. It is manifesting Itself into form, then out of form again. Then re-manifesting more of Itself through differing and various other forms of Itself. This expression in and out of form is what we will call the Divine Process and it is through this Process the Universe is Being what is referred to as "God".

Through us, this Process is energised through one vehicle and one vehicle only. It is desire. Desire is the impetus behind anything. From the Universal perspective, it may be said the only desire of the Universe is to grow and evolve. It is desire through which the Process evolves more Life in whatever form into which It manifests. It is this same Process which desires to be expressed uniquely through each one of us. It is this Process which calls us and which initiates all of our own desires within us. Through our desires made manifest we evolve into who we are all here to Be, which is what we have to say. It is through this Process the Universe grows and expands more Life. Simply put, desire is the Process of the Universe seeking to experience and express more Life through us; to evolve.

UNIVERSAL DESIRE

As far as we currently know, we are the highest form of consciousness through which this Process can express Itself physically, spiritually, mentally and emotionally. This is because we are endowed with individualised awareness. We know that we are ourselves. We are both conscious and self-conscious. We have a brain, a mind, a soul – we have intelligence – and we all have desire. All of these elements mould our Being and give shape to our unique expression of the Universal. Each Being is endowed with a voice, an avenue if you will, through which we are to provide this expression. And, because we are these things and more, the Universe Itself can experience more conscious and self-conscious awareness through us.

There is no greater emotion than love. It is within the space of love our intentional desires are made manifest. Love is the foundation for the greatest longing we all have and crave to experience. It is the *only* longing we have, really. This is happiness, peace, joy and love.

Happiness is all that we seek. Happiness is at the core of our Being. The reason we do anything, want anything, or want to Be anything is for the sake of happiness. It is for the sake of happiness we and the Universe manifest desire.

We will get into the intricacies of desire in a later chapter but for now, think about it this way. True desire is the Process of the Universe seeking expression and expansion through us. The Process of expression culminates in the manifestation of the desire, which promotes happiness. This is a Co-Creative Process and because it is Co-Creative, it is what gives us our divinity. As the desired is made manifest, the experience of the Process expands God, or the Universe. Whatever the desire may be, the experience of manifesting it allows the Universe to experience it as well. When we experience having it, we are then Being the physical manifestation of the desire. The Effect of this manifestation Process is what we all seek; happiness, peace, joy and love.

Because each one of us is a unique expression of the Universe, then logically each one of us must possess a unique *way* of Being that is perfectly honest to this expression. This is a Universal principle. If we are resistance free, the Universe easily finds the voice through which It may manifest Itself, Co-Creatively, through our Being. If there is resistance, It cannot grow and evolve. It cannot manifest Its desired form. The more resistance there is to the Process seeking expression through us, the more we ourselves cease to Be and are condemned to merely exist. Mere existence is the cessation of the Divine, Co-Creative Process through us. It is extinction. If It cannot Process through our individualised expression, whatever that expression is goes extinct.

By now, it is commonly accepted that *everything is energy*. Energy is all and through all and is in a constant state of flux. Energy is Life. It never ends. It never begins. It is never made. It is never destroyed. It is never not. It is always. Energy is the Universe and therefore, energy is God. We are made of energy, as is everything else. This makes us individualised points within the greater consciousness known as God.

By Its own nature, the Universe is an expressive force; a creative force; a feeling force. The force is with us, in us, and *is us* always. Through us, any true desire we have means we are called to be divine Co-Creators. Desire fuses together our creative divinity with that of the Universal creative expression further expanding the Process that is God. Our desires and our manifestations are at the borderland of the Universe Processing Its evolution and through us It becomes the powerful *Presence of Being*, what is called "I AM". I AM is the Universal statement of Being and it is our model of Being as well.

The Intention of Being

> God said to Moses, "I AM WHO I AM. This is what you are to say to the Israelites: 'I AM has sent me to you'."
>
> Exodus 3:14 NIV

I AM is the very model of intention, and it is this first model our Being must follow if we are indeed to Be Masterful. I AM proclaims Being the intention of our desires. The declaration of I AM is the announcement of its reality. "I AM a musician. A musician is what I have to say." "I AM a sculptor. A sculptor is my unique expression." "I AM a teacher," "I AM a dog walker." It doesn't matter. I AM is the statement of power and intention that springs from the Co-Creative, Universal desire. Each one of us is an I AM seeking expression through what each of us is here to say.

We, the most conscious expression and highest form of Universal consciousness, seem to struggle with understanding just how powerful we are, *with or without intention*. Our power is Divine power and some of us are afraid of it. Many of us make ourselves wilfully ignorant or wilfully unconscious of it. We try to ignore or hide away our unique expression of Power by surrendering or rejecting our Being. We reject the intentional for the unintentional. This can only provide the opposite of that which all desire; the opposite of happiness. It is the unintentional pathway of being which surrenders to external circumstances upon which are blamed the very suppression of the unique expression we ourselves gave up willingly or otherwise.

From beginning to end, from cradle to grave and beyond, we are all trying to say what we have to say, or express what we have to express. We crave it. We hunger and thirst after it. It is called a hunger of the soul. It *must* come forth in some way. It must manifest. It is sometimes called a "black hole" inside us and it must be filled with something.[1] Those who are aware willingly provide the expression, while others fight against it. Those who choose the latter opt to lock away their Being behind layer and layer of stuff. Whether by cloistering it away out of fear, or by an unintentional and unconscious resistance, the stuff begins to fill that hole and, by default, squelch our happiness. But, it doesn't go away. Browning wrote that the spark within us may never be completely extinguished or hidden regardless of how hard we choose to believe otherwise.

Our unique expression is always there, trying to get out and to be articulated in whatever modality it is so inclined. For as little regard it may be given by some, that expression is the Source of our power.

The Kabbalists tell us of "the lost word", the word of power which mankind has lost. To him who discovers this word all things are possible... It is indeed true that the "lost word" is the one most familiar to us, ever in our hearts and on our lips. We have lost, not the word but the realization of its power. And as the infinite depths of meaning which the words I AM carry with them open out to us, we begin to realize the stupendous truth that we are ourselves the very power which we seek.

Thomas Troward[2]

"We are ourselves the very power we seek." That's a profound truth. It doesn't come from outside of ourselves. It doesn't come from some image of God in Heaven. That power remains as close to us as the atoms and molecules from which we are formed. It is never truly lost. It is always there. It has to be. It is locked in the very DNA of our physical, spiritual, and emotional Being. We may just choose to "forget" about it, and for that there are consequences.

For those of us who choose to forget, the power of our Being becomes unrecognisable to us. It becomes an alien, a thing lurking in the shadows; a foreign invader. We don't understand its language. We don't understand how it moves; how it thinks, where it is going, what it is doing and why it is always, always following us. The fear pulls us into the darkness with it and we become more afraid. We react by hiding or we attack.

When our Being is cloistered away, this fight-or-flight reaction often shows up in very negative ways. That "black hole" gets filled up with alcoholism, drugs, addictions, depression, divorces, marriages, offences, defences, sex addiction, shop-a-holism, celebrity worship, or artificial personas which we try to adopt as our own to mantle over that which is aching to be set free. This serves nothing other than to increase our fear causing us to supress it even more. We push it away; hide it in the deeper recesses of our selves, which uses up a lot of precious energy – our power. Our Being, which is our true Self, is held prisoner by the unconscious, unintentional self and we wonder why we are so unhappy.

Jim Carrey, the American actor, comedian, and entertainer tells a story about his father, Percy, and growing up in Canada. He refers to his father as a very funny and talented man; not surprisingly so. Jim tells us his father was a fantastic saxophonist with his own band in Toronto and *would have been* quite successful had it not been for one thing.

He tells us the thinking of the time was that in order to "make it big" in Canada in that sort of business you had to prove yourself in the United States first. With a growing family to support, Percy was afraid of making such a huge, life-altering commitment. So, he became an accountant. This is not to say he did the wrong thing. There is no right and wrong here. He just made a decision and that decision took a toll – it had consequences.

Jim Carrey says his father's choice to chuck it all and compromise for the so-called security of accounting wore on him greatly especially when, in his fifties, he lost his accounting job, a job he did not love – it wasn't what he had to say. Jim says he became bitter and regretful as life wore on him; a very painful place to be. The lesson he offers is this. Even if we fail at something we do not love, it is far more painful than failing at something we do love, because even if we so-called fail, we are Being in love with the Process. So, do what you love. In other words, say what you are here to say. Be it. Master it. It is your unique expression.

I believe Percy had his "something to say". His unique I AM. His expression of Being was through his music and the saxophone. His band was his desire manifesting, growing and evolving. However, fear covered it up and he buried it deep inside but it still yearned to be let out. By supressing it, it seeped out as bitterness and regret. This kind of thing happens so often to so many of us. Our true Self; our Being; our expression cannot be got rid of. It must come forwards in some way and unless given the expressive outlet it needs, it will show up in some other way which is often unpleasant – again, consequences.

The story above highlights a very important point. What anyone has to say may not always be "said" or "spoken". Some of us, like Percy, play the saxophone and have a band. Some of us say it by building empires like Richard Branson or building cookbooks and bake-off's like Mary Berry. Some of us dance it like Darcy Bussell, some of us sing it like Whitney Houston and some of us dream it like Martin Luther King, or innovate it like Walt Disney. Some write it like J. K. Rowling and inspire it like Maya Angelou. Some paint it. Some climb it, some play it, some teach it. Some cook it, some eat it, some build it, some knock it down. We plant it, drive it, read it, colour it, run it, ski it, lift it… you name it. What is common to all of these Beings is intention.

Those who are on the intentional journey, Masterfully expressing their I AM, those who know what they have to say and are willing to say it, are those in whom we find inspiration. We are drawn to them, magnetically. Their Being-ness shows; It produces; It grows and It evolves the Universe. They are those who make big differences in small places and small differences in big places. They are those who are both inspiring and who are themselves inspired. They are called those with gifts, or talent, or genius, or charm, or magnetism or personality. They are those who vibrate somehow differently, and we are captivated by them. Yet, they make up such a small percentage of us, which is profoundly sad. The truth is we ALL have this power within us; we are the power we seek. The power *is* us and we are supposed to Be all we came into this world to Be.

> *The first rule is to obey your genius. All men and women have their inheritance, their share of the divine.*
>
> Ralph Waldo Emerson

I have a very dear friend with whom I have been friends for many years. Her I AM is a musician; a pianist and an organist and she's brilliant at both. She has made a living by the piano and the organ, playing for musical theatre, auditions, rehearsals, weddings, funerals, birthdays, bar and bat mitzvas, and any other avenue in which she may express her Being-ness. She gives lessons, accompanies soloists, plays for choirs, churches, schools and composes her own music to this day. Well into her nineties, one could say she knows her stuff. Her Being has something to say through music and it is finding Its expression through her.

From a very young age, her unique expression of the Universe was bursting to get out and evolve Itself. She tells of her early childhood when her brother was given piano lessons in their home. It was my friend who, at around the age of four, with each lesson her brother learned on the piano, would walk right over to the instrument and play the piece by ear. Each lesson her brother received was instantly memorised and performed as if she had been given the lesson herself and had the opportunity to practise it to perfection. Her parents had to finally make the decision to give her piano lessons as well, fearing she would develop a habit of knowing only how to play by ear and of never learning how to read music. Without doubt, she has something to say as a unique expression of the Universe experiencing Being a musician through her and she is a Master of the Way. Furthermore, she is a Master because she works on it. She practises nearly every day!

The story is told of Gandhi who, compelled by something deep within, started and won a movement for Indian independence from the British in 1947. Through non-violent civil disobedience, he continues to inspire freedom movements across the globe even today, long after his death. The Gandhi that was Being the unique expression of the Universe had something to say and manifested it through that Being-ness.

I am doing this because a voice within me speaks.

Gandhi

He remains one of the most referenced and inspiring models of civil rights we have ever known.

Nelson Mandela said, "There is no passion to be found playing small – in settling for a life that is less than the one you are capable of living." His Being, his I AM, was to be a force to end apartheid. If Nelson Mandela was not clear on what he had to say, he could not possibly have survived twenty-seven years in prison, through torture, beatings and solitary confinement, to come out of it all as the inspiring leader we know him to have been.

If you watch any of the talent search shows; *America's Got Talent* or *Britain's Got Talent,* for example, once in a while someone comes along that absolutely, drop-the-mike smashes it. In spite of outward appearances and all that they seemingly have against them, the minute they open their mouths, what they have to say is clear. It moves the house, and it moves us while we sit in our living rooms, far removed by time and space. This is because what they have to say is true to their Being which means it's true to our own Being-ness, otherwise – and here is an important point – it wouldn't resonate with us.

As I write this, a contestant on the American version of the talent show in question recently got his moment in the spotlight. The clip currently circulating like wildfire on Facebook, Instagram, Twitter and the dozens of other social media outlets plays out his audition and it currently has millions of views.

Being led out on stage by his mother is a young man using a guide cane. Within seconds, we can see he is clearly disabled. The irony here is, he can't see that. His mother holds the microphone to his mouth as the judges begin to ask him the usual string of questions. "Who are you?" "How old are you?" "What are you going to do for us today?" As the young man answers each question, it becomes more clear by his speech, blindness is not the only handicap he is experiencing. He struggles with articulating the answers to each inquiry. When he is finally led to the piano… yes, he will accompany himself…he sits at it, and a hush comes over the crowd.

He begins to play. He plays each chord of the accompaniment perfectly. His body begins to change somehow, morphing into some other being right in front of us. His posture changes. His energy shifts and becomes brighter. He opens his mouth to sing and what comes out of it is not the voice of the young, autistic blind man we saw at the beginning of his audition. It is the voice of a young man whose Being is a deeply talented musician and singer who fills that Beingness to the rafters of the fully-packed auditorium in Los Angeles, and through the ethers into our living rooms. He receives a standing, tear-jerking and highly emotional ovation. We are all moved. After the thunderous applause finally dies down, and the judges try and articulate what they just witnessed, he gets the Golden Buzzer sending him straight through to the semi-finals of the show, and rightly so.

WHAT IS TO FOLLOW

What you are about to read is not another book about the Law of Attraction. It is far more. This book is about an incredible journey of Being a Well-Manifested life. But more importantly, it is about uncovering what you have to say. It was born out of a synthesis of the many tools I have used over many years and the evolution of those tools through my own experience. It was formed out of the words and works of many of my teachers such as Ernest Holmes, Napoleon Hill, Wallace Wattles, and Thomas Troward just to name a few, and to whom I remain eternally grateful. This book adapts themes and ideas from many different resources and religions such as Judaism, Christianity and Buddhism. From ancient, as well as more modern philosophies, and Universal truths. It includes references taken from Jungian Psychology, the Kabballah, Mindfulness, meditative practices, personal observation, Shakespeare, the Peanuts, and Doctor Seuss. There is a great value in all of these resources and more besides.

If you follow a particular religious practice, nothing here *should* interfere with any of that. And, by the way, nothing here should interfere with *not* having a religion or religious inclination. Either way, it doesn't really matter. Furthermore, you do not have to form a belief or anti-belief system around any of the ideas which follow or the resources from which they came. They just are. The principles gleaned from resources such as the Bible are stable and true enough to have been said or expressed in much the same way throughout time religiously and culturally for millennia. Jesus said it. Buddha said it before him. Pythagoras said it before both of them. Rumi. Khalil Gibran. Aldous Huxley, Einstein, Emerson, Newton, Tesla, Thoreau… the list goes on. They all said very similar things about the Universe in ways that were unique to their expression of Being. They all spoke of these Universal truths in their own way. So why so many *versions* of the same Truth? There is, I believe, a good and logical reason.

> *The shoe that fits one person pinches another; there is no recipe for living that suits all cases.*
>
> Carl Jung

I believe the Universe gives us so many versions because we all hear things in a different way and at different times. When people are ready to receive, the messenger will express and the message will find them. I realise that statement is a bit clichéd, however the truth is no two people are exactly the same. We may speak the same words, but we all speak different, individualised languages. We may see the same things, but we all have different lenses through which we experience the things we see. One person's language or lens may be *similar* to a lot of other people's, but every one of us has our own unique way of understanding. We all vibrate differently from one another, which is what makes us unique. It only makes sense the Universe would give us a variety of ways of knowing Its Truths. One way can be right and resonate for millions, another for dozens, and another for one or two. The point is, we all have something to say from which we all benefit one way or another. So, this is my version of Universal Truths and my desire in Co-Creating it is that it will resonate with you.

What is to follow is frankly nothing new. It never has been. It is not the next version of New Thought. It isn't the next generation of mysticism. It isn't the missing link in the Law of Attraction people seem to be so keen to find lately. You probably won't find the exact formula, or the right word order of the next great incantational affirmation here to suddenly make it all work for you. If you are open to it, however, you very well could and should find something contained herein to indeed make it all work for you. My intention is that something here may help you on your Masterful Way.

All of this is about Being the Self you truly are. This is not the Self you are *becoming*. That which you are becoming implies a Self that is stuck in a future place which doesn't yet exist. The Self you truly are is also not a made-up Self you are *trying* to be; some mask you are wearing hoping to fool the Universe. It is also not forcing the Universe to bend Its power to the force of your will. It doesn't work that way. The Self you truly are is the intentional manifestation of your unique expression. It is your Truth. And, not to drop too big of a bombshell this early on, it *does take some effort to expose it*, in spite of what many manifesting authorities out there may say. Here is the good news about that, however. *Almost all the effort of The Masterful Way is simply getting out of your own.* And, keep in mind, this is the

Way OF Mastery, not the Way TO Mastery. The Being part is the easy bit. Mastery takes a little work.

Lastly, I want to frame what is to follow properly, so you don't close yourself out of any lessons which may be waiting to reveal themselves to you. In the following pages there are a few things to keep in mind. I use the terms God, the Universe, Spirit, Energy, Source, Law and other such familiar references *interchangeably*. I believe these terms are all describing the same thing. These words are simply labels for a force that is deeply profound and profoundly simple. I am a Buddhist, however I pull references from the Bible frequently as I am smart enough to know it is one of the best collections of Universal truths around, in spite of its being so misused and misunderstood. The Bible itself is not "religious" – it is just another label.

In fact, I pull apart and re-perceive many Biblical references, the majority of which have been the source of what has caused many of us so much disappointment and angst around all things "religious". I synthesize bits and pieces from a dozen or more other resources as well and use them interchangeably because they are *all saying the same thing*. If there is something in the following pages that causes something to come up for you, I offer this challenge.

My friendly advice is, "snap out of it!" Stop resisting something that will only work for you if you'll just stop making something wrong about it. Now, my coaching advice is this. If you do trip over some reference, or some manner in which certain concepts are strung together, or over whatever reference source from which it may have been gleaned, think about it from this perspective. Whatever it is, or whatever you make up about it, it just *may be* the Universe tapping you on the shoulder, whispering in your ear telling you to take the time to explore whatever it is you stubbed your toe on. It just may be Your Truth calling out to you to stop wasting your power fighting against something you haven't really grasped yet. I would suggest you go with that. You may be ready for some growth. Take it.

Take some time to examine whatever pinched you. Do so through your Being; do so through your Truth. In my experience once you get pinged, it generally means you are due for a little evolution. Take that step. It is a step in the Masterful direction. Whether you go with it now, or go with it later, I am confident that lesson will find you again. Somewhere, someday, somehow, the Universe will set it up for you and, hopefully, you will grab it and go with it the next time.

Your journey of Mastery must be expressed in absolute truth and belief; your I AM. If so done, the Universe, and all of us who are Co-Creating it along with you, will finally be privileged to experience it and it will bring us all joy, happiness and peace, so long as it brings these emotions to you. This is, after all, why we are here. It is why I AM here. It's just the way it works. So, this is *my* voice. This is a part of my Being and a lesson I have to share from my own Way of Mastery. I invite you to take this journey with me because, *I have something to say*.

And so do you…

Chapter Two

The Mastery of Being

Being is the general concept encompassing objective and subjective features of reality and existence. Anything that partakes in being is also called a "being", though often this usage is limited to entities that have subjectivity (as in the expression "human being"). The notion of "being" has, inevitably, been elusive and controversial in the history of philosophy...[1]

Part One of this volume has to do with understanding the tools of Mastery. Any set of tools needs a toolbox and the toolbox in this case is the following foundational truth. The Masterful Way of Being the Well-Manifested Life has no destination point. It has no finish line. You don't get to cross it and get your prize. There is no "The End" like the final frames of a film or the last page of a book.

Don't let this scare you. This is not to say The Masterful Way has no purpose. The Way of Being is not an aimless journey so long as you travel with *intention*. It is Being OF the Way, not ON the Way. It is also about not getting IN your own way. Those who travel along by default are adrift, wandering a darkened road looking for that illusive end point, or even beginning point, neither of which exists. By so doing, they miss out on the intentional journey we are all here to Master by stumbling around in the dark.

As with all things in the Universe, this journey has two directions opposite each other by Law. On one side we have the true state of Being, which is conscious, intentional and purposeful Mastery. The other condition is what we will call a state of *becoming*. It is a less conscious state, far less intentional, and bound to a destination in some future so-called reality.

THE STATE OF HAPPINESS

Whether one is on the intentional pathway, or the unintentional one, each traveller is seeking the exact same thing, but is going about it in vastly different ways. The object sought after is the most desired condition of all. It is happiness; it is peace, it is joy, it is love. This is the true object of any and all desire. It is the only desire of the Universe of which we are an integral part.

To begin with, we must create a distinction between happiness and pleasure, and the objects and artefacts which tend to define them. Happiness is internal – it is the stuff of Being and living that which is *what you have to say*. Happiness is what we will call "the object". Pleasure is generated from external sources and it is most often defined by what we will call "artefacts". Artefacts are corporal and temporary. Those who are Being the individualised expression of the Universe expanding and evolving are naturally in a state of happiness, peace, joy and love. Those who are becoming are confusing happiness with pleasure and mistaking one for the other; mistaking artefacts with the true object. In addition to the error of artefact versus object, they misplace where the object itself lives.

To understand the distinction between Being and becoming, one must understand the placement of the object of happiness. Intentional

Mastery recognises the object of happiness as a natural state; the *result* or the Effect of consciously Being, which is the Cause. It is contained and released through the Process of all desires made manifest in the space of the Present/Now. Happiness, peace, joy and love are an inner state of Being, which is reflected in the outer world of physical existence. This, too, is by Law.

What we call *becoming* seeks happiness outside of itself. Becoming tends to believe happiness occurs by a different result. As the by-product of something, of some event, or of some time when some *one* manifests into the lives of those on this road. Becoming believes there is an artefact that must manifest before the true object of desire, happiness, is experienced. The artefact manifested produces pleasure, in this case. Because the two emotions are similar in feeling, this is how happiness and pleasure get all muddied up. While the sensations are similar, pleasure is always relatively short-lived.

Becoming carries a big stick from which is dangled a big carrot. It tempts with a false vision of happiness that lies at the end of the string. Becoming is mistakenly guided by the thought that if and when that carrot is caught, happiness will be achieved. Happiness will *become* real. The object in this case becomes an artefact. If the artefact is not caught, happiness remains elusive; out of reach. Therefore, the carrot, the stick, the road they are on, as well as any other external circumstance, may be faulted or blamed for the artefact of happiness being out of reach. This is sometimes called fate.

> *At a certain point in our lives, we lose control of what's happening to us, and our lives become controlled by fate. That's the world's greatest lie.*
>
> Paulo Coelho[2]

By this way of thinking, if the artefact of happiness lies at the end of the journey, then the time spent on the journey itself is time not spent in the state of happiness, peace, joy and love. The road can be long and the journey may take some so-called linear time. A year on the journey to have an hour of happiness at the end is far less desirable than a year *plus that hour* spent with joy by virtue of Being on the journey. Through the Mastery of intentional Being, we will come to learn happiness is the *journey itself because it lives in the Present/ Now.* Through desire, we experience happiness every step of the way of its manifestation. This is the distinguishing shift in the perception of the object. It is this perspective which distinguishes Being from becoming.

Through our desires, thoughts, actions, emotions and focus, we are manifesting either intentional Being or the unintentional becoming each and every day. Those of us who have awakened to Being conscious of certain Universal Truths, understand we Co-Create our own life experiences. We are the power we seek. Intentional or not, our thoughts, actions, emotions, focus and desires are the conduit by which we manifest things, people, situations, experiences etc., into our lives. The only difference between the intentional and the unintentional versions is in the perspective and the placement of the object of happiness.

Let us use a common example; money. For those *becoming*, the focus on the object of happiness is seen through two obstacles in front of it. One obstacle is the future; the other is the artefact of money. Once that obstacle is conquered, happiness ensues, or so it is believed. For those intentionally Being, a desire for money isn't a desire for the artefact itself. Being Mastery is a state in which money has already manifested in the Present/Now vibrationally, so the joy of having it is to be lived in this space. The focus flips from the artefact of money to the state of Being. The object is happiness, not the artefact of money. The object is joy, not the artefact of a big home. The object is peace, not in obtaining the artefact of a great relationship and a lovely family. While all of these desires provide a channel *through which happiness IS*, the physical manifestation of the artefact of a desire is not where happiness lives. It is the journey of it and Mastery of the Process.

"I will be happy with a truck load of money in my bank account." "I will be happy when I have that big home." "I'll be happy when I am in a great relationship." "I will be happy when I have a better job." This cart-before-the-horse logic is a broken construct – it always has been. It is not the manifestation of the artefact that ignites happiness; it is the road of its manifestation. Happiness, peace, joy, love etc. cannot be found at the end of some finish line, as a prize to be had once you have broken through the tape. It is in the running of the race.

TRUTHS AND LAWS

So, before moving on, there are a few suppositions or truths to be made which will be vital to understanding the remaining content of this book. The first assumption is that everything is energy. Energy is power. The Mastery of Being is to understand the power of energy, which is to understand the power of everything. Wisdom of how energy works is the key to using this power intentionally. The second supposition is to understand the power by which this energy is governed is through certain principles or Laws of the Universe. The most familiar of which in our Westernised culture is the Law of Attraction, and in more Eastern cultures, the Law of Cause and Effect. The Law of Attraction in particular has received a great deal of attention in the last several decades. However, this Law is just one of the 12 Universal Laws which unite together to construct the Process that is God or the Universe expanding and evolving more of Itself. And, with the Co-Creative Process It evolves us along with it.

THE 12 UNIVERSAL LAWS

Primary Laws of the Universe	Static Laws	Actionable Laws
The Law of Divine Oneness The Law of Perpetual Transmutation of Energy	The Law of Polarity The Law of Gender The Law of Rhythm The Law of Attraction The Law of Cause and Effect	The Law of Relativity The Law of Compensation The Law of Action The Law of Vibration The Law of Correspondence

THE PRIMARY LAWS OF THE UNIVERSE

1. The Law of Divine Oneness – This Law acknowledges the Oneness of all things energy. Since energy is all things and all things are energy, all things are One. Everything is connected to everything else, seen and unseen, through all dimensions, physical and non-physical. Every person, every living thing, every "non-living" thing. All is One. This is the Law that describes what we will call the nature of God Itself.

2. The Law of Perpetual Transmutation of Energy – Energy is in constant motion moving in and out of form. Energy is never created nor destroyed. It is the substance of *Oneness*, or the substance of the nature of God. Combined with the Law of Oneness, these two Primary Laws are the Process of God, or the Universe, manifesting Its Being as It evolves ever forward.

Static Laws

3. The Law of Polarity – Everything has an opposite state or, as it is sometimes described, a polar opposite. There is both an up and a down. There is both a right and a left. There is both a bad and a good. What is between the two opposites, or extremes, is simply varying degrees of each. Distinguishing where one extreme begins and the other ends on the pole or plane of varying degrees is not possible. The extremes are on opposite ends of *one* pole or plane. Therefore, the extremes are literally One and the same thing. There are two ends to a stick, for example, but no matter what end you are holding, you are still holding a stick. The degrees in between merely provide distinguishing characteristics of their own polar opposites along the Oneness of the pole or plane.

   This law is vital to understanding the root of our desires. Knowing what we consider to be bad creates consciousness for a desire to manifest something we consider to be good. Both are one and the same thing, however, just to varying degrees of opposites. By being conscious of bad, we create a desire to experience good. By Law, once the desire for good arises, the manifestation of it does as well. It manifests at *the same time as the desire for one over the other.* Just as good and bad are on the same pole, desire and the manifestation of it are on their own same pole. They are one and the same thing, just on different ends. This will be an important point to keep in mind for later on.

4. The Law of Gender – Everything has both masculine and feminine characteristics, or masculine and feminine energy. The masculine energy is always in the position of the giving of something; or the position

of action. The feminine is always in the position of receiving something.

Gender manifests in all things on all planes; the physical, the mental, and the spiritual. In the physical plane, this Law manifests as sex; a physical act of both masculine and feminine energies. In the mental plane it manifests as left brain and right brain. The masculine left side is responsible for logic, the will and is more mathematically inclined. The feminine right side of the brain is the creative hemisphere. It controls the imagination and gives birth to new thoughts and ideas. In the spiritual plane, the Law of Gender manifests as the ego and the soul – the conscious and the subconscious. The ego is the social mask, validated by the external world, or artefacts. The soul is the internal expression of love, unchangeable and unable to be influenced by forces outside of itself.

Whereas the masculine and feminine energies of the Law of Gender appear to be opposites, they are in reality complements to each other; interdependent with each other. Yin and Yang, creating a wholeness, or a Oneness. Both are required for life to exist on any plane. Together they are One.

5. The Law of Rhythm – Everything is in constant motion, which creates its own vibrational rhythm forming patterns, flowing in and out like a pendulum. The four seasons, the tides, the stages of development, economies, the orbit of the moon around the Earth, all of it has a predictable rhythm; a cycle; a pattern. Everything has a season; a journey from beginning to end, and back. The key to this Law is recognising the passing of one season to another and maintaining a balance of non-resistance and peace.

6. The Law of Attraction – Like attracts like. What we focus our energy upon consciously or unconsciously, intentionally or not, attracts more of it. Things that vibrate on harmonious wavelengths attract other things vibrating in the same harmonious way regardless of whether we consider them to be good or bad. We create things in our lives by our focused thoughts, emotions, words *and actions,* which produce belief energy which attracts like energy. Because the energies are the same, they seek each other out. They are seeking Oneness with each other so they attract each other.

7. The Law of Cause and Effect – For every action, there is a reaction. With every thought, emotion, intention or desire, its vibration creates a Cause, which eventually returns to the source of its emanation in the form of an Effect. This is because Cause and Effect are One and the same thing.

    Any Cause will produce an Effect whether or not the Effect is a desirable one. The energy and actions of the focus are the Cause. The result, or Effect, is the artefact of the focused energy, whatever that may be. As in the case of poor Job who, having lost everything, said the following.

    > *What I feared has come upon me; what I dreaded has happened to me.*
    >
    > Job 3:24 NIV

    The fear of losing everything was the energy of Job's Cause. The Effect was Job's loss.

    The Law of Cause and Effect is measurable and predictable. It contains involution and evolution. Involution is the Cause; evolution is the Effect. Involution is the idea generation, or the desire.

Evolution is the unfoldment of or the manifestation of said desire. Involution is masculine. Evolution is feminine. This is how beliefs become things. This Law forms the basis of Buddhism and, it may be said, the basis of Judeo-Christian faiths as well.

Actionable Laws

8. The Law of Relativity – Nothing has any meaning or value in and of itself. The Law of Relativity states everything is relative to something else. Therefore, it is in this relative relationship that value and meaning find their place. Everything just IS until *we* compare it to something else. That comparison gives it its value. There is no good and there is no bad. One is only good or bad when it is compared to its opposite. Light is so because of its comparison to darkness. Hot is so because of its comparison to cold. Good is so because of its comparison to evil. Nothing really has any meaning except that which *we give it* based upon comparing it to something else.

9. The Law of Compensation – Similar to the Law of Cause and Effect, this Law states everyone is compensated in a manner equal to the amount he or she has contributed. This Law may be called the Law of Measure. It is the measure or degree of the Effect. And, as with any type of compensatory model, you must perform the Action first. You must give before you receive. You must forgive to be forgiven. By grasping this Law, one understands performing even the most mundane of tasks takes on a greater meaning. Performing the task to your greatest ability produces a compensatory result.

10. The Law of Action – This Law addresses the necessity of taking inspired and intentional Action. By engaging in activities that support the manifestation of the object of our desires, we are in fact Being said desire. All actions must be in full alignment, or One, with the object of our desires. This means our actions must vibrate harmoniously with our desired state of Being. In this state of Being, any action taken is a Cause in further support of the desired state.

11. The Law of Vibration – Everything is energy and all energy is in a state of vibration. The vibration is the energy of everything in constant movement whether it is within an artefact, within a thought, or within a desired state of Being. The whole Universe and everything in it is vibrating and all of it vibrates at its unique tone. Our desires have a vibration. The vibration of our desires is real; just as real as the so-called tangible things we see all around us.

12. The Law of Correspondence – As within, so without. This law states our outer world reflects the world within. Both are One. Your inner world of thoughts and feelings shows up in the tangible outer world. There is a direct correlation or correspondence between how you think and feel inside and the way you behave and experience your environment. There is a direct correspondence to your internal, emotional atmosphere and how the Universe reflects that back to you. The internal is the Cause; the external reflects the Effect. They are mirror images of each other. Change in any circumstance of life begins with changing the inner world. Then, the outside environment changes in relation to that world.

THE PROCESS THAT IS GOD

The two Primary Laws of the Universe are The Law of Perpetual Transmutation of Energy, and The Law of Divine Oneness. The Law of Perpetual Transmutation of Energy simply states everything is energy. It always is, always was, and always will be. It is constantly moving in and out of form, always manifesting more of Itself from Itself. This Law explains how thoughts in formlessness, which are pure energy, are moved into form; how invisible Cause produces a visible Effect.

The Law of Divine Oneness permeates everything comprised of energy. Since everything is energy, everything is of this Oneness. It is everything that ever is, ever was or ever will be. It is the Godness of everything, including us. Our individuality is how Universal Oneness manifests distinct entities within Itself and of Itself. Individualised and indivisible. And, this is an important point right here. We are not individuals. We are *individualised*, which is our uniqueness within the whole. Whatever is created is so created out of the stuff of Oneness and shares It perpetually. The more we accept the knowledge that we are separate from nothing and nothing is separate from us, the more powerfully we are capable of manifesting anything into our lives.

It may be easily seen how the 12 Laws together operate as One. Upon examination, it may further be seen how the two Primary Laws are woven throughout the others. The main distinction between the Static Laws and the Actionable Laws is the degree to which *we have an active part* in the way they work with us and for us. The way we actively engage with, and intentionally use, their power is their point of, what may be termed, "separation" only.

So, let's get clear on what is God. For many of us, the very idea of God is a turn-off. There is some validity in those feelings to be sure, simply because of how misunderstood the concept of It has been historically. The truth is, God is this Oneness; we are this Oneness. We are made of God. It is not some personality or entity outside of ourselves. We are made of the Universe, and the Universe is made of us. We are made of each other. So is that tree, that rock, that puppy, that wad of gum on the street. Yes, God is that wad of gum. There is really no separation between anything because everything is the same energy, just manifesting in different ways. It is the Law of Oneness that holds all the other Laws in place. It is this Law that is the essence of our Being.

It is the combination of the two Primary Laws that helps us understand another important point. These two Primary Laws together are *that which is Being God*. The two Laws work together in a Union-ship of masculine and feminine energy. The Law of the Perpetual Transmutation of Energy is feminine as it is always the creative unfolding. The Law of Divine Oneness is masculine energy, giving to the Law of the Perpetual Transmutation of Energy the impetus for that movement to manifest into form through the feminine energy. The Law of Divine Oneness is the Mind of God. The Law of Energy is the Spirit or Soul of God. The union between the two is a Process. *This Process is the basis of what is understood to be God.*

As Energy moves in and out of form, It is ever expanding and evolving It's Oneness. The Process of the evolution and the growth of energy is the Intelligence of God creating. God, or Energy, is wholly dependent only upon Itself to make It what It is. It evolves more of Itself out of Itself. It is totally dependent upon only Itself, Self-driven and Self-determined. This makes God, the Universe or Energy, Infinite.

Together, we too are the Process of God, and *we* make up the ever-expanding Consciousness of God Co-Creatively. This Consciousness is at the border of what we know to be the evolutionary journey of Itself. The Way of Mastery is intentional and conscious Co-Creating with the Infinite Oneness of God, the Universe or Energy. As we intentionally manifest our desires, God is experiencing desire through us, Co-Creatively. The Oneness we share with the Universe is our Being; the creative is what gives us our divinity. As each one of us is a unique expression of the Oneness of Energy in the Process of Being, no two people, no two expressions of the Universe, ever experience the same creative unfolding. All desires are different and all desires manifesting and manifested are the steps we take along the never-ending Way of Mastery.

THE STATIC AND THE ACTIONABLE LAWS

Essentially all of the 12 Universal Laws are what they are. They are impersonal. They work the way they work without any help from us. However, in terms of the Way of Mastery and intentional Being, the Static and Actionable Laws necessitate a Masterful perspective.

The Static Laws are by no means in a lesser position to the two Primary Laws. They are simply Laws that state those things that just *are*. The Law of Polarity, the Law of Gender, the Law of Rhythm, the Law of Attraction and the Law of Cause and Effect operate in a capacity more or less along the lines of statements of and about the Universe; impersonal. They are declarations about Energy.

Similarly, the Actionable Laws could be considered in a comparable position to the Static Laws without a distinguishing difference; a slight variation. The difference is the Actionable Laws are those *with which* our vibrational energy has a more of a direct effect, intentionally or not. Left alone, they would be in the same category as the Static Laws. With our energy involved, however, these Laws are moved and stimulated. Therefore, they are Laws of Action.

For example, by engaging in Actions in support of Being one who is intentionally manifesting the object of desire, happiness, the Law of Action is energised. It responds to our activity. The Law of Compensation is another example. This states the things we experience in life are the consequences of the amount of, and to the degree of, time and effort we give into manifesting our experience. The Law of Compensation acknowledges and then rewards our time and effort in direct proportion to what we have given into it, measure for measure.

If we are to receive we must give. If we give, we will receive. Said in another way…

> *Give, and it will be given to you. A good measure, pressed down, shaken together and running over, will be poured into your lap. For with the measure you use, it will be measured to you.*
>
> Luke 6:38 NIV

The Law of Relativity is dependent upon *our* perception of X in relation to Y. In other words, *our* comparison of one to the other. This perception gives both X and Y their relative value. Between X and Y is nothing until the perception of X is more desirable than that of Y. As the desire for X grows, so should the lack of desire for Y. This creates a greater relative distance between the higher energy of desire for X and the lower energy of non-desire for Y, both of which are on the same pole. Then the vibration of X and the desire for X are drawn closer to each other, becoming more One with each other, and manifestation occurs.

This also works in the opposite way. If the desire for *less of Y* is greater than the desire for *more of X*, then the vibrational alignment of Y becomes stronger than the vibration of X. There is no way to distinguish where X ends and Y begins from the Universal perspective because they are one pole. The stronger desire for *less of Y* has a vibration, which Universally speaking translates to desiring Y and the Law of Attraction will bring more Y to you. This is why fear-based manifestations seem to be a more regular occurrence for many of us.

The Law of Vibration responds to our actions. Everything made of Energy vibrates. By changing *our vibrational output*, we are able to match the vibration of the desired state of Being. This Being has already then manifested in a vibrational state. It moves into form accordingly. Our role is to Be the vibrational match, and to enjoy it.

Desire is the evolution of God. *Working through us*, desire is vibrational output seeking a vibrational match to itself in the form of the manifestation of the object or artefact of desire. What we focus on, intentionally or not, is changing the energy of the Universe. It is forming the thing thought of, felt, or desired into another iteration of Its own Energy.

As stated, all of the Laws are essentially plastic or non-personal, meaning they work the way they work without regard to who uses them, intentionally or not. However, we can see both the Static and Actionable Laws differ slightly from each other by virtue of the powerful energy we put into them. We can consciously or unconsciously, intentionally or not, affect the way in which they work – for us or against us.

All of these Laws are *interdependent*. You cannot isolate one's use without the others. They all need each other to function, as they are all governed by the Law of Divine Oneness. One Law cannot work independent of the others. They are all inextricably interconnected. Therefore, I believe some of the power of working with these Laws is lost by a single-minded focus on just one or two of them and not consciously understanding what Laws we are working with and at what time. This is why I believe overly focusing on just the Law of Attraction, for example, without understanding the other 11 Laws often results in not manifesting the object of desire and, therefore, manifests itself as unhappiness, frustration or what have you.

Non-Resistance to The Laws

The law of gravity is often used as a discussion point in manifestation circles, so let's go with it and use it here. It could be argued that we don't really need to fully understand the law of gravity to work with it. Well that is true, in part. I want to tell you why this idea is different from the use of the 12 Universal Laws.

For example, I know about gravity and its basic workings. Most of us do. However, the people at NASA need to know a whole lot more about it than I do to launch a space shuttle and put it into orbit. To put a man or woman into space, they need to know more than I do about the laws of physics and how they work with the law of gravity as well as the workings of a half-dozen or so other laws – for all I know. In fact, they need to know enough about all that stuff to know how to effectively work *against* gravity to launch something into space. I could never do that with my limited knowledge and experience of gravity. Their grasp of this collection of laws increases their power to manifest their desires over my limited knowledge of just the law of gravity. Working with all the laws they need to know is the key to manifesting the object of their desire; space flight. So, too, wisdom of the suite of Universal Laws increases our intentional use of them exponentially, versus the knowledge and use of one or two of them in isolation of the rest.

Carrying this thought further, most of us don't argue with gravity, therefore we have no resistance to it. When some of us occasionally do argue with gravity, most often unintentionally, there is usually some unpleasant consequence involved. Just watch one of those home video shows and see how many ways people mess up working against this law. We really don't *have* to understand gravity very much, nor do most of us seek to. Its basic ins-and-outs are enough for us to work with it as effectively as we need to, so we just let it be to do its business. The difference between the law of gravity and the Universal Laws is that with the latter we are talking about deliberate and intentional manifestation through them.

We don't choose to be deliberate and intentional with the law of gravity very often – we don't have to. We don't have much resistance to the way in which it works. We do, however, need to be intentional with the 12 Universal Laws until we reach a point whereby these 12 Laws are, in our experience, no different to us than our use of the law of gravity. That is why we need to understand the Universal Laws on a more intentional and intimate level and experience how they work within our lives.

Here is another important truth. The Process of God is not personal. The Universal Laws do not care who uses them and the truth is, everyone does use them one way or the other. The Laws work whether we understand them or not. They respond just as much to the unkind as well as the kind, just as the sun rises on the so-called evil as well as the so-called good.[3] There are some awesome manifestors out there who, *as people*, just don't seem to be very good at it; powerful manifestors who I personally would never want to meet. Yet, they seem skilled at using the Universal Laws whether they call it that or not.

There is a difference between intentional and conscious manifesting by working *with* the 12 Universal Laws, versus the unintentional use thereof, however. If you have been on a conscious journey for even a little while, you probably found out early on how much we *unconsciously* manifest some things which trip us up. Wisdom in, and the intentional use of, the Universal Laws helps us better understand where we may be taking a pratfall in this regard. And, by better understanding the Laws we are better equipped to intentionally tap the right Laws, at the right time and in the right way to manifest our desires.

The Universe works in a certain way. It doesn't consciously pick and choose the way It works; It can't. Whatever you believe about the power of your own Beingness, the Universe will respond to it in kind by Law. So, intentional Mastery involves *creating a space* to evolve into more powerful and greater manifestors who wisely and deliberately use the Universal Laws, Co-Creating with It. This is the essence of Being. This is The Masterful Way.

Many say it is the easiest thing in the world to just accept the Universal Laws and go with them and that's very true, but only to a degree. Going with that idea *alone* can lead to a little heartburn when what we are manifesting isn't showing up, or we are manifesting its opposite. What I am saying is *if* one can just accept and get on with the intentional manifesting bit, bless you. That is the point, after all; to accept the Laws as we do the law of gravity. Not many accomplish this with ease, however, and there is a reason.

For most of us, getting to the place of Mastery with the Laws just like we have with gravity is *work*. It is the work of cutting through our resistance. If we had as much resistance to gravity as we do to these Laws, it would logically take some time and effort to get past that resistance long enough just to get up out of our chairs.

To that end, to those who say all of this should be the easiest thing in the world to do… I totally get where you are coming from, but I say poppycock. Being is the easiest thing in the world… yes. You don't really have to do a thing to Be except Be it with intention. The process of shedding layer upon layer of the stuff of resistance, however, is not necessarily so simple. So, let's be realistic about this upfront. Mastery takes effort. All Mastery does.

A Silent Lesson

I love the story of the Buddha and the Sermon of the Flower. It's a terrific example and a great lesson on Being. There are a number of different versions to this story, so I'll just give you the gist.

As it goes, towards the end of his life the Buddha had something to say. He had a sermon to deliver to his followers. Some consider it to be one of the Buddha's most profound teachings, actually. The quirky bit is that he delivered it without speaking a word. He delivered his sermon to the assembled crowd by holding up a lotus flower he had just plucked from a muddy pond in which such flowers grow. Still dripping with mud from its roots the Buddha simply held it out for all to see.

One version of the story says he silently held the flower up to each of his disciples who, in turn, did their confused best to expound upon its significance, and how it represented the Buddha's teachings. The Buddha remained silent. How loud that silence must have been to his disciples. One could only imagine what they must have been thinking. After a short time, however, one of the Buddha's disciples, Mahakasyapa, began to smile. The Buddha observed him smiling and commended him to the crowd for having been the only one to have "heard" the Buddha's very important teaching. Mahakasyapa was to become the Buddha's successor from that day forwards, and this event is credited with being the story of the creation of a form of Buddhism known as Zen.

While the story certainly expresses the concept of the fleeting nature of everything, as well as the Oneness of it, I believe it also expresses Being in a very profound way. The lotus flower didn't work at being beautiful, it just was – no resistance. The mud dripping from its roots in front of the assembled crowd didn't have to struggle to do so. It just did – no resistance. While the crowd tried to understand in their heads what the Buddha was teaching, the one who "got it", just *got it*. He felt it in his heart with no resistance. He was Being the receiver, a Co-Creator of the message. You see, Being the highest and truest Self you are is very simple. Getting there, getting rid of the resistance and out of your own way, is the work.

> *And why worry about your clothing? Look at the lilies of the field and how they grow. They don't work or make their clothing.*
> Luke 12:27 NLT

While the oft-quoted verse above is lovely and reflective, very few of us just wake up one day as Master manifestors – powerful performers on the stage of the 12 Universal Laws. Very few of us just get the message like Mahakasyapa. Remember, he was just one in a crowd, and the only one to have "got" it. This is not to say Being is an elusive, one-in-a-million shot at living our highest Self, either. What it does mean is the better we recognise our resistance to manifesting, the better equipped we are for shedding the layers of stuff more easily, and to Co-evolve the Universe more consciously.

Doing the work is also not a contradiction to the allegories of the wildflowers and the lotus, who were just really good at Being. The difference is they didn't have a lot of built-up stuff to work through. The truth is, most of us have managed to cover over our Being with years of junk which is too small for us, too dirty and which trips us up. Getting through it, past it, or as rid of it as we possibly can be takes some effort. Give yourself a break. *This is work* but it's good work – the best work ever, really. Be whatever it is you are manifesting through yourself and Master the work of getting out of your own way.

DEFINITIONS

So, now that we have provided some framework, let us recap these suppositions as a prelude to what is to come. These understandings will be further expounded upon in the chapters that follow. In no particular order, some of these definitions are as follows.

1. Being is the physical, emotional and spiritual representation of your desires. With each new and true desire, your Being and the Universe evolves *through it* Co-Creatively. Each true desire represents an element of your unique voice; what you have to say. Combined, these elements are the evidence of your Being-ness and your divinity. Your Beingness is *your own unique True Self*. Your desires are the journey. Getting out of your own way is Mastery.

2. Being is not becoming. Being is a state not experienced as the result of thinking and acting of becoming as an external objective. Becoming implies a future state, which does not exist. Being is experienced as the *Process of thinking and acting from the state of Being in the Present/Now.*

3. Being is your Self in its Truth. Being is the ultimate expression of the Universe as it expands and evolves through you. Therefore Being is the highest individualised and indivisible vibrational expression of Oneness to which the Universe responds powerfully.

4. Every Being is his or her own expression within the space of Oneness. In Being that unique expression, the Universe expands and evolves through it, or through the conscious desires of said Being, and experiences them with us. Therefore, any true desire we have is growing and expanding the Universe; or growing and expanding Life – which is Life's only purpose. True Being, then, is the conscious Co-Creating, evolutionary Process of Life through desire. Without this Process, evolution could not happen.

5. Every action undertaken in the Being state is an Action in support of Being all of the physical manifestations of your desires. This is according to the Law of Action. These Actions become Causes, the Effects of which manifest the physical and non-physical object or artefacts of desire. If, for example, you desire a new vehicle, in a state of Being the physical manifestation of someone with the new vehicle in the Present/Now, even a mundane task such as walking down the street becomes a Cause in support of Being that person Now – the Effect. Outside this state of Being as described, the action of walking down the street is not an action in support of that Being-ness. It is not consciously directed and remains a mundane task to get you from point A to point B on foot.

6. Here is an important distinction to be aware of. A true desire is something that supports the evolution of the truth of your Being. I may have an honest desire for a pretty new Rolex, and I could certainly manifest one. However, that desire would not make or break my Being-ness. If, for example, my Being is the expression of the Universe as a successful dog walker – in other

words Being that dog walker is the deep-in-the-core expression of *what I have to say* – then a true desire would be to manifest into my experience dogs to walk. A true desire would be to manifest the time necessary to walk them and any of the artefacts that would support that Being-ness.

I could, however, approach this from the perspective of desiring the income from being a successful dog walker, which is a valid desire, but it's not the income I am actually after. That is an artefact of Being a Masterful dog walker. So a true desire is Being a successful dog walker and supporting this true desire would be to manifest those things which will contribute to that Being. These are Causes. An Effect of Being that successful dog walker would be the income generated by so Being. By Being the proper Cause, the income as the Effect could provide the opportunity to manifest the pretty new Rolex. Too many of us have the whole idea backwards, desiring the Effect before the Cause.

7. Happiness, joy, peace, love, etc. are the ultimate goals of intentionally Being. It is the goal of the unintentional and unconscious journey of becoming as well. However, happiness is not achieved as a result of the physical manifestation of artefacts. Rather it is achieved through Being the physical manifestation of the desired state regardless of its form and physical presence in the moment.

8. Happiness is in the Present/Now, not in some future state. Nor is happiness found in the past. The only state that exists is the Present/Now. This is the only state in which your Being exists and the only state in which God or the Universe exists as well.

9. Man is an expression of his beliefs; whether they are conscious beliefs or not. Man is belief expressed,[4] regardless of what those beliefs may be. Being differs from this general construct in that Being is an intentional and conscious expression of beliefs through Actions that support the manifestation of the intended desires. This is Mastery.

Now, let us understand a few truths as related to the above.

In his teachings, Wallace Wattles (1860–1911) described the work of the Mastery of Being as the hardest work in the world. Why it is so challenging is because it is the work of *maintaining sustained thoughts on the manifestation of your desires*. It is of maintaining sustained thoughts on Actual Truth; your Being. It is the work of Mastering these sustained thoughts. It is the power of the will to keep your mind steady and unwavering – it is to will belief, to control feelings and to direct your own thoughts.

What is the hardest work in the world? To think.

Ralph Waldo Emerson

It is this work itself whereby most of us find failure or hardship in Being truly Masterful manifestors. Mastery requires spending a lot of energy to keep our minds focused and to keep our will in its proper place. There is energy spent in constantly searching out and ridding ourselves of resistance to the manifestation of our desires. There is energy spent in keeping our Being true to our Truth. There is energy spent in noticing even the slightest twinge of doubt showing up from somewhere. There is energy spent in sussing out where that somewhere is, and further energy spent in keeping it from re-entering our space.

Energy is spent in uncovering those things that are taking energy in a lot of other ways as well. There is energy spent in order to what the Bible calls, "pray without ceasing" – which basically means focus

– and the energy spent being deeply "grateful for all things",[5] at all times even when you can't see or touch the manifestation of your desires. And, there is energy spent in dedication, meditation, self-control and a big helping of NOTICING what you are putting into the Universe ALL THE TIME as it expresses Itself, evolving and Co-Creating through your Being.

Masterful Beings know this. They know that the energy invested in the work is a reward worth having unto itself, because "unto itself" is where the happiness lies. Further, they know there are Universal Laws that define powerful energies and it is their responsibility to *work with them* to manifest what they desire. Master manifestors know there is a reward that is found only on the *road* of manifesting the objects of their desires, which illuminates the whole world just a little bit more. As happiness grows one person and one desire at a time, it contributes to being the proverbial *Light of the World*.

We are admonished to let our light shine for all to see. Why? Is it because it highlights some sort of egoic accomplishment? Not at all. It's not a spotlight beaming down on you. I believe Being the *Light of the World* helps us all to see the road a little better. Being a shining example of how all of this works is the greatest privilege there is. To Be the example of one who has evolved past the unintentional and unconscious journey, to Being on the intentional road of Mastery will, by its own volition, light the path for others. You are the distributer of that light and that light, that happiness, raises the vibration of the whole Universe, one harmonious note at a time.

The 12 Universal Laws operate though one thing, through one avenue of focus only. That is desire. It is desire that drives all we do. So intrinsically powerful is desire that the Rigveda, ancient Vedic Sanskrit hymns millennia old, call desire the seed of the Spirit; or that which birthed the Universe. So, let us now begin to gain a deeper understanding of that which is called the creative force of the Universe itself. Let us look deeply into desire.

CHAPTER 3

THE MASTERY OF DESIRE

Desire is a power seeking expression. You cannot desire what is not potentially within you; and therefore, you can be what you want to be. The fact that you want to be is proof that you can be.

Wallace Wattles[1]

Desire is the divine impulse. It is God, or the Universe, urging a movement through us towards Its own greater expansion and experience. Therefore, it is important to understand desire in its truest sense so we may better grasp the powerful Process that sparks desire within us, and what our role is in the Co-Creative Process that desire is seeking through us.

The etymology of the word desire is the Latin *desiderare*. It translates to "long for, wish for; demand, expect". We will discuss some of these words in greater detail a little further on. Going back into the deeper root of *desiderare*, we have the phrase *de sidere*, translated as "from sidus" which means from a "heavenly body, star, constellation". *De sidere* literally means "from the stars", or "await what the stars will bring".[2] In the broader sense then, the phrase can be understood as "to see what the Universe will bring", or "to see what God will bring". Therefore, a desire is literally a divine thing. Joseph Murphy calls desire a gift of God. It is what God brings through us and we should treat our desires and the actions they Cause with this perspective in mind.

To reiterate, any desire fuels our unique expression. Each desire, step by step, creates *what we have to say* and it shapes our experiences, which in turn shape our Being. Desire is the foundation of that which we are all seeking; happiness, joy, peace and love. However, desire itself is the very thing which trips a lot of us up due to our lack of understanding of how all the Universal forces work together to achieve these elevated states of happiness through it.

From a Universal perspective, desire and the manifestation of that which is desired are inextricably fused, like the Gordian Knot. The trouble is, many of us approach desire with an Alexander the Great complex. We wield a heavy sword at our desires and slice them in half. We then place one half in the present moment and the other in some future point in time. The problem with this approach is it not only breaks a few Universal Laws, it tends to destroy the knot. For us to properly demystify this idea, let us discuss a few deeper truths about desire beginning with what desire is not.

THE PROPER USE OF WORDS

All words carry energy to which the Universe responds accordingly. Negative words produce negative energy, and positive words produce positive energy. As energy is energy and the Laws are the Laws, the Universe responds in kind.

> *The tongue has the power of life and death, and those who love it will eat its fruit.*
>
> Proverbs 18:21 NIV

Words have the power to both destroy and heal. When words are both true and kind, they can change our world.

The Buddha

By faith we understand that the universe was created by the word of God, so that what is seen was not made out of things that are visible.

Hebrews 11:3 ESV

Words have power. Words are power. Words could be your power.

Mohammed Qahtani[3]

The power of words was and is perhaps the greatest lesson I ever learned. As it relates to intentional Mastery, it is vitally important to understand how to use the power of words properly. This begins by understanding words such as "desire" and the many synonyms with which it is often confused.

One such word is the word "need". Desire is not need. We often freely substitute the word need for the word desire very inappropriately. Desire is not related to need except on the level of the description of the two words as being either a noun or a verb.

As with many words in the English language, the word "need" is both a noun and a verb. The first-level definition, and its strongest usage, is as a verb. Verbs are words of action. Need is an action word usually associated with some sense of urgency, the requirement of something essential. "I need air" or "I need help" would be examples. It is something that is necessary. To need is to require something with speed. The word need carries a sense of desperation. As a noun, need has similar applications, all of which provoke thoughts of some necessity, or of lack. "The basic need for food", or "help us in our hour of need".[4] Both as a noun and a verb, the word need always denotes necessity, a sense of urgency and usually a sense of speed.

Generally speaking, I believe we are very lazy with the word need, given its proper meaning. We toss it around lightly when it is, in fact, not a very useful thing to do, especially for those of us who are Being intentional. "I need a drink", or "I need a cup of coffee", for example, when we are actually saying we *want* a drink or a cuppa. Using the word need when we really mean want, or even desire, slows down or stops the intentional manifestation of that which is in fact desired because the vibration of the two words is different.

If you *really need* something, it carries a power-packed vibration. It focuses our energy on the need-ing of whatever it may be, to which the Universe responds rather quickly by providing you with more needing of the something, because whatever is needed is required rather quickly. The needing of something is always from the space of a lack thereof. Because it is associated with urgency, the word need will always highlight a lack that requires speedy assistance. Need will produce more needing in order to inspire urgent action. Unlike desire, which manifests as the object of it, which produces the emotions associated with happiness, peace, joy and love.

Desire is a word also associated with strong feelings and emotions, but there is a big difference, vibrationally speaking, between desire and need. It is in this difference where I believe the confusion between need and desire catches us off-guard.

Whereas need is first and foremost a verb, desire is first and foremost a noun. Desire has a verb side as well but in second position. Need is usually associated with emotions of lack in a given situation or circumstance which is most often urgent. As is the way with all verbs, it automatically carries action and emotion. Need has a strong emotional attachment already associated with it, if for no other reason than it is first and foremost a verb. On the other hand, desire as a noun is a thing. As a thing, our role is to breathe life into it, to provide the emotional attachment and give it its value and its action.

No-*thing* is any-*thing* to us until we give it some relevant value or worth. This is by the Law of Relativity. Unlike need, which comes packed with actionable energy, desire as a thing requires an attachment of our own making. This attachment must be in the form of an emotional energy. If you can't breathe and need air, the emotional attachment to the need for air is self-evident. Desire, however, has only the degree of emotion we place upon it.

For example, let's say you have two desires. One is for a horseshoe, the other for a pile of money. The reason why you have either or both desires is irrelevant. You desire them and that's enough. Ask yourself, what is the level of attachment to the horseshoe? How about the pile of money? I very strongly make up the emotional attachment to the pile of money is far greater than the horseshoe because it is more relevant to your life. We give the desire for money a greater emotional attachment over the desire for a horseshoe. We give each of the two desires a different value. This is how desire works. With the object of our desire, it is our job to give it a degree of life, thereby giving it its energy. Once we have done that, we may then give it to the Universe and enjoy the state of Being or receiving. This is the Process of Co-Creation, which will be discussed in detail later.

Through the lens of the Law of Gender, the *Process of desire* is both masculine and feminine. Whatever desire we may have, the intention is to receive whatever the object may be. And, that is the key. The *receiving* of it is therefore feminine energy. The *desire* for something comes first, however. It is then followed by our Action of attaching the appropriate emotion and meaning to the desire through creative, intuitive feminine energy. As we attach a degree of emotion to the desire vibrationally speaking, and we have become clear on the object of said desire, the desire is asked for, or given back to the Universe through masculine energy. In feminine energy the Spirit or Soul of the Universe receives the ask which then works with us in masculine energy to manifest the artefact or object of the desire. This becomes the Process of Being Co-Creators with God or the Universe of both that which is desired, and Being the recipient of it in feminine energy.

While also both masculine and feminine, the process of needing something is a much more masculine endeavour and is different. The true needing of something is not the same as the two-sided Process of Co-Creating a desire. Using the action of its verb-ness, needing produces the hope of *getting* something; as a hunter goes and gets food to satiate the need for it. It is not open to negotiation or the creative process. If there is a need for air, you either get it or you don't and let the consequences be what they may. Desire, on the other hand, must be nurtured and grown. *Desire* shares the energies of both the masculine and feminine more equally than that of need. It is a more equal exchange of both of these energies, assuming we do our part in the Process. Need does not provide happiness, joy, peace, etc., nor the road of it. Rather need highlights a void that must be filled. Desire and manifestation *are themselves* happiness, joy, peace, etc. which is the only reason for desire in the first place.

Akin to the term need is the term "wish". Wish, too, is a verb that carries its own emotional proclivity and action associated with it automatically. Wish, however, differs greatly from need in that its energy is very, very weak for several reasons. A wish is usually connected to some thing or some event that may not, or probably will not, occur. A wish is a desire without any intention attached to it. As a result, the action of a wish is erratic as is the emotion it may or may not come with, versus that of need, which is more straightforward.

Another reality about the word wish is wishing always lives in a future state. As we will grow to understand, a future state does not exist. Therefore whatever is wished for also does not exist in that state. When something is wished for, its energy goes up and away like an untethered balloon, whereas a *need* is a direct target. You need food; you either get food or you don't. The consequences of the lack of food are fairly obvious. If you *wish* for food, on the other hand, you can sit and ponder food for as long as you like. You can think about all the lovely things you can eat, and all of the different types of food there are and then walk away from thinking about it at all with no consequences, save maybe a hunger pang or two. You can easily see how the use of the term wish as a synonym for the word desire is erroneous. Wishing is a low-vibrational energy to which the Universe responds lowly and slowly if at all.

Need and wish are also related to another misused term; *want*. Want is also primarily a verb. It too has its own energy and emotions automatically attached to it. Most often, it is understood through the emotions associated with possession regardless of whether the thing, or sometimes the person, to be possessed wants it as well. It has the sentiments associated with ownership and control.

Want is also used as a noun and, as such, it carries the emotional vibration of a deficiency of something. "I want a banana" for instance highlights the fact a banana is not had. Similarly, as a noun, it is defined as a state of being poor and of lacking essentials. "In want of basic necessities," for example. Putting the terms want and desire together, we can clearly see the vibrational differences between the two. Furthermore, we can see how using the term want in place of desire may not be providing the proper space from which, and into which, the manifestation of the object of our desires may take place. The misuse and misappropriation of the words "want", "need" and "wish" as synonyms for "desire" is not helpful. Neither is it suitable to apply the use of the word desire when we really mean want, need, or wish.

Truths About Desire

The primary truth about desire is probably the most profound truth of all. When we have a desire, we must realise *the Universe has the same desire because it is the Universe's desire*. To restate, desire is the Universe, or God, seeking to express and experience more of Itself through us as it continually advances into Its own Process of Being. Therefore, to have a desire is a divine act seeking greater happiness for us all through the Co-Creative Process.

> *There is one great truth on this planet: whoever you are, or whatever it is that you do, when you really want something, it's because that desire originated in the soul of the universe... The soul of the world is nourished by people's happiness.*
>
> Paulo Coelho[5]

For God is working in you, giving you the desire and the power to do what pleases him.

Philippians 2:13 NLT

The words I speak are not my own, but my Father who lives in me does his work through me.

Jesus[6]

As a desire is sparked within, the manifestation of the artefact or object of it has been created within as well. They are bound together in that Gordian Knot fashion through the Law of Polarity. Desire and the object of it are on the exact same plane of existence vibrationally. They are on one pole. Therefore, desire itself is the first evidence of the physical manifestation of the object, straight away. It is not in some future state.

... Every kingdom divided against itself will be ruined, and every city or household divided against itself will not stand.

Matthew 12:25 NIV

When we split the desire from its manifested self, the desire becomes isolated from the object. This leads to us being of two minds. One mind believes having the desire for a fine wool coat, for example, lives in this moment in the present, while at the same time the other mind believes the manifestation of the coat is somewhere in the future. If desire and the physical manifestation of the artefact are on the same pole or vibrational plane, this cannot be the case. If desire is in the Now, then the full manifestation of the object of desire is also. They are one and the same thing. One Pole.

Put as plainly as possible, *desire and the manifested artefact of desire, always and only live in the time zone of the present.* Furthermore, the present is the only space God, or the Universe, inhabits by Its own Laws.

I am the Alpha and the Omega, the First and the Last, the Beginning and the End.

Revelation 22:13 NIV

The meaning of the verse above is just that. In between the Alpha and the Omega, the First and the Last, the Beginning and the End is the only space there is. Now; the Present. Your Being also *only* occupies the space of the Present. Your Being, your desire, and God or the Universe all co-inhabit the same place. The Universe is not limited by perceptions of time and space as we believe we are. It knows what we desire before we do. We are ever so slightly catching up to It when a desire occurs to us.

> *… your Father knows what you need before you ask him.*
> Matthew 6:8 NIV

This is not like *need, want,* or *wish.* These three states live in a different place altogether. Need, want, and wish all occupy a future state. The state of the future does not actually exist. Because it does not exist, God cannot be found there. Because it does not exist, your Being cannot be found there. Because it does not exist, neither your desire nor the physical manifestation of it can be found there. They can only live in the Now.

Once the Universe creates a desire through us, It asks us to make an agreement with It to be on an intentional journey of Being someone manifesting the object of desire in the Present. It is already done and we can either agree to be the vessel through which the Universe experiences the physical manifestation of the desire through nurturing the Truth of our Being, or we can choose not to. By Being it, we sign on the dotted line and the Universe begins to work towards the physical manifestation. We need only remain in that state of Being, happy, peaceful, joyous, loving, etc. with the vibrational manifestation already had.

We break the contract, and our agreement, when we begin to focus on the lack of the desired object made manifest. When we notice the opposite of having it and when we are miserable because of it, this violates the contract. If we can relax, agree with the Universe, and allow It to manifest through us acting in accordance with the state of Being, or receiving, I believe our manifesting powers would grow exponentially.

A further truth about desire and the manifestation of the object of it is when we have a desire, especially a big, audacious desire, there may be times in which we feel as if we have to prove or convince the Universe of our worthiness to have it. The state of Being is not a state in which we need to somehow convince the Universe that we are worthy of, or that we deserve, the object or artefact of our desire. It knows we are and we do because we are the vessel through which the Universe had the desire in the first place. It is the so-called will of God. To think otherwise is a mistake and a violation of the Universal Law of Oneness. The idea of worthiness is a rejection of the desire of the Universe. It is a false notion that we are separate from It in some way and must prove ourselves. This impresses muddy and confusing energy into the Universe and we know muddy and confusing energy is much less effective to work with.

A further truth about desire is that *we can only physically manifest the object of the desires to which we bond ourselves mentally, emotionally and vibrationally.* This is by the Law of Vibration together with the Law of Correspondence. This is true of both those things we desire and of those things we do *not* desire depending upon our vibrational situatedness. If we do *not* desire a given thing or situation more than we desire its opposite, the vibrational match is more closely aligned with the thing or situation *not desired.* The Universal Laws respond to the strongest vibrational match first so, in this case, the Universe will produce more of the thing not desired.

To the Universe, desire is desire from a vibrational perspective. If we bond vibrationally with something we do not desire, it will manifest just as the things we do. Remember, desire can only have the emotions with which we provide it as we nurture the Process of manifestation. The things we *do not* desire are usually injected with fear; a powerful emotion. The things we *do* desire we inject with the emotion of love, or happiness; also powerful emotions. If we can get it through our heads to love more of what we desire and fear less that which we do not, our Well-Manifested Life would be far more enjoyable.

Desire is the angel of God, the messenger of the Divine saying to each one of us, "Come on up higher." Desire is behind all progress. Let your desire captivate and hold your attention… The greater the expected benefit from the desire, the stronger is our desire.

Dr Joseph Murphy[7]

THE FORMULA AND THE LAWS

Ask and it will be given to you; seek and you will find; knock and the door will be opened to you. For everyone who asks receives; the one who seeks finds; and to the one who knocks, the door will be opened.

Matthew 7:7–8 NIV

The above contains the mechanics of the manifestation "formula" many of us are so familiar with. It is the most basic of all tools of manifestation. It precedes the intentional statement of Being; I AM. This formula is the framework into which the statement is situated. We will be going into greater detail on these ideas a little further along. For now, however, the simplicity of the ask-receive formula is better understood as seen through the lens of some of the key Universal Laws.

Let's take a closer look at desire through the Law of Gender. As stated, desire begins as masculine energy. When your desire becomes an "ask" of the Universe, when it becomes your Being, your I AM, you *give it* to the Universe in masculine energy. The Universe receives your ask in feminine energy which begins the Co-Creative Process. Next is a piece of perspective that is often missing in this mix. That is, there is a *necessary* reversal of roles that must take place at this point, vibrationally speaking.

Masculine energy is always in the state of giving, or the Action thereof. The feminine energy is always in the state of receiving. Once the ask has been received by the Universe in feminine energy, the Universe must turn it around in masculine energy in order to give us the manifested desire. It remains in that energy until the Co-Creative process is complete as it relates to that particular desire.

Now, here is the part that is often missed. As this is a Co-Creative Process, our part is to *switch masculine and feminine roles* with the Universe, energetically and vibrationally speaking. We must change energies to those of the feminine, receiving mode to manifest the object of our desires. This back and forth dance of energies relative to the object of a specific desire becomes the vibration of it, its rhythm, according to the Law of Rhythm that governs such energies. When the Universe begins to make the object of desire manifest, It takes the role of the masculine energy by "giving" the object of the desire to us in the Now, as the energy dance of both the desire and of us Being the physical manifestation of it seek Oneness with each other.

Feminine energy is not passive. It is the powerful knowledge of Being clear and the activity of allowing. Unless we *actively* take on the feminine energy of receiving the manifestation of the object, we remain stuck in the masculine energy of asking. How we take on the feminine energy most clearly and easily is by Being the physical manifestation of the object or artefact of our desire, vibrationally speaking, in the Now. This puts us in the purest receiving state we can get into, resistance free. However, when we focus more on the lack of the object made manifest, we produce the masculine energy of asking, or of *giving* the desire to the Universe over and over again. By focusing on its lack of manifestation we keep giving the Universe the masculine energy of the ask. At the same time, the Universe is still producing the masculine energy of *giving* the object of desire to us. Therefore, two masculine energies are pressing against each other unharmoniously and everything stalls or stops.

Both masculine and feminine energies working together are necessary to manifest any object of any desire. The Universe is doing

Its part by Law, yet we sometimes forget the Law also applies to us. The second half of the masculine/feminine, feminine/masculine energy transference is *our* part in this Co-Creative Process. Masculine gives to feminine; then we must become the feminine energy to receive it. The faster we get clarity on this bit, the faster we get into the Being state and the faster the physical manifestation.

A CLOSER LOOK AT THE PROCESS

Let us go deeper into the mechanics of this Process. Desire is born from the Law of Polarity, which states everything has an opposite. Desire springs from a state of noticing that which is undesired, or of not having whatever is desired, then desiring the opposite state. If we have manifested or are experiencing something undesirable, we can focus on something more desired by transforming the energic vibration from the undesired something to the more desirable something. This engages the Law of Vibration, which places these energies into the Law of the Perpetual Transmutation of Energy.

The undesired thing is on the same pole, plane or stick as the desired thing, just to different degrees. They are one and the same, however. Experiencing the undesired thing means you are vibrating at a closer proximity to the undesirable end than that of the desired thing on its opposite extreme. The level of energy being devoted to the undesired state, condition or thing must be transferred and applied in greater measure to the opposite state, condition or thing to achieve the desired result. Said in another way, the focus on Being someone with the object of desire must be greater than the focus on being without it. The work here is about learning how to focus attention, intention and energy because wherever attention goes, that's where the energy goes and, subsequently, our manifestations.

As soon as we control where awareness goes, we control where energy flows. As soon as we control where energy is flowing, we control what is manifesting in our life. This is a great secret to learn and it can change your life.

Dandapani[8]

Controlling awareness can be a little tricky when one is in the weeds with the undesired state and it's pulling your focus. This is why the Law of Perpetual Transmutation of Energy and the Law of Polarity are so important to understand, most especially when you are deeply involved with something undesired. It is so important to work on a perpetual habit of knowing *you* have the power to change your energy and to exercise that power through your Being state. On the pole of desired/undesired, the vibrational energy associated with the thing or circumstance that is undesired must be transformed by tipping the pole more towards the desired end and vibrating at the higher levels of it. This is easily achieved by Being the desired state, Now.

The Law of Action states we must engage in activities that support the manifestation of the object of our desires. The first Action is accepting the desire, followed by the Actions associated with gaining clarity. Acceptance is the first Action of manifestation. The activities of gaining clarity are subsequent Actions. Once clarity is achieved, your next Action should be your ask of the Universe as stated in the formula above – ask and receive – then to move into the receiving state of Being which is the intentional statement of I AM. It is the proclamation of your desired state. Examples include the following.

"I AM the physical manifestation of Being # weight."
"I AM a professional musician."
"I AM a straight-A student."
"I AM loving my work."
"I AM Being the physical manifestation of success in my industry."

Then the work is to Be whatever is your statement of reality. If you are truly Being the person with the object of the desire manifested vibrationally, every Action in this state from that point forwards is an Action in support of the physical manifestation of whatever it may be. Being is a state of Now. Now is the state where the manifestation resides. Being is *physically embodying the object of manifestation regardless of its appearance in form*. Therefore, Being is Action, and with each action, greater belief and faith in that Being becomes stronger. The stronger the vibrational agreement with the object of desire, the faster it is produced.

A CAVEAT

Now, with all of this in mind, here is a very, very important piece of this Process which is never spoken about and rarely, if ever, mentioned in most manifestation circles. You must be OK and make peace with the position in which you find yourself. You must be "good" with whatever situatedness you are presently in as the desire for the next facet of your Being makes itself known; whatever that other experience, artefact or situation is.

For example, if your Being is a "professional musician", if your Being is a "straight-A student", if your Being is "loving his or her work", this most often comes from a position of not necessarily being that musician, student or worker as your current situatedness or context. While your Being is someone who loves his or her work and makes a huge, positive impact is as true in the Present/Now as anything that it is currently not, you must not use the personification of Being that person who is in love with his or her work as a destination point to escape from the person in the situation you are in currently; as a "running away from", of sorts. I know that was a really long sentence with a lot packed into it, but read it again. Then continue…

Let's simplify this concept a little bit. Let's say your Being is THIS. The context within which THIS finds him or herself is other than THIS. It is THAT. THIS is the space of working in a lovely environment, making a huge contribution, enjoying the work itself and being richly compensated. THAT, which it is not, is what helps facilitate the desire for Being THIS. The recognition of this disparate context is what highlights the contrast between THIS, your Being, and THAT other situatedness. You must find peace, and be "good" with THAT before you can manifest THIS. You cannot use THIS to escape from THAT. You must come to terms with what THAT is, your responsibility within it, and get yourself to be grateful for it, if for no other reason than it contributed to a new Cause for your Being. As we will come to understand in the following few chapters, you will not be able to honestly manifest THIS Being until you can see THAT as "good" and perfect in itself.

Let's look at this Process through the Law of Cause and Effect. Desire creates the need for a Cause. Action produces said Cause. Those Causes will produce Effects by Law. Now, here are two truths about Cause and Effect that many of us get sort of bent out of shape. The first truth is the desire is not the Cause. *Desire is the urge to produce a Cause.* Causes come from inspired Actions, such as your ask and declaration of Being. Belief, non-resistance and Being the one with the object of desire are some more of the basic Actions or Causes. This is what is meant by phrases such as "a leap of faith", or "a step of faith". Leaping and stepping are Actions. It is also the Action of getting to the OK-mindset of how you are situated within the current context. Each action builds belief; Cause and Effect. As the Causes build up, so do the Effects and the manifestation of desire is achieved. Simply put, you cannot have a desire and sit on your hands waiting for it to appear. This idea lacks Action or Cause and, in that case, it is nothing more than wishing.

The second truth is most of us operate under the mistaken notion the whole Effect of the Cause, or the effect of the desire, is the complete, physical manifestation of it. This is a very shallow and incorrect perspective. The manifestation of the desired artefact, situation, or whatever it may be, *is only a tiny fraction of that whole.* The rest of it is the Process to the physical manifestation of the object of desire where *most of the manifestation of it resides in the Now* through each Action you make and its subsequent Effect.

THE REALITY OF PERCEPTION

Being the person with the desired object in the Present/Now, and being happy because of it, is the whole reason for desiring the object in the first place. This allows us to intentionally perceive a different reality as it pertains to the physical-ness of it. The Effect is immediate and therefore so should be happiness, joy, peace, love, etc. Assuming we did the work associated with the Process of manifestation, the desire is manifested. Allow the Law of Rhythm to take its course in creating the season for the manifestation to occur in the physical Universe. Receiving is allowing. In the meantime, you have already received it vibrationally which should result in greater happiness and joy. Set about Being it.

Condensing all of this down to its most basic substance, desire itself *is happiness*. It *is* happiness because ALL desire and all that is desired boils down to this one thing. The reason we desire anything is because we believe that having it will help us live happier, more fulfilled and juicier lives. Where we stub our toe on this is we tend to focus our attention on the physical manifestation of our desires – the Effect – without putting in the Actions of Cause. As we discussed earlier, some of us are in a habit of belief that states when the physical manifestation of our desires materialises, then we will be happy. This is a cart-before-the-horse way of thinking which is way too small. Even Master manifestors sometimes get stuck on this bit.

With the manifestation formula of ask-seek-knock, our Co-Creative role is to place our focus upon the "… it will be given to you", the "… you will find", and the "… it will be opened to you" bits which is a focus on receiving or Being the object of desire and on the road to its manifestation. However, we forget that by asking, seeking, and knocking, the manifestation happens at the same time vibrationally. We may not see its physical-ness just yet. So, the formula is telling us the secret. It is telling us not to keep asking, seeking, and knocking for the same thing over and over again. If we have already been given something, what is the point of continually asking for it? If we have found something, do we keep looking for it? If the door has been opened, what's the point of standing on the step knocking? Just Be the parts of receiving, finding and the open door Now and enjoy.

MORE TO DESIRE

The more of your desires you receive, the more desires you may have. Why? Because once you are Being the one with a desire already manifested, the logical next step is to have another desire. It is the continuation of the natural Process of creation and evolution modelled so brilliantly to us by the Universe Itself. The more desires are fulfilled, even vibrationally, the more we desire. This is because, once again, the desire is happiness and the more happiness, joy, peace and love there is in the Universe, the higher the vibrational level of us all. This is the meaning of the following verse.

> *Whoever has will be given more, and they will have an abundance. Whoever does not have, even what they have will be taken from them.*
>
> Matthew 13:12 NIV

Said in another way;

> *The more things you have, the more fully God can express himself through you. God is also in the things you want; so that they desire you as much as you desire them…*
>
> Wallace Wattles[1]

The quotes above speak directly to the phenomenon of desire and manifestation being One at the same time. If we can get clear on that idea, manifestation takes on a whole new level of truth. These lines are saying, whoever has the desire already manifested regardless of physical-ness is primed to have more desires. Abundance of desire is now, therefore, the joy of it. "Whoever does not have, even what they have will be taken from them" is because if the Present is lost in the future space of thinking the object can manifest only into that space, an abundance of desires cannot manifest through you. That space doesn't exist yet, so the manifestation is taken away as well as the enjoyment of not only the journey of manifesting current desires, but the enjoyment of what has already been manifested. The happiness is mis-placed into that future state rather than in the abundance of Now. The focus is off which puts us into a better vibrational match with not having our desired manifestation. There is not much happiness there.

The thinking that if we manifest or achieve our desires, happiness follows, is false. A belief in this falsehood will only serve to weaken our ability to manifest anything because it chips away at our ability to Be, or to believe. Therefore, even what we have manifested will start to slip away along with faith in our Being. Why? *Because of the attachment to the outcome.* We falsely believe the physical-ness of the manifestation somehow makes it more "real" to us over the actual reality, which is the Process or the journey of it. Happiness lies in the Process of unfolding the desire. Think about it. Once a desire is physically manifested, what happens next? We move on. We actually desire the next manifestation. Why? Well, two reasons...

The first is, once we physically manifest the object of desire, the object becomes a symbol of the past which, much like a future state, *no longer really exists.* It is an artefact representing a past journey of Being. A trophy, if you will. Trophies or ribbons on a shelf are symbols of past achievements. They may be very lovely to look at, even talk about now and again. You can pick them up and *remember* the events that led up to receiving them, but the *experience* of acquiring them was the fun bit. The experience of the race, the experience of the bake-off, the experience of the swim meet was the rush. Once it's over, and you have accepted your victor's trophy, what then?

I have known people who have manifested a fine life. They have a lovely home, a nice lifestyle, have manifested great business success, and are happy. In talking to them, it's funny how they sometimes reminisce about their early days just starting out and how much more "fun" it was to get it all going. Not that they are unhappy now. It's just interesting to hear them talk this way. I am convinced the reason why is because it's the journey that is happiness. Their fine life and lifestyle suits them, and they certainly enjoy it, however, the road of its manifestation was really were the fun was.

The journey is what brings us happiness not the destination.
Dan Millman[10]

It is the *experience* we are after because it is what the Universe is after in this Co-Creative Process. As God or the Universe evolves a desire through us, It is seeking greater experience of Itself. Once It reaches that bit of expression, it is time to evolve more. The Universe is continually evolving and growing. It never stops. Our manifestations are constantly evolving and growing too. *But it is not the manifestation of the object where evolution occurs.* If it were, any and all evolution would cease to be, covered over by the silt of the past. A physical manifestation is just the next step in the Process of evolving. It's a never-ending cycle and it will never end.

Buddha said all phenomena are rooted in desire. Since there will never be an end to all phenomena – all that ever is, was, and will be manifested is desire. This being the case, if you can get your head around desire being happiness, and happiness is Being, then there is never an end to Happiness.

There is no path to happiness: happiness is the path.
Buddha

The Turning Point

As we become better manifestors, there is always a turning point. I hope for you this is it. It is the point at which we finally realise the acquiring and accumulation of the artefacts of our desires, the trophies, ribbons and plaques, are not what we were after at all. The manifestation of the artefact of the desire is secondary – always. This is why so many of us become frustrated in our manifesting efforts which keeps flinging us back into the space of *not* having the desired object physically manifested. We look for happiness in the wrong place, with our backs turned to where it really lies.

I once read somewhere humans are less human *beings* and more like human *desire-lings*. While that is chuckle-worthy, it is actually quite profound. Many forms of Buddhism teach that desire and ignorance are at the root of all suffering. One of the Noble Truths of many major sects of Buddhism advocates the letting go of all attachment to *desire* as the pathway to Nirvana. I do not believe this is the intention of what the Noble Truth is encouraging. Additionally, I believe letting go of desire robs us of what the Universe desires to Co-Create through us.

What I believe this particular truth is referring to is *the attachment to the object of the manifestation of the desire*, not the desire, or the Process itself. Desire is emotional, but it is not the emotion of the *desire* that sometimes trips us up. It is when we shift the emotion from the desire itself to the artefact of the desire as an avenue to happiness that it causes us to stay stuck, suffering from not having whatever it may be and feeling it all being taken away from us.

Being is not attached to the results of manifestation. Mastery knows it is never the manifestation of the desire that will make us happy because nothing external to ourselves can *make anyone happy*. Happiness is an emotion; it comes from within our desires; from within the Law of Perpetual Transmutation of Energy. If you desire happiness, Be happy first. Let desire be your happiness without attachment to the outcome.

I know this sounds easy and I know it's not for many of us, especially depending upon what we are manifesting. Remember, the powerful emotion of happiness lies in the Process, or on the journey of the object of desire. Be happy Being on the road to it and the Universe will bring it about. It has to. It is The Law at work. The ask, the seek, the knock comes first. Then, the "it will be given"; "you will find"; "it will be opened" follows. Trust it. Be happy with that.

Take delight in the Lord and He will give you the desires of your heart.

Psalm 37:4 NIV

This is another Biblical affirmation of the Process. Said in another way, *taking delight* is Being happy. The *Lord* referred to in this verse is "how it all works" or the Process. In other words…

Be happy in the way the Process works…

And how does it work? Ask – receive; seek – find; knock – it opens.

… and the Universe will give you the desires of your heart and more to boot.

… And subsequently, more to be happy about. You must follow the steps, however. You must work with them, not against them. Allow the desire then let go of forcing attachment and allow it to unfold. It's the masculine energy transference to the feminine. Our role is to enjoy the Process Itself, every bit by bit of it.

CHAPTER 4

THE MASTERY OF YOUR TOOLS

Our last chapter gave us our toolbox. Desire. Let's begin to get very clear on what goes in it with a discussion about the tools of manifestation, some of which many of us are very familiar with.

At some point, most of us fall a little short of manifesting the objects of our desires. It happens. I have a theory as to why this may be. If you believe as I do, then we agree the Universal Laws operate scientifically, meaning they work for all equally. Therefore, if we assume the tools of manifestation are steeped in these Laws, then they must help us all achieve our desires in equal measure. It only makes sense.

At some point, in some form or another, we all use tools to assist us in our manifestation efforts, whether we are consciously using them or not. Tools such as affirmations, vision boards, mind movies, chanting, visualisation, even goal setting and other such aids are usually in our manifestation toolbox. If the tools of manifestation are steeped in the scientific Laws of the Universe, then it stands to reason they must be scientific as well. As scientific tools, then, what works brilliantly for one, should work equally as brilliantly for all. That's pretty much the criteria for any scientific method. I used to think that too. I have come to believe there is a flaw in this line of thinking.

From my observations, experiences and personal applications, I believe we tend to get too hung up on the tools of manifestation; the specific mantras, systems, or other methods. The Laws of the Universe are indeed scientific and work exactly the same for everyone. The tools of manifestation, however, are *not* scientific and simply do not work evenly across the board. The reason is simple and it took me a while to figure this out. There is a *craft* to tool use. As such, the use of them relies upon a unique expression: a personal, individualised application. This takes the tools of manifestation out of the realm of science and into the realm of creative art.

The Tools of the Craft

To reaffirm what will become our watch cry, *we are individualised and indivisible expressions of the Process that is God evolving, expressing, experiencing and expanding through us Co-Creatively.* Our Being, or what we have to say by Being, is an individualised, unique expression of this Process. As such, the way we use the tools of manifestation, or the craft of it, must be unique and individualised as well. Much like the use of a pen. We can all use a pen, but we all sign our names differently. Same pen; different application, which forms the unique expression of our signature.

The purpose and use of any manifestation tool is to accomplish several things. The first is to *reduce resistance*. An affirmation, for example, is to counter the thought, the voice in our head, or the feeling associated with its opposite. If you desire a new coat, the desire comes from noticing not having the new coat. The affirmation is to counteract the thought of not having a new coat with a new thought. This thought becomes a new Action, or a new Cause, in support of the manifestation of the new coat. A further Action is being grateful for the old coat and its service to you. In other words, Being OK with wearing and enjoying the old coat now, as addressed in the last chapter. By the Law of Vibration and the Law of Polarity, these Actions should begin to change the vibrational alignment with the lack of the new coat and slide you closer to the end of the pole, which is more of a vibrational alignment with the new coat manifested. The use of the affirmation is to reduce the resistance you may feel against Being the person wearing the new coat Now.

The second use of the tools of manifestation is to increase belief; the belief of Being that person with the new coat. Belief is an Action or a Cause. As resistance becomes less vibrationally sound, each Action you take as a result of the affirmation in agreement with the belief that you have the new coat strengthens such belief. As resistance decreases, belief increases. It is a shift in energy through the Law of Transmutation.

The third reason for the use of tools is to *raise the emotional levels* of happiness, peace, joy, love, etc., which come from vibrating at a closer level of alignment with the manifested artefact in the Present. The resulting increase in belief should make you feel good. That high, emotional feeling is what we are trying to achieve. The result is, the Universe responds to the greatest level of emotional vibration. It is from this place of Being, believing and happiness we should produce our "ask" for the new coat, according to the formula. Then the continued use of the tools should keep us in the receiving mode.

The manifestation of our desires is a unique and personalised Process. No one gets to the Being place in exactly the same way. Not everyone *believes* in exactly the same way, through the exact same process. Everyone's vibrational "tone" is different. What would make us think, then, the use of a specific tool such as an affirmation, which worked well for one, said in the same incantational way, will produce the same results for all in equal measure?

Most of us have come across and grabbed hold of a tool that has worked brilliantly for someone else, then tried to make it work for us just like it did for them. The difficulty is, that specific tool has their signature all over it. There is certainly nothing inherently wrong with this idea so long as the tool meets a basic criterion; the tool must be wrapped in the Universal Laws. However, I believe someone else's exact "formula" may not *entirely* work for every person in the same way.

I'm not saying using someone else's formula won't work at all, but it has a significant margin of error if you exclude from its use your own unique expression of the Universe – what you have to say – in a way that is in alignment with your personalised Being. For example, if someone's particular affirmation is in Greek, and you do not speak nor understand Greek, using this exact affirmation will not benefit you. If you translate it into a language you understand and the words match the meaning you intend them to, then the tool is in much better alignment with your Being. However, the exact translation from Greek to English does not have the same tense or word pattern from one to the other. Therefore, you would naturally change the pattern to suit your unique preference.

The Universe is in a constant state of evolution and growth. It is always expanding and moving from one expression to another; experience to experience. This being the case, the Universe cannot help but evolve us along with it. In fact, as far as the *conscious* evolution of the Universe is concerned, it can only evolve more consciously through us. Therefore, I believe the Universe helps bring us to a point where we must grow past someone else's ways and means and find our *own* way; our own voice… our own something to say and how to say it, using manifestation tools through our own unique way of Being powerful manifestors.

DEPENDENCE, INDEPENDENCE AND INTERDEPENDENCE

This Process of evolving is one of those Universal principles. It is the principle of dependence, independence and interdependence. Children, for example, are born and are raised dependent upon external forces such as parents. Then as they grow, they tend to evolve past the dependent stage to the stage of independence, much to the consternation of many a parent. There is another stage, however. Most stop at the independent stage, but that is not where the process ends.

The state of Being is *interdependent*. Being is interdependent with the Universe in the Co-Creative Process and the Universe is interdependent with our Being to produce a desire through us. This becomes the Process of Co-Creation and both the Universe and our Being benefit equally. The use of manifestation tools operate in the same way.

Going back to the tool of an affirmation, for example, let's say through some means we are exposed to a certain affirmation; a string of words that seems to link perfectly with a desire we have. Obviously, we begin to use it the way it came in the box, so to speak. We have an emotional attachment to it so it fits. We are dependent upon it. After a while, perhaps that string of words in that particular order may begin to feel stale, or to feel like our emotional attachment is waning. Two things are happening at this point. The first is your Being, the one with the physical manifestation of said desire, is moving along with the Law of Polarity. You are starting to vibrate closer to the end of the pole of having the desire manifest in the physical and away from the end of the pole that doesn't have it. That's a good thing.

The other thing that is happening is you are becoming independent. You are moving past being dependent upon a particular string of someone else's words. The staleness you may feel is the Universe nudging you to take the tool and make it your own. It's time to take that particular string of words and put your signature on it.

Much like we all learned to write. We all started printing in exactly the same way and were graded upon the uniformity of the letters. One child's paper looked much like any other's. As we graduated to cursive, we started to develop our own style. We stopped printing our names, for example, and began to develop our signature and, I make up with some certainty, we practised that signature until it resonated with us and became our own particular mark, which most likely looks nothing like the letters of which it is composed.

That affirmation we once resonated with is seeking some personalisation. That feeling of low energy around someone else's specific affirmation is a call to practise your signature with it. It is a call to make it your own and, if you do and do it right, that feeling of high energy will return. It will resonate with you and the place at which you are along the pole. You are independent with said affirmation.

The further you slide towards the end of the pole in which you truly are Being the one with the physical manifestation of the object or artefact of your desire, you slide into interdependence with the Universe whereby together you are firmly grounded in the Co-Creative Process, regardless of the physical-ness of the object itself. At this point, the tool as such is no longer necessary. The job is complete in your Being. Both your Being and the Universe have Co-evolved through this Process. This is how this Universal principle works. It's the same pattern whether we are talking about the growth of a child in the normal process of maturity, or of your Being.

THE TRUTH ON TOOLS

My personal journey towards the Mastery of Being a much more powerful manifestor did not take all that long once I *finally* turned the elusive corner and figured out this particular truth. It took years to get to that place, however. So, to save you some time, let's break it down just a bit more.

The most basic truth is there are tools we can use to work with the Universal Laws to more consciously and effectively manifest our desires. And, frankly, these tools are necessary up to the point at which we move through the manifestation Process; through the dependent-independent-interdependent stages. This is until we reach a state of Co-Creatively Being in which we move just as effortlessly as we move through the law of gravity.

You see, we don't need tools to work with gravity as we do to work with the 12 Universal Laws. We just accept gravity and go about our business. We are interdependent with gravity to the degree that serves us. We have little or no resistance to it, so it just works effortlessly in our lives. On the contrary, we have spent a good deal of time creating resistance to the way in which the 12 Universal Laws work, so working with them without effort is a bit more challenging. We need tools to help us cut through the crap. We use tools to help us better align with the 12 Universal Laws, or the resistance to them, before we flow with them effortlessly. That's OK. It is not a question of whether or not we use these tools. It is a question of *how we use them until we evolve past the need for them.*

The next truth about tools is this. If we can imagine and assume our manifestation tools are just like any tool in any mundane toolbox, then we also understand this fact – *the tool cannot use itself.* And it is at this point where I believe some of us fall short. Unless we move into the independent stage with the tool, we are expecting the tool to do just that; we are dependent on it doing all the work. Without our active, engaged participation, the use of any tool is pretty much useless.

We don't expect a mundane tool in our mundane toolbox to get up and work on a piece of pipe by itself. Why do we think a manifestation tool will do so? There is a Law of Action necessary to the effective use of any tool in either toolbox at play here. We can't drive a nail by observing a hammer and hoping it will pick itself up to drive that nail. That is a stage of dependence. We must engage with a hammer in order for it to be useful in driving a nail. We must perform the Action of picking it up and assess its efficacy for the job. This is the independent stage. Is it big enough, sturdy enough, small enough? Then, we engage with the tool to accomplish the task and reach the desired outcome interdependently. By so engaging, the tool becomes a part of us; *an extension of us.* We become interdependent with it. Without that level of engagement, the tool is of little use. If we cannot engage with a manifestation tool that works brilliantly for someone else, to the same degree or better than it did for that person, we cannot expect to achieve the same level of result for ourselves.

We must also choose the right tool for the right job. You wouldn't use a hammer to saw a branch from a tree. Nor would you use a saw to hammer in a nail. The tools of manifestation are no different. Furthermore, it is our own unique way of handling that tool that will determine the result of our outcome. If we are right-handed, we use a tool in a different way than a left-handed person would. Some tools are in fact made to be right or left-handed. If a right-handed person tries to use left-handed scissors, neither the process nor the result is equal from the left-hander to the right-hander. Manifestation tools are no different. We become independent with the tool to the degree we choose it as it fits our dominant hand; our personal Being. Only then can we become interdependent with it to produce the desired outcome.

I remember years ago, my grandmother used to have her own box full of what she called "ladies' tools". Simply put, they were just smaller versions of "men's tools", and they came in fancier colours. It's weird, I know... The point is my grandmother wouldn't use her version of a hammer, a thing about the size of a man's thumb, to tackle a huge nail. It would be a waste of time and would very likely cause some level of frustration. It may even cause some damage to the hammer, the nail, or even the wall. Most likely she would engage a different tool, e.g. she would call my grandfather with his "man's tools" to tackle that big nail. Again, the tools of manifestation aren't any different. Not every tool is right for every purpose, even if it is essentially the same tool, just a different version of it.

Let's assume I have a choice of toolboxes here. My grandmother's and my grandfather's. My desire is to manifest a cleanly and *efficiently driven* large nail into a wall. It would be pretty silly to do but, theoretically I *could* choose to use my grandmother's small hammer to pound a very big nail. It *may* accomplish the task...eventually. It may also wear me out in using it for that task. The nail, or the hammer, might bend after so many whacks. The wall might suffer a few misfires as well. While my grandmother was a fairly patient person and could probably accomplish this task with her ladies' hammer, I personally cannot and do not wish to engage her tool in such a way that it becomes an extension of myself sufficiently enough to do the job properly and get me the results *I'm* after. I cannot be interdependent with it.

My grandmother would use her hammer to put a *small* nail into a wall, or to loosen the lid of a jar. Given the same task and the same tool choices, I would choose her hammer to do the same. Both of us can engage with that particular tool in such a way as to accomplish the desired result because that tool works *for both of us used for a similar task*. Additionally, she wouldn't pick up my grandfather's heavy "man's" hammer to put a small nail into the wall or to loosen the lid on a jar. It wouldn't work for her, the nail or the jar for obvious reasons. The truth is a hammer is still hammer, big or small. It is what it is. Metaphorically speaking it is steeped in the *Universal Laws of How Hammers Work*, so it works as a hammer. One would work for my grandmother and the reason for which she would need it, and one would not. Similarly, her tool is not necessarily going to work for me in the way I need to use it.

So, to recap our truths about tools…

1. A tool cannot use itself. And, we must engage with it to the extent to which it becomes a part of ourselves to accomplish a desired outcome. We must be interdependent with it.

2. Not every tool is right for every job. Independence seeks a right fit and a proper purpose.

3. Not every tool is the right fit for every person for every job. To assume so is the state of dependence.

Again, *any tool of manifestation will work* as long as it is grounded in the Universal Laws, much like my grandmother's hammer. However, it will work only to the degree it is grounded in the right Universal Laws, that we can engage with it enough to become an extension of ourselves to achieve the desired result *and* that it is a right fit for the intended job.

I spent years receiving only moderate results using some of the basic tools of manifestation… the vision boards, the affirmations, etc., using the directions provided "on the box" for how they should work. I spent a great deal of time in a mild level of frustration as well because of the low-level engagement factor. Now, this isn't to say that these tools didn't work at all. They did and do. Just not to my desired degree of manifestation.

I am offering no offence to those who have gone before us and made such huge advancements with certain tools. I am very grateful for these folks and their tools. There isn't a day that goes by during which I am not reminded of, and touched by, their brilliant work. All of these tools are the *absolute truth because they are grounded in the 12 Universal Laws* and I have personally benefited from these brilliant people and many others. However, I am saying using the *exact* methods some of them proposed, used in the exact ways as described, began to get in the way of manifesting my desires to the degree I desired them, and I suspect this may be the case for some others of us out there. I hadn't yet figured out how to move through the dependent-independent-interdependent cycle.

For me, these tools began not to be very useful anymore. I was feeling my independence. That's when I made the connection with the original truth at the beginning of this chapter. Evolution and growth is all a part of this work of Being on the journey of Mastery. The intentional journey of Being is unique and personalised. Therefore, any tool we use should be tailored to our individualised specifications. The tool may work for you right out of the box, and it may not. Just be aware of how you feel using it and adjust, if necessary, from there.

Tools Evolve

Sometimes we outgrow a tool much like we outgrow toys as children. Nothing stays static in a Universe always growing, always evolving and always on the move. In order for me to evolve I had to grow past these wonderful tools to find what worked best for *me in my own way* if I wanted to continue Mastering the Well-Manifested Life. I had to expand my knowledge of the Universal Laws and create tools that resonated with me. When I did, things began to shape up. I strongly encourage you to do the same.

Think of the tools of manifesting as just that; basic tools. As mentioned, these could be affirmations, vision boards, chanting, meditation, focus wheels, grids, gratitude journals, etc. There are a million methods and tools out there and I will be sharing some of mine with you further along. And, again, any tool will work, as long as the absolutely necessary elements are in place – the tool or tools must be grounded in the Universal Laws to work for you or anyone else, and you must *engage* fully with the tool through the interdependence stage. If those two bits are in place, the tools will work for you… *until they no longer serve you.*

Use them but be flexible. Flexible with yourself, flexible with the tool and flexible with the results. If something doesn't work for you, or resonate with you, or you evolve *past* it, put the tool away for now and grab one that resonates better. Or even more effective, make up your own tools. The best manifestation tools are those of your own making because the use of them is the purest level of engagement. Something you create yourself is far more energising than any other tool. Above all, don't be afraid to try something new or adjust as you go along. It is the evolutionary process at work. And, don't knock yourself out trying to pound a big nail with a small hammer.

I have worked with people who tried very hard to use a tool that didn't really suit them. They insisted that because it worked for so-and-so, it would for them in the same way. Often, exhausted and frustrated, they would achieve minimal results if any at all. The state of "exhausted and frustrated" is NO place from which to manifest *anything* except more exhaustion and frustration. If you find yourself in this space, examine whether the tool or tools you are using resonate with you. Unless the answer to that question is a resounding "yes", put the tool down and work with another, or tinker with the one you have until it fits you again. Figure out what works for you and your unique way of Being. The Universe will guide you if you will listen. This is the meaning behind the verse…

Whoever has ears to hear, let them hear.

Jesus[1]

Remember, do not let the tools use you. Do not fall into a trap of being bound by the tool simply because someone else had some success with it. YouTube is full of examples of "This is how I manifested winning the lottery – and if you do it my way, so can you," and "Use my personal steps to manifest your dream home." Do yourself a favour. While you may, just *may* achieve some modicum of success using someone else's manifestation tools in this way, remember the rules of engagement we have discussed so far. To ignore them is a sure-fire recipe for disappointment at the level of the unique Being the Universe is expressing through you and you alone.

Let us be perfectly clear on the above point. Any tool you choose must be used wholly and completely without reservation, to the stage of interdependence with the Universe to be effective as an extension of your Being. If this is not the case, the enemy of all manifestation efforts will surely challenge you. It is the Devil incarnate – *Doubt.*

DOUBT IS THE ENEMY

Our doubts are traitors, and make us lose the good we oft might win, by fearing to attempt.

Shakespeare, *Measure for Measure*

It is interesting to me that the Bible mentions the Devil or Satan actually speaking exactly three times and each time it was to inject *doubt* into the situation. Disclaimer, once again… it doesn't matter whether you believe any of the stories from this material to be fact or fiction, the principles are valid in and of themselves.

The first mention was to Eve in the Garden of Eden.

He said to the woman, "Did God really say, 'You must not eat from any tree in the garden'?"

The woman said to the serpent, "We may eat fruit from the trees in the garden, but God did say, 'You must not eat fruit from the tree that is in the middle of the garden, and you must not touch it, or you will die.'"

"You will not certainly die," the serpent said to the woman, "For God knows that when you eat from it your eyes will be opened, and you will be like God, knowing good and evil."

Genesis 3: 1–5 NIV

And, most of us know what happened next. We can clearly see here the serpent, the Devil, Satan or whatever you wish to call it, was casting a web of doubt over the eyes, ears and heart of Eve in this instance. One minute she was perfectly happy with her life. Beautiful home, lovely garden, plenty of food and comfort. Then doubt came in and mucked the whole thing up. The manifestation of an idyllic life in Eden was shattered forever.

In the second instance, we are given a glimpse into the life of a man called Job in the opening lines of the book of the same name. We are introduced to Job's wealth, stature, and right-standing. One day in a heavenly court, the angels came to present themselves to God. Satan happens to tag along. As God questions him as to his purpose for being there, they get into a conversation about the character of the man in question and his devotion to the ways of virtue.

Then the LORD said to Satan, "Have you considered my servant Job? There is no one on earth like him; he is blameless and upright, a man who fears God and shuns evil."

"Does Job fear God for nothing?" Satan replied.

"Have you not put a hedge around him and his household and everything he has? You have blessed the work of his hands, so that his flocks and herds are spread throughout the land.

But now stretch out your hand and strike everything he has, and he will surely curse you to your face."

Job 1:8–11 NIV

We can see again the Devil is trying to tempt the Almighty Himself into doubting his servant Job, and vice versa. While He is not fazed by this flagrant attempt, He does permit Satan to put Job through one heck of a time and then kick him while he's down. Of course, if you know the story, everything works out in the end, but this idea of doubt is a reoccurring theme as it relates to the Devil as shown in the third example.

The third and last time the Devil actually speaks in the Bible is when he shows up to tempt Jesus in the wilderness. After fasting for a very long time, Jesus admits to being hungry, and rightly so. While it is generally agreed Jesus could have pretty much taken care of this situation without help, his desired outcome was to fast for a certain length of time and to get into the proper headspace to begin some important work. Enter Satan who places doubt on his mission by tempting him. First to make bread out of stone, second by tempting him with worldly wealth and comfort, and lastly by casting doubt on his own divine nature.[2]

In several other Biblical references, doubt is certainly scorned. The case of Doubting Thomas for example. Or any one of the following.

But when you ask, you must believe and not doubt, because the one who doubts is like a wave of the sea, blown and tossed by the wind. That person should not expect to receive anything from the Lord.

James 1:6–7 NIV

Then Peter got down out of the boat, walked on the water and came toward Jesus. But when he saw the wind, he was afraid and, beginning to sink, cried out, "Lord, save me!" Immediately Jesus reached out his hand and caught him. "You of little faith," he said, "why did you doubt?"

Matthew 14:29–31 NIV

Now whether or not you believe such stories as those above to be allegorical or based upon some true-life events is irrelevant. The fact remains they reveal a pattern – even by way of allegory. I am convinced the Devil so reviled in the Bible, and other iterations in other sacred texts, is synonymous with doubt. I am further convinced the antithesis of doubt is belief and trust. And, I am absolutely sure that trust and belief, along with gratitude, are the paving stones of The Masterful Way.

If you grab a hammer from your toolbox, you have no doubt it will work as a hammer is supposed to. You don't believe the hammer will turn around and use itself on you. In a sense you trust in the tool; you have faith in it. Essentially you and the tool are Being One. If you use your choice of tools properly, and use them to the extent they become a part of you, at the very core of your Being you may realise something. If you can reach that level of Oneness, that level of belief and faith; if you are actually Being *whatever it is you needed the tool for* in the first place, the result the tool was intended to be used for will automatically flow into supporting you, resistance free. It's the Law. Belief is the greatest influencer any of us has on our Being. Indeed on our life.

So, Which Tool is Right?

How do you know if a tool is right for you? It's hard to answer that question concretely because the answer is different for everyone. What I can say from what I know is, you will *feel* it. If it is right for you, it will resonate with you. It will excite you. The use of it will make you happy. Envisioning the results of its use will bring you joy. Using a tool or tools should be fun, not a chore. It should make you want to jump out of bed in the morning to spend time with them. You should experience evolution and growth by using them. They should work towards helping you manifest your desires and you should see and feel tangible results. If your tools do not do these things, put them down and reach for ones that do.

On that note, here is another very sticky and sloppy use of manifestation tools that is very prevalent in modern culture. I have been banging on about your own uniqueness and how the Universe wants to manifest through you in your own individualised way. Not to overuse a metaphor, but here I would like to hit a fairly big nail with a big hammer squarely on the head.

Most people don't even realise they are using or mis-using this particular tool of manifestation. It is not a new tool by any means. It is a sort of visualisation tool with a kick – most often in the backside – and in modern society, it seems to have reached manic proportions. The tool in question is called "celebrity".

Now, let's draw a distinction here so we may be clear on what is about to follow. Celebrity is a two-headed coin. On one side is actual celebrity. There is absolutely nothing wrong with anyone Being a celebrity for whatever reason, assuming it is ethical of course. A celebrity is a great visual, living-breathing representation of a powerful manifestor. They are such because of this very fact. They can be inspiring and there is nothing wrong with using a celebrity as a tool of visualisation. Remember, of course, a celebrity is a celebrity at Being someone – themselves.

The other side of this coin is celebrity *worship*. There is growing evidence that celebrity worship is an actual condition, or syndrome in modern society. Along those same lines is celebrity envy, which too is gaining support for being its own version of a syndrome or condition today. This is because celebrity is saturated within our modern culture and it tends to skew what we believe to be reality.

Overarchingly, celebrity and the need for it is projected at us from every angle; through social media, television and so-called reality shows where celebrities are manufactured en masse. Once so christened, these reality-show celebrities then make round after round of *celebrity* reality shows; that is doing a reality show as a celebrity of another reality show. Culturally speaking, we celebrate celebrity to the degree that it becomes overwhelmingly and I believe inappropriately venerated.

Celebrity envy is where the line between who we are and what they are becomes blurred. We desire celebrity for celebrity's sake. We desire to have their lifestyle, their money, their fame and all the trappings of celebrity to the degree we want to be just like them. In many cases, exactly like them and as such we commandeer this desire as a tool for manifestation. As a manifestation tool, however, used in this way, it is actually damaging to our own manifestation efforts.

So, let's be clear on the use of the tool of celebrity. Using a personality as a tool to emulate, or try to be just like in some way in order to manifest some of the things and situations they have can be tricky…and here's why. Many celebrities and personalities who have reached a certain level of social status – those who have "made it", who have become kings and queens, superstars, famous singers, huge politicians etc. – have all used some version of a manifestation tool to get them where they are, even if they *didn't know they were using one*. The most common tool is what this book is all about. They became who they are by Being who they are, resistance free. Awesome!

In numerous interviews I've heard many say they were just being themselves and worked hard. Absolutely true and I would say that is a good percentage of what got them where they are – hard work. I contend, however, part of the hard work is the work of Being; of Being the Self they really *are* regardless of outward appearances and circumstance. By using their focus on Being the successful and abundant *fill-in-the-blank* self with the *fill-in-the-blank* bank account and the *fill-in-the-blank* lifestyle. They may have been such while only slinging hash at the local Burger Barn, but Being it they were. The *fill-in-the-blank* stuff just had to catch up with their Being. Where they were before to where they are now manifested as a result of their *Being there Now*. Once they were just "Being themselves", Mastering their Being, the rest followed; the rest manifested to support their Mastery.

The way Jim Carey tells of his pre-fame Being is an awesome example. As he tells it, his early years in Hollywood were not terribly bright by Tinsel Town standards. His Being was and is an entertainer. His circumstances had not quite caught up to that Being in the earlier years, however. In interviews, he tells of driving himself regularly up to the top of the Hollywood Hills, which provides a breath-taking vista view of the Los Angeles basin, particularly at night. That's where I grew up and it is quite something.

In spite of his outward circumstances, he would support his Being the manifestation of the successful entertainer by envisioning Being just that; of having made it – a manifestation tool I am sure most of us are familiar with. Then, he enhanced this tool by writing himself a $10 million cheque for "acting services rendered" and post-dated it several years in advance to be made payable on Thanksgiving Day. He carried that cheque around with him day and night as a reminder of his Being a successful entertainer.

Several years passed. He started Being the success he envisioned so many times on top of Mulholland Drive. As film roles and greater success became more the rule rather than the exception for him, a few years after writing that cheque for $10 million, he found out a few days before Thanksgiving of the year for which he dated it that he would be receiving $10 million for his role in *Dumb and Dumber*.

The Universal Laws were brought into play, and manifestation occurred. Being, regardless of circumstance, was followed by the physical manifestation of situations in support of that Being. As with many celebrities, the magnetism that drew Jim Carrey's resulting manifestations to him is the same magnetism that captures our attention. We are naturally drawn to them because we are always drawn to powerful manifestors.

Let's take another classic example. There are some discrepancies to this story but, as an example, it works so let's go with it.

Growing up in Hollywood as I did, everyone hears the stories of how some movie stars get "discovered" and are catapulted into fame and fortune in motion pictures. While there are some who have made it to the top in this way, it is certainly the exception not the rule. Take the famous case of Lana Turner who skipped a class at Hollywood High School one day to have a soda with friends supposedly at Schwab's Drug Store on the Boulevard (it was actually the Top Hat Café). While enjoying her soda, the publisher of *The Hollywood Reporter*, Billy Wilkerson, who was also enjoying a soda, spied the beautiful teenager and arranged through the shop manager to meet her.

Not long after, Billy Wilkerson organised a meeting between Lana and her mother with then agent Zeppo Marx with full commendation. She was quickly signed under contract with Warner Brothers Studios and, just like that, a star was born. She appeared in her first film at the age of 15 or 16, accounts vary, which launched a legendary career encompassing over fifty films, and in the 1940s made her one of the highest-paid women in the United States.

These two celebrity examples highlight distinct points. The first point is with regard to tools. In the Jim Carrey example, we have a brilliant use of manifesting tools. A clear vision, a $10 million cheque, and a Jim Carrey Being the superstar entertainer regardless of outward circumstances. The tools of manifestation, as long as they support our Being, work. They decrease resistance and increase magnetic energy towards circumstances physically catching up with who we are Being.

As long as these tools resonate with you, you can use them successfully. If carrying around a cheque for $10 million energises you, makes you feel great, helps put you in the emotional space of Being someone with that chunk of change in their pocket regardless of outward appearance, then by all means use it. If it does not, then find some tool that does these things for you as strongly as it did for Jim Carrey.

In the Lana Turner example, we have an aspiring actress who manifested a miraculous thrust into stardom. While many accounts of the story do not overtly mention the use of any tools per se, as does the Jim Carrey example, it is said she had a *strong desire* for fame and fortune in the Industry. Desire always fosters vision, and if that was her tool – which I suspect it was – it certainly worked for her.

In these examples, it isn't the tool itself to be discussed here. It is the method, or the way in which the manifestation occurred that is noteworthy. What worked for them may not exactly work for all, however. Do you know how many young people spent hours at

Schwab's lunch counter (and the Top Hat) making themselves sick on ice cream sodas, hoping to be discovered *just like Lana Turner*? Not one of them manifested anything out of those efforts except, I suspect, a bellyache. I have actually known not-so-successful actors who carry around $10 million cheques in their wallets or purses hoping this will trigger the same results for them as it did for Jim Carrey. Lightning might strike twice but you won't be another Lana discovered in a drug store while drinking a soda, or another Jim Carrey by sitting on top of the Hollywood Hills at night with a $10 million cheque in his back pocket, and that's just the point.

Using the same methods as some of the great celebrity manifestors out there, essentially trying to *be* them, or be "just like them" won't get you very far, I'm sorry to say. Carrying around a $10 million cheque just like Jim Carrey, to achieve the same results in the same way, probably won't work. It has Jim's signature all over it. It's a fine line between admiring someone, and trying to copy-cat who they are Being for the purposes of manifesting your *own* Being-ness. The desire to Be the next Oprah, Bill Gates, or Rihanna gets a little fuzzy when your desire becomes an obsession with the mechanics of who *they are* and you lose sight of the greatest thing we all possess; who YOU are.

This kind of imitation used in this way is what Ernest Holmes calls suicide; the death of one's unique Being. Taken to an extreme, which it often is, people become somewhat lost in a celebrity to the degree those who try this route choke off their own unique expression of God and the Universe. They essentially add a very thick layer of make-up to hide a face not being ready to receive the Being they are supposed to Be. While some success may be achieved, the Universal Laws only work so far this his regard. Eventually, they must wash their face and evolve towards interdependence or fail.

Another reason this method of manifesting goes a little crooked is simply because the mould has already been made and broken. It's a done deal. By this I mean no one else can ever be the *next* Oprah, or the *new* Bill Gates or the *next* Rihanna. Everyone is a unique expression of the Universe, Being a copy of someone else is impossible.

Be yourself. Everyone else is already taken.

Oscar Wilde

Besides being a colossal waste of time, being a copy of someone else is beyond futile because the Universe can't help you get there. It doesn't even recognise what it means for someone to try and be someone else. Trying to follow *their* formula, precisely how they manifested what they have manifested in exactly the same way will not get you far in the end. It may help you get started in a dependent kind of way and if that is how you use the tool, go for it. Remember though, those folks were and are successful at manifesting whom they were and are because they were and are clearly themselves and no one else; Being themselves and no one else. It's their journey, not yours. Ernest Holmes wrote that one's individuality is the most precious thing anyone can possess. Even for a moment, to allow influences outside of that individualised expression to take control over what I call "Being you" is a crime against said Being.[5]

When you are content to be simply yourself and don't compare or compete, everybody will respect you.

Lao Tzu

In my experience, being the next or new anyone or anything will cause heartache at some point. While we admire what these wonderful manifestors and others like them have accomplished, it's best to stop there and not cross the line. It's fine to adapt techniques or tools from these folks such as their fashion sense or gym bod, or admire the cars they drive, the houses they live in – the by-product of their Beingness. Trying to be just like them actually puts you in competition with them and yourself. This does not work. You can't *be* them and you know it on a very deep level. It's just the truth. And, you *knowing that you know* you are not them is the where the Devil lies, because knowing that you know creates doubt.

It's not just you who knows or doubts the attempt at Being someone else's journey. Deep down, everyone else knows it too. It is similar to certain artists and entertainers who, for a living, imitate certain personalities. They are very, very good at mimicry and imitation, but we and the Universe all know they are not the real deal. Everyone knows they are *faking it* – including themselves and that's the key. When the lights go down, the audience goes home and the hair and make-up comes off, they are not whom they were pretending to be. To be truly and deeply successful at manifesting the results you want, *you must find your voice*; find what you have to say in the way of Being who you truly are. This can, and probably will, take some time but it's well worth the effort, which is really what it's all about anyway. This is the Process of Mastery.

Speaking of faking it… I am about to say something here that will shake some of the manifesting gurus out there to their very core. What I am about to say flies in the face of some very powerful manifestors, including some of my favourites.

There is a very, semi-probably-not-so useful manifesting tool that has been around forever, it seems. Some have success with it; most do not. It's called Fake-It-'til-You-Make-It. Here is my big, audacious statement on this one. The Fake-It-'til-You-Make-It method as a tool of manifestation has a built-in self-destruct mechanism as far as the Universal Laws go, and it most often *does not work*. Hold on… hold on… don't get all huffy. Allow me to explain before you get all carbonated on me.

We all know everything is energy. I don't believe I am sharing anything new. The Universal Laws are themselves energy and serve to explain how energy works. All energy works through the Law of Vibration. All energy has a specific vibrational frequency; high, low and everything in between. High feels good, low feels bad. The Law of Attraction is where those vibrations find their foothold. How you feel emotionally, or your energetic vibration, is your barometer regarding how you are manifesting anything. Therefore…

As long as you are faking it, like celebrity impersonators, you *know* you are faking it somewhere deep inside. You can feel it. Much like the feeling you may have when you tell a huge lie, you have an awareness of non-truth that has an emotional vibration on the low end of the scale. That energy is palpable and, guess what? Others can feel it too because the energy of it lives in the atmosphere of who you are Being, which is the atmosphere we all share, and your Being is telling a whopper.

You yourself instinctively know when someone is not being honest with you as well; when someone is not telling the truth. The Universe knows it too. Because that person knows it, he or she is putting out a vibrational energy of "not-being-honest", the frequency of which can be felt; it can be picked up. We might feel it in our gut, or something just doesn't quite compute. Wherever you feel it, the fact remains it can be felt. You may not be able to put your finger on it but if you could, you know you'd have to wash it. The Law of Divine Oneness is in operation, here. We all share the same Oneness, so it only makes sense.

As far as Fake-It-'til-You-Make-It is concerned, you can fake it all day long but if, while faking it, there is even a *glimmer* of recognition within you that you are indeed not being honest, it'll be a huge waste of time and a big disappointment in the end. Even calling it Fake-It-'til-You-Make-It makes it a failure in waiting. The title of the tool itself has the word *fake* in it! So, while you put out the vibrational energy of fake, the Universal Laws will supply you with more examples to highlight the fake you; of you not being truthful with yourself until at some point you realise this tool may be a bit dangerous.

Now before you take an even longer ride on that huffy bike of yours concerning what was just said, here is the flip side of that record. I wanted to get your attention first. I will stick by my truth about the Fake-It-'til-You-Make-It method but will add a little twist to it. The Fake-It-'til-You-Make-It method will not work *unless* you are 100 per cent totally convinced, crystal clear, and *completely in belief* that you are not a fake. You must be completely committed to the image. You must have total faith in it. In other words, Being the Master of it. And, you cannot BE the Master of it as long as you are faking it on any level.

If this is your chosen method to help you manifest, go for it. Use it to play with. That is perfectly fine. Don't, however, go off the deep end with it. Do not even call it "fake" to begin with. Change that straight away. Move into independence. For example, when I use my form of this tool, I use the term Rehearsal, and treat it as such.

REHEARSAL FOR BEING

The purpose of a rehearsal is to allow the time necessary to memorise lines, to get to know the blocking and the phrasing of dialogue between one actor and another. Rehearsal is the time to work out the lighting cues and where the lighting placement is, where the sets fit in, where the cameras are located for the scene, and to learn your blocking. It's a time to learn what the score and music cues are and how the character you are playing fits into the story being told. Rehearsal is not a *performance* and you certainly don't perform the entire script on the first day of rehearsal. You take it in and get it down pat *one scene at a time.* You rehearse and rehearse to the point of *Being* the person you will be playing, not faking the person you are playing. Actually Being it; believing it until it becomes a part of you. Some of the greatest actors out there are such because they are really, really good at being the characters they are playing. They *believe* they are the character and that belief comes from the heart and lives in the atmosphere around them. As a result, we believe it too. The character moves us and maybe even touches us on an emotional level. That's why we believe them, and that is why they are stars.

> *Assume a virtue, if you have it not.*
>
> Shakespeare, *Hamlet*

I can tell you, though, most stars didn't start out that way. Like Master manifestors they had to grow their craft and hone their skills. Most had to take smaller roles; bit parts before landing a starring role. I would bet some of their earlier roles were probably not all that good. Even some of their earlier starring roles may have been rough around the edges. Furthermore, no one would expect an actor to be thrown onto the big stage with a full audience in a starring role without a script, without a rehearsal, without a clue and expect them to be any good. That is a sure-fire flop waiting to happen and the stuff of nightmares. Furthermore, nobody likes bad acting. So it is with the Fake-It-'til-You-Make-It method. Many of us try faking a leading role before we even know what we are doing. You can't fake being a successful actor, entrepreneur, artist, teacher, scientist, CEO, dog walker or what have you, if you can't imagine what one looks and feels like. No one would believe you, least of all yourself.

Unless you can Be the starring role right off the bat, without doubt, and give a better-than-Oscar-winning-performance to the point that *you* totally believe it, don't perform in public. Keep rehearsing. Rehearse at home until you can believe whatever it is you are Being with your whole heart, one scene at a time. When you get Act One, Scene One down pat, and you can feel it in your bones, when you *are* it, then feel free to play that scene in public.

Go out and spend an afternoon Being your Act One, Scene One self while shopping, or getting coffee at Starbucks, or taking a drive, if that's the scene you rehearsed. When you have that down, work Act One, Scene Two. Put them together and play those two scenes in the public eye if you want to. Go to Starbucks *and* go shopping. Being whatever it is you are manifesting one scene at a time is a lot less difficult than forcing a fib in two acts into the Universe, much less on to yourself.

Trying to Be the star of a full-blown production which is bigger than you are ready for simply won't work. Said in another way, it's absolute *truth* you are going for – the absolute truth or nothing. Once you have that, you'll be ready for that starring role on the Universal Stage of Mastery. You will believe it. You will have faith in its truth. As Ernest Holmes writes, faith is an attitude that is so convinced of its truth that anything outside of that truth is unimaginable.[5] Or, said in another way...

Now faith is confidence in what we hope for and assurance about what we do not see. This is what the ancients were commended for. By faith we understand that the universe was formed at God's command, so that what is seen was not made out of what was visible.

Hebrews 11:1–3 NIV

… Truly I tell you, if you have faith as small as a mustard seed, you can say to this mountain, "Move from here to there," and it will move. Nothing will be impossible for you.

Matthew 17:20 NIV

This book is about The Masterful Way of Being and that's the antidote to faking it. You can't fake Mastery. You can't fake believing. You must just Be it and believe it. If you are wanting to become wealthy, *Be* wealthy. If you want happiness, *Be* happy, *Be* abundant, *Be* a rock star, a banana split – it doesn't matter what it is. Use the Law of Action and put your Actions into harmony with that Being.

Be it, one completely belief-filled scene at a time. The caveat is to understand who you *can't* be is another George Clooney, Jennifer Lopez, or even Julius Caesar – which should be quite a relief, actually. Whatever it is you desire to Be, *Be* it. Be on your *own journey of Mastery*, not someone else's. Live it right now interdependently with the Universe. That's how you vibrate on a frequency that the Universe responds to and it responds to you because it must. It is the Law.

So, use your tools and know that any tool or method you engage with is only effective to the degree to which it puts you into the emotional state of Being, also known as receiving, also known as believing. We have been given vitally useful gifts by those who have gone before as tools. Learning from them is like using training wheels. Use them, feel them, work with them, modify them until they resonate with you completely. Someday, however, it will be time to take off the training wheels, find your own stride, and ride like the wind into your journey of unique Mastery.

Use your training wheels as long as you need them. Get used to what it feels like to manifest one pedal-push at a time. Read those books, listen to podcasts, get into a manifestor group or start one yourself. Get a coach if you can. I could have really used one myself at one time, which is why I became one. At some point it will be time to take off those training wheels and you will know when the time comes.

It is also true that if Being on a bike with training wheels is the way you wish to ride your bike forever, so be it – it's OK. Be a Master at Being someone with training wheels if it makes you happy. It is your choice. A girl on my street growing up had training wheels on her bike until she was 13. That's as far as she wanted to take the whole bike-riding thing for herself. One day she put the bike down and was done with it. It's all good. Just be clear and know that the Universal Laws will only give back what you put in.

Be clear on what it is you are Being. The Law of Action works with the Law of Cause and Effect and responds through the Laws of Compensation and Attraction. Don't expect to receive anything from the Universe for which you didn't put in the effort. Don't expect a starring role when you haven't mastered bit parts and one-liners. And, don't expect to be on a ten-speed Schwinn racing in the Tour de France when you are still riding a Disney Princess Pedal Pal with training wheels.

Find your teachers and their tools and celebrate the training wheels they provide. Remember though, they cannot ride your bike for you, neither can I, and neither can any of the powerful, celebrated manifestors out there. Your choice, your voice, your way, your unique expression of the Universe. Use the Universal Laws; evolve and grow. Above all, enjoy the ride. In short, Be that interdependent, Co-Creative force of Mastery with what you are uniquely here to say. Sing your own song…

Chapter 5

The Mastery of Time

I believe those of us on the road of Mastery really desire only two things. The first is to be more powerful manifestors. To experience and express the fullness of our Being. We want to have powerful and beautiful manifestations and to be very good at Co-Creating them. We want our Being-ness to be happier, to have more fun, to live a juicy life and enjoy our desires manifested – and especially to enjoy the Process of getting there. Behind all of this, just beneath the surface, is an even greater desire although we may not actually realise it. I believe that in order to accomplish Being such Masterful manifestors, what we really desire is *integration*.

In the course of using our tools and expanding our desires to manifest, at some point many of us may begin to understand something. Most of the tools we use and the time and effort we put into *noticing* what we are sending into the Universe vibrationally are all efforts towards lowering resistance. They are all working towards diminishing the push-back from what we perceive to be reality. So, if this is true, it begs a question or two. Exactly who or what is resisting? We know we have a strong intention to Be the person with the manifestation of our desires. We engage in Actions that support our desired state of Being and our tools help us with this. So, what's the problem? Where exactly is the push-back coming from?

First, let's take a look at the programme; the Playbill of what's really going on. We need to recognise there is the cast of characters on the grand stage of Being Mastery. Sometimes those in the cast are supportive of each other, mostly they are not, and it's a little frightening that we, perhaps, may not have even noticed them all hanging out in the wings. So, without further ado, allow me to introduce you to your ensemble cast of three.

- There is *you* – the *you* reading this book. We will name it You. Your You is completely made out of the past.

- There is your Being – the Self you *really* are. We will name it Being. The ultimate goal is to know your Being more than you know your You.

- There is *your truth* – let's call it the gatekeeper between your You and your Being. We will name it simply Your Truth. This is the Universal Soul.

The starring role always belongs to Being, of course. It is the highest, greatest Self and deserves top billing as it is the Co-Creator of the Universe. The other two roles just don't always happen to agree with the casting. Well, here is the truth. The Mastery of Being is not just the Process of happiness, but also the road to integrating these three cast members into one triple-threat super star. In order to do that, we need to unfold a few truths.

Truths on Being and Time

The first truth is that Being happy, joyful, peaceful, loving, etc. is the goal of anything we desire. If you have read this far, that point has been made abundantly clear. But, it is not in the physical manifestation of the object of our desire where happiness resides. As we discovered earlier on, that would be considered *becoming* happy and, in my experience, the Universe doesn't support that cart-before-the-horse idea. I am convinced the Universe simply isn't able to support it because it doesn't understand the constructs associated with becoming. This is because becoming is steeped in an artificial construct of time; specifically the future. Becoming is an abstract based upon a misunderstanding of time and space. Happiness isn't discovered at the end of the journey, as we have discussed, somewhere in the future. You don't become happy. Happy is the journey, and Being in the journey is happiness. *To Be Happy is your true and only function in the Universe.* The Masterful Way is a state of Being through which happiness inevitably flows. Choosing whether or not to engage in your true function is simply a choice of whether or not to be happy, peaceful, loving, joyous, etc.

The second truth is that your Being – the Self you really are, is only Being because of the journey of the physical manifestation of the object of desire which is happiness. In other words, your Being IS the object of your desire. It is the Spiritual Self. It isn't the stuff, the money, the trappings or trimmings. What you really yearn for is Being the Well-Manifested Life in full Mastery. Having and desiring is in the journey of Being just that.

The third truth is what this chapter is all about. We have a huge problem with our current understanding of time. If we are going to make any headway into true Self, into true Being, into true Mastery, we must alter our beliefs, our perceptions and even our fears about time.

To most of us, time is a linear construct consisting of the past, the present and the future. This comes from our relative experience with this idea. We are born, we live and we die and we have been doing this for millennia. The only reason we have a personal experience within this construct is due to our fear of death, and the regression from that point to this point right now is how we live in so-called time. Even though we don't know when that end point will be, we stick it in the "future" so we can forget about that inevitability, then run a backward race against it in what we call time.

Because we fear death, it naturally informs our fear of time, of which we are so fond of saying we don't have enough. "I don't have time to see my kid's play at school." "I don't have time for your problem." "I don't have time to sit in this traffic." "I don't have enough time in a day…" All of these are statements confirming our fear-based construct of death and our slow march towards this certainty, which, by the way, we don't want to think about too much.

All of these statements, and the thousands of others we make up, are nothing more than choices. The problem with this is we give our power to something we made up and created out of fear, so we may falsely exonerate ourselves from the responsibility of having to make choices concerning the only element in so-called time we are actually a part within. The Present/Now.

> *Time is a created thing. To say "I don't have time" is like saying "I don't want to".*
>
> Lao Tzu

All time really consists of, from our fear-based perspective, is a label we apply to the Law of Rhythm. This Law states because everything in the Universe is made of energy it all vibrates at a certain frequency, according to the Law of Vibration. This vibrational movement coalesces into a certain pace; ergo a rhythm. We observe this rhythm in the seasons, the orbits of the planets, etc. In order to make sense of what all of this means to us, we label this as time, seasons, days, months, years, and so on. Because the label we attach to this rhythm is based in fear, we hurry, we worry, we wring our hands because when the pendulum of time swings in one direction, it will swing in the other. We know this. And, somehow by that swing in the other direction, we feel we will lose something. We will lose time.

This also works in the other direction. We can have a fear-based experience with the swing of the pendulum in the present within the expectation of what will happen as it makes its way back. For example, "I can't wait for tomorrow." "I can't wait for our holiday." "I can't wait for this day to be over." Why? Because we know the Law of Rhythm will take effect and produce the rhythm of another day, which will certainly be better than this one, we tell ourselves. See, we instinctively know about the Law of Rhythm, and call it time. As stated in the first chapter, the secret to working with this Law is to accept it, and to go with the flow as it were. Which points to another element we made up and which we fear. Waiting involves patience and patience is a virtue we are collectively not very good at. We will chat about patience in another chapter – so...be patient.

Now, this isn't to say we can stop being responsible with what we know as time. We need to get to work on time. We need to get home on time. We need to get to school on time, need to get the crops in, or to take the cookies out of the oven and all on time, otherwise there will certainly be consequences. Our collective belief in time dictates we work with it, at least to these degrees. Ultimately, though, we don't *have* to do anything except choose. And, it is the power of our choice I am asking us to reclaim. If you are OK with the consequences of not taking the cookies out of the oven on time, then so be it, and this is the key. The power of choice. And, for the purposes of reconstructing our ideas about time, I am asking us to choose to think about it differently; to surgically remove our fear of time and look at it from a Masterful perspective.

Since Albert Einstein manifested the Theory of Relativity, both our general and specific understanding of traditional time has shifted dramatically. In the most basic of nutshells, the theory states that both time and space are one integrated substance called "spacetime". Spacetime is malleable. It is relative to the observer's frame of reference within the realm of our friend, gravity. This is called time dilation; a concept of physics concerning changes in the passing of time as related to general and special relativity. For the purposes of our conversation, we will just tackle general relativity. Usually, all of this is explained using the prop of a clock, so I'll continue the tradition with this brief example.

General Relativity states two observers under different gravitational influences will have two different experiences of time. The observer whose clock is under the influence of a strong gravitational mass will experience a slower running clock than the observer under a weaker gravitational influence. Clocks in space, for example, move faster because they are under less of a gravitational pull than clocks on the ground. Said in another way, if you want your weekends to last longer, stay as close to the ground as possible. If you want a dull lecture or the time spent in the doctor's office to move faster, both should be held on the highest point to which you can get yourself.

All joking aside, the concept of General Relativity is significant because what it is saying is that time is not written in stone. We just made ourselves believe that it is. It is not the linear and immovable Newtonian time which believes time to be more absolute. Therefore, if time is relative, it can be manipulated by how it is perceived, or by our frame of reference within our personal gravity force, which is totally within our power. The gravitational heaviness we tend to feel in our space is the resistance, the junk, the "stuff" that holds us back. It is the stuff of getting in our own way. It is our work and our choice to rid ourselves of this junk in order to fully actualise our Being.

We have all experienced our own gravitational pull and how time is perceived within it. Let's say we are having a brilliant day. A day full of friends, family and fun. Each moment is brighter and lighter than the next. We laugh, we play…it's a juicy day. Before we know it, hours have passed, the day is over and we find ourselves saying, "Time sure flies when you're having fun."

Flip it over. Same day, different experience. You are at work. Your whole day is spent doing the most mundane things. Your boss is grouchy. Your co-workers are in a snit. It's damp and cold both inside and out. You watch the clock. You keep glancing at your wristwatch. And, you wonder why both appear to be broken all the while waiting, wanting and wishing that each moment would just get itself over with. The more you think about it, the longer everything takes and when the day is finally through, you feel as if you have lived through two days in the space of one. Same day, two different feelings.

The day of fun had a lighter and brighter gravitational tug on us. Our atmosphere was uplifting and joyous. As such, time moved faster through that day because of our gravitational pull on ourselves. We perceived time to have moved faster because, frankly, it did. Whereas, the "day that wouldn't die" seemed as if would never end. The gravitational tug on us was heavier. Therefore, time moved more slowly, relatively.

This isn't a book on relativity, nor physics, nor even Albert Einstein, so I'll stop here. What is highly significant about this is we all tend to be stuck in a Newtonian absolute time conundrum in a relative time reality. Ideas of past, present, and future are outdated at best. For the purposes of Mastery, it is imperative we adjust our thinking about time and how to work it intentionally. To shed the stuff that increases our gravitational pull.

Time: the Past, Present and Future

There is only one thought about time with which we need concern ourselves. Time is not the past, and it is not the future. While this is true of itself, for the purposes of manifesting desire and Being fully joyful, it is even more significant. The only element of time of interest to us is the Present/Now. We need to get our heads around the fact that time is not linear. Time is relative.

I know over the last several years in particular, the concept of the present or of "presence", of "being in the moment", or of "mindfulness" has received a lot of press. They are good tools and being well versed in certain techniques of mindfulness, or presence, can only do us good. While these thoughts are true at their core, this is not what is being discussed here. While mindfulness and presence help us "be in the moment", most of them still operate from the platform of the unholy trinity of past, present, and future. I am certainly not picking on mindfulness. I have personally taught many a mindfulness seminar. What I am saying is this is not what is being discussed here.

> *Realise deeply that the present moment is all you ever have.*
> *Make the Now the primary focus of your life.*
>
> Eckhart Tolle[1]

In terms of Being, then, let's start with a peek into the construct of the *past*. Look around you. Look at the room you are sitting in, the chair you are sitting on, the floor the chair is sitting on. Look all around that room. See the various objects in the space. Let your eyes just land on this or that object and rest on it for a moment. The pictures in frames, the various pieces of furniture, the books on the shelf, the clothes you are wearing. Just let it all slow down and sit with you for a few minutes. When you have explored your immediate surroundings, cast your gaze out the window.

What's out there? Let your focus land on the things outside that are within about ten yards. Are there houses, cars, people, trees, hedges, lawns…? Then, move further out to the end of the block, the next street, the next row of houses if you can. Keep going systematically further out in ten- to twenty-yard increments until you put your focus on the farthest away thing you can comfortably see. Take it all in. Sit with it for a minute or two. Now, ask yourself this question. *Who is looking at all of these things?* Let all of what you observed and who observed it just remain in your consciousness for a few minutes. Then, think about this.

All of what you just observed and who observed it…ALL of it… is the past. Even those of us on the intentional road of Mastery, let alone those on the unintentional one, spend a lot of time looking in the rear-view mirror at what has already passed beneath our feet. We are completely surrounded and inundated by the past, inside and out, and we believe it to be what we call "real". What we tend to perceive as what is real is nothing more than *what has passed*. Everything tangible that we see, touch, feel, taste, even what we think is the past.

We have never been out of our right path, only we have been walking it backwards instead of forwards, and now that we have begun to follow the path in the right direction, we find that it is none other than the way of peace, the path of joy, and the road to eternal life.

Thomas Troward[2]

The things we see around us are things we have already manifested. That table, this chair, those flowers in that vase, that painting on the wall…all past manifestations. These things are relics; artefacts of past thinking, of past action, of past vibration, past intention and past desire.

Because the past is so clearly and visibly manifested into something we consider palpable, we have confused this with something that is real, that we can understand within the context of being in the *Present*. In fact these things are misplaced. They are not in any context of the Present; rather they are in a construct of history to which we cling as reality. We believe in it and believe it to be true. Even the You who is reading this book is a construct of the past. A remnant of past thinking and past believing. The true reality is, the past does not exist.

For the most part, your brain is a product of the past. It has been shaped and moulded to become a living record of everything you have learned and experienced up to this point in your life.

Dr Joe Dispenza[3]

Only remnants of the past remain in our thinking. The past is all a memory that tries to make us believe it is the present. What we think about the stuff surrounding us, what we think about the person staring at us in the mirror every day, what we think about our spouse, our partner, our friend, our dog or cat, all of it is historical. It is important to understand this. The You you see in the mirror is a shadow of the past.

Now, there is nothing to fear here and, unless you just intrinsically "get" this point, you may struggle with the whole idea a little bit. However, ponder the significance. The stuff all around you which we believe with our whole heart to be real, simply put, isn't. This includes the You that you see in the mirror, for the most part. Now, let's ratchet this up a notch.

The Future Doesn't Exist Either

When we give birth to a desire and create a vision of what the artefact of that desire might be, there are two things of which we must be aware. The first is we tend to believe the object will manifest in a *future time and space*. This is because it may not have physically manifested in the Now and therefore, we regard it as not "real" yet. Because we all have a powerful tool – our imagination – we instinctively know it must be somewhere, so we plunk it down in the most convenient space which seems to be available to us; the future. In the future we can believe it will be so-called real. Our vision of the future, however, is based solely upon the past, which is also not real. What we envision to be the future state is based upon nothing more than past experiences, memories, feelings, etc. So, the future does not exist in itself, and it also does not exist because it is a construct of the past. The future is constructed by our images, feelings, thoughts and emotions of our past. Both are not reality.

We should never limit ourselves to any perspective of Being that is based upon our past. Remember, the physical manifestations all around us are relics and our past-centric thinking believes our desires must physically manifest in order to exist; to be real. So, we plop our manifested Self and the objects of our desires into the bucket called "the future". This is illogical; *ill*-logic. We mistakenly tell ourselves we just have to catch up to that place in time when we will rendezvous with the object, or artefact of our desire and then it will exist; then it will be real. Of course, this is a false premise if not a false hope. The future hasn't happened. The future does not exist. Anything we place into a non-existent future is also non-existent, even the non-existent past. So we must do something about our ideas of time and its malleable nature. We must get into the habit of belief that it is only our *perception* that alters time, because time is relative. Thank you Einstein.

This is why I believe setting a specific date for our manifestations to happen may set us up for a potential failure because this technique always places the object of our desire in that future state. Very often, that date comes and goes without our manifestations appearing, which leads to disappointment, doubt, maybe even anger and none of that helps anything to occur except more of the same.

So, with our ideas of reality and of the past actually projecting into the future, we are confused and this confusion scatters our energies all over the place. Our vibrations are disseminated and muddy. We make ourselves a little schizophrenic, which by its own definition is a condition characterised in part by *a failure to understand reality* and by confused thinking. We then take it a step further and create confused Actions in the Present/Now in support of our desired outcome with confused thinking and confused feeling about the past and the future. Then, the Universal Laws work to give us more confused thinking based upon our confused vibrational energies.

> *Whatever your action is to be, it is evident you must act NOW. You cannot act in the past…and it is essential you dismiss the past from your mind. You cannot act in the future, for the future is not here yet.*
>
> Wallace Wattles[4]

So what does it mean to act now? It means Being. You cannot postpone Being until whatever you are desiring manifests in some future state. You cannot Be in any past state either. Besides these obvious truths, the main reason you cannot act in the future nor in the past, however hard we may believe we can, is it breaks a big Universal Law. The Law of Cause and Effect.

Cause and Effect

As everything around us is the past, and everything in the future does not exist, by placing our attention on either past or future as a reference point for what is real, we are directing our energies on an Effect, placing it before Cause. What is the Effect of this so-called reality? The stuff around you is the past; an Effect of a prior cause. Our vision of the future, or future desire, is based upon our understanding of everything that has past, or upon Effects. That is the only way we can visualise it. So, the future being populated by the past makes the future, in this way of thinking, an Effect placing it before a Cause. It creates a future state full of Effects. We have missed the Cause part. "When I physically manifest yada, yada, yada, I will be so happy," places Effect of happiness before the Cause of Being happy. This breaks the Law.

> Nothing must be postponed. Take time by the forelock. Now or never! You must live in the present, launch yourself on every wave, find your eternity in each moment.
>
> Henry David Thoreau

Being the happy, joyful, peaceful ones, manifesting our desires in the Present/Now is supposed to be the Cause. The Effect is happiness. In the realm of that Effect, our desires manifest physically. But, we must Be the Cause of them Now and allow the Effect of happiness to be the next Cause and set the Universal Laws in motion through that. The Law of Attraction and the Universal Laws that support it *cannot* facilitate the materialisation of the object or artefact of our desire in the future. Our perception of the future is only a projection of what has past. Logically, then, the Laws cannot Co-Create the object or artefact of our desire into a made-up future constructed from a non-existent past. That's done and dusted already so technically is not real. It does not exist. The Universal Laws can only facilitate the manifestation of our desire in the Present/Now because it is all that exists.

So, let's be clear. The past does not exist. The future does not exist. Now, picture both of these elements on opposite ends of a flexible pole called linear time. By Being the physical manifestation of our desires in the Present/Now, we have the ability to bend the pole to the point at which each end can touch the other. It is at this point the pole represents relative time. We now have a circle called the Present/ Now. Within the space of that circle, created by joining the two states of non-existence together, lies the only thing that really does exist; Now. The Present. This is Reality. *This is where the manifestation of everything we desire exists.* It is the most important place of all because it is the only thing that is actually real.

> *I am the Alpha and the Omega, the First and the Last, the Beginning and the End.*
>
> Revelation 22:13 NIV

Notice the wording of this deeply profound passage. We discussed the power of I AM earlier on. It is your pronouncement of that which is what you have to say. It is the essence of your Being and the basis of all that is desired through you. "I am the Alpha and the Omega, the First and the Last, the Beginning and the End…" means your I AM, your Being, exists only when you can take the beginning and the end, the first and the last, also known as the past and the future, and bend them into a touchpoint. This eliminates them both in favour of the only thing that is real. The circle resulting from the two points being joined together creates a space of the Present/Now. This is the only reality there is.

The Present/Now is so powerful that it is tasked with sheltering and caring for the one thing that is most important to us, our Being; our happiness. Our Being exists only in this space. The Universe exists only within this space. God exists only in this space. This is spoken of in the Bible in the following way.

God said to Moses, "I AM WHO I AM." This is what you are to say to the Israelites: "I AM has sent me to you."

Exodus 3:14 NIV

"Very truly I tell you," Jesus answered, "before Abraham was born, I am!"

John 8:58 NIV

Neither God nor Jesus said, "I was who I was", or "I will become who I will become". They specifically used the term "I AM". "I AM" is a statement in the present tense, which is all that exists. I AM is a statement of Being. I AM is an affirmation of truth unfolded.

The Suppression of the Present/Now

In keeping with a linear perspective of time, we have unfortunately managed to compress the powerful space of the Present/Now between the two artificial existences of past and future. The Present/Now is squeezed into a layer so thin we hardly notice it; we barely perceive it being there. We have given it a name, however. We call it "a moment" which, by definition, is a very minute portion of time. And, because we believe a moment to be miniscule enough to be insignificant, we don't energise it with much importance. However, as the song made famous by Whitney Houston says, it is in one moment in time where all of eternity and everything else exists.

Try this experiment. Ask yourself this question; "Where does the past end and the future begin?" If you find difficulty in defining the answer, as does everybody, it should tell you how entrenched within us are our ideas of linear time. It is virtually impossible to pinpoint that place and yet that place is what is Now. That thin, almost imperceptible layer is where both our desire and the attainment of the object of our desire *are already manifested.* This is what is real and the only thing that truly is.

What untold misery is suffered through the burdens imposed by our yesterdays and the bitter prospects of our tomorrows! The good of the present day is too often sandwiched between these two impossible situations. The day in which we live is sufficient.

Ernest Holmes[5]

Therefore do not worry about tomorrow, for tomorrow will worry about itself.

Matthew 6:35 NIV

Because the noise of the past and the perceived noise of the future is so loud in our heads, we can't hear our manifested desires calling to us. "HEY – I AM HERE, right in front of you!" If we can turn our attention to the correct place of the Present/Now and realise our desires are here, we can embrace the *emotion* of having whatever is the object or artefact of our desire in Truth without resistance, through the emotions associated with having our desires Now.

It is through these emotions that we build *new* thoughts, feelings, and behaviours free of the dust of the past and illusions of the future. These new thoughts, feelings and behaviours are our true Being manifested. When we have a desire and are clear on why we desire it, when we make our ask of the Universe and declare our statement of Being – I AM...– the object manifests in the Present/Now. According to the Law of Vibration, everything in the Universe including our thoughts and desires has a vibration unique unto itself. The object of our desire manifests in its own frequency because of this Law. When we are Being our desires, we are vibrating at the same frequency as the manifestations themselves and we are being drawn to each other through the Law of Attraction. These vibrational energies will coalesce into physical form when the pendulum swings.

According to the Law of Polarity, both our desire and its manifestation are on the same Pole. The object of our desire is made from the same stuff as you, me and everything else. When we practise Being in the Present/Now it keeps us in the reality of Relative Time in which the desire and the object become One according to the Law of Divine Oneness. Therefore, we can experience the happiness of having and Being whatever it may be in perceived reality. This concept is foundational to The Masterful Way.

When we experience the *feelings and emotions* of the manifestation of our desires, they become as real to us as anything that we can see, feel or touch. In linear time we may experience a lag in the object manifesting physically, but it is no less real. It is our perception that is skewed. If we could just *Be* the object of our desires in the only space that is real, just think how much more powerful manifestors we would all be! This is the true meaning of the following passage regarding the Kingdom of God.

> One day the Pharisees asked Jesus, "When will the Kingdom of God come?" Jesus replied, "The Kingdom of God can't be detected by visible signs. You won't be able to say, 'Here it is!' or 'It's over there!' For the Kingdom of God is already among you."
>
> Luke 17:20–21 NLT

In other words, the Kingdom of God, or peace, love, joy, etc. is already in the Present/Now. God, the Universe, Being is already among us in the only place that exists.

Speaking of lag times, I believe there is a physical lag time for a good reason. The Law of Action states we must participate in activities that are in full support of Being our desires. This includes activities such as our thoughts, dreams, words and emotions. Done properly, participating in those Actions is the road of Being and the journey is in the Present/Now. The Universe Itself, in Its entirety, is in that space. What is often misdiagnosed as merely "a present moment" is in reality all of the moments of time. Not past time, and not future time. The so-called lag time is only a space in which to fine-tune our vibrational instrument and to better align it with our manifestations. Meanwhile, we may partake in a lot of joy and happiness by Being the manifestation of our desires however long the perceived lag time.

THE TOOLS IN TIME

What most of us fill our lag time with is the utilisation of the tools of manifestation. Whatever tools you have with you on the road of Being, use them. As long as they work for you, use them to strengthen your desires and towards finding the joy in the Present. In addition to the obvious use of these exercises, the more important by-product is that their use carves more space from the past and the future and creates more prime real estate in the Present. What we are doing is spreading open that paper-thin space of a moment by creating a vibrational match to the artefact of our desire. It is in the widening and deepening of our perception of the Present/Now where happiness evolves and grows. It is in the pushing back of past and future where the evolutional journey of our Being, and the evolution of the Universe, takes place. The *evolving* is what makes us happy desire after desire. And, the Universe uses us and our desires to evolve through us. Remember, we are one and the same thing.

Use whatever tools you have to expand your understanding of this space. Use them to get you into fully engaging with the 12 Universal Laws. Use whatever tool or tools resonate with you to get you to the place of total confidence the object of your desires exists Now, because it *does*. It is called belief; it is called faith and faith is tangible. It has matter, substance and must be used as a tool.

> *Now faith is the substance of things hoped for, the evidence of things not seen.*
>
> Hebrews 11:1 KJV

Let us then reframe the "lag time" in our heads because for most of us it has negative energy around it and tends to keep us in the space of asking and a space of fear. That so-called lag time is your time for Being the person who manifests all of his or her desires and who loves the ride! Don't toss it away. That only compresses the Present/Now back into that paper-thin layer once again.

Let's unpack an example. Some may argue if someone desires a degree in physics it will take some linear time to make that happen. That's certainly not untrue. It is also not entirely the whole truth. Let's examine this example more closely.

If that desire is clear, and the one desiring it knows why it is desired, the image of the so-called future state appears in reality – in the Present/Now – as complete in the space of Being one with a graduate degree in physics. The achieved degree can be felt. She sees herself walking down the aisle to be awarded that piece of paper she worked so hard for, with her friends and family cheering her on. She sees herself working in her chosen field and being richly rewarded for it. As she sees all of this and more, she feels it. It is done. And, guess what, it isn't done in the future which doesn't exist. It is done *Now*. She and it are vibrating together now. The lag time is necessary, so she may enjoy the Process of so-called getting there.

I have several degrees so I could almost guarantee if you asked her post receiving that piece of paper and the honours it bestows, how it feels to have finally achieved that desire, she would probably say she couldn't believe how fast the time went. Why? Because intrinsically she enjoyed the journey, even in spite of the all-nighters and lost social life. She evolved and grew. That's what made her happy. It's what makes us all happy. The evolving; the growth. Of course, the degree is a marvellous accomplishment as well. Well done!

AN EXERCISE IN CLARITY

With the intention of knowing the purpose of the following tool, as well as any tool in our toolboxes, is to diminish resistance to manifesting our desires and to put us in vibrational rhythm with them, let's play with an exercise of clarity to demonstrate the power of the Present/Now.

Think about any artefact you desire. That new vehicle, for example. If you are like many folks out there, the idea of a new vehicle springs from over-noticing the old one, or lack of one at all. Therefore, just having a desire for a new vehicle is a bit vague. So, let's tuck into clarity here.

Thought: I want a new car.
Clarity: That's not good enough. You can do better than that.
Thought: … I desire a new car.
Clarity: Good. What kind of new car?
Thought: … I desire that new *Mercedes CLS*.
Clarity: Better, but still not clear enough.
Thought: … that new *black Mercedes CLS*.
Clarity: Getting better… go on.
Thought: … that new *matte black Mercedes CLS*.
Clarity: OK, pretty good. Keep going…
Thought: … that new black matte *Mercedes CLS* with dark grey and cream leather interior with red brake callipers and the wood inlays…
Clarity: Even better, keep going…

I'm just making all of that up, however you can see how this desire is becoming clearer with each pass. Keep going with any desire you have until you are crystal clear. Hold that crystal-clear picture in your mind. Get clear on *why* you have a desire for this Mercedes CLS, as well. That's an important step in this clarification exercise and we will go into that in more detail in another chapter.

Do this clarity exercise with all your desired manifestations. If it is a *true* desire, and it is the absolute truth for you, you will have a growing feeling of excitement and happiness as you gain further clarity with each pass. *Notice that feeling is Now, in the Present, not in the so-called future.* You should get to the point where you see, feel, and smell that new car smell, and see yourself driving your new Mercedes with all the bits and pieces involved, resistance free. You should have an emotional response to it being yours. To you *Being* a person with that kind of vehicle and knowing why you want it. Your true Self, your true Being, is driving that Mercedes CLS in that picture, Now.

Here is the truth. This particular artefact of desire, your Mercedes, *has* manifested. Your ask is complete. If you are like most of us manifestors, the lag time between the Present/Now reality, and our perceived future reality, is our opportunity to connect with the Law of Action and go with the flow of the Law of Rhythm. In other words, participating in the activities, or Actions, like the one above, in support of the physical manifestation of that Mercedes.

> *It is here we find the importance of realising the Spirit's independence of time and space. An ideal, as such, cannot be formed in the future. It must be formed here and now or not be formed at all.*
>
> Thomas Troward[6]

What is the description of your state of Being someone with that new car? How does Being that person feel? What conversations do you have about it with friends? Where do you park it when you go shopping? Feel all of these exciting emotions. Be all of these emotions, right Now.

What you are manifesting should be as "real" to you as is the physical presence of your past manifestations. If they are not that absolutely real to you, you need to adjust your way of putting your attention on them; to stretch the space of the Present/Now and shrink that illusionary space of what we believe to be the future. We have so trained our thinking to believe that, firstly, there *is* a future and secondly, that it is hiding our desired manifestations, that we completely lose sight of the truth and of our power. Keeping them in the future is energising the enemy of any manifestation… Doubt.

You, Your Being and Your Truth

The following is a very important point, which needs some attention. Remember our cast members? Our star is our Being, and it is sharing a stage with the ensemble of our Truth and our You. Let's unfold this idea. Most often, the reason we fail to manifest is *because we get stuck in an argument between our Being and our Truth,* even though we may not be aware we are arguing.

Assuming we agree with it, all of us give our Truth a heck of a lot of authority precisely because we believe our Truth, regardless of what may be considered objective reality. From this belief we make hardcore decisions about this or that based upon the interpretation of our Truth. *These include decisions regarding the truth of our manifestations.* If our Truth recognises our manifestation as not being in the Present/Now, it interprets it as something belonging to the future because it is interpreted as not real yet, but may be someday. Our reward is doubt.

Every affirmation; every acknowledgement of our Being, every vision of our desire gets blasted by a shot of a low-energy vibration called doubt, and the arguments between our cast members keep doubt alive. Doubt slows the physical manifestation of our desires way, way down. If our desired manifestation is not wholly and completely real to us, our Truth will literally question it away from manifesting entirely and that's what we will believe in. So, our dialogue with the Universe, as does the ensuing argument, goes something like this. Pay attention to who in the cast is saying what…

> *Being*: I have a beautiful new *Mercedes CLS*.
> *Your Truth*: No, you don't. That's not true. You're playing one of your little "manifestation games" again…
> *Being*: I can feel the hum of the engine.
> *Your Truth*: No, you can't. That's not true. There is no engine; there is no hum.
> *Being*: I can see myself driving it.

> *Your Truth*: Driving what? Your imaginary car?… It's not real.
>
> *Being*: I can feel the leather seats and can see my hands on the steering wheel…
>
> *Your Truth*: A *Mercedes CLS* is way out of your league. Now, stop pretending and get to work…

And so on and so forth. Your Truth is trying to convince your Being that it is right and will find evidence from the past to stick pins into your new Mercedes balloon. Your Truth is battling against this new manifestation idea. You may see yourself driving that new Mercedes, you may feel the leather seats and the steering wheel in your hands, but Your Truth may not be convinced, and can prove it – with a little help from a friend which we will discuss shortly.

The proof may come in the form of the "real-world" car you are driving breaking down on you. It could show up as *wishing* you had that new vehicle, over and over again as you sit in the mechanic's waiting area. It could show up as envy whenever you see someone driving a Mercedes CLS, especially a black one. There are dozens of ways Your Truth can appear to win this virtual argument. It may be very subtle, it may be in the background so we don't really notice it, but this vibrational argument your Being is having with Your Truth is a very powerful one.

The argument causes messy and confusing vibrational energy. It unintentionally energises the vibration of resistance into the Universe, along with the vibration of that which your Being is intentionally putting out there. Add to this a third energetic vibration, which may be even more subtle than the argument itself. The vibrational energy of the *confusion your You is having while stuck in the middle of the disagreement.*

With each piece of mental imagery, with each line of affirmation, Your Truth needs convincing. This is because Truth lives in the Present/ Now – an important distinction to keep in mind for later. Unless Your Truth recognises whatever it is you are manifesting to be the truth, in the Present/Now, then at the very best it will hand it back to you. Your You, a relic of the past, puts the manifestation of your desire into the only place it has left…the future which doesn't exist. So, the more of a vibrational match you are to your manifestation residing someplace which does not exist, the less whatever it is you are manifesting will exist and the more the Law of Attraction will keep it in the place of not existing. Because you are more of a vibrational match to that idea, Your Truth agrees.

All of this keeps the manifestation of your desires in the asking phase. Any and all asking always has a question mark attached to it. Confusion does too. Confusion is another form of asking. "What's going on?" "When will my car manifest?" "How long will it take?" and similar questions along these lines. All such questions turn your ask into a wish. Wishing is powerless and only produces a clear picture of the lack of what you are desiring. All of this produces low-level, negative energy. Snow White may have *wished* for her prince to come and he did. But, that was a fairy tale, and the conversation she had with herself was with her head stuck down a wishing well.

A Few Law of Action Tools

So, we can see we have some work to do in reframing our Truth, shutting down the argument and clearing up the confusion. We need to expand our Present/Now so all of it lines up vibrationally in order for our ask to be clean. Use whatever tool in your toolbox you like to make this happen so long as it doesn't cause more of the vibrational resistance of doubt or argument. Be very clear on this. Make sure you know whatever tool you engage with is clean and clear of the grime of confusion and does not turn into noticing your lack of whatever it may be.

I'll share one of my favourite Law of Action tools with you. If done correctly, there is zero resistance, zero argument and it is in total alignment to my Truth. There are three stages to the process and all three stages need to go in proper order, at least at first, because the first bits are exercises in clarity.

I assume most of us at this point on our manifesting journey have some sort of list of desires in the works. I highly suggest keeping some kind of journal for your own benefit and to use for the exercises in this book. In your journal or on a pad of paper, make a space to record all these artefacts of desire. I encourage you to be fairly specific in writing down your desires at this point.

Once you have recorded the artefacts of your desires, the next step is to look for themes. A theme consists of several related ideas from your list. Are there several entries related to money? About what you will do with more money? Are there several entries related to your physical body? About losing or gaining weight? Are there several entries related to work or business? Or several about being a more powerful manifestor? If you have three or more related entries about something, that's a theme. Define the themes, name them, then put all of the entries which would naturally fall under that theme into that "bucket". So, as in the above example, you will have a Money Theme, a Body Theme, a Business Theme, and a Manifesting Theme.

Most often, this exercise produces around five-ish themes. I would recommend keeping to around that number, and certainly no more than seven, because it has been shown that holding on to and energising more than that is very difficult to keep a strong focus on for any length of time. It's like having an internet browser with seventeen tabs open. Three are generally frozen and, as for the rest, you can't find which one the music is coming from. Personally, I am most comfortable with four themes. Choose the themes that are most desired for you right now. You can work on the others later.

Now that we have worked on getting clear on our desired manifestations thematically, the next step is to clean them up, stop the vibrational argument, and ask the Universe for what we want. By way of an example, I'll use a common desire that for most of us carries a high emotional charge. I use very specific wordsmithing here because of the resistance thing. Let's work with the money theme, or money bucket.

Let us say you are manifesting a cool million. I normally would not advocate anyone start out with a manifestation goal of a million anything, but just for the sake of illustration let's go with it. If you are clear on that desire, if you have a crystal-clear understanding of *why* you want this amount of money, who would benefit, and what you intend to do with it, then you are ready to ask. The process of getting clear on what, why, and for whom is usually a powerful ask in itself. I encourage you, however, to make it more formal. Go for it and ask. Announce its reality with an I AM statement.

The Action of asking usually takes the form of some sort of affirmation or declaration. It is a declaration of Being. Most asking, or affirming, usually goes something like the following dialogue. The addition of the argument will help illustrate what usually goes on.

> *Being*: I AM wealthy! Yay!
> *Your Truth*: Sorry… I don't believe you.
> *Being*: I have a million pounds in my bank account.
> *Your Truth*: You have exactly £462 in your current account.
>   You just looked this morning.
> *Being*: I am a millionaire!
> *Your Truth*: What are you smoking, the lint in your pocket?
>   You're not even close…

Three conflicting things are happening right at this point. Your Being and Your Truth have entered into a disagreement with each other, and there is a part of You which is confused. The argument defaults into an unintended Action which counteracts the intentional Action you were trying to create by the ask itself. This becomes a Cause, but not the one you are going for.

The energies you are putting into the Law of Action are three distinct vibrations. One, "Yay! I have a million pounds!" Two, "Sorry, you don't have a million pounds". And, three, "I'm confused. Do I or don't I?" The Universe is receiving messy, jumbled-up energy. It will do what the Law is supposed to do, though. It will just work. It will communicate with the Law of Attraction by telling it to attract back to you more messy energy. More argument, more confusion, and more of your lack of that million. It must, it's the Law. So, let's do this a different way. Let's play a game of *Is It True?*

Your desire is to manifest a cool million. Awesome! Now, ask yourself, how does it feel to have a million pounds or dollars? If it is a true desire, your answers will be along the lines of, "Amazing, great, powerful, free, generous…" or, any other feelings associated with having a million pounds in your hot little hands would produce. Now, keeping those feelings aloft, take the specific amount of money out of the picture. Instead of *telling* the Universe you have a million pounds, which Your Truth doesn't believe, try something a little different and *ask yourself some questions from the space of Being.* We are involving all three cast members now. Please pay attention to who is saying what.

Being: Money is a useful tool.
You: Is that true?
Being: Yes, it's the truth.
Your Truth: I agree. Money is a useful tool.
Your Being: I love receiving money.
You: Is that true?
Being: Absolutely! I love receiving money in any way it wants to show up.
Your Truth: Correct. You DO love receiving money.
Being: I can use the tool of money to pay off my credit cards.
You: Is that the truth?
Being: Yes. It is true I can use the tool of money to pay off my credit cards.
Your Truth: I don't have a problem with that. I agree.
Being: I love to spend money.
You: Is that true?

Being: Yes! I love to spend money, not only on myself, but
　　on friends and family.
Your Truth: Oh boy do I agree. You *do* love to spend money.
　　Proceed…

Do you see how much different this conversation is to the previous one? There is no resistance in the statements you are making. There can't be. You are working *with your own Truth* instead of against it. I suggest you continue this until any resistance Your Truth is putting on your ideas about money has shifted. Now, perform your ask from *this* space. Declare your I AM. "I AM Being the physical manifestation of wealth…" for example.

All of the statements in the above are clear and truthful. They have a much cleaner vibrational energy to them. Free of doubt, resistance and gravity. The Universe receives the emotional vibrations of happiness, wealth, abundance, joy, fun and excitement. How different are these vibrational energies over the former ones? The Law of Action communicates these energies to the Law of Attraction and, bound by Itself as *Law*, it will attract back to you more of THAT. Each truth is a Cause to which the Universal Laws will produce the desired Effect.

Once you play with this game for a while, you can manipulate it in any way that works best for you. You may use a different version of *Is It True?* in your own wording; in your own scripting. It doesn't really matter as long as two things happen. One, you are clear, and two, you wordsmith it in such a way as to have little or no resistance nor doubt creep into what you are determining to be true in the Present/Now.

For example, sometimes I play the game from the perspective of "What's real to me now"… If you were to say, "What's *real* to me now is that fancy new home, packed with cool new furniture and nice things, in ABC neighbourhood," most of us would have a little voice in the back of our head, aka our Truth, saying, "Sounds lovely but, no, it isn't. You don't have it yet, so it's NOT REAL." That's Your Truth disbelieving you. Your Being will know whatever is real to you Now by the answer to the following question. "Is that true?" If it *is* true and there is no resistance, then it's real now. If it isn't true for you to the very core of your Being, then you'll need to wordsmith the "What is real to me now…" statement. Try something like this.

Being: What is real to me now is… that fancy new home, packed with cool furniture and nice things, in Alderley Edge.
You: Is that True?
Being: It will be once I manifest it.

STOP! That's what most of us do. This will stop you manifesting it. Keep going with what is true about the statement.

Being: I love Alderley Edge. It's real to me now…
You: Is that true?
Being: Yes.
Your Truth: That *is* real to you…OK, I agree…
Being: I *really* love the Alderley Edge area. It's real to me now…
You: Is that true?
Being: Yes.
Your Truth: Alderley is very nice. Proceed…
Being: What's real to me is I am manifesting a home in Alderley Edge.
You: Is that true?
Being: Yes, I am manifesting living in that area. This is real to me now…
Your Truth: Yup I know you are…
Being: What's real to me is I enjoy looking at cool furniture and lovely things I can put in a home there.
You: Is that true?
Being: Absolutely!

Your Truth: Indeed, you do. And, you have fun with it.
  That's real.

Similar to the first version of this exercise, you are validating your reality, and everyone in the cast is on the same page of the script. Whichever version you use, have fun with it. You know you are on the right track by how you feel and whether you have *any resistance come up for you* in response to anything you say. So, it's very important to pay attention to even the slightest twinge of resistance. If you experience a pinch, explore it. Don't ignore it or be afraid of it and never just let it go. For example, the following...

Being: What's real to me is I see myself living in Alderley Edge. I can see myself standing in my front lounge and loving my surroundings.
You: Is that true?
Being: Yes.
Your Truth: Hmmm, that's not *totally* true. You *wish* you were living in Alderley Edge... that I agree with, but it's not quite the same thing, is it?

OK. There isn't a huge amount of resistance with a statement like this from Your Truth. However, *any* resistance can grow into a lot of resistance very quickly. Furthermore, any resistance at all, big or small, is enough to put the brakes on the intention. Just remain very in tune with the dialogue that is going on with all parties concerned. Again, if you notice any slight twinge, go back and dissect the statement you are making about your reality and restate it until it has no resistance. Working with any of your buckets of desire or themes, your intention should be to just keep going until you feel on top of the world with the Truth of Being. Once resistance free, you are ready to Be your I AM.

Another version of this exercise I use is more along the lines of general vibrational up-ticks. It will help get you into a higher vibrational state and can keep you there for a while. It's one of the most fun exercises for me and the Universe really resonates with the higher vibrational tunes you are putting out there. So, any opportunity to keep yourself on the high-vibe is a very good thing. This one is called the "What's Fun For Me" game. It uses the same basic principle as the others in that it should generate zero arguments from Your Truth, therefore exercising a new reality from which your Being may operate. This version should produce emotions of happiness and, well... *fun*.

There are no major "thematic buckets" to work with this one. Just start by speaking, writing, or otherwise identifying what is fun for you. For example...

What's fun for me is...Disneyland
What's fun for me is...shopping
What's fun for me is...sleeping in
What's fun for me is...getting up early
What's fun for me is...Christmas
What's fun for me is...having guests over
What's fun for me is...travelling to Greece
What's fun for me is...gardening
What's fun for me is...reading
What's fun for me is...theatre
What's fun for me is...putting money in the bank
What's fun for me is...manifesting more money
What's fun for me is...autumn
What's fun for me is...spring
What's fun for me is...going for brunch
What's fun for me is...(fill in the blank)
What's fun for me is...(fill in the blank)
What's fun for me is...(fill in the blank)

Fairly quickly, you should be feeling pretty happy and excited about all that is fun for you, and you are feeling it in the Present/Now. That's a great place from which to produce a few new desires and to feel the feeling of Being the person with the object of your desires manifested.

Play with this game often. Use it when you take the dog for a walk or when you drive to work. Use it when you are at the gym, when in line at the checkout stand. You may even desire to find time to establish a routine for this. Sometimes, I use a part of my Buddhist practice for this activity as well as the others mentioned. It is especially useful when you start to get carried away with low-range vibrations. Like when you start to feel annoyed, irritated, angry or unloving about anything or anyone. Quickly pull out this tool and get yourself off that stuff. It will work to flip that energy back to the high-vibe very quickly. There is another side benefit of this particular exercise. It makes you feel good from a really good place. We know that we get what we focus on and focusing on fun is a great thing to manifest more of.

As with most of these kinds of things, there is a caveat. Do not let these exercises become more asking. Unless we remain fairly conscious of what we are doing with them, they may quickly spiral into asking mode. Once we have got very clear, we have essentially already done our ask. However, once again, I encourage you to make it formal. Ask the Universe. Announce it and expect it. I AM…

The proper use of these exercises is to practise Being. This is also known as Receiving. If your use of these exercises begins to highlight any lack of having whatever it is you are manifesting, you are back in the ask mode. If you notice yourself slipping back into ask, shift your focus back to Being. You will know it when you feel fabulous. And, you know when you are in the ask mode when it doesn't feel like so much fun.

In all of this Your Truth may raise an eyebrow at these games you're playing because it may feel it's being duped. After all, it may not have had an argument with your Being in a while, so something must be up. With the help of that friend I mentioned, Your Truth usually comes at you with something around the physical manifestation of your desire, or lack thereof. It may be subtle, and it may be over some minor element in your thinking. Don't worry. Just hit it with another truth and get back to Being. Speak to Your Truth when this happens; talk it out. *Eventually, Your Truth will get the picture and will begin to agree with you more and more freely.* Remember this last sentence for later.

TALKING BACK TO THE BACK-TALK

The technique of speaking to the undesired thought or experience is a fairly powerful practice to get into. In fact, there are dozens of examples of Jesus himself engaging in this back-talk technique when things didn't go well. When Jesus calmed the storm, he spoke right to it. In Matthew and Luke, it says He rebuked the storm, while in Mark, it records the actual words used.

> *"Quiet, be still."*
>
> Mark 4:39 NIV

When He took on one or two men possessed of "demons", he spoke to the demons telling them to get lost (Matthew 8:32; Mark 5:13; Luke 8:33). Or, when a hungry Jesus tried to find some juicy figs on a tree that had none, he spoke to it and the poor thing withered (Matthew 21:19; Mark 11:14). It is also at the fig tree incident that one of the most famous quotes Jesus ever uttered on faith and belief is recorded.

> *Jesus replied, "Truly I tell you, if you have faith and do not doubt, not only can you do what was done to the fig tree, but also you can say to this mountain, 'Go, throw yourself into the sea,' and it will be done."*
>
> Matthew 21:21 NIV

> *Truly I tell you, if anyone says to this mountain, "Go, throw yourself into the sea," and does not doubt in their heart but believes that what they say will happen, it will be done for them."*
>
> Mark 11:23 NIV

So, make it OK to talk back to Your Truth when it points out a disbelief. Then restate what is real to you now. Your Truth, after all, works for you. *He just needs a good talking to once in a while until he sees things your way; the way of your Being.* Your Being is the only reality and you have to believe in it first. Remember these last two sentences as well.

The really big news about these and other such exercises is probably the most important bit to keep in mind. What we are doing with these workouts is, in reality, pushing those illusionary boundaries of past and future further apart, thereby making more room for what is Universally real to continue to wedge itself in there and to expand – the Present/Now. The Universal Laws will work to fill that space by giving you more to desire, and therefore more to manifest and have fun with. Your main role is to Be the desires you have in your ever expanding Present/Now space.

> *The creation of something new is not accomplished by the intellect but by the play (-) instinct acting from inner necessity. The creative mind plays with the objects it loves.*
>
> Carl Jung

Your desires are the Universe and your Being Co-Creating from the most powerful vibrational space there is; love. Love is always resistance free, in the Present and fully believing in Itself. Desire that space above all. This is the purest meaning of the following.

> *But seek first his kingdom and his righteousness, and all these things will be given to you as well.*
>
> Matthew 6:33 NIV

"These things" being spoken of here are more desires; more elements of joy. "His kingdom and his righteousness" is your Being. So, putting this verse in our manifestation language…

> *Master your Being-ness first; Be your desires, and more to make you happy – more desires to make manifest – will be given to you.*

Chapter 6

The Mastery of Truth

In the last chapter, we discussed the dialogues Your Being has with Your Truth and what your You is doing in the middle of it all. Here, we will gain more clarity about the argument that goes on, what it's doing to you vibrationally, and how the Universe responds to it.

As is the case with all of us, much of our work on this road of Mastery is to expand our version of what is True in the space of the Present/Now. A greater portion of the work is about getting out of our own way in the Process. The result is the Universe evolves and gains a deeper expression of Itself through our Journey of manifesting the objects or artefacts of our desires. Now, let's scratch a little deeper and unpack more truth about Your Truth.

One of the greatest experts in the field of mind science and intentional manifestation was Thomas Troward. He spoke directly to the truth about Your Truth in a lecture he gave at Dore Gallery, London in 1909, called *The Worship of Ishi*.[1]

In speaking of the argument, or the resistance, Your Truth has with your You as you manifest your Being, Thomas Troward called this friction. This friction occurs when you have slipped out of Being and have moved back into asking or doubting mode; the You side of you. Or, when you are as yet unclear about your desires causing your Being to doubt. The work here is to *consciously notice when this friction happens* so you can do something about it before it has a chance to take hold.

> *... you may be sure that the friction is being caused by some error in your own thinking – you are limiting the Spirit in some way. Set to work to find out what it is. It is always limiting the Spirit that does this... The remedy is to go back to the original starting point of the Cosmic Creation...*
>
> Thomas Troward[2]

The Cosmic Creation spoken of here is, of course, the birth of desire. What he is saying is when the argument or the friction comes up, get to work. Go back in and mine for more clarity on your desires.

What do you desire? Why do you desire it? Are you placing restrictions on how it should manifest? Who are you manifesting this for? What's true about it in the Present/Now? What is real for you? How are you Being with it? Once you are clear again, be a grateful manifestor and move back into Being; back into receiving.

It may seem on the surface that Your Truth is working against your Being and your intentions. You have a desire to Be a vibrational match to your manifestations. It should be a no-brainer. We know the way the "formula" is supposed to work is that you ask and you receive. However, it can sometimes seem Your Truth is hell-bent on arguing you out of it. It may feel like it disbelieves every word you are saying. You may start to believe Your Truth is stubborn and bull-headed and that it's keeping you from manifesting your stuff. It may feel like you just can't win against it; as if your desires are just too big and too far out of reach if you can't get Your Truth to believe your Being and your ability to manifest them.

Well, I know it can feel that way sometimes. I get it. There have been times I have felt that way too. That was until I figured out what is *really going on.* I found out a little, albeit profound, secret and I will share it with you now. A few truths about Your Truth.

THE TRUTH AND THE MASK

As briefly mentioned in the last chapter, we need to be very clear on our intended desire and it has to be as real to us as anything that surrounds us which we can touch and feel. In other words we have to Be it. We have to Be the One with the manifestation of our desire in the Present/Now. A vibrational match to it, which can only happen in this space. It is in this space where it truly exists. If it is anything less than that to you, your ask of the Universe is merely a wish and a wish is nothing but superstition. Wishes are powerless towards manifesting your desires. Wishes are full of power towards manifesting the lack of it, however.

> *There is a difference between wishing for a thing and being ready to receive it. No one is ready for a thing until he believes he can acquire it. The state of mind must be belief, not mere hope or wish. Open-mindedness is essential for belief. Closed minds do not inspire faith, courage or belief.*
>
> Napoleon Hill[3]

Two things stand out in the quote above. The first is, as previously mentioned, that wishing is a futile endeavour. It is a powerless energy that does nothing and produces nothing. Wishing is not even an ask of the Universe. It's too weak to be one. Honestly, I believe the Universe doesn't know what to do with a wish. So, as a result, It does nothing which is why wishes never come to pass. Wishing has no intention, no direction, no purpose and no power.

The second point of interest in the quote above is about belief. *Belief requires Mastery and discipline.* The discipline of keeping an open mind about what is real and what is possible. This is where the proper use of willpower comes into play, and it is the only constructive use of it. Belief requires your willpower. The kind of belief we are talking about takes a hefty dose of determination to filter out any information, internal or external, which does not support belief in your Being.

It takes belief to think the way you want to think; to think Truth regardless of appearances. It takes the kind of faith and belief OF God to work by Its own Laws. This is a level of belief which believes 100 per cent in Itself, otherwise it wouldn't Be. This is different from a faith and belief IN God. The Universe believes in Itself to the point of Its own Being in which it is inconceivable to believe otherwise. *It is the level of belief that renders the need for belief unnecessary.* This is, in fact, the level of faith required to believe in Your Being. It is the belief OF God. This is also why, I believe, many people fall short in their manifestation efforts.

The friction your Being, Your Truth and your You are having is the belief OF the Universe struggling to find Its way through what your You currently holds to be true. It is struggling with your closed mind. The friction you feel is nothing more than the growing pains of your current thinking as it is compelled to loosen its grip and open to wider truths.

Once you start to understand and tune into the interactions between your Being, Your Truth and your You, you may begin to realise that something very deep is actually going on. You may start to figure out something about Your Truth. It took some time for me to figure this one out so in order to save you the trouble, I'll provide you with this understanding right now.

The reality is this. *Your Truth is wearing a mask.* The entity you are having an argument with is showing you what Jung called *The Persona;* a mask that is covering up the actual Truth behind it. Just about anything behind a mask can feel a little scary, or maybe a little mean. Because Your Truth is wearing this mask it may feel like it is being a bully. It may feel like Your Truth is trying to be the boss and is being very unkind by keeping you from your desires. The mask Your

Truth is wearing can feel exhausting sometimes because you just can't seem to crack its veneer. However, the reality is *it is only the mask that is bullying you, not what is behind it.*

Here is *the truth* about what is actually behind the mask *Your Truth* is wearing. Your Truth is not bullying you, not tearing your desires apart and trying to intentionally cause you grief for the sheer joy of it. Your Truth is not trying to keep you locked in a state of frustration. Your Truth is not trying to cheat you out of obtaining your goals and desires. That said, here is the big, bold statement. *Your Truth is actually working with you, not against you.* You just don't see it because of the mask Your Truth is wearing and your inability to see what's behind it.

Behind the mask is, in fact, *The Truth* honestly loving the heck out of you in those conversations, those arguments and that friction you are all having together. The Truth is only seeking your highest Self, your greatest good, and deeply wants the happiness of your Being. The Truth wants you to have the artefacts of every desire. It absolutely and with no reservation wants you to be thriving on your journey of Mastering that Being and to find the happiness you seek along the way. This is the only desire of the Universe because The Truth is your Being, which is the Mind of the Universe, seeking the highest expression of Itself through you and Being the Master of it. As Jesus once said…

For it gives your Father great happiness to give you the Kingdom.
Luke 12:32 NLT

In the last chapter I asked you to keep in mind the following statement in speaking about Your Truth. The statement is intentionally worded in this way.

He just needs a good talking to once in a while until he sees things your way; the way of your Being. Your Being is the only reality and you have to believe in it first.

He is, of course, Your Truth. Now here is the clarity about that statement. The fact of the matter is behind the mask is *The Truth* seeing things your way – the way of your Being – and the argument is *purposefully designed to make you see things in the way your Being is desiring and The Truth already knows it to Be.* The Actual Truth knows the highest Self your Being is capable of. You are the one who has to believe it of your Being. The problem is your Being has too much You in it, keeping you from Being *The Truth.*

Here is an additional fact about the nature of The Actual Truth. *The Actual Truth is that which is called God,* or the Force, or the Universe, or the Source, or whatever name you want to call that which is expanding Itself through you. This Truth is the essential energy that is the same energy whether we are talking about galaxies or guinea pigs; planets or peacocks. This Truth is Your Truth and it is love seeking the integration which only your Being can provide. It is simply behind a mask.

We are the Oneness of the Universe *because* of Your Truth. We are One with God *because* of this Truth. We are inseparable from the Source *because* Your Truth and Being are inseparable from It. Your Truth is seeking out your Being; that which is an individualised representation of the Law of Divine Oneness. All is consciousness of God and we are Co-Creating and evolving It though our intentional Mastery of Being. When you are Being, it is You and your Being at One with Your Truth, fully integrated, fully whole.

You may ask, therefore, what is up with all the fussing? Why the argument? Why the need for it? Well, here it is. *The argument serves a vital purpose.* The friction is actually producing a Cause, the Effect of which is putting you into greater alignment with your Being, bit by bit, battle by battle. The argument is the Process of The Truth leading you incrementally into agreement with the highest level of your Self; your Being. The reason the argument exists at all is because Your Being doesn't yet believe in what you are manifesting, and The Truth behind the mask is gently guiding you into lowering your resistance. If there is argument, your Being is still looking through the eyes of your You;

through the eyes of the past. The argument is because your Being is straddling an unclear space between The Truth and your You. When The Truth and your Being come into alignment, The Truth becomes Your Truth.

When you don't have a crystal-clear belief in Being the person with the manifestation of your desires already done in the Present/Now, The Truth comes to your aid and gives you a tap on the shoulder, otherwise known as the argument or friction. If you choose to engage with It, the friction will force you to take one step closer to clarity. Or, it will force you to abandon the desire altogether, which is what most people end up doing. The former is Mastery. The latter is misery.

Many people who try to engage with the Universal Laws intentionally, who "try and see if this stuff works" meet with the same arguments we all do between their Truth, and their Being. Assuming they tune into it at all, when the friction comes, they begin to question the *Process*, not their Truth. They point the finger of blame at the wrong entity in the trinity. They cannot see the reality of their desired manifestations in the space of what they consider to be real, which is the past, so they run in fear and doubt, all the while collecting much-needed evidence in support of "See I Told You So".

This is why it is so vitally important to be constantly on the alert for this friction; this argument. It happens almost all the time when we are manifesting something new into our Being, at least at first. Even the slightest bit of friction can snowball into a semi-silent avalanche of doubt if left unattended to. Doubt will take away your power to manifest anything you are desiring. This is the meaning behind the following.

> *The thief comes only to steal and kill and destroy. I have come that they may have life, and have it in all its fullness.*
> John 10:10 NIV

The thief figuratively spoken of here is the Devil, or doubt. Doubt will kill and destroy the work of your Being. "I have come that they may have life, and have it in all its fullness" is speaking of Being. The Truth is here to guide you to the fullness of all of your desires because The Truth desires them too. The fullness of life is the full life of Being. Any form of doubt separates The Truth and your Being, breaking the Law of Divine Oneness.

For reasons such as these, I believe whomever says this Process is easy is not providing the whole picture, unintentionally, of course. You can see how this Process is work. It's great work, but work it is. Until we can get completely out of our own way, this takes some effort. We must change our thinking and change the way we think about our thinking. We must become intentional. We must exercise our willpower, not over the Universe by willing It to do our bidding. Rather, we must exercise our willpower over *ourselves* to keep us in alignment with how our Being thinks through Truth. And, sometimes our Being thinks, acts, sees, hears, and feels in a way which is different to what appearances may show us. What your You sees is very often unlike to the vision of your Being through Your Truth. Until we get fully integrated, it's work.

> *Every individual has the natural and inherent power to think what he wants to think, but it requires far more effort to do so than it does the thoughts which are suggested by appearances. To think according to appearances is easy; to think truth regardless of appearances is laborious and requires the expenditure of more power than any other work we are called upon to perform.*
>
> Wallace Wattles[4]

The Big Reveal

So, a quick review. Your Truth is wearing a mask and behind the mask is The Actual Truth working out your highest good. Your highest good is your Being. If you understand this so far, you may sense a question or two hanging in the air. What is the mask? Who made it? What is it a representation of? Glad you asked…

There is a huge irony here regarding the mask Your Truth is wearing and it is vital to recognise what that is. The mask can be frightening, mean, threatening, argumentative, etc. At least that is how you perceive it to be. Here, however, is a little bit of wisdom which may hopefully help you see it for what it really is, what it is made of and who made it.

The reality is, *you made the mask Your Truth is wearing*. You fashioned it carefully out of doubt, disbelief, fear, a lack of self-confidence, the past and a lack of trust in how all of this works. You made it very realistic. And what does the mask look like? The mask is an image of yourself; the doubtful, disbelieving, fearful, lack-of-self-confidence you. A mirror image of a darkened You is looking back over the negotiating table during the argument you are having. The friction you are feeling is your own argument and it will remain quarrelsome as long as the mask is worn over The Truth.

The mask can only be removed when your Being is ready and able to remove it. Once you are clear and out of the asking mode, once your desires become a part of your Being, you can reach out and pull the mask off. Once you remove it, you are at integration. You are at Oneness with your Being, resistance free. You, your Truth, and your Being are whole. You have reached atonement; at-one-ment.

When the alignment happens there is no doubt or resistance evident. You have reached a level of Mastery when there is seamlessness between you Being and The Actual Truth. Once Being and Truth are aligned and in agreement, you are Being in Truth, in the Present/Now. It is at this point your actual *biology* changes into that Being and you begin to evolve into Its form.

You move differently. The way you walk down the street changes. The way in which you interact with your friends, family, neighbours, co-workers, your boss and anyone you meet is in this state of Being. The way you eat may change. The way you dress and present yourself to the world may take on a new appearance. Even how you see and perceive the relics of the past all around you may seem different. From the space of Being, you have physically embodied your desires and it feels different; lovely, happy. This is what is meant by having new thoughts and new feelings not bound by images and behaviours of the past.

When you are Being, the Present/Now expands and can never regress again. This is because the space you created within the Present/Now is permanent. The *substance* of your belief cannot be mis-believed once you have it in your Being. It's in your Beings' DNA; its biology. You have successfully carved out more Present, more reality from the false past and future. As Being, through the Law of Action, each step you make and each breath you take in that state are indeed Actions which build greater belief, one well-intended Action at a time. Action is belief. Belief is Being.

Engaging in the Conversation

A second statement I made in the last chapter can now be clarified. As in the previous statement, the wordsmithing of it was intentional. In the last chapter I said the following on which I can now provide more clarity.

Eventually, Your Truth will get the picture and will begin to agree with you more and more freely.

This statement has two meanings. The first is, after you become more aware of what is going on with the friction, it becomes much less difficult to get into alignment or integration with your Being and Your Truth. Much like exercising your physical muscles, or building a new skill, it becomes easier with use. The work at this point is tuning in to more subtle frequencies of the argument as it grows less and less robust and the time the friction take grows shorter.

The second meaning of the phrase above may have already occurred to you, but here goes. If Your Truth is wearing a mask that you have made, and the mask is a darkened, fearful image of You, then the argument you are having is with yourself. The Truth is only trying to convince you of your Being; patiently sitting there, waiting to be relieved of the mask. Once you believe in your Being, it shifts completely into alignment with Truth, seamlessly. Therefore, the entire argument is under your control. You have the power to cease the friction at any time and remove the mask.

So, I will now reword that sentence above so it reveals its true meaning. Here is that sentence as it sounds from this perspective. *"Eventually, Your Truth will get the picture and will begin to agree with you more and more freely"* is more appropriately worded this way.

> *Eventually, your Being will get the picture and begin to agree with The Actual Truth more and more freely.*

Feels different, doesn't it? Until you understood what is *really* going on, it wouldn't have made sense to have said it in this way. Now you understand how all three players are interacting on the grand, Universal stage of Oneness and the integration of all three is the real Self – the Highest Self; the most pure expression of God evolving through you. It is Mastery.

All of this is why it is so vitally important to engage in the conversation your You, Your Truth and your Being are having. This is why it is so important to tune into it and to work with it intentionally towards Mastery over resistance. The dialogue is happening whether you are aware of it or not. The problem with being unaware is the friction part of manifesting your desires will be as far as you get. Without having the conversation and unifying all parties involved resistance free, all you will receive is more resistance; more friction.

Truth is only seeking your Being. The mask is of your own making. The faster you can remove the mask, the faster your Being can Be. It is in this state of Being that you achieve a vibrational match with all of your desires; where you become united with them. When you are united with them, they are as real as any other thing you determine to be so. The more you manifest your desires, the more the Universe can express Itself through you in the Co-Creative Process which is the entire point of Being in the first place. It starts with belief, with unity and with Oneness. This is the road of Mastery.

> *The first step toward becoming united to a thing in the outward world is to become united to it in the inward world. If you will unite yourself with it internally, you will certainly come to be united with it externally...*
>
> Wallace Wattles[5]

PART TWO: THE SKILLSET

THE MASTERY OF A CLEAN HOUSE – THE 5-STEP PROCESS
THE MASTERY OF CLARITY
THE MASTERY OF MAPS
THE MASTERY OF PHANTOMS
THE MASTERY OF MONSTERS
THE MASTERY OF WHAT'S TOO SMALL
THE MASTERY OF JUDGMENT
THE MASTERY OF FORGIVENESS

Part Two introduces us to the skillset; The 5-Step Process of Manifesting a Masterful Life. This section gives us a thorough understanding of how to use these steps and, more importantly, how to identify and rid ourselves of the many things that get in the way of our Being.

CHAPTER 7

THE MASTERY OF A CLEAN HOUSE – THE 5-STEP PROCESS

So far, much of what we have discussed are ideas concerning clarity. We have grown to understand truths about our desires, the past, the present and the future. We have moved from dependence to independence into the space of Co-Creation; interdependence. We have gained clarity around the tools of manifestation and gained some truth about Your Truth. All of this is guiding us towards cleaning up our space and getting out of our own way. Now, let's discuss a larger construct; the bigger clean-up job. Let us discuss cleaning up the house of our Being; the space into which our intentional manifestations may be realised, and introduce the 5-Step Process of Manifestation.

I am a huge theatre buff. I'll admit it. It's one of the things I enjoy most. One of my favourite genres is musical theatre and one of my favourite musicals is *Fiddler on the Roof*.[1] I just love the glimpse into the heart, soul and life of the lead character, Tevye, and his journey along a path to define himself, his relationship with God and his traditional Jewish heritage in a world that no longer has a place for him, nor for his people.

For Tevye, a poor, philosophical milkman living in a pre-revolutionary Russia, Jewish Orthodoxy is his entire world and the world of his friends and neighbours; the villagers of Anatevka. Throughout the story, his familiar, cherished traditions begin to crumble all around him. He clings tightly to his traditions and his values, only to realise that the more firmly he grips on to them, the less he has to hold on to. Deeply, he understands that the only thing constant in this world is change, growth and evolution. On the other hand tradition is important too.

We are privileged to see and hear his internal dialogue clashing against his external world as he tries to loosen his grip on orthodox customs and rituals in order to please his five daughters, who are just one step ahead of him in their interpretations of Jewish life in the modernising world. While this journey is heart-warming, frustrating and captivating all at the same time, the story is packed with some very Universal truths as far as the Laws go. One of the most important, I believe, comes nearly at the end of the show. It's a very poignant moment and is delivered not from Tevye's perspective, but from the perspective of his wife, Golde.

The Dirty House

The Jews have been expelled from Russia. The traditional hopes and dreams of Tevye and his family, humble though they were, are all but gone as they hastily struggle to pack up what little they have into their wagon. All their belongings are tied down to cart, which will be pulled by Tevye himself through the mud and muck of the dirt roads of a Ukraine winter.

The knots are being synched, villagers by the dozen are walking past their gates beginning their own personal exodus; a dusting of snow is on the ground. The air is bitterly cold as the last-minute details are being checked. Beside the great unknown before them lies a long, arduous journey, on foot. The humble house they have lived in for decades is being abandoned; the farm animals left behind. Emotional and physical doors are closing all around them. Any moment they will take their first steps towards a new life in America. Then Golde, in a moment of clinging on to something familiar, suddenly looks around, turns, and goes back inside the house. She tells Tevye she has to sweep the floors.

Let's paint a more detailed picture. *Everyone* in the small village of Anatevka has been forced to leave. There is no one to sell the house and farm to. They couldn't give it away, even if they wanted to. The house on a good day is unassuming at best. No one will want the place, ever. They are leaving everything behind. Why on earth is she cleaning it?

Tevye is puzzled, frustrated and, I imagine, a bit genuinely curious at Golde's actions. As he follows her into the house, he asks, "Golde what are you doing?" Through tears, anger and uncertainty she says, "I cannot leave a dirty house!" She snaps back around and continues cleaning. Even though the house is of no value to anyone, she cleans it.

Let's go a bit deeper…

There is a very entrenched, cultural facet to Golde and the role she plays in life; in fact in all of their lives. For all Orthodox Jews, roles are clearly identifiable, expected and taken as written in stone; always and forever. Tevye is the papa, the man of the house and head of the family. He makes the living for his household. He says the prayers. He makes all final decisions. It is expected of him. It is tradition.

For Golde, and generations of women before her, her role is deeply ingrained into her very DNA. It defines her reality. The back-breaking work of a woman's role, the role of the mama, is a place of familiar comfort for her; her own place of tradition. She is a woman, and a woman is the cleaner of the house and keeper of the home.

She instinctively knows she cannot leave this role and begin another without making sure the work is complete, at least in her own head. It would crush her. She cannot begin a new chapter in her life, head for America, and *leave a dirty house behind.*

As for an earth-shattering and defining moment in the story, it isn't, really. It is one six-word line of dialogue very few people truly understand, and it is usually tossed away for the laugh it generally creates. Whether or not the writers had this intention in mind when they wrote the scene is irrelevant. There remains a very deep, Universal truth within it, however, and it contains a lesson for all of us to explore. Here it is.

Whatever our desires may be, Being the Master of the Well-Manifested Life is transformative. Yet, before any of us can move forward on this Journey, we are compelled to follow Golde's example. Consider the house in question as the house of our Being or Its space. As such, *we need to clean our house before we may move into it.* We need to put things in order, turn on the lights and scrub the floors. Before we move into the next chapter of our Being, before receiving the physical manifestation of our desires, understand these two truths. You cannot leave a dirty house behind, and you cannot take a dirty house with you.

Clean the Crud or Double the Dirt

Too often when charged up by the desire to manifest something "shiny and new" into our lives, we want to plough full-steam ahead with a power-packed sense of urgency to receive it. Most often the impetus for wanting something shiny and new is because the "dirty and old" is dragging us down. The dirty and old is getting to be too small for us. But, the dirty and old serves a great purpose. It highlights the desire for something different. That's the way the Process begins.

Listen to what I am saying and do yourself a favour. If you launch into the next chapter of your Being before putting in a little elbow grease, you may waste a lot of time and energy along the way. You will most likely become really frustrated by the lack of manifestation, or some very slow progress. The Law of Correspondence states our outer world reflects our inner world. If the darkened corners of your dirty house remain so darkened, the Universal Laws will manifest more of the dirty and old. You will create more frustration, more of *not* journeying towards your new Beingness, and more of *not* manifesting your passion-fuelled desires. You haven't cleaned the inner world so the outer world reflects the clutter.

> *...there is nothing outside of yourself that can ever enable you to get better, stronger, richer, quicker, or smarter. Everything is within... Seek nothing outside of yourself.*
>
> Miyamoto Mushashi

There is an order to the Universe and an order to all this manifestation stuff. If we get out of sequence, we are doomed to repeat ourselves until we get back on track. Before we can move forwards with what we need to say and how to express our Beingness, how to manifest our deepest desires, we need to clean up our house. Easier said than done.

Call it what you will... it's your dirt, your stuff, your baggage, your junk... it's all the same thing. Your dirt shows up as your fear, your jealousy, your wilful ignorance, your anger, your trust issues. It's your grudges, your judges, your wounds, your ego, your making-others-wrong. It's self-loathing, false expectations, the blame-game, a lack of confidence, a lack of forgiveness, doubts, feelings of superiority or inferiority... on and on. Genevieve Davis, author of *Becoming Magic*, calls this "the dross"; telling the story of a bleak and bitter life.[2] Charging ahead before you clean this stuff up essentially causes you to take a dirty house with you. This will follow you wherever you go and carrying around a dirty house is exhausting. Somehow, some way, that dirt will need to be cleaned up at some point. If you don't cut the grime, it will keep showing up in one form or another until you do.

By the way, I am not making all of this up. There is a sequential order to all of this, which has been around forever.

Therefore I say to you, all things for which you pray and ask, believe that you have received them, and they will be granted you. Whenever you stand praying, forgive, if you have anything against anyone, so that your Father who is in heaven will also forgive you your transgressions.

Mark 11:24–25 NIV

It is not what we eat or drink, but what we think that defiles. The issues of life are from within. If a man is clean in his mind, then he is clean indeed. We must keep the mental house free from any thought which contradicts the truth of being.

Ernest Holmes[3]

It stands to reason… that if man will not take charge of his own house, the propaganda, false beliefs, fears, and worries of the phenomenalistic world will act as a hypnotic spell over him.

Dr Joseph Murphy[4]

I'm sure you get the picture. But, let's explore this further. How many times have we done this to ourselves? Some event in our life prompts a shift and from it we jump into forwards motion. But, how many of us actually do the whole job of cleaning up properly? How many of us leave some mess behind? How many of us attempt to intentionally ignore said mess? You know, it's that last bag of rubbish in the corner that you hope will go unnoticed. How many of us simply try to just cut ties altogether and run away from someone, or something, or someplace, somewhere? There is a predictable chain of events that usually follows in cases like this.

At first, most of us experience a temporary euphoria, a swipe of the brow, "whew", and look forwards excitedly into the dawn of a new day for us. Ties severed; dirt gone. However, how long did it take before we began to realise the new day in our lives looked remarkably like the old one? Perhaps our new day has a new cast of characters, is in a different city, a new time zone, whatever… but the same old stuff we tried to run from or leave behind is following us into our new beginning. We start noticing the dirt in the corners, under the carpet, over the doorframe. We end up being wildly disappointed and frustrated when we discover we have a mess on our hands that is even bigger than the one we left behind. We essentially doubled the dirt.

If you are even the least bit self-aware, you may have noticed this phenomenon. The dirt you create follows you around until you clean it up. It comes with you into your new direction like it has a computer chip implanted and it's on a sharp GPS. It finds you wherever you go. It doesn't go away and, if anything, it gets messier and dirtier as you go along adding more stuff to the pile.

I grew up loving the Peanuts cartoon characters by Charles Schulz. They are such an allegory of life and often hit it right on the money. One of the characters is known as Pig-Pen. He was named that for a reason. While he's a nice enough fellow, friendly, even charming in his own way, he always had a dirty face, wore dirty clothes, dirty shoes and was always in a cloud of dust and grime which followed him around everywhere he went.

What's funny about that dirt cloud around Pig-Pen is that the dirt didn't just affect him. It *polluted the space around him*. Everyone he got near to was enveloped in his personal dust storm. As nice as Pig-Pen was and is, it's not quite fair to contaminate those around him. It isn't quite right when all he would have to do is take a bath, clean up the dirt and the whole thing goes away and everybody's happy.

But, guess what? He resists the whole idea of cleaning up his mess. To Pig-Pen, the dirt is familiar. He is used to it. He may even like it. It's his namesake! For Pig-Pen, it's his tradition and he has no intention of taking that bath in spite of how clean-smelling his new Being would be. He doesn't expect anything different of himself. If, one day, he did in fact desire to manifest a clean Pig-Pen who wears nice clean clothes and who hangs around his friends without covering them in a mess, he certainly can't expect the Universe to help facilitate that Being if he doesn't clean up his junk, take that bath, wash his clothes and polish his shoes. If he doesn't change the *behaviours,* in other words, take Action around cleaning up all that caused Pig-Pen to be, well, Pig-Pen, his new, cleanly clothed and sweet-smelling self won't last long. In a very short time, his old behaviours will manifest the old mess-cat Pig-Pen who will go right along polluting himself and everyone around him.

I'm sure most of us are familiar with *The Wizard of Oz.* It is the story of a young girl, Dorothy, who is whisked away from her home by a powerful tornado. From a common, grey life on a Kansas farm, she is transported to a land where she finds a colourful world of beauty, wonders, friends, helpers, strange creatures, witches, wizards and, more importantly, a deep life lesson.

If you pick the story apart and look at it through the lens of the Universal Laws, we can very clearly see what Dorothy was attempting to do. She tried to leave a dirty house. When she ran away from home, she tried to run from her troubles and the life they were tied to. She tried to run from the mess she had made. When she ran into Professor Marvel, con-man extraordinaire, she believed going with him to visit the crowned heads of Europe and the exciting new life that would bring for her would be far better than her hum-drum life in a world where no one understood her. She could leave all her dirt behind and move on.

Not so fast. If you remember what happened, all the while in Oz, two distinct things were going on. The first was the dirty house she tried to leave behind followed her right into her bright, new world. The troubles she had with a nasty old lady in Kansas found a new outlet in the Witch of the West, who was worse than the one she left behind. The second was she felt compelled to return home. She felt drawn to the lesson she was placed in Oz to learn and to apply it. She would certainly miss everyone she had become so close to through all her adventures, but she felt the need to go back home. At the end of the film, when she was asked by Glenda, the Good Witch of the North, what her lesson actually was, she replied with one of the most famous lines in motion picture history…

If I ever go looking for my heart's desire again, I won't look any further than my own back yard. Because if it isn't there, I never really lost it to begin with.

L. Frank Baum – *The Wizard of Oz*

Behind the obvious meaning of the words, there is a deeper implication of course. In our manifestation language, if you try to leave a dirty house without cleaning it up, you will either take the dirt with you or it will follow you around until you do. In Dorothy's case, she took the dirt *and the house* with her into Oz and she was forced to take it all back to Kansas for a fresh start and an opportunity to clean up her mess. She couldn't run away from a life in which no one understood her. *Her life lesson was that she needed to understand herself,* get clear on her desires and define where to begin anew, which was in her own back yard. This is true for all of us.

I am not saying that in every case you have to return to the actual scene of the grime in order to clean it all up *before* you can manifest anything on the road of Mastery, unless the Universe compels you to do so. In most instances, merely noticing and recognising the dirt, then performing the work of cleaning it up as you go, is a powerful enough Action. While Dorothy landed right back where she started from, it is not always necessary, nor advisable, to make that kind of Action happen. Listen to your internal guide and follow that. The more in tune you are to that guidance system we all have, the better you are able to achieve the results you are after in an expedient way.

Keeping it Clean

In *The Science of Mind*, one of my favourite lessons is, "Only those thoughts which are helpful and life-giving can find entrance to my house."[3] It is very similar in thought to a verse from the Bible in Philippians 4:8, "Finally… whatever is true, whatever is noble, whatever is right, whatever is pure, whatever is lovely, whatever is admirable – if anything is excellent or praiseworthy – think about such things." Both contain the same profound truth. Whilst cleaning your house is vital, it is also crucial to understand that after you have cleaned it up, your work isn't done. *You must keep it clean by engaging in, and continually Being, the Cause of Actions that support the clean house and what you are filling it with.* A big part of this work is noticing when things need a polish; of noticing when we start to get off course before we are very much off course and we find ourselves stuck in a corner, sitting in the dark, surrounded by dust bunnies.

As a Buddhist, I practise in front of an altar upon which are laid the tools that support the Actions or Causes of my method. One of the daily Actions is to dust the altar and to clean the pieces on and around it. I used to think that was a sort of silly thing to do. After all, I thoroughly clean the altar once a week anyhow. How dirty can it possibly get from one day to the next? Then, quite a while ago, I realised the power-packed Universal truth behind the Action of daily cleaning.

The altar is considered an extension of your highest Self. It is a *reflection* of your inner world. It is a physical representation of the house where your Being lives. The daily practice of dusting and cleaning it is a beautiful metaphor highlighting the importance of the daily cleaning of your own internal house; the new behaviours of your new Being. Of clearing out old patterns of thinking. Of ridding yourself of mental models that no longer serve you. Of shutting the door on doubt and fear as they come for a visit. All of these cleaning actions are in support of your Being the person with your desired manifestations in the Present/Now.

There are some manifestation gurus out there who advocate the thought that you don't have to clean up the stuff in your life in order to manifest a wildly better one for yourself; that you don't have to scrub the dirt, get rid of the junk, or clear out the second-hand goods to manifest a much better Being. I have heard it said you get over it by ignoring it and to allow the Universe to steer you around it. I cannot say I agree with this idea at all.

I'm certainly not trying to make anyone wrong about this, but you cannot just ignore behaviours, vibrations, relationships, wrongs, or what have you – the stuff you are getting in your own way about – and expect the Universe to give anything different back to you. You cannot expect the Universe to just fix everything. You have to take Action by Law for any and all of this to operate. A refusal to take responsibility for your dirt just isn't sound. It's like the saying goes, if you keep doing what you have always done, you'll keep getting what you have always got. Or, as a quote loosely attributed to Albert Einstein goes…

Insanity is doing the same thing over and over again and expecting different results.

You don't necessarily have to cover yourself in sackcloth and ashes and beat your breast until all things are put right. I am saying, however, it is your responsibility to notice what's not really working for you and to change it. I am saying that if, for example, you have issues with money, you will need to clean them up if you expect to manifest more money into your life. If you have trust issues, you'll need to clean them up before you manifest a trusting relationship. If you have issues with food, you will need to clean them up before you have a healthy relationship with food and manifest the results you are trying to achieve. If you desire a better job, doing lousy work in the one you have now and hating it all the while will not help you manifest a better one. All that junk needs to be cleaned out.

Here is how most of us work with cleaning up our space. Let's say you've become very clear on your Being and what that Being-ness has to say. Through gaining clarity you notice you are holding on to a full-to-the-rim glass of Coca-Cola. And, the clarity you have achieved recognises you can't stand Coca-Cola, at least not anymore. Your Being-ness loves lemonade. The glass is full of Coke, however, and cannot hold any more liquid. In order to fill your glass full of your desired refreshment, you will need to empty the glass. Once empty, then you can fill it with lemonade.

Sadly, many of us are impatient, or don't really want to do the work of emptying and cleaning out the glass, so we pour lemonade into the already full glass of Coke in the hope that this will suddenly be a glass full of lemonade. We keep pouring and pouring becoming more frustrated wondering why we still have a glass full of Coke. Eventually, by pouring enough lemonade into the glass, the ratio of lemonade to Coke may reach the desired result. But, look at what you've managed to accomplish in the meantime. A big, gooey mess and you have lost a lot of lemonade in the process. Now that you have that glass of lemonade, you'll need to clean up the sticky lemonade-Coke puddle on the floor in which you are standing. Wouldn't it have been much more effective to have cleaned out the glass first?

> *The usefulness of a pot comes from its emptiness.*
>
> Lao Tzu

Clean up the present job, doing the best work you are capable of doing and do it just for yourself. Figure out what's behind the kinds of poor relationships you seem to manifest. Uncover why your relationship with food or money causes you such unhappiness in your current situation. Otherwise, the Universe will continue to provide you with opportunities to have these issues, and more of them, manifest into your life until you change your vibrations around them and how you relate to them.

> *If we wish to change the exhibited subject, we do not manipulate the reflection on the screen, but we alter the slide. And, in like manner, when we come to realise the true nature of the creative process, we learn that the exterior things are to be changed by a change of the interior spiritual attitude.*
>
> Thomas Troward[5]

To be completely and wholeheartedly on the road of Mastery and the Well-Manifested Life, we must create the space in which to receive it without any clutter and without any resistance – an empty glass. This doesn't come from simply ignoring the clutter and the mess hoping it will all go away. Nor does it come from dumping it in someone else's space, which some of us do, by the way. Furthermore, it doesn't come from expecting someone else or the Universe to clean it up for us; to fix us, to complete us, or to make us happy. It comes from cleaning up our own mess, ourselves. We need to turn on the lights, get to work, start sweeping and Being happy in the Process.

As mentioned, there is a sequence to all of this and the clean-up part is mandatory. It is just the way the Universe works. You either get in sync with this or you don't. If you don't, you will get results alright, just don't expect them to be the results you are trying to achieve.

The 5-Step Process

The manifestation Process to follow is the work that precedes your "ask" of the Universe. It comes before the "it will be given" bit. It is the process of creating the space into which the manifestation of your I AM, the declaration of your Being, may be realised. *This Process is really THE ONLY formula whether it is for something you are manifesting or something you are de-manifesting in the state of Being.*

Now, I believe it's time here to re-affirm what has been laid out already concerning God, the Universe, Source… call It what you will. There is no personality called "God". It is not some entity "up in Heaven" somewhere waiting for us to die so He can judge our eternal souls. God does not "make things happen" to us. God does not cause calamity or mayhem in our lives any more than God causes some people to be prosperous and others poor. God does not damn any more than It blesses. Any of these ideas, and those related to them, are separating us from that which is called God, violating a Primary Law – The Law of Oneness.

God did not make man in his own image. We made God in our image in order to put our ancient heads around a Force that is as profound in Its simplicity as It is simple in Its profundity. We took our innate connection to this invisible Force, named it something, and gave it very human characteristics as a way of relating to It. This is how we innately disintegrate mystery or fear. It is no different an idea than what polytheistic cultures did in the past. Rather than pulling apart all of the characteristics of man, and forming and naming different gods after them, our traditions of God stuck them all together into one lump and named it "The One True God". The main difference is our theological ancestors didn't put clay around it and put it on a pedestal to which we bend our knee.

While that concept of "One true God" is essentially true through the Primary Laws, by pulling that construct away from us and making it something outside of ourselves, we broke the Law and we have perpetuated this violation for eons. What this has succeeded in doing is to fool ourselves into believing we are somehow absolved of our responsibility as Co-Creators of the Universe seeking expansion and evolution with us. And, we can also foist blame upon It when things don't go our way.

So, let's grow up a little bit, stand up, and be the Masters we are meant to be. While we go deeper into this in the next volume of *The Masterful Way*, for now let's be clear on this before going any further here. *God is Energy. It is through all, in all, of all. It is all there is. It is never made nor destroyed. It always has been and always will be. It is perpetually moving in and out of form, evolving more of Itself, by Itself, from Itself through Its only desire – Life.* And it is to evolve more Life for ourselves that we have any desires at all.

This does not, however, negate the truths found within ancient texts such as the Bible and other writings. We have things like this around to use as tools and it is from such tools as the Bible we have been given perspectives and methods to use. The 5-Step Method to follow is one of these and it's a big one.

One of the best and most well-known illustrations of this principle comes right from the first lines of the first book of Genesis. It is told through the story of creation. Whether your belief system regards this story as literal, figurative or poetic is of no concern. This is the manifestation Process revealed and it is this formula on which we will focus regardless of the allegorical way in which it is presented.

Most of us know the basics of the creation story. God spent six days creating the universe, our planet, the stuff on it and us. On the seventh day He rested. It is a fairly familiar story. To begin with, however, I would like to point out the fact that the seven-day process of creation, as we understand it, was not actually a story of creation until the third day. As God was creating what we know and understand to be the Universe, even HE set out to clean it up first, and systematically put things in order, which took place in the first couple of days. Cleaning up the space, as it were, to express Himself and make ready the space into which His creations could manifest, dirt free. Let's take a walk through it.

As we are introduced to the story, we see here a mess so great, so deep and dark, that one can almost feel the sticky darkness like tar.

The earth was formless and void, and darkness was over the surface of the deep...

Genesis 1:2 NIV

That's a pretty profound mess. The void, darkness, the deepness of it, all of that chaos... There are some very interesting bits to notice here, however. While the Bible says, in the verse just before this, "In the beginning, God created the heavens and the earth", and leaves it at that before continuing on, we have to notice the words "darkness", "void" and "the surface of the deep" in the verse that follows.

Applying the Law of Polarity which tells us everything is on a continuum and has an opposite side to it, "darkness" could not be darkness without light, "void" could not be void without fullness, and the "surface of the deep" could not be a surface without something above it. It sounds like something really messy was already there and needed a big, deep clean up before proceeding. It is clear what we are looking at here is an extreme end of a pole or two.

What is the first thing any of us do when we enter a pitch-dark room? Most of us *turn on the lights* so we can see what we are doing. That is exactly what happens next, as you may know…

Then God said, "Let there be light"; and there was light. God saw that the light was good; and God separated the light from the darkness. God called the light "day", and the darkness He called "night". And there was evening and there was morning – the first day.

Genesis 1:3–5 NIV

We see here that the first thing God did was turn on the lights. The force of "Let there be light" created a distinction; light from the darkness; the Law of Polarity. We now have light on one extreme and darkness on the other. We have some sort of order and balance. Darkness has been cleaned up and light is now in collaboration with darkness on the continuum. It is more than that, however. What the cooperation between light and darkness also does is introduce the element of *time*. Time is a key point in how this whole Process works as we have seen.

God then categorised it, He called it something… He named it. Light was "day" and dark was "night". This illustrates another key element. The naming of something recognises *clarity*. If you cannot name whatever it is you are manifesting, you are simply not clear enough.

It also illustrates a point made in a previous chapter. God called the light "good". The light and everything it shone on was good, even at that yucky, dark, chaotic stage. He didn't take a look at it all and say, "this sucks". He called it good. In other words, He made it OK. Just like manifesting something new into our lives – a new job, a new coat or whatever it may be – we can't say, "this job sucks and I want another one" and run out and get it before we make peace with it and clean up the mess. Let it be "good" and perfect just the way it is, then use it as a platform to manifest the next iteration of your Being from that space of "good"-ness. As we have seen, we must clean up our space before moving ahead.

And God said, "Let there be a vault between the waters to separate water from water." So God made the vault and separated the water under the vault from the water above it. And it was so. God called the vault "sky". And there was evening and there was morning – the second day.

Genesis 1:6–8 NIV

The next day He separated and categorised another part of the workspace, those messy, troubled waters. The separation of those waters above from those below created the element of *space* in which to work, and herein lies the lesson. *You must create the space in which your desired manifestations may show up.* It must be clean and clear – or at least in the process of being so – otherwise your intentional manifestations will have no place to go.

So now, by the second day, we have two key elements linked together; time and space. Both key elements are necessary to the manifestation of our desires. These key elements cannot be ignored.

And God said, "Let the waters below the sky be gathered into one place, and let dry ground appear." And it was so. God called the dry ground "land" and the gathered waters he called "seas". And God saw that it was good.

Then God said, "Let the land produce vegetation: seed-bearing plants and trees on the land that bear fruit with seed in it, according to their various kinds". And it was so… God saw that it was good. And there was evening, and there was morning – the third day.

Genesis 1:9–13 NIV

The work of day three shows us a shift in the Process and a shift in focus. In a final act of cleaning, God gathered up the waters below the sky separating it from the land. What we find now is that the house, as it were, has been cleaned up; spic and span. We have working lights, the water problems have all been fixed, we have a clean floor and we have the tools of *space-time* to work with. It's all good. Up until this point, there has really been no expression or manifestation of the Universe. It's all a clean-up job. However, it is in this third day we begin to see God actually expressing Himself through what He creates in that cleaned-up space.

Grasses, plants, trees – all sorts of vegetation. Each blade of grass is different from the next; each leaf on each tree is different from every other leaf on every other tree. Each and every element, uniquely expressing itself fully, unreserved and unapologetic, passionate and complete enough in itself to continue this expression through millennia filled with potential to create an endless supply.

> *And God said, "Let there be lights in the vault of the sky to separate the day from the night, and let them serve as signs to mark sacred times, and days and years, and let them be lights in the vault of the sky to give light on the earth." And it was so. God made two great lights – the greater light to govern the day and the lesser light to govern the night. He also made the stars. God set them in the vault of the sky to give light on the earth, to govern the day and the night, and to separate light from darkness. And God saw that it was good. And there was evening, and there was morning – the fourth day.*
>
> Genesis 1:14–19 NIV

On the fourth day, we see God working specifically with the tool of spacetime. We further see Him using the mindset spoken of earlier. "It was good." Although the work had not been finished, each element of the job, as dirty and messy as it was, was good. There is a pattern here.

We also see ways to measure and manifest using the tool of spacetime. Stars, planets, galaxies… the elements necessary for observing the construct of time and all of it in the Present/Now. This Action established the Law of Rhythm; everything has a season. Now the tools of time and space are no longer conceptual. They are more tangible; easier to handle, and something we are supposed to use, properly of course, and with the proper perspective through Universal Law.

Into the fifth and sixth day, we see God expressing Himself through the animal kingdom. Fish, birds, sea creatures, then land animals, livestock, etc. What is interesting here is that after the third day, we see an end to the specific naming of things. Along the way of cleaning and manifesting each step, He just "saw that it was good". I believe He was waiting to make the naming of things a model for teaching His finest creation, which was to follow.

We see the Process continuing through the rest of the creation story until we see His most unique expression; the one through which He can expand and experience more of Himself intentionally, intelligently, more consciously and emotionally… US. You, me, men, women – people. *And,* He used another tool of manifestation. The ground; the dirt. All manifestations of energy. Here is a significant element. God breathed LIFE into the man and he became a Living Being. That is the only desire of the Universe. To expand more Life. And we, through the Co-Creative Process expands it through our desires; through our Being.

Continuing the story…

Out of the ground the Lord God formed every beast of the field and every bird of the sky, and brought them to the man to see what he would call them; and whatever the man called a living creature, that was its name. The man gave names to all the cattle, and to the birds of the sky, and to every beast of the field.

Genesis 2:19-20 NIV

I believe when God stopped naming things Himself, He was holding off in order to teach His most magnificent creation how this whole Process works. We see that God then lets the man exercise his God-given creativity to name each thing whatever he wanted to – just like the Creator; essentially Co-Creating, interdependently and with clarity. God empowered the man to say whatever he had to say without a dirty house to get in the way of things and mess everything up; a Garden of Eden. Which, as we know, didn't last for long.

> *Then Lord God took the man and put him in the Garden of Eden to work it and take care of it. And the Lord God commanded the man, "You are free to eat from any tree in the garden; but you must not eat from the tree of the knowledge of good and evil..."*
>
> Genesis 2:15–17 NIV

And, we all know what follows...

Once again, whether you believe the story to be literal, figurative or, maybe just a lovely story is absolutely beside the point. What we have is the pattern; the sequence of steps that must go in their proper order. Imagine if He'd gone out of sequence and started randomly putting seas in place without cleaning up the space for dry ground. Or, doing everything in darkness and chaos. How would that work? The Universe, thankfully, just doesn't operate that way by Law. We cannot properly manifest and create what we desire unless we follow the rules of engagement; the Process of manifestation.

1. Turn on the lights.

2. Clean up the space.

3. Take the time to get clear.

4. Name it – Ask and announce your intention.

5. Receive it – aka, The Mastery of Being.

GOING OUT OF SEQUENCE

What happens next in the story is a fine illustration of acting out of sequence and the consequences of doing so. Eve saw something shiny and new in the tree of "knowledge" and she desired it, right away. And she wasn't going to be selfish, either. She wanted her husband to share the swag. She wanted them both to jump ahead a few spaces on the board game of Mastery.

> *When the woman saw that the fruit of the tree was good for food and pleasing to the eye, and also desirable for gaining wisdom, she took some and ate it. She also gave some to her husband... and he ate it.*
>
> Genesis 3:6 NIV

But, she didn't prepare, she didn't take the time, and she didn't get clarity on even *why* she wanted wisdom in the first place. What exactly *was* wisdom, anyhow? All she saw was something bright and appealing and it clouded her judgment. So much so that she, and then he, fell into a manifestation trap; a giant boo-boo of Being. That is wanting the artefact of our desire to instantly show up without preparing for it. While instant manifestation is certainly not out of the question, this is not usually the way things work. The both of them bit into something they couldn't chew *before they were ready to receive it.* They went out of sequence, out of synch and got the boot – kicked out of the Garden of Eden. In addition to the example of sequence hopping evident in the story, there is a deeper message within it.

What do you think is the purpose or symbolism of the so-called forbidden tree, or more specifically, the forbidden fruit? What purpose would it serve to put something in the middle of this beautiful garden that man could not touch? It is absolutely nonsense to think that God would put something so bright and shiny, so fragrant and lush, into their space just within reach, but keep it untouchable forever. From what I know, that is not a characteristic of the Universe. I understand the traditional interpretations of this part of the story concern obedience. I agree, actually, but not the way it is usually discussed. I believe it demonstrates obedience, or the opposite thereof, to the Universal Laws.

God showed them a pattern, a sequence of events in the manifestation Process. When they had done the necessary work, I believe they would have been allowed, if you will, to partake of this luscious fruit *when they were ready for it*; when they had trust and belief enough to have handled it. When they fully understood what wisdom was and what to do with it. When they had made the space, gained clarity and were ready to receive. Symbolically speaking, I believe God, or the Universe, was waiting for them to get clear about their understanding of how the Process works. The lag time existed for them to grow their experience of manifestation sufficiently enough to be able to receive with intention. Instead, what they got was an unintentional disaster.

We on this journey of self-discovery and self-expression have all stumbled on this one. We see something we desire and, being the powerful manifestors we are, we try to jump ahead and manifest our luscious, sweet and juicy desire before we are ready for it. When you put the cart-before-the-horse, there are consequences. You get a pissed-off horse with a bruised nose and a cart that no longer works the way it's supposed to. In short, you make a mess you will need to clean up before moving on.

Fortunately for us, that instant physical manifestation thing is a rare occurrence. If we succeed in manifesting something for which we are not ready, what would usually happen would be the quick loss of it – with damages as in the case of our tragic couple above.

The result would be, we would find ourselves working really hard trying to manifest our desire with very minimal results, if any, over long periods of time, collecting more dirt in the form of frustration, doubt, depression, anger… you name it. We say more affirmations, we fall into the incessant trap of asking, day in and day out, instead of readying ourselves to receive. We read the next manifestation book or try to cheat the process by using some magic formula that worked for someone else and wonder why we are so frustrated. Wanting something before being ready to receive it is a ridiculous game to play. It's self-destructive and a complete waste of energy. We must do the work upfront and we cannot cheat the Process.

The Manifestation Method

1. *Turn on the Lights!* Even God didn't manifest anything without the lights on. So, let there be light and see what you have to work with. What has caused the desire in the first place; what is it you desire instead and why?

2. *Clean up and clear out the space.* Clear out the rubbish and the clutter. Get the dust under the rug, and in the corners. Scrub the walls. Do the laundry, wash your hands and face.

   Get rid of your junk. Take that bath, Pig-Pen, wash your clothes and clean your dirty house. *You can't move on without this step sans consequences.* You cannot manifest the results you are trying to achieve unless you do so. You must clear out the old stuff before manifesting the new. You can't be both clean and dirty at the same time. You cannot be in the past, present and the future at the same time. You cannot be dependent, independent and interdependent at the same time just like you cannot both believe and doubt at the same time.

   > *But when you ask, you must believe and not doubt because the one who doubts is like a wave of the sea, blown and tossed by the wind. That person should not expect to receive anything… Such a person is double-minded and unstable in all they do.*
   >
   > James 1:7–8 NIV

   If you have to make amends for an old wrong, do it. If you have to forgive someone, forgive them. Forgive those folks you still have not let go of and the hurt they may have caused you. Forgive yourself. Forgiveness is probably the most powerful solvent in the Universe and we will be discussing forgiveness in some detail further along. Forgiveness is a tool; use it.

3. *Take the time you need to gain clarity.* Some of this baggage, this dust, this dirt, this junk is so subconscious that it will take the key element of time to bring it out of hiding. Equally as important as cleaning, is gaining clarity on what it is you are actually desiring and why you desire it. So, take the time you need.
   Take the time to soul search. Respect the time. Respect and enjoy the pause between your desire and the physical manifestation of it. It could take all of a moment; it could take a month or a year. Be flexible through this Process. In the space between desire and physical manifestation is the fun of it as well, don't forget. The road of Mastery is the happiness thereof.

4. *Name it.* Whatever it is you want to manifest, once you are clear, call it out in specific terms. God named the land, the seas, the heavens. He was clear. He was specific. Be specific; be intentional. Are we absolutely ready for the luscious bite of fruit? If not, put in the work and go back to step one. You will *know* when you are ready. You will feel it without a shadow of doubt, resistance free. Then make your ask and declare your I AM…

> *Ask, and it will be given to you; seek, and you will find; knock, and it will be opened to you.*
> *For everyone who asks receives, and he who seeks finds, and to him who knocks it will be opened.*
> Matthew 7:7–8 NIV

5. *Receive it.* This is another way of saying Be it. Master the habit of Being the person who already has manifested the object of his or her desire for "fill-in-the-blank", Now. Live it. Breathe it. Feel what that's like. That is where you find the happiness in the Process. Receiving it by Being it is the ultimate key to making this work and it is the work of Mastery.

Ask-receive, ask-receive. But, do the work first! Clean up the space. Prepare the house into which the manifestation of your desires may Be. If you don't, you could end up biting off something you can't chew, creating a big mess, and getting the boot in the end.

CHAPTER 8

THE MASTERY OF CLARITY

In the last chapter we discussed the need for clarity as it relates to the object of our desires. In my experience, and the experiences of those with whom I live and work, gaining clarity is a vital part of the effort of manifesting anything. We cannot ask for something about which we are unclear. If we can't name it, we can't manifest it.

The Law of Vibration states everything in the Universe is moving, and that movement causes a specific vibrational frequency. This includes our desires. If our desire for something or some outcome isn't clear, if our desire is a bit muddy, the Universe will bring us a muddy result or no result at all. This is by Law. If the Cause is muddy, the Effect will be as well.

Being unclear is a lower and slower vibration that will get us a lower and slower manifestation. Low frequencies are not very magnetic from a Law of Attraction perspective. Additionally, being unclear with our desires will not allow us to muster up a positive emotion about them and without that emotion, they will remain low frequency and slow-going. This may result in frustration, which is not a vibration anyone needs more of.

If you were going to send a wireless message to a friend, you would not send the letters of the alphabet in their order and let him construct the message for himself, nor would you take words at random from the dictionary. You would send a coherent sentence, one which meant something.

Wallace Wattles (1)

WHAT'S THE WHY?

In his book, *Start With Why* (2), Simon Sinek discusses the principles of inspiring leadership. Leadership that inspires is emotional. It touches the head but most importantly the heart. As such, inspiring leadership causes a higher vibrational output, which attracts the best out of followers.

Inspirational leaders help their people understand not just what they are doing but *why* they are doing it. If people can get behind the *why* of a thing, he says, the *what* of it and *how* to get the results you are trying to achieve with whatever it may be is easy. The why provides clarity and an emotional connection. On the darker side, getting to *why* may even blind people into doing things they would otherwise have never conceived possible. Propaganda and organisational blindness is built upon this principle.

Speaking from an organisational perspective, Simon Sinek says many leaders get the whole lot backwards. They promote the *what* of it first – the product or service itself, followed by the how of it – how it's made or how it works, and finally why anyone would want it, assuming that bit is ever explained at all. Organisations rarely get clear on the why, except to wonder why the consumer is not buying their product, or why leaders do not inspire great followers. How you get to the vibrational level of inspiration is basically gaining clarity. The best and fastest way to gain clarity on anything, whether it's a product you're selling or the followers you are leading, is by knowing the *why*.

Concerning your desires there are a couple of important distinctions to be made at this point before we go further. First, let's make sure we are clear about the difference between the object of desire and the artefacts of desire. The object of desire is always happiness, peace, joy, love, etc. At the core of this object is your purpose. It's what you have to say at the very heart of your Being. Artefacts of desire are what I call one-offs. It's the Rolex, or the racehorse. It's the sixty-inch television. It's the Mercedes CLS in the driveway. All of these things are fine as far as manifesting is concerned. However, getting to the why of them always reveals the truth of your Being.

Gaining that kind of clarity will always point you towards your Being. No one is born into this current existence whose sole purpose is to manifest a flat-screen TV. No one is born to BE the owner of a nice house in the country. If understood properly, these things are the *result* or by-products of the Cause of Being whatever it is you have to say and Be in this life. There is nothing wrong with manifesting one-offs, but if you can get clear on your Being-ness first, your purpose, your mission – whatever you wish to call it – the faster the bling manifests into your life. The watch, the ring, the new set of Le Creuset is properly positioned as a Result of the Cause of your Being. Many of us get it backwards and manifest the watch or ring, the Results first, without figuring out the Cause which is your Being. Oh, you can manifest the Results in a one-off way, but the truth is it will take longer to do it that way than it would by getting clear on your Being and moving in that direction first. The one-offs are generally classified as pleasure, not happiness.

It is never the artefacts you are manifesting. It's never the stuff. And, you don't get an emotional spark from artefacts of desire itself – at least for an extended time. Pleasure doesn't last forever. You don't get deeply emotional about that big diamond ring or that fancy new car – the artefacts themselves. You get pleasure from them. The ring is a just a ring and a car is just a car and again, there is nothing wrong with manifesting a ring and a car. How you do that is by putting an emotional attachment upon these artefacts. The emotional attachment comes from how these things make you feel. That's the *why* of the diamond ring or the fancy new car. It makes you feel great, special, sumptuous, opulent – all of which are very powerful vibrational emotions to which the Universe responds more quickly. This is why Being someone with a diamond ring and a fancy new car in the Present/Now is so important to the Process of Co-Creating it. The feeling of opulence Being one with the diamond ring engenders will attract more of that to you. It's the Law. However, getting to Being first is always the best and more effective route. We will see an example of this in just a bit.

It's not about *what* you are manifesting but *why* you are manifesting that gets things moving towards the receiving of it. If you don't have an emotional attachment to whatever it is, all the affirmations in the world, all the prayers, all the many forms of asking will do absolutely nothing towards manifesting it. All of these efforts equate to nothing more than worthless repetition.

So for me, gaining clarity involves getting clear on *why* I have a desire for this or that to manifest into my life. In almost every case, this can be distilled into the emotion of happiness, joy, peace and love – which is the purpose of your Being. I think many of the manifestation gurus out there would agree.

Feeling the Why

I recall when *The Secret* hit it big. It really resonated with me at that time. I bought the book, read and re-read it. I still have a copy of the book somewhere. I purchased the CDs to listen to in the car while sitting in that glorious Los Angeles traffic, where I used to live. I can still here Rhonda Byrne's voice telling me, "you've got to FEEL it… FEEL what it's like to have or be XYZ" manifested. For some reason, that often proved to be the more difficult accomplishment for me on certain things I was manifesting. I mean I could feel it, but I didn't really FEEL it and the bigger problem was I didn't know how. And, of course, as a result my manifesting was weak on those certain things or was non-existent.

I know now there were several reasons why feeling it was sometimes a challenge. In the first place, I can admit that some of the things that I was manifesting back then I was very unclear about. So, my manifestation techniques were really nothing more than wishes and asking. Wishes do not serve a purpose, as we know. Secondly, because I was unclear on my desires and why I wanted to manifest them, my wishes were coming from a place of *not having what I was desiring.* You cannot feel emotionally attached to something about which you are unclear. You can't believe in Being it if you can't sense it on an emotional level. As a result, I was vibrating on a low-level frequency. It's not surprising the Universe wasn't working with me – I wasn't working with It. The more I operated from this level, the more "lack-of-it" I put out there, and that's exactly what I got. Being a powerful manifestor, I powerfully manifested the lack of the desired object or circumstance and kept perpetuating it. Fortunately, those days are long gone. Since then, I have created and continued to use an exercise that works for me and I use it every time I am manifesting something into my life. I will share it with you now.

When you have a desire to manifest something, make 100 per cent sure you are clear on *why* you desire it. Sounds simple, right? Trust me, it can be a bit of a challenge sometimes. Let's work an example that resonates with almost everyone. Let's say it is money you are manifesting. Let's make it a big sum. Let's use the cool million we discussed earlier. It would be awesome to receive a million pounds or dollars, wouldn't it? You can really get all jazzed up about what you could spend the money on, right? That's pretty easy. Now let's ask the million-dollar question. *Why?*

Why is it that you want that kind of money? Aside from how amazing it would be to have that loot just drop from the sky and right into your lap, *why* do you want it or anything you are manifesting? *Why do you desire it?* Take some time to gain some clarity around this.

AN EXERCISE IN WHY

Grab a piece of paper, or your journal if you have one, and work out at *least* twenty-five answers as to why you want that money and what your feelings about having it are. If twenty-five elements are super easy for you to write down, go for twenty-five more. Go deeper than what you could buy with it. That kind of thinking is too small. Go beyond the easy answers such as "because I'd like to have it", or even the real and most obvious, albeit erroneous answer, "It would make me happy". Too easy, too shallow and too weak. Low vibrational stuff, which will keep it in a slow to no manifestation mode. Genuinely ask yourself, *Why do I desire a million pounds or dollars?* Then answer the question.

There is another caveat here, which is the necessary perspective towards gaining real clarity on this or anything you are manifesting. In all cases of desired manifestation, answering the question of *why* you want this or that has a technique to it. The answers should NOT be in any form of… *"it will allow me to buy that new car"* or… *"it will give me time and freedom…"* or… *"It will get me out of debt"*. Anything to do with any form of answer such as these will keep you from manifesting it, or significantly slow it all down. There are a few reasons why this is and why it is very important to understand what these reasons are.

The primary reason answers such as the ones above are dangerous is that you are essentially giving some *thing*, some artefact, power over you and then reinforcing it. "Money will give me freedom…" for example, only feeds the fear factor in your vibrational field whether you know it or not. Your vibrational energy shifts away from the feelings of manifesting it, to begging money for freedom. With money now in power, what you believe it could "give you" can also easily be taken from you, and more besides. That's the Law of Polarity. Therefore, you become afraid of it, consciously or unconsciously, and that's what the Universal Laws will start to manifest for you. The fear of money.

Money cannot give anything. It cannot allow anything. It can't get things for you. It cannot *give* you time, space, freedom from debt, etc. Handing your power over to money in this way will definitely cause you some grief. The Universe responds only to energy. Energy comes from our emotions; how we feel. Our emotions come from our desires, which create a vibrational output in accordance with the Law of Vibration. This further stimulates the Law of Attraction. The vibrational output is also known as a Cause, which will create an Effect by Law. Posing answers in a way such as, "It'll get me out of debt" is highlighting your debt, or your lack of a new car, or your lack of time and freedom and turns your power over to money. You are putting focus on the lack thereof. The only fear-less purpose lack serves is to cause a desire to spring from it. Don't allow it any more power than that. Lack is not to be feared. It is to be recognised only.

With the exercise of why, what we are developing is a new or stronger vibrational Cause to create a different behaviour with money, or a different Effect. While the new behaviour is being nurtured, the old and very powerful vibrations of being in debt often come rushing back to chase the new, much happier vibrations away. Those old vibrations don't like to be uprooted no matter how ineffective they may be for you. We will get very clear on where all of that comes from in the next chapter.

The reason those old feelings are so powerful is because they are loaded with fear and fear is a very powerful vibration. The Universal Laws will blindly respond to the predominant feelings or vibrations you are putting out there. What is most predominant? The vibration of the fear of being in debt, most likely – at least for now. You haven't tipped the balance of vibration more towards the new desire, which will affect the new behaviour, vibrationally. Until you are used to the new feelings and vibrations about money, the fearful aspects will try and stage a coup against your manifestation of a million dollars. You will wind up with more to put you in debt because that's what you are telling the Universe to provide you with by focusing on answers of why in such a way. So, let's get clear on money.

The Love of Money

For the love of money is a root of all kinds of evil. Some people, eager for money, have wandered from the faith and pierced themselves with many griefs.

I Timothy 6:10 NIV

Again I tell you, it is easier for a camel to go through the eye of a needle than for someone who is rich to enter the kingdom of God.

Matthew 19:24 NIV

Jesus looked around and said to his disciples, "How hard it is for the rich to enter the kingdom of God! … It is easier for a camel to go through the eye of a needle than for someone who is rich to enter the kingdom of God."

Mark 10:23, 25 NIV

Jesus looked at him and said, "How hard it is for the rich to enter the kingdom of God!... Indeed, it is easier for a camel to go through the eye of a needle than for someone who is rich to enter the kingdom of God."

Luke 18:24–25 NIV

The reason I stuck these passages in here at this point is because I believe it is these Biblical passages, particularly the first one, which are behind so many fear-based relationships people have with money, and their distaste for the book from which they come. These very misunderstood verses from the Bible speak directly to the point just made about giving money power over you. Let's pick it apart to get a sense of why this may be.

In the first verse regarding the love of money, the sentence uses very specific words, which have big emotional charges to them. It places the words "money", "love" and "evil" in close proximity to each other in one short sentence. This adds to reasons why this verse is so often misunderstood and mis-applied. Let's look at it.

Love is a powerful *emotion*. Money is a powerful *tool*. Evil is a powerful *fear*. The *love of money* is where the sticking point in all of the confusion resides. However, I do not believe the phrase *the love of money* as it is traditionally thought of, or preached about or taught, is quite accurate. This verse is usually used to demonise money, which seemingly gives it an evil power over the person who has it.

I have a different interpretation. I believe the love of money is essentially a matter of *loving a tool* over what the tool is to be used for. It is out of alignment with how the Universe works. The Universe doesn't actually support falling in love with any sort of tool, regardless of whether that tool is money or microchip. There are very specific reasons for this.

Love is an influential emotion and the most powerful emotion in the Universe. However, when love is one-sided it loses its creative power and becomes uneven and weak, vibrationally speaking. As we know, love can turn to a less than positive emotion very quickly when it is not reciprocated. Love only really and truly works when love is loved back, and that is precisely the problem with the love of money. *No tool can love you back.* The love of money is putting an emotional attachment on a tool, which is a big waste of energy. Sitting there, doe eyed, fawning over a tool, over that large wad of cash, won't get the job done. The tool is to be used for creating Causes, which will produce Effects, just like any other tool.

It's like loving the barbeque instead of loving the taste of the juicy steak it can be used to cook for you. You can try to love the barbeque all you like but it won't love you back, and it won't get you that steak unless you use it. Using the tool gets you the result you are trying to achieve – the juicy steak – and that's something that produces pleasure and joy – emotions. Unless you are a vegetarian, it makes you happy. It's the emotion of the taste of the steak that's loving you back, not the barbeque. The result of love is how it makes you feel when love is loved. It's emotion *feeling* emotion, and emotion *feeling* it back. The truth is nobody actually can love money because money can't love you back; neither can a barbeque. If you don't use the tool, it's useless.

The other verses regarding the rich entering the Kingdom of God are addressing the same issue. If we are to understand the Kingdom of God as being within, we must understand it is a representation of Being happy, peaceful, joyous and loving from within in the Present/Now space. I believe what was being referred to in these three verses from Matthew, Mark and Luke was not money or riches per se. I believe they are referring to the power one often gives to riches, wealth, etc. and the fear this generates. It is hard for someone to enter the state of Being when the tool of money has been given power over them and they become subject to the fear of it, or of losing it. This is explained by the interaction Jesus had with the young man that prompted the statements in the first place.

In all three versions of the story, the quotes about the rich entering the Kingdom were the result of an interaction with a rich young man or a ruler. After asking Jesus what must be done to enter into the Kingdom, Jesus eventually told him to give all his money to the poor and follow him.

> *When the young man heard this, he went away sad, because he had great wealth.*
>
> Matthew 19:22 NIV

All three versions say the man went away sad. Now why would this man be downcast? Simple, he was bound to his wealth having dominion over him. If he gave it all away, what would become of him? Do you see the fear and doubt in this? Fear and doubt is the destroyer of all that is the Kingdom of God; happiness, joy, peace and love. So it was not the fact the man was rich that keeps him out of the good stuff. It is the love of, and his trust in, the tool of riches over Being that which the tool of wealth could provide.

Let's take another example. You can't muster up much love for a hammer and a saw but you sure can enjoy the house you can build with it. This only goes so far, however, because the house itself is only a tool as well. The house can't love you back. It can't, of itself, produce loving emotions, so falling in love with a house is not Universally sound, which is where I believe many people go astray when manifesting a new home.

So let's say you have a desire for a new house. Why do you want a new house? The question goes deeper than the paint on its surface. A new house can be used for shelter. It can be the stage for happy Christmases, birthdays, anniversaries. It can be decorated with things you enjoy and which give you pleasure. It can be used for gatherings of family and friends, which deepens relationships. It can be a place of inspiration and art. All of these things and more are what the tool of that house is supposed to be used for. All of these things promote the happiness emotion and therefore, it is through the use of the tool of the house that the emotions involved in having it as described above love you back. If you fall in love with the tool of the house without any of the stuff the tool can be used for, the house is just a house and may quickly become a prison. Even the most aesthetically beautiful house can quickly become a dilapidated shack if not used properly.

Here is another bit of clarity when it comes to the precision-use of tools. You certainly didn't pick up a hammer or a saw and become an expert at it the very first time you used it. It took practice and knowledge. With each good and bad hit of the hammer, with each stroke of the saw, you became more clear on how the tools worked and, more importantly, how they don't. Eventually, you got pretty good at it and, I imagine now, most of us don't have to concentrate too hard on gaining clarity into how to drive a nail, or how to use a saw to cut a two-by-four in half. Our tools of manifestation are no different.

If the artefact of your desire is money, but instead of desiring the manifestation of what the *tool can do for you*, your love of money will bring you to a place of fearing or maybe even hating money, consciously or unconsciously, especially if it is slow to manifest. Let's play out a love scene here.

The love interest in this scenario is money. Simply put, you *love* money and, as we know, money cannot love you back. Money has a wondering eye and a very fickle nature. All of us spend money and you must spend the money on something… bills, expenses, and fun things too, of course. If, however, you're in love with the object of money, the spending of it is equivalent to your love interest slowly *losing interest in you*. It begins to leave you, you see? It has eyes for someone or something else. With the mindset of money-love, each credit card you pay off or new car you buy, the spending of money is *causing* your lover to put its attention on someone or something other than you.

As the money starts to be used up, the *effect* is that it will scare you. Now your vibration is something very different to the vibration of attracting money. You begin to feel insecure about it and distrustful because it's leaving you. These are strong emotions. You will want to cling tightly to it but the tighter you squeeze, the faster it goes. Why? The Universal Laws are bringing you what you want… the *fear* of losing money. So, more things needing to be spent on will show up until you no longer have it, and probably won't have it again because the Universe will give you whatever vibration you are putting out there. This happens, by the way, even if you are *unaware* you are doing it.

There are numerous examples of this happening with people who have won a lottery. Suddenly a big chunk of money comes to someone who is very unclear about it. They have the behaviours of *not* having money deeply engrained. Oh, they desired to win the lottery alright. Otherwise why play? In spite of manifesting a win, the vibrational energy of the lack of money was still with them and manifested as getting back to a lack of it. This is why certain lottery winners become flat broke within a couple of years after winning it big.

From listening to dozens of these kinds of winners speaking on this, although they don't explain it quite in these terms, the reason is, was, and always will be because they did not have clarity about money. They hadn't changed their behaviours from the behaviours of lacking money to those of having it and being responsible with the tool.

Do not be confused. Winning the lottery and *knowing what to do when you win the money* are two different things. When they attached their focus on winning the lottery, I can almost guarantee they also had a long list of things on which they would spend the money. But, the connection wasn't made between spending money as a tool, and getting rid of what they had manifested because their behaviours were more closely aligned with the lack of it. There's nothing wrong with wanting to spend money on the good stuff but old behaviours, vibrationally speaking, remained pretty much the same. The new vibrational and emotional behaviours about money hadn't solidified yet. They didn't prepare themselves to receive it. They hadn't cleaned their house. In other words, because they hadn't created a new behaviour and vibration around money, they did what their old behaviours compelled them to do. Be lacking money. So, they got rid of it, spent it and spent it fast because a lack of money is what they were putting out there vibrationally. That's what they were used to. Old habits die hard, as they say.

I believe this comes from the fear of money. They may believe that money is somehow evil, or they feel they don't deserve it. They may feel guilty they received it. Somewhere deep inside they may even resent rich people for being rich. So, they turn their resentment upon themselves, and the money disappears. The money tool is no different than any other tool. Before we use it expertly, we need to practise using it. We need to be clear on how money works and how to manifest more of it. Gaining clarity is a Process. It gives you the opportunity to align yourself towards receiving the object or artefacts of your desires.

I intentionally use the term *Process* here because it's important to respect it. I know you want that pile of money this instant but allowing the Process allows you to gain the clarity you need in order to receive it and use it properly. Said in another way, it gives you time to clean out the space, clear out the storeroom, air out your money house and gain Mastery with the tool. It gives you time to think about it, dissect your behaviours and intentions, to clear out any doubts, or even guilt, and allows the Universe to provide you with *precisely* the thing/person/event/situation you are manifesting at just the right time. All the while, it has already manifested vibrationally so enjoy!

THE WHY GAME

So, let's dig a little deeper with this. Let's use the "Why Game" to gain clarity on money. The Why Game provides a space in which to ask the *right questions* about money, or anything else, which will produce some very clarifying answers. Walk through it with me. Why do you desire that pile of money? Use your list of twenty-five and choose one of those answers.

> Desire: One million pounds.
> *Why?*: I can use it to pay my debt down.
> *Why?*: Being free from debt will create the space for me to apply financial resources somewhere else.
> *Observation*: You have used the word "free". It must be important to you to harness that feeling of freedom.
> *Question*: What does freedom feel like?
> *Answer*: Open, exciting, happy, light, fun, rich, powerful, restful, peaceful, in anticipation…

OK, pausing here, do you see how emotional these words are? We could probably find a dozen or so more words to describe specifically what having a pile of money at your command could help facilitate with you. Do you get how much stronger the vibrational energy of these words is? Do you see how clear these feelings are? The emotional nitty-gritty is what we are after. Let's continue…

> *Question*: You mentioned other ways to use your financial resources. In what other ways could you use them?

Answer: I could start that business I've always wanted to start.

Question: Why start your own business?

Answer: I can engage full time in doing work I am passionate about – working full time with animals – dogs to be specific. I would be working for myself. Rehabilitating unwanted or unloved dogs and finding homes for them can help bring joy to both the dogs and the new families.

Question: What does doing the work you are passionate about feel like?

Answer: Exhilarating. Joyful, empowering, exciting, enriching, peaceful, energising.

Question: What does working for yourself feel like?

Answer: More exciting every day. More creative, flexible, fun, autonomy, independence…

Question: Why does helping animals seem important to you?

Answer: Helping animals makes me happy, it makes them happy and it makes their new families happy.

Question: Why is that important to you?

Answer: Expanding my own happiness through making others happy gives me more energy and greater impetus to do more of it.

Question: So, happiness is important?

Answer: Absolutely…

We have now gained a huge amount of clarity on just *one element* of what having a million pounds is like. We went from gaining freedom from debt to *joy, happiness, peace, light, fun, creative*. We gained clarity on starting a business and the joy that would bring to you and others. Additionally we went from a dependent state in using money to pay off debts, to independence with how working for one's self can feel, to interdependence by making you, the animals and their new families happy. This is the Being coming through these answers.

Can you feel how much richer the vibrational energy is at the end of the string than it was at the beginning by exploring the whys and the whats? You can almost feel how clean the intention is. This type of clarity is the space of your asking the Universe for the object of your desire. Your "I AM a rescuer of dogs" declaration is much more vibrationally sound than "I have a million dollars". Now the work of Being the open, exciting, happy, light, fun, rich, powerful, restful, peaceful… and all of the other strongly emotional words described, begins. This is now the work of Receiving. Being is Receiving. In this state you will find the work the easiest thing in the world because it's fun! Then, start engaging in Actions which support that Being – a vital component to how all of this works. Action.

Do this exercise with all of the twenty-five or more elements you wrote down about what having a million pounds would be like, or with whatever your desires are. Why do you want a better lifestyle? What does that feel like? Why do you desire that new car? What would having that new car feel like? Why is that important? Keep asking why, and what until you are truly excited and clear with the object or artefact of your desire. Then make your ask of the Universe. Declare it intentionally and go to work on *Being* happy, excited and clear all the time; in other words, receiving.

Receiving is operating with the Law of Cause and Effect. You are putting out a new Cause with your Being in this state. Expect a new Effect. *Being* the person with a million pounds will feel different. It will create different behaviours for you, stimulating the Law of Action to match those new behaviours with the object of your desire through the Law of Attraction. The Universal Laws working in harmony will bring your desires forwards.

Do not rush this Process. Keep going until you find it more difficult to come up with things around *why* you want this or that. It could take a day, a week, a month… the time doesn't matter, just don't rush it. Allow however much time it will take. When you think you have exhausted all the why's, and what's, you are ready to Be; to Receive. Now, make your ask and state your declaration.

CREATING THE SPACE

You have mined for higher vibrations, got clear on your ask and have given a clear shout out to the Universal Laws. As always, the job of the Universe is to provide you with your manifestations. Putting out mixed, fuzzy signals and expecting the Universe to do all of the work for you is a massive time-waster. That is not any part of how the Universal Laws work. You must do your part of Co-Creation. Clean the house, clear the path, set the stage, make a plan. Think about it, this is how everything works.

Once you have found the higher vibrational positions of your desires, go in for the deep clean. Create the space. This is where Being the person with the money you desire comes in to play in a very tangible way. By Being, you move out of *asking* and move into *receiving*. Where, for example, are you going to put the money? In your bank account? Investments? Do you need a money manager? A financial planner? An accountant? A lawyer? Get them all lined up now. Know which lawyer, which accountant, which bank. Look up their client reviews, check them out, call them. Get a binder, write it down, and sift through all of the noise out there to find your perfect match. Remember, with that kind of cash, you are an employer. You will be employing these folks to help you. Be a good boss and do your homework. Look for the best employees out there. If you are afraid of being a boss, get yourself over that or find someone who can manage your affairs for you. Nothing you do will come to fruition until you clean that up.

Learn about investing. Imagine calling your investment firm and talking to them about a venture you are interested in and getting some good advice. Get yourself prepared to receive it, whatever *it* may be. All of this movement is tapping the Law of Action with activities supporting the object of your desires. And, as you know, all of the other Laws as well.

Live in the new house, mentally, until it takes form around you physically. In the mental realm, enter at once into full enjoyment of the things you want… See the things you want as if they were actually around you all the time. See yourself as owning and using them. Make use of them in imagination just as you will use them when they are your tangible possessions.

Wallace Wattles[1]

Clarity Through a Cornfield

Field of Dreams (1989) is another of those very profound films that on the "feel-good" surface is just a nice film. However, underneath that feel-good layer are some very deep, Universal truths. Let's deconstruct the film for just a moment.

If you've never seen the movie, stream it, rent it, whatever… just watch it. It's quite the story of manifestation and Being told in a very light-hearted and sentimental way. Until then, here is a quick synopsis:

If you build it, he will come.

Ray Kinsella is a novice Iowa farmer. Emphasis on the word "novice". He and his wife Annie have always had a dream of living the farming life. This is their desire; their Being-ness. To be connected to the earth, the seasons and a farming community. Ray knows he has a lot to learn in order to be the expert farmer he desires to be. He frequently seeks the advice of more experienced neighbours. His learning curve is great, but his time is short. The farm is going under.

While out checking on his crops one day, Ray hears a voice coming from his cornfield that no one else can hear. "If you build it, he will come." Startled at first, he hears it again. "If you build it, he will come." He is clearly hearing voices. Not knowing what "it" is, nor who "he" might be, a frustrated Ray thinks he may be going a little bit out of his mind. Then he has a vision. In the centre of his cornfield, he sees a baseball field emerge. It appears, then disappears, then reappears, finally fading back into the ethers.

He begins to ponder the words. He talks with his wife, Annie, about it and tells her he believes he must follow the instructions. He must plough under a portion of his crops and construct a baseball field in its place. He believes the "he" who will come is "Shoeless" Joe Jackson, made famous not so much by his incredible batting average, but by his participation in an alleged plan to throw the 1919 World Series of Baseball in Chicago for money. Although Jackson was never indicted for the incident, he and all the other players of the Chicago White Socks involved in what would be called the Black Sox Scandal were banned for life from playing professional baseball and from receiving any post-ban honours. If he builds it, Ray believes, he will come.

Ray has never done a spontaneous thing in his life, he explains to Annie. Furthermore, he shares with her a deep concern he has. He does not want to end up like his father who also never stepped outside of the box. His father must have had dreams and desires, he explains. He just never tried to fulfil them. At thirty-something, Ray does not want that to happen to him.

The bond between Ray and the game of baseball is a deep one. His father, John Kinsella, in fact played in the minor leagues and lived in Chicago when the 1919 World Series events occurred. John knew every story about each player better than he knew his own. As a boy, John would keep Ray spellbound with story after story about "Shoeless" Joe Jackson and the players of the Black Sox Scandal. Sadly, as Ray grew up, he and his father grew apart. When his father died, they were deeply estranged, which left Ray alone to carry the heavy load of regret, guilt, anger and hurt.

With Annie's support, and in the face of all good sense, Ray ploughs under a good portion of one of his corn crops to build a regulation-sized baseball field in its place, sparing no expense. A decidedly poor move he and Annie can ill afford as their farm is losing money fast and may be repossessed at any time. After weeks of work, after many visits to the hardware store for supplies, after enduring the sideways glances from the neighbours who believe him to be beyond help, and after spending most of his and Annie's savings, the baseball field is complete. The voice goes quiet. Ray is frustrated and annoyed.

The summer fades to winter; seasons slowly pass. The baseball field lies there, stoically refusing to give up its secrets. However, one day in the early part of the following summer the lonely baseball field begins to come to life, in a manner of speaking. As Annie and Ray are discussing what appears to be the impending loss of their farm, their young daughter Karin interrupts their discussion to inform them someone is standing in the baseball field. Ray and Annie look out the window, and it's true. There is a baseball player, dressed in a uniform clearly from days gone by. It is "Shoeless" Joe Jackson. A young man full of life and the love of the game.

Ray goes out to meet him. They exchange greetings and find themselves in a game of one-on-one. Ray bats first, then Jackson, who was known as an incredible hitter. With each pitch, Jackson hits the ball out of the park and into the surrounding fields. Ray is gobsmacked. He is playing baseball with the incredible "Shoeless" Joe Jackson.

As Annie and Karin come out to the field to be introduced, it becomes clear Jackson cannot pass beyond the baseball diamond and he must soon return to the cornfields. He informs Ray there are others who would like to come and play and asks if it would be OK for them to use the baseball field. Ray enthusiastically agrees. As Jackson heads back into the corn, he turns to Ray and asks, "Is this Heaven?" "It's Iowa," Ray replies and with that, Jackson is gone.

A short time later, the field is full of the ghosts of the disgraced players of the Black Sox Scandal from 1919. Ray is dumbfounded and soon begins to realise what a miracle is occurring right in his own back yard. The players visit daily, using the field to practise and play the game as best they can without enough players necessary for a full team. At least everyone is having fun and Ray, Annie and Karin enjoy the free entertainment they provide.

The family quickly discovers they are the only ones who can see, hear, and communicate with these guys. To everyone else, especially the neighbours, they are acting like a bunch of nuts, sitting on the bleachers watching a game no one else can see. To the community, ploughing under a perfectly good cornfield is crazy enough. To put a baseball field in its place is madness. To Annie's brother, Mark, who tries to buy the farm from Ray before it's too late, they are out of their minds. But, Ray, Annie and Karin feel privileged to be involved in such an unbelievable experience.

In spite of the nagging worry of losing the farm playing in his head, and the unsettled feeling that the baseball field is not just for ghostly kicks, Ray hears the voice again with a different message. "Ease his pain." What could it possibly mean? Who is in pain? What exactly could Ray do about it anyway? He'd already done one very crazy thing for this mysterious-whispery-voice-thingy calling from the corn. Now, it wants more from him?

After some soul searching about what this message could mean, Ray is compelled to contact author Terence Mann, a literary guru to both he and Annie from their college days. He was the "voice of reason" in the tumultuous 1960s. Terence Mann often wrote about the golden days of baseball, and lamented that he himself had always wanted to be a ball player and play with the Dodgers on Ebbets Field in Brooklyn, but was unable to fulfil his dream. Ray believes he has solved the mystery and, once again with Annie's support, he is off on another spontaneous adventure.

Ray drives from Iowa to Boston, Massachusetts, the now home of Terence Mann and, with considerable difficulty, he finally locates his college hero. Ray is going to ease his pain at all costs, whether Terence Mann wants it or not. Convincing Terence to come with him by force if necessary, they end up at a ball game at Fenway Park. It is night-time and they are sitting in the bleachers when Ray hears the voice again.

"Go the distance..."

At the same time, Ray sees something on the scoreboard, which incidentally doesn't belong there. He sees a message telling him to find Archibald "Moonlight" Graham, a ball player from the 1920s.

Figuring he's made a mistake virtually kidnapping Mr Mann, they leave the game behind.

Later, as Ray drops Terence off in front of his apartment, he cautiously tells Ray he saw the message too. Incredible as it may seem to them both, the two of them are now all-in and head out on a quest to find Archibald "Moonlight" Graham.

Travelling to Chisholm, Minnesota they eventually do find Mr Graham… now Dr Graham, who quit baseball in the 1920s to become a man of medicine. Now an old country doctor, Ray and Terence try to convince him to return to Iowa with them to see the field and, hopefully, solve the mystery. That's the message they feel compelled to deliver. The doctor refuses, choosing to stay where he is and do what he was meant to do; be a small-town, country physician. Disappointed, Ray and Terence Mann begin the long journey back to Iowa, tail between their legs.

Along the way, they pick up a young hitchhiker, full of life and hope. His name is Archie Graham; a young, vital, and eager Archibald "Moonlight" Graham. Both Ray and Terence are blown away. Archie climbs into the back seat, aching to fulfil his dream of becoming a real, live professional baseball player and the three return to Iowa together.

Upon arrival, they find the ghostly ball players have grown in number. There are enough players to play full games now and all are thoroughly enjoying themselves. Young Archie Graham is invited to play. At the same time, brother-in-law Mark again shows up to try one final time to convince Ray and Annie to sell the farm to him before it's too late. Then, mysteriously, Karin offers a prediction. People will pay money to see the baseball field and relive their childhoods. Mark is having none of this insanity and believes Ray and Annie have deluded the poor child. But, Terence Mann is inspired by what Karin says and confirms people will come for reasons unbeknownst to them. They will pay for the chance to regain carefree days of baseball and of their youth.

Mark is determined. All of this nonsense is fanning the flames of upset between them all. As Ray, Annie and Mark argue, daughter

Karin gets knocked from the bleachers lodging a piece of the hot dog she's been eating into her windpipe. Ray tries unsuccessfully to revive her. As panic starts to build, from the field young Archie sees what's going on. Instinctively he knows what to do. He steps past the boundary of the baseball diamond and leaves the field to attend to Karin. As he crosses the base line, he transforms back into old Dr Graham. He revives Karin, but that's not the only miracle. Suddenly brother-in-law Mark can see the players too. Shocked and awed, he implores Ray NOT to sell the farm to anyone, ever!

Meanwhile, the game ends and the players have to go. As they head back into the cornfield, they extend an invitation to Terence Mann to come with them. Ray is upset, feeling he should be the one to go. After all *he* built the ball field. *He* drove all over creation to find Terence Mann, and "Moonlight" Graham. *He* put up with all of the insults and creepy stares from the neighbours. He even spent all of his and Annie's savings on this whole enterprise. He feels it's his right. But, there is more here than meets the eye.

Before leaving, Terence gently convinces Ray that going with the baseball players is not in his best interests. He has a wife and a daughter who love and need him. He must stay with his family. As Terence Mann disappears into the cornfield with the team, the first player to ever show up in Ray's cornfield remains. It's "Shoeless" Joe. Grinning silently at Ray and his family, Ray asks him why he's staring at him. What does he want? *"If you build it, he will come…"* he reminds Ray and then gestures towards home plate.

Ray turns and notices a new player standing near the plate all alone. He is not one of the regular guys, but Ray recognises him almost instantly. It is Ray's father, John Kinsella from 1919, young and full of life. Ray approaches his father, cautiously but with a full heart. He introduces himself and his family to John. John doesn't know who Ray is, and Ray keeps it that way, for now.

After introductions, John asks Ray, "Is this Heaven?" "It's Iowa," Ray replies. "Is there a Heaven?" Ray asks. "Yes. It's the place where dreams come true," John replies. Turning over his shoulder, he sees

Annie and Karin back at the house, rocking carefree on the porch swing. Ray replies, "Maybe this *is* Heaven."

The full understanding of the voice from the cornfield starts to become clear. "If you build it, he will come." It all makes sense. "He" is Ray's father – not "Shoeless" Joe. Ray and his father needed to reconnect. The meaning of "Ease his pain" was to ease the pain of their strained relationship, spoiled so long ago; a dirty house. They needed peace and to rekindle their lost connection which caused them both heartache. They enter into a game of catch, as fathers and sons do, under the bright lamps illuminating the field.

The camera pans out, highlighting the sharp contrast of a brightly lit baseball field against the blackness of the surrounding cornfields and the waning purple shadows of the disappearing sunlight. As the camera pans further back, a line of car headlights, miles long, is revealed. They are all heading to the baseball field which Karin and Terence Mann predicted. Implication? The farm is saved with a true Hollywood ending… and they all lived happily ever after. Fade to black…

So, let's look at this through the lens of the Universal Laws.

In the story, we can see the 5-Step manifesting sequence play out. Ray hears the voice telling him "If you build it, he will come." Desire is born. Although it confuses him, he has a strong urge to follow the instructions, although he doesn't know what or who "it" or "he" are yet.

Often that is how our desires begin to form. Something triggers us to birth a desire with little or no clue as to how it may manifest, or without much clarity around it. How it may manifest is not the issue. Clarity is the focus. We need clarity *and clarity comes through Action.* You can see in this example he is not a vibrational match to anything except confusion and maybe mild irritation at the beginning. If you watch the film, you will see the Law of Attraction does in fact bring him more of the confusion as a vibrational match until he takes some *Action.* Action was inspired by a moment of clarity; the vision of the baseball field and the burning desire to create it. More importantly to get out of his own way and get past the fear of being like his father, and the fear of losing a sizeable chunk of his cornfield.

His Actions begin as he ploughs under his crops. He is creating Cause and cleaning out the space. Bit by bit, each day the field begins to take shape. Causes creating more Effects. More energy builds around it. More clarity ensues. You can see and hear it in the interactions he has with his wife and daughter. You can see it gaining momentum as he goes about the business of purchasing materials at the local hardware store, trying not to notice the way his neighbours keep looking at him and what they may be thinking. He has clarity for now, and his Actions are confirming his desire. Ray is Being someone with a regulation size baseball field on his farm and all for "Shoeless" Joe Jackson. That's as far as he got with the *why* for himself up to that point.

Then, the field is finally complete. Ray manifested his baseball field. Now what? He knows he should be happy with his accomplishment, but he is not... quite. This is always the barometer; how you feel. Something is missing but he doesn't know what. He believes "he", "Shoeless" Joe Jackson, will come. However, the baseball field just sits there, day and night. He built the house, so to speak; created the space and works daily at keeping it in excellent shape; clean and clear. However, summer turns to winter and the field sits. Applying the principles of our Laws, we can see that the clarity he received earlier which resulted in a burst of Action only brought him to a certain point through The Law of Attraction. How do we know it's not a clear desire manifested? It could be felt.

"Shoeless" Joe Jackson does indeed show up, and a lot of other folks besides, Things then got muddy again, however, with the second voice – "ease his pain". Whatever he was hoping to receive from all of that Action just became seemingly more out of reach. Yes, he has ghosts having a right good time using his ball field, but that couldn't be the ALL of it. If it were, he would be *feel* satisfied. What we can see is Ray hadn't answered the question of *why* he felt he needed to build the baseball field. He still didn't know why after he had completed it. Why was it there? Why did he want it? What would having it do for him and his family besides having "Shoeless" Joe Jackson as a regular visitor? At this point, the answer would have been a shrug of the shoulders to all of those clarifying questions. What he *had* succeeded in accomplishing was creating the space – the baseball field. He manifested the tool and one desire births another. Evolution. He needed to engage the third step – taking the time to get clear.

The Universe was then forcing him to go in for the deep clean. His Being and his Truth were in a disagreement. It was asking him to reach inside for more clarity. Think about it, if the accomplishment of the baseball field alone was the object of desire, he would have been thrilled to have succeeded in manifesting that and he would have moved on to his next manifestation, happy and content. He wasn't. It niggled him to see it sitting there and not know why he had put all of that action and attention into manifesting it. His Truth nudged him into finding more clarity, which came through the next message. "Go the distance."

He searches and fumbles along finding bits and pieces of clarity here and there, but he's still not finding what he's after. Ray did what a lot of us do in similar circumstances. He tried to force an answer into the Universe instead of reaching for clarity within himself. He convinces himself that taking Terence Mann to a baseball game is his clarity and the answer to the question of whose pain he might ease. He finds the author Terence Mann who unenthusiastically joins him on his journey towards clarity; an initially unwilling partner who sees the same message as Ray on the scoreboard at Fenway Park. This is an example being back on track. So together they "go the distance"; Action. Eventually, he brings Terence Mann back to the Iowa farm and, of course, to the baseball field which has obviously connected them. Terence, too, can see the Chicago players, and the others they brought with them. This is evidence of clarity sifting itself through the fog.

Mark, Annie's brother, comes to make one last appeal to Ray to sell his farm to him to avoid complete disaster and bankruptcy. Ray and Annie, of course, refuse. They are clear about their desire for the farm and the ball field. Then more clarity makes itself known. Mark can now see the players too. While stunned, he encourages Ray *not to sell* the farm, ever. Terence tells Ray to charge a fee for all who want to see the field, a plan that will, if it succeeds, save the farm.

It is then we see the players heading back to the cornfield bringing Terence with them. Ray is left alone once more in his quest for clarity. Until he sees a different player show up – John. Crystal clarity. He had to build the field because he had to see his father to make reparations and reconnections; to clean up the space. To forgive and be forgiven. To expand his Being. To move on. It wasn't the manifestation of his father happening before clarity was had. The manifestation of his father provided the clarity of what really needed to happen. Reparation, atonement; At-one-ment. And, a means by which to fund the ailing farm. All the things beforehand were still just tools.

But, that's still not quite the "why". Besides the reparation of his tragic relationship with his father, Ray's true desire was to be a fully functioning farmer, which couldn't happen if he lost his farm to bankruptcy. It was his desire to reconcile with his dad as well, which couldn't happen until he created the space for it to manifest into. "If you build it, he will come." The field was a tool to bring about not only the reparation of his lost relationship with his father, but as a means of attracting another tool. Money. Judging by the miles-long line of vehicles heading towards the farm, for reasons beyond the drivers' comprehension, money was on the way.

Ray's Actions were Causes supporting his desire. Each Action moved him closer as clarity was realised. Did every Action produce the desired end result? Of course not. But that's how gaining clarity works and with each seeming mis-step, deeper clarity ensued inspiring further Action in the right direction. In most cases, clarity is reached one step at a time; one inspired Action after another.

Take the first step in faith. You don't have to see the whole staircase, just take the first step.

Martin Luther King

The Law of Action working through the Laws of Attraction and Cause and Effect brought about the clarity he really needed. It brought him forgiveness, an opportunity to forgive and means through which to evolve – he cleaned up his space. It also brought him what he was seeking for himself and his family. Freedom from the debt of the farm, and a constant stream of income whilst he pursued what his true Being wanted; to be a farmer. A *real* farmer, not a novice farmer. Happiness for him and his family. His desire to Be the life of a farmer, for his wife to Be the life of a farmer's wife, and for their family to Be the family they have always desired from the beginning of the film. For Ray and his family, this is his Kingdom of Heaven, an Iowa farmer on an Iowa Farm.

While we don't know if the writers of *Field of Dreams* ever meant to explain their story through the Universal Laws, what is evident is how much of these Laws played out in this film. Let's recap.

1. Turn on the Lights – "If you build it, he will come." Lightbulbs on!

2. Get Clear and Clean the House – Ray builds the baseball field. Go for the deep clean.

3. Take the Time – Ray took the time and got very clear on his desire for a happy farming family. "Maybe this *is* Heaven." And, right in his own back yard. He took the time necessary to forgive his father and himself, which helped create the space. He took the time to manifest what needed to be manifested along the way.

4. Name it – Ray named his desire to Be a farmer by his words and actions at the beginning of the film. The novice farmer stumbling around his farm and his community, desiring to be better at farming than he was at present. He named each Action-filled step. He

declared his I AM by declaring his desire to build that field of dreams.

5. Receive – No more ask. While the film leaves us with the line of cars stretching to the horizon in the waning twilight, we can conclude that he *received* the object of his desire though his tools. The Universe was providing. Throughout the film we see he managed to get out of his own way, dared to ask – even if it was just to not be like his father – then he received one step at a time. That's the way this stuff works.

CLARITY ON BEING CLEAR

I want to add a final few bits of clarity on the subject of being clear. Let's say we are still talking about money. I am not advocating being steadfastly attached to the exact amount of money you are manifesting down to the dollars and cents or pounds and pence. While this can be useful in getting you started on thinking about *why* you want the money and what you will do with it, it can also lead you to frustration. Being overly exact disallows the Universe to provide you with other avenues and resources, which may be better for you than the exact amount of money you are desiring. Ray, for example, needed resources to save his farm. If he had it in mind the only way to accomplish that desire would be a bank loan, being in bankruptcy would probably not be the best space to ask for money on credit. He did, however, manifest resources. Remember it is not the money itself; it is the Being you achieve through having resources such as money manifest into your life.

The Law of Action states we participate in Actions that support the manifestation of the object or artefacts of our desires. Once you are clear on the amount of money you are manifesting, let that amount completely go. The amount of money is a tool to get you to the *feeling* place of having it. Stop fussing about the specifics and get even more clear on *why* you want it and how to feel about it. These are Actions. Get to the emotional core of the desire, then just BE the person who already has the tools and resources associated with money. That's the Receiving part.

The second piece of advice about manifesting is to not put too much energy into a specific date and time for your money manifestation to occur. That may work for some people, albeit rarely. For most of us, however, getting stuck with a specific date tends to keep it in the ask zone. The worst part about this method is it keeps putting our desired outcome into the future, which, as we know, doesn't exist. Putting it in the future instead of in Present/Now keeps you from Being it and away from Mastery. Once you are clear, and you have made your ask of the Universe, you must put yourself into the space of Receiving and keep yourself there by Being a Co-Creator interdependently. As long as you put something you are manifesting into a future someplace, you're still asking until that date comes and goes. Additionally, when that date does come and go you run a mighty big risk of conjuring up an unhealthy dose of doubt. That will definitely slow things down.

A third bit of advice is to not be overly fussed about the specifics of how and in what manner your manifestations occur. When we are talking about clarity, we are talking about the *why* not the *how*. By overly focusing on the how, we shift focus off the why. The why is the emotional part of it, which is the only real part we need concern ourselves with. The *how* is the tool and just like any other tool, it won't be effective until we know why we need it.

By letting it go it all gets done. The world is won by those who let it go. But when you try and try. The world is beyond the winning.
                                                                          Lao Tzu

Here's a sidebar to the prior suggestions. You don't need to convince yourself or anyone else of your Being whomever you are Being, and the object or artefacts of your desires. Nothing in the Universe ever tries to convince you of anything, nor Itself. It just is. *We* are the only ones who try to do this. We tend to feel a need to justify our Beingness; to convince the Universe, and everyone else, we are somehow worthy. Guess what? The Universe already knows you are and celebrates your Being. It wants to celebrate it more if we would just do the work of getting out of our own way, like Ray. We can't do that unless we are willing enough to turn on the lights and see what needs cleaning; to see what's been sitting around in the darkness in need of some attention.

You will know when you are Being whatever is the object of your desire. You will know when you have the emotional state of Being the person with the artefact of a new car. Being the person with the tool of money. Being the happy, experienced farmer. It should feel happy, joyful, fresh, free… all of what those very positive and very emotionally descriptive words imply. The feeling may go in and out from time to time, which is OK. Just notice. It only means you are not totally 100 per cent of the time Being that person. Don't get weird about it. Just notice and get back to Being. The noticing is part of the Process of Mastery.

I am not saying you have to jump up and down every minute, shouting to the Universe and whomever else is nearby how exciting it is to Be You! That can be fun as well but probably not very practical. If you are Being that person, a simple noticing is the vibrational equivalent of jumping up and down. Then, jump up and down when you're alone. It can be quite fun! Both activities are stimulants to the Law of Action, which further stimulates the other Universal Laws. Just receive it and, in the meanwhile, enjoy the feelings of Being the fullness of your unique expression of the Universe. It distributes your manifestations to your Being, not to your need; to the person you Are not the person you are trying to be.[4]

The work of gaining clarity can sometimes feel like getting into the weeds. To be fair, sometimes it just is that way. Like Ray, the process often uncovers many other hidden blockages that need to be dissolved; things that may need to be cleaned up. Be prepared and allow them to present themselves to you. You may have kept them very much in the closet for some time. Usually because of fear. You may have them so well hidden you may not even know they are there anymore. Let it out. Let it go. Discover those monsters behind the curtain, or in the closet. Turn on the light and look them in the eye. They are not part of your plan. Your role is to have the desire, create the space and to enjoy the Mastery of Being.

CHAPTER 9

THE MASTERY OF MAPS

In the next few chapters we will be getting very specific with some things that clutter up the space of every one of us. Furthermore, we will begin to gain Mastery over these things and take back the power they use up unintentionally, freeing up more energy for our intentional manifestations. Let's start by thinking about the mind and the brain.

The mind and the brain are two distinct entities and, as far as intentional manifestation is concerned, we must be clear on their differences. The brain and the mind are certainly related, but are very separate things. Beginning with the mind, the easiest way to think about it is to understand the mind as awareness. It is aware and conscious, and it is aware of being aware and conscious. It is aware of knowing, and knows that it knows. It knows what we are doing, it controls what we are doing, and solves the problem of doing it. The mind allows us to *think*. The question then becomes, what is the thinker?

There is only One mind. It is the mind of God, or the Universe of which we are all a part; separate entities within It but sharing in the Oneness of It. Our minds are individualised centres of a greater Universal or God consciousness thinking through us.[1] The mind is non-physical. It cannot be seen nor felt nor touched. It is the invisible Cause. The mind is mental. The mind is emotional; the mind is perceptive; the mind is imaginative; the mind understands. Because it is all of these things, the mind must be consciously controlled; to be consciously focused. As Nichirin Buddhism teaches, we must become Masters of the mind, and not let the mind master us, that is unconsciously.

Now, if the mind is the mind of God or the Universe thinking through us, it may be asked why do we need to control it? The reason is because the mind, as the mind of God, is the creative power of us all. It is the power of our divinity. As such, it is always creating whether or not we are in conscious control of it. Conscious Mastery of the mind is not Mastery over God. It is the Mastery of our divine power; of our creative power. It is our divine nature to create and we are doing it all the time. The Mastery of it is simply *intentional* creating; Co-Creating with the Universe as Masters of Being. Your statement of Being, your I AM… is that conscious Mastery. You cannot manifest an I AM declaration without being conscious and clear about it. All other creation is unconscious which may or may not be manifesting our desired results.

> *The brain does not think, the person thinks and expresses his thought through the brain.*
>
> Wallace D. Wattles[2]

The brain is none of these things. The brain is the physical organ in which the mind resides. Said more simply, the brain is where the mind lives. It transmits impulses and coordinates the movements that the mind communicates to it. The brain is a physical thing; it is the tool of the mind. Just like any tool, it doesn't use itself. It doesn't think for itself. It needs something to "think" for it. That's what the mind does with the tool. As René Descartes aptly stated…

I think, therefore I AM.

Where the brain and the mind find a connection, or where they overlap, is within the three levels of consciousness. The conscious, the sub-conscious, and the unconscious. It is estimated the conscious part of the mind-brain relationship takes up about 10 per cent of full capacity. The conscious is the communicator, both internally and externally. Externally to the outside world, and internally through our inner dialogue, which is comprised of language, speech, pictures, sounds, writing, even movement.

The sub-conscious takes up a large chunk of the mind-brain relationship. The estimates are around 50–60 per cent. The sub-conscious stores recent memories and the acquisition of new skills. For example, when one learns a new language, it can be challenging. Each new word needs to be learned and used, consciously. Each new sentence, paragraph, and application of the language needs to be thought out, consciously. Assuming you stick to it, after a while, you don't have to think about it so hard. Things become a lot easier. They do so because a lot of it has slipped into the sub-conscious and out of our conscious awareness. We can pull it out of our sub-conscious if we have to, but for the most part, things are on autopilot.

When you first learned to drive a car, all the bits and pieces had to be coordinated consciously. You had to think about looking in all of the mirrors to see what was behind you. You had to learn what it felt like to go different speeds and to know the distance between you and the car beside you. After driving for many years, however, I am fairly certain most of us don't even give it a second thought anymore. The skill of driving a car resides happily in the sub-conscious.

Pausing here, let's connect a few dots. The sub-conscious is the creative substance of the Universe. That is where the connection is made between our creative divinity and the creative nature of God. It is where Your Truth lives and also the space wherein your Being is grounded. When we have a true desire, it comes through our sub-conscious into our conscious awareness. It is there where we have to consciously receive it, attach our Co-Creative power to it, and send it back into our sub-conscious where it grows and evolves the Being of who we are.

When we have a desire for an artefact, the pathway is somewhat in reverse. We consciously see and desire that new Aston Martin. Then the work begins of gaining clarity on why, and all the other bits associated with belief in it. It is the work of getting your Being to believe in Your Truth residing in your sub-conscious.

Now, think about this. The desire for the artefact of the Aston Martin comes from that roughly 10 per cent of our brain capacity and usually comes from the egoic perspective. The work is to form a belief around it that resides in our sub-conscious – the fertile ground comprising 50–60 per cent. A true desire – a desire of the heart which supports that which we are Being, comes from the 50–60 per cent space into our 10 per cent conscious awareness. It already comes with a lot more creative juices than the other way around which explains why it is often more of an energy user to manifest an artefact than to manifest those ideas that support our "what we have to say", and why it may generally take more time to manifest into our lives.

The pathway of desire is much easier if that Aston Martin is the Result of the Cause of your Being than it is by working the artefact of the Aston Martin into your Being-ness. It is just less work. Not invalid, just less involved. Like learning how to drive a car went from your conscious to your sub-conscious, it took work and practice to get there.

The unconscious takes up the rest of the 30–40 per cent. It's like the basement of your house, so to speak. It is where memories you no longer really need or want are stored – all of them. It stores memories like what you wore on your first day at school. Or, what you got for Christmas when you were three years old. It is also the place where more traumatic memories are stored; things you don't *want* to remember consciously. It's all in there tucked away, and without some psychoanalytical tool, like hypnosis, or some trigger event to help bring it back into the daylight, it's in there to stay locked in the unconscious.

MAPS

Now, I would like to introduce a way of thinking about how we think. The mind thinks through the brain, and the brain is a repository of what I call our *Maps*. Maps have been called different things by different people. Some have called them mind models, mental mock-ups, scripts, etc. It's all pretty much talking about the same thing.

All of us live through our Maps. All of us act and react according to our Maps. Maps are the programming in our sub-conscious and, sometimes, unconscious brains that cause us to react a certain way to a certain stimulus. We receive the stimulus, we have a response, and it gets us a familiar result. As long as the result is the result we are trying to achieve, we don't have to pull out and examine our Map and the result it gets us. It is when we are not getting the result we are trying to achieve that the Map attached to that particular result needs updating. For the purposes of Being, we need to Master our Maps.

A physical map (lower case "m") is a tool which helps us understand where we are, where we want to go, and which route we need to take to get there. Maps are very useful tools, and pretty handy things to have around. Let me offer a few truths about maps, however.

The first is, having the *right map* is absolutely essential. A map of Los Angeles will do you no good if you are lost in New York. The second truth is, a map will do you no good if you don't know where you are *on* it and in what direction you are pointed. If you can't find your bearings, a map will only get you more lost. Thirdly, almost all maps need updating at some point. The geography changes, the streets get renamed, highways are put in, etc. Things on a map from 1929 most often look very different to the present day. Our mental Maps work in exactly the same way.

I remember years ago, when I was a relatively young driver, everybody I knew, including myself, carried around a bulky set of bound maps called *The Thomas Guide*. They were undeniably necessary for navigating the streets, roads, and freeways of Los Angeles, California where I grew up. They were great; very detailed and very helpful but not very practical. They were heavy, bulky things that didn't fit anywhere except the footwell of the passenger seat. Additionally, there was nothing quite so frustrating as finding yourself lost and needing to locate your position on one of the pages of that book. There was many a time I could not figure out how the heck, by using a map, I could get more lost.

It would be almost unthinkable today to pull out a guide like that, or to unfold a huge paper map to figure things out. Map use has been updated. We have the modality of GPS, if not built into the car itself certainly on our mobile phones. It not only locates us on the planet but can easily tell us how to get to where we are going by talking us through it, in any language we want and any sort of accent we prefer. Pretty cool stuff.

Here are a few truths about Maps (upper case "M" this time). Our Maps consist mainly of deeply held beliefs about things, people, the world at large... you name it. And, if you can name it, or even if you can't, you have a Map about it. Maps are made from lots of bits and pieces such as culture, parents, upbringing, education, religion, experience, emotions, laughter, tears, fear... all kinds of things go into the making of a Map, and it is our Maps that form our personal reality.

Thus every mind lives in a world to which its own perceptions give objective reality. Its perceptions may be erroneous, but they nevertheless constitute the very reality of life or the mind that gives form to them. No other life than the life we lead in our own mind is possible.

Thomas Troward[3]

Now, here is an important distinction. It is often said our Maps are habitual ways of thinking. This idea, however, leans towards the implication our Maps reside on a more conscious level and that we regularly think about them. Actually, this isn't the case. Rather, they are habitual ways of *not* thinking. They are modes of habitual, sub-or unconsciousness recordings that guide and direct us. We are mostly unaware of them. We don't necessarily have to think about them very often, if at all, so they run under the radar. This is a good thing from a certain perspective because if we did have to consciously sift through all of our Maps about everything, it would drive us mad. So, Maps sub- or unconsciously inform the course of our lives. In effect, just like any lower case-m-map, they tell us where we are and help us get to where we believe we need to be, sub- or unconsciously.

Here is another truth about Maps that applies to both Maps and maps. All Maps are an artefact of the past. Maps are comprised of past thinking, past life-lessons, past emotional experiences, past relationships, etc. All of the Maps we are operating from are formed and moulded from past stuff. Therefore, since Maps inform our reality, our reality is consumed by the past.

When you fire and wire the same circuits in your brain over and over again because you keep thinking the same thoughts, you are hardwiring your brain into the same patterns. As a result, your brain becomes an artefact of your past thinking, and in time it becomes easier to automatically think in the same ways.

Dr Joe Dispenza[4]

We know, for example, what chocolate cake tastes like because of a Map. We've had chocolate cake in the past. We know we like it. We have a *Chocolate Cake is Good Map*. That's why we can order it off a menu without any hesitation, except, perhaps, about the calorie or sugar content it may have, and even *that* is a Map. We have Maps about everything. If we don't have a Map about something in particular, we are in the process of making one up. Maps are our neural pathways; the grooves in our brains that help us make sense of stuff.

When you learned how to tie your shoes, the learning of it was creating a Map, which by now has slipped into the sub-conscious level. I still remember the day I actually did it correctly. Most of us, however, don't recall that event. The *Tying My Shoes Map* is tucked away so you don't have to think about it – consciously.

How often do you pull your *Tying My Shoes Map* out into your consciousness in order to tie your shoes? You don't. You filed that one away years ago. You Mastered it. But, let's say your right hand was temporarily incapacitated. Tying your shoes would become a little bit more challenging. You would need to pull out your *Tying My Shoes Map* and polish it off; update it so you can learn to navigate your way through tying your shoes with one good hand and one incapacitated hand.

THE CARETAKER

Now, I'd like to introduce you to a little helper we all have in our heads. It's a little cartographer, a geodesist. Our very own, one and only Map keeper; our Caretaker. Our Caretaker lives in the Map Room we all have inside of us. He or she straddles the three regions of the brain – the conscious, the sub-conscious, and the unconscious, and informs the zeitgeist of our own unique experience of life.

Most often, he or she works in the realm of the sub- or unconscious because the Maps he keeps for us do not often need examining or referring to, consciously and specifically. He keeps them safe, however, quietly using them to inform our navigation through life, day-in and day-out. We hardly notice. He performs his task of holding on to and caring for our Maps with relish and pride.

In addition to storing all of our Maps, his primary work is to *reinforce* them. I say reinforce versus update, which is an important distinction. He reinforces by taking bits and pieces from our conscious experiences every day and places them into the appropriate Map file to strengthen it. That chocolate cake you ordered a minute ago? How does that taste? Like chocolate cake, right? And, it's good! The confirmation that chocolate cake is delicious is added to your *Chocolate Cake is Good Map* by the Caretaker who is just doing his job.

Now if you had one bad experience with chocolate cake for whatever reason, it probably wouldn't affect your *Chocolate Cake is Good Map* very much. In fact, it may have just reinforced it. With that one bad experience you and your Caretaker compare it to all of the other good experiences on that Map which only strengthens it. Two bad experiences? Maybe he would raise an eyebrow. Three or more bad experiences? Now, your Caretaker is probably removing your *Chocolate Cake is Good Map* from its cubbyhole, and together you both examine whether this is still true for you. Maybe you have gone off chocolate cake and it no longer tastes good to you. Maybe you have consciously decided that too much chocolate cake makes too much of you, so you are curbing your appetite for it. Whatever the reason, a Map Room summit needs to take place. Your *Chocolate Cake is Good Map* needs updating.

For another simple example, let's take a traffic signal. Three colours: red, yellow and green. The Map says a traffic light that is red means something. Red means stop. Furthermore, it means that it is unsafe to proceed until further instructions by the traffic light. In our Map about traffic signals, green means something too. Green means go. It means it is safe to proceed.

Most of us have a similar *Traffic Signal Map* going on. Every time we stop and go at a traffic light, our Caretaker collects more data to support our Maps about traffic lights. Red, stop. Green, go. We don't sit and ponder the meaning of red and green traffic lights and make a conscious decision as to their meaning every time we stop at one. That is the job of our Caretaker. It is his job to gather up that information to support our *Traffic Signal Map*. We simply stop and go without too much conscious mental energy being spent. That Map is stored in the Map Room in our sub- or unconscious brain. Our Caretaker handles it all.

Let's continue with our traffic signal example. As mentioned, most of us have very similar Maps about traffic signals, what the colours mean, and what we are supposed to do when we come to one based upon the colour it is showing us. Let's say, by way of example, while stopped at a red light, we come into relatively close proximity with someone driving a car with a different set of Maps about traffic lights. One whose green light is going red at the cross point just as ours is turning green. Our Map says green means it is safe to proceed. This other person has a Map that says any red light is *merely a suggestion* to be followed or not. You have begun to accelerate into your "safety zone" when, whoosh! The person in the other car with the Map dissimilar to yours barely misses you. As your car rocks lightly and your heart pounds heavily, your *Traffic Signal Map* is being taken from its slot and is about to be updated slightly.

Now let's look at our *Traffic Signal Map* and the meaning of the colours. The near-miss experience has forced your Caretaker to take the *Traffic Signal Map* from its dusty shelf and bring it to your consciousness for inspection. While the basics of "red means stop, and green means go" don't necessarily need to change, you may need to update it slightly to include a piece of imagery – your near-miss experience and how it felt – and include a further instruction; a codicil to the part which reads, *"Green means it's safe to 'go'."* To it we add "We might want to look to see if anything is coming at us for a second or two before proceeding into the safety zone." There. You have just updated a Map.

Until this new bit of updating has been sufficiently recorded on your Map by your Caretaker and filed away in its proper place in the sub-conscious, it will remain fairly sentient for a while. Every person you tell about your near-miss story informs this new Map. Every time you think about it, dream about it; every time you hear the song that was on the radio at the very moment it happened will remind you of the amendment to the "green means 'go' *but...*" piece of your Map. It may even start you thinking about some related maps concerning personal safety that could use a touch-up, so you start having your Caretaker pull them out for you. That would be natural because no Map lies in isolation. ALL of our maps are connected in some way.

A Personal Map

Most of us have a story about ourselves we show to the world. This is perhaps one of the biggest, most comprehensive Maps we have in our Map Room. This Map is another instance of what Carl Jung referred to as "The Persona", or the mask we wear in certain situations, much like the mask Your Truth is wearing when friction arises regarding your Being. This would be the mask we wear at work or the mask we wear at home, for example. It is what some have called the "public relations" part of ourselves. Again, this is a Map we don't often think about too much. In some cases, however, this particular Map can be the most insidious because it can work against us.

In England, we have a television show called *First Dates*. It puts together couples who have never met, on a sort of blind date in a restaurant. Everybody involved, including the restaurant staff, knows they are being filmed and voice recorded, by the way. At the end of the date the couple are brought into an anteroom where they are asked a few questions and then asked whether they would like to see each other again.

For a bit of light entertainment, it's an OK show; nothing earth shattering. However, what I find to be the most interesting bit is the study of how strong people's *Persona Maps* are. They can be pinpointed fairly quickly. Then it's even more interesting to watch how, throughout the date, they work to reinforce this Map. They share bits and pieces of it as they go along, and pretty much ask their date to agree with them. This, as we know, becomes evidence their Caretaker uses to reinforce their *Persona Map*.

For example, "People tell me I look like this or that celebrity…" This is a Map-ball lobbed into the court of the dinner partner in the form of an unasked question, to affirm and confirm this piece of the *Persona Map*. The partner then answers something to the effect of, "I can totally see that…" There, we have evidence. Or, the partner can say, "Really? I don't see that at all…" This particular piece of evidence is immediately rejected by the Caretaker because of all the other evidence supporting the "celebrity lookalike" piece of the *Persona Map*. The rejection itself then becomes evidence of support as your Caretaker presents you with the many other pieces of evidence in the file, and you affirm its validity. All the while you start to build a Map about the person you are sitting with being too dumb to see what is so obvious to so many others, and the date begins to go south. If possible, I would suggest watching this show, or some other like it, just to study the way *Persona Maps* play themselves out. It helps you to see your own *Persona Map* and decide whether it is really serving you.

Now why I say the *Persona Map* can be insidious is because, in most cases, it is often built from a great deal of fear and can show up as a bit of a shield, the energy of which can be felt and misunderstood way too easily. The way in which this shield is pieced together can be a real turn-off, which is not necessarily a Map that works for someone on a date. In extreme cases, the *Persona Map* can actually take over as in examples where someone is so identified and obsessed with their Persona Map that it carries over into every other aspect of their lives.

Bless her, but a certain popular actress and model – who shall remain nameless – is a good example of this phenomenon. One evening in a fit of rage, she allegedly hijacked a car to pursue a woman with whom she had been arguing at a party. It was hijacked, by the way, with two passengers stuck in the back seat. It is alleged she ran red lights and drove very dangerously down the Pacific Coast Highway in the chase. Evidently, feeling no remorse, she said to those who were stuck in the back seat that she couldn't get into any trouble for this. She boasted she was a celebrity and could do whatever the "bleep" she wanted, recourse free. It's a shame but it is clear her *Persona Map* has taken over causing her, and some like her, a great deal of grief.

A Peek Into Your Maps

Here's a Map game for you. Two identical women apply for jobs at the same company. The women are virtually the same in almost every way. They have the same mother, the same father and the same birthday and they look exactly alike. The interviewer asks, "Are you twins?" to which they honestly reply, "No". How is this possible?

This is a pretty classic brain bender. Keep thinking about it while you read on. I'll give you the answer in a little bit…

While the *Traffic Signal Map* example above is a very simple one, think about how many Maps we have about everything and how interrelated they all are. Further, think about how many of our Maps about people, places and things may be in desperate need of updating because they no longer serve us. The difficulty is, our Caretaker is very good at his job and keeps our Maps tightly sealed in the Map Room. He may bear a mild-mannered demeanour on the surface, wise and scholarly, quietly doing his research, but know this. Unless pushed emotionally in some way – like our traffic signal example – he can prove to be VERY strong and VERY stubborn when challenged to change a Map. He will put up quite a fight to protect certain Maps that he's worked on so hard, particularly if the Maps have a strong emotional attachment to them and have been in service for a long time. This is most true of our Maps concerning people. Our Caretaker will fight tooth and nail to protect a Map even in the face of the closest thing we can come to objective reality. This is the little helper, spoken about earlier, who shows up when your Being is arguing with the mask Your Truth wears in manifesting a new artefact.

Try this. Read the following poem and read it aloud if you can…

Today was the absolute worst day ever.
And don't try to convince me that
There's something good in every day
Because, when you take a closer look,
This world is a pretty evil place.
Even if
Some goodness does shine through once in a while
Satisfaction and happiness don't last.
And it's not true that
It's all in the mind and heart

Because
True happiness can be obtained
Only if one's surroundings are good
It's not true that good exists
I'm sure that you can agree that
The reality
Creates
My attitude
It's beyond my control
And you'll never in a million years hear me say that
Today was a good day.[5]

How does that make you feel? When I use this poem with some of my clients and I ask that question, most often the answer is something along the lines of "lousy", "a bit depressed", "sad". Totally get that. It does me too. That's because you have a bunch of Maps firing off about your own past "worst days ever". Maps about "convincing" you of something. Maps about the "world being an evil place". Maps about the fleeting nature of "satisfaction and happiness"; about "no good existing"; about "reality creating attitude". Even the length of time that is a million years, etc., etc. It goes on and on.

Now, try this. Read the same poem, again out loud is best, and start from the bottom up. Read each line left to right as you would normally read but start at the end and work your way up…

How did that make you feel? Different than the first time? Exactly the same words with different Maps attached to the way they are strung together. That's really the deeper meaning to Maps and why it is important to make sure your Maps are serving you. In spite of the fact that most of our Maps operate in the sub- or unconscious level, they carry a vibrational energy and are subject to the same Universal Laws as our *conscious* thoughts and feelings. If they are carrying lousy, fearful, cantankerous, woe-is-me energy, that is what you'll get more of. Remember our Caretaker uses a lot of our energy keeping our Maps safe and is always looking for evidence to continue supporting them. Even if they are bad Maps that no longer serve us! And, sad to say, our Maps are manifesting whatever is on them all the time because of our creative divinity. If we could just clean up, get rid of, or update our energy-sucking Maps, we would have more energy to devote to intentional manifestation, intentional Co-Creation and the Mastery of Being.

Oh, the answer to the twins question? They are triplets…

If that came as a little bit of a surprise to you, in the first place, you're not alone… it does to many people. Secondly, what that experiment did was to shift a Map most of you had about twins, even if slightly. The next time you come across a set of twins, I make up you will think about them differently. Even if they are in fact twins, the Caretaker in your Map Room will be pulling out your *Maps About Twins* file, which will help you to remember this little experiment, and whatever you now think about twins *maybe* being triplets is snatched up as evidence to support the newly updated *Maps About Twins* file, now re-named the *Twins May Actually Be Triplets Map*.

He probably won't be putting up too much of a fight about that one because most of us don't have a particular emotional attachment to a Map that says, "two people, identical in almost every kind of way imaginable, *have* to be twins and only twins until the end of time." If he is putting up a fight using that logic, he would not have entertained them being triplets in the first place, in spite of the fact that they are triplets. This is what was meant by our Caretaker putting up a fight against changing a Map even in the face of objective reality. That's the way he works. As said, he can be very stubborn, even if it doesn't serve us well.

When Maps Do Not Serve

The Bible gives us a powerful, if not a bit grizzly, example of the absolute necessity for changing a Map that does not serve you. Many times Jesus referred to the Kingdom of God as being "in our midst"[6], or within. In speaking of the pursuit of this Kingdom, Jesus uses hyperbole to illustrate the importance of this quest and to never lose sight of the purpose of it. He said that whatever should cause you to falter, regain clarity and get back on track.

> *If your hand or foot causes you to stumble, cut it off and throw it away. It is better for you to enter life maimed or crippled than to have two hands or two feet and be thrown into eternal fire. And if your eye causes you to stumble, gouge it out and throw it away. It is better for you to enter life with one eye than to have two eyes and be thrown into the fire of hell.*
>
> Matthew 18:8–9 NIV

Now, I am fairly certain no one would take any of this chopping off, gouging out, and burning in eternal fire imagery literally – hopefully. However if we look at this through the Universal Laws and Maps, we see an interesting correlation. I believe the Kingdom of God is the idea of the Mastery of Being, with all the joy, peace and happiness that comes with it. A Map that doesn't serve this state of Being needs to be adjusted, changed or thrown away entirely if Being is to Be. In the reference above, the foot, hand or eye that causes you to stumble on the road to the Kingdom is a Map that causes you to stumble on the road to Mastery. So, if an old Map gets in the way of this state of Being, cut it off, gouge it out, and throw it away.

Jesus used some pretty strong words and some vivid imagery to get his point across. However, I have a firm belief that we of the journey need to be equally as vigilant with our Being. This is Mastery. This Journey is an amazing one and not to be taken lightly. We need to be diligent with our energies and where we put them. If old Maps are sucking energy by running unintentionally and, by the way, creating unintentionally, it becomes imperative we cut the flow of energy to them and redirect it to our intentional desires.

When a Map is created and established, even if we are not conscious of it, the evidence our Caretaker continually collects to support the Map creates vibrational energy. That energy is constantly putting out into the Universe that Map as a desire. It is a Cause. The

Universe will give us what we desire, even if it's not good for us, as an Effect. The Law is not partial and doesn't know the difference between things that are good or bad for us. The stronger the Map, the stronger the vibrational energy and the more the Universe responds to that energy by way of manifesting more of it.

Depression, particularly clinical depression is, in our language, an Effect. Most often it is the result of a Cause. Something in the past, some event, some relationship, has created a Map, or a Cause, which has been deeply buried by the person affected. The Map is reinforced over and over again until the Effect becomes depression. Depending upon how deeply buried it may be in the unconscious, it will take the caring help of a professional clinician to work that one out.

Aversion therapy is a sometimes painful way of forcing a significant change in a strong Map and the behaviour associated with it. It is often used with addiction to unhealthy habits such as smoking, or alcohol abuse. If, for example, one is trying this method to quit smoking, a simple form of aversion therapy involves the wearing of a rubber band around one's wrist. Every time he or she smokes or even thinks of a cigarette, they are supposed to snap the rubber band against the wrist. This causes a slight pain, which begins to be associated with the *I Enjoy Smoking Map*, incrementally shifting it to a *Smoking is Painful and I Don't Like It Map*.

Most diets don't work because the diet itself isn't strong enough to counter the Map many dieters have about food. When someone takes on a diet, they usually have a desire to lose weight. The actions associated with dieting are a Cause, the Effect of which should be weight loss. But, here is the rub. The Map one may have about their relationship with food is still putting out into the Universe the vibrational energy of the old *I Love Yummy Food Map*, and the Caretaker is staunchly defending it. So whenever a dieter orders a small salad with a lemon wedge instead of a bacon cheeseburger with fries and a shake, the resulting argument one has is only fodder for the Caretaker to use in support of the *I Love Yummy Food Map*. The internal dialogue of, "I really want that burger instead of this crappy salad" is adding to this Map. The reactions one may have to those first bites of that crappy salad are all screaming, "This stinks!" which becomes evidence. The going away from the dinner table with the gnawing feeling of dissatisfaction of eating a salad over a bacon cheeseburger with all the trimmings is further evidence the Caretaker will use to reinforce the *I Love Yummy Food Map.* It is no match for the *I Love Eating Healthy Food Map* that the dieter may be trying to establish, at least at first.

It is only when the desire to lose weight is approached from the proper emotional perspective that the diet will work. Only when the dieter is aware of the potential battle with the Caretaker, and understands this process, will the result change favourably. If we are getting an undesirable result, we cannot expect a different one to materialise unless we are willing to do the work of changing our Maps, and subsequent behaviours, about things. This is why most diet programmes which offer their own pre-packaged food for every meal fail after the dieter goes back to "real life". The behaviours never changed. Only the choices. Once those choices are no more, the old behaviours take over.

> *And this can be done only by giving some sufficient reason for accepting the new idea in the place of the old. For each one of us our beliefs constitute our facts, and these beliefs can be changed only by discovering some ground for a different belief.*
>
> Thomas Troward[7]

In other words, the "why".

INTENTIONAL MAP MAKING

As with the Universal Laws and the way things work, intentional Map making or updating has an order to it; the 5-Step Process. When a Map no longer serves you, and you desire to change it, recognise you are essentially lost, just like you would be in the middle of unfamiliar territory with an outdated map. Your Map is taking you around in circles. Don't let it scare you. You've simply discovered you took a wrong turn and lost your way on the journey of Mastery and that's OK. As long as you desire to be *not* lost, all you need to do is follow the signposts to a new Map; a new way of thinking that will serve you better. The signposts read…

1. Turn on the Lights – Recognise and accept you are lost. Don't beat yourself up about it. It happens to us all. Just notice you're not where you think you ought to be. Pull over to the side of the road and turn on the light.

2. Clean Up the Space – Break out your Map and locate where you are on it. What caused you to notice you were off track? How does it feel? What have you been holding on to that is no longer serving you? What deeply held beliefs have been challenged? What new Map or opportunity may be emerging for you? What did you notice that you would have missed by relying upon this old Map?

   Questions such as these and others like them may take some time to answer. Just like any clean-up job, *take the time necessary to gain clarity*. Take the time necessary to locate yourself on your Map before starting your engines again. You didn't build a Map overnight, and it doesn't get updated overnight.

3. Take the Time to Get Clear – Determine where you want to go. Once you've located yourself on the Map in question, decide where you want to go from there. It may not be on this particular Map at all. In that case, you will need to discard the Map entirely and create a new one.

   With the *Twins Map*, we only just shifted it a little. In many cases, creating a whole new Map is necessary. What does the new Map look and sound like? Why do you want to go where it leads? How does the new Map feel? What opportunities does it create? Does the new Map feel right to you? Does it match your desires – your Being?

Whatever Map or Maps you are designing at this stage must be in alignment with your desires; with your Being. In most cases, the reason you noticed you were off course in the first place was because the Map you were using was out of alignment with your Being; with what you were desiring. That's a good thing so don't get frustrated. You noticed it! A lot of people don't.

Many just get irritated because they continue to be lost and off course and they just don't know it. All they know is they keep going in circles, but it never occurs to them to stop and figure out why this is. One thing is for certain. This won't get them to their destination. That circular frustration will keep manifesting because frustration is a powerful vibration. The more powerful the vibration, the faster the Universal Laws respond.

4. Name the Desire – Name the destination. Once the determination has been made, start your engines. You may have to backtrack a little but that's OK. You may feel yourself repeating the same patterns of thinking for a while. That's OK, too. Just notice and replace those patterns with those of the new Map. Reaffirm your I AM declaration.

5. Receive – Step on the gas. Go the distance. Stay the course. You know where you are headed now so enjoy the ride. Take in the scenery. These are the very things you would have missed by relying upon your old Map. How does this feel? Stay in the feeling as long as possible and remember it.

Here are some other Map shifting or Map making questions to ponder.

- What other Maps are limiting your ability to achieve your desires?

- What are some of the core Maps you use to guide your thinking and actions?

- What Maps unconsciously impact your relationships?

- What Maps do you think people have about you?

- What is something "certain" you have been holding on to which is no longer real for you?

- What if you were to let limiting Maps go?

- What would an updated Map look like?

- What would be a first step forwards? What would that look and feel like?

Truths About Maps

Four last truths about Maps that may help in this process. Like all the other steps involved in getting out of your own way, intentionally making a Map which is in alignment with your Being, is work. It can be fun, but it's still work. The Maps most of us have are sub- or unconscious. We don't have to think about them very much so we become a bit lazy. It's like starting at the gym. You know you want to. You know you should. But, you can always find 106 different excuses why you can't start today. Just do it. Take a first step. Just choose the gym as a first step. The next could be joining that gym. The next step could be just driving or, better yet, walking to the gym. You don't have to do a three-hour routine just yet. Just go there, and go home. Get into the habit of it with Action.

The second truth has already been discussed but bears repeating. Our Caretaker generally hates to shift or give up a Map. Depending upon the Map itself, he will put up quite a fight so be prepared. Use your tools. In making a new Map, use language that will provoke the least amount of resistance. If your Being supports a Map about having more money, for example, don't come at your Caretaker with statements like, "I have a million pounds", or "I have won the Lottery". He will resist that because it doesn't match the Map you have going that says, "I need to have more money".

Use non-resistant language to build your new Map. Say instead, "I love receiving money". Or, "I love manifesting money". If you do in truth love to receive and manifest money, your Caretaker cannot resist that and must agree. You are engaging with the Law of Action by doing this and you are creating Causes. With each agreement you make between you and your Caretaker, he uses it as data to support your new Map. As you become more vibrationally aligned with your new Map, the Universe will respond in kind via the Effects of those Causes, or by the intentional results you are after.

The third truth is, once you and your Caretaker take a Map from its cubbyhole in the Map room, it leaves an empty space where the old Map used to live. The space and the old Map were a perfect fit. The space loved the Map and the Map loved the space, so to speak. The separation of the two will cause them to call out to each other occasionally. The old language of the old Map will show up for you once in a while. The old behaviours, the old pity-party, or the old thinking will make itself known. It's phantom energy connected to the life of the old Map. It will haunt you for a bit and you will have to consciously and intentionally stay vigilant to supporting your new Map. We will go into this in more detail shortly. In the meantime…

Be on the lookout. Always be noticing how you are feeling. Remember how it felt to be on the road with your new Map; on the road of Mastery and Being the person with a new Map? If you are not feeling *that*, you are most likely stuck in somewhat of a tiff between the old and new Map. Consciously and intentionally unroll the new Map and get that feeling back. You'll know it when you have it.

The last truth is, until the new Map is as comfortable in the space as the old Map was, and the space is comfortable with the new Map, you will need to be on-call. Remember, the Map Room is in the sub- or unconscious. Until the new Map is as familiar as the old Map was, you'll have to keep up the work of making the new Map as detailed and clear as possible and of consciously putting energy and focus on it.

> *Emerson said, "A man is what he thinks all day long." By your habitual thinking, you make your own mental laws of belief. By repeating a certain train of thought you establish definite opinions and beliefs in the deeper mind called the subconscious; then such mental acceptances, beliefs, and opinions direct and control all of the outer actions.*
>
> Dr Joseph Murphy[8]

If you have ever driven to someplace new, you probably used a map of some sort to get there. Like most of us, you probably fired up the GPS and let it guide you to where you needed to be. If you drove there about every day for a year, the GPS is not really helpful anymore. It's just noise. The map is unnecessary. This is because the route has sunken into your sub-conscious, or even unconscious, and it just becomes a part of the routine. It is the same with Creating new Maps. It will take some time for the new Map to be as comfortable as the old Map. Just keep thinking about why you are moving Maps around in the first place. And, above all, enjoy the scenery; admire the view. These are things you would have missed by holding on to that dirty old Map.

CHAPTER 10

THE MASTERY OF PHANTOMS

As previously stated, I grew up in Los Angeles and when I was young, I was fortunate enough to be able to go to Disneyland several times a year. Over time, I became so familiar with that place it felt like my own back yard.

I had several favourite attractions at Disneyland. I loved the Pirates of the Caribbean, Tom Sawyer's Island, Space Mountain and The Matterhorn Bobsleds. I paid my usual visits to It's a Small World, the Spinning Teacups, and Sleeping Beauty's Castle. My hands-down favourite, however, was the Haunted Mansion in New Orleans Square.

That old Victorian mansion stuffed full of precisely ninety-nine haunts intrigued me. I would go on this ride several times a visit if the lines weren't too long. I was always fascinated by the ghosts flying around, dancing in the ballroom, creeping down the halls, haunting the paintings on the walls and singing their ghostly hearts out in the cemetery of the mansion's back yard. A ghost would even follow you home. You could see it sitting behind you as you made your exit from the ride. I loved it, and still do.

Now, living in England, I get my Haunted Mansion fix by occasionally watching a couple of those paranormal shows about "real-life" haunted houses. I have never been overly impressed by them but still, it's fun to play along. Once in a while, I do get a little spooked, and for me, that's fun. Don't judge, now.

Most paranormal experts believe many so-called hauntings consist of what is termed residual energy. Some believe it is the most common of all hauntings. These types of hauntings are caused by some event, sometimes a significant or traumatic event, which leaves an imprint on the atmospheric energy of the place in question. The energy produced by the people involved in the event leaves a footprint on its atmosphere, which gets stuck in a kind of loop. At times, this residual energy discharges like gasses from a distant star and replays a certain snippet of the incident. It could replay as unexplained noises such as the common footsteps down the hall. Or, as disembodied voices, laughter, or groans coming from behind closed doors.

It's like seeing the proverbial "woman in a white dress" walking down the hallway of some 600-year-old inn in the Cotswolds somewhere. Many guests would report seeing her over the years. She is *always* in a white dress and she is *always* walking down the hall. The scene repeats itself over and over again. When conditions allow, she haunts the hallway ready to spook the next guest who stays in room 13.

Some residual energy imprints itself on the atmosphere of a place through the repetition of a certain activity and the energy expended in the performance of that activity. For example, in homes that have staircases, the most common of these activities is walking up and down them. The number of times people go up and down and the energy it takes to climb a flight of stairs leaves a footprint, so to speak, on the atmosphere of the staircase. This is often used to explain why so many hauntings actually involve staircases.

From a quantum physics perspective, the explanation provided by paranormal experts actually makes sense. We know everything is energy and energy never dies. It just takes on a new form by the Law of the Perpetual Transmutation of Energy. Therefore, I don't doubt energy can be impressed on the atmosphere of a place and move into visible or audible form when conditions dictate. But, this isn't a book about quantum physics. Nor is it a book about the paranormal, so we don't have to get all tangled up in that right now. There is a certain Universal truth surrounding this idea of phantom energy, however, and this is why I bring all this up.

As with everything else in the Universe, our Maps consist solely of energy. Energy is what holds them together. Our memories, our past, is all energy and it is these memories, whether conscious or not, which form our Maps. It is this energy that draws to itself the continual flow of evidence to support the Map it is reinforcing. The impression of this energy is what guides the outflow of physical or mental activity that we put into our actions. Map energy is what guides the way we perceive the world and how we move through it. Whenever we change our Maps about someone or something, it causes the energy of the old Map to change form through the Law of Transmutation. It doesn't mean our old Map instantly goes away, however. Most often, the shifting of an old Map produces phantom energy that gets stuck in the atmosphere of our Map Room, much like the residual energy of the hauntings described above. Ernest Holmes calls this a "hangover".

As discussed earlier, when we are consciously putting together a new Map, or shifting an old one, the attention we must put on creating it causes a disturbance. The atmosphere surrounding the old Map frequently discharges as the phantom of it. It could show up in the form of lapsing into an old habit that no longer serves us. It could take the form of old ways of thinking which creep back into conscious awareness. It could make an appearance as a thought which is completely contrary to the new Map; one which is very characteristic of the old. This is the most common kind of phantom energy as it concerns Maps.

The Haunting of Old Maps

When we shift a Map or form a new one in opposition to an old Map, the phantoms will, for a while, haunt our thoughts. This will happen until such time as the new Map we are consciously making firmly takes hold and can take the old one's place. Remember, too, our Caretaker doesn't take well to letting go of old Maps. He will cling on to them for dear life. Depending upon how deep our Maps are, how much evidence there is stored to support them *and* how much emotion there is attached to them, silencing them for good will most likely never happen completely. As an example, let's work with a Map about weight loss.

> *Old Map:* Losing weight is difficult for me.
> *New Map*: I lose weight quickly and easily.

The old Map probably has a fairly strong gravitational tug on it, with a lot of reinforcement over the years, and a lot of emotional baggage attached. As a result the Universe brings you more of the difficulty in losing weight. Additionally, your Caretaker keeps adding fuel to the energy furnace by resisting your new Map while, at the same time, pulling forwards evidence in support of the old. He has a strong grip on the old Map. He hates to be wrong, loves to be right and will absolutely refuse to entertain the thought of a new Map, at least at first.

> *Your New Map*: I lose weight quickly and easily.
> *Caretaker*: No you don't. Diets can't work for you because losing weight is difficult. See, right here on the *Losing Weight is Difficult for Me Map* how many times you have tried to lose weight and how many times you have failed. Losing weight is difficult for you.
> *Your New Map*: Losing weight is easy for me.
> *Caretaker*: Of course it's not. Don't you remember last

spring and last winter when you tried to lose weight, twice? Here, I'll show you on this Map. Right here… Both times you actually gained weight, remember? Look at the Map.

Your New Map: I don't have a problem losing weight.

Caretaker: Losing weight is too hard, for you. And, it's no fun. See, on this Map right here how miserable you were when you tried that diet? The food you were allowed to eat was tasteless. Why would you want to put yourself through that again? Losing weight is difficult for you…

And, so on and so forth. To be honest, it can be challenging, this game of tug-of-war. After a while of sparring with your Caretaker and the Old Map, it's quite possible you may start to give in especially if progress on the new diet is slow. You may begin to feel defeated and depressed, discouraged and alone. Slowly, you may begin to go off your new eating regimen and eventually let go of it entirely. You forfeit the game and let the Caretaker win. With this victory, he can prove himself right once again. With that task out of the way, he leaves you alone for a while; game done and dusted.

Because the *Losing Weight is Hard For Me Map* is still there, strengthened by recent activity, the Universe will agree with the Caretaker by sending you more evidence in support of that Map. In your depression, you eat a packet of biscuits, a half a cake, a tube of Pringles and you end up feeling sick. Until one day you get fed up and try to revive the *I Lose Weight Quickly and Easily Map*, which you may try to sneak past your Caretaker. The trouble is, you can't sneak anything past the Caretaker. There are no shortcuts. Working against him just won't bring you the result you are trying to achieve. What will bring you the desired result is working *with* him.

If you have begun the effort of cleaning your house, of clearing out the cluttered spaces and scrubbing down the walls, you may have noticed this phenomenon. Once you sweep the dirt out the front door, it always wants to come back. The old thought patterns, the old Maps and subliminal records want to replay themselves over and over in your head. The old jealousy, envy, superiority/inferiority complexes, you name it. The Map about losing weight is old dirt. The new Map about your ideal weight is a clean floor. When the old Map comes knocking and you open that door, you will quickly discover the old Map has very muddy feet, and should not be allowed in.

That old Map you are struggling with, knocking at the door or tapping at the window, is phantom energy; a hangover. It is the residual ghost energy of your old Map trapped in a loop, wanting to replay itself over and over again in the great hall of the house of your Being. If you wish to be successful at changing your Map about this or anything else, you have to be very diligent, especially at first, with what and about whom you let into your clean house. If you open the door of your house to the dialogue, feelings and emotions of the old Maps, they will feed on the energy being used to create that new Map, weakening your efforts.

TENDING TO NEW MAPS

The new Map is fragile. Protect it by blocking the door. Nourish it with your attention, emotions and the feelings of what it is to Be the person Mastering your ideal weight.

> *Only those thoughts can enter my mentality which I allow to enter. I do not and cannot accept adverse thoughts. Only those thoughts which are helpful and life-giving can find entrance to my house.*
>
> Ernest Holmes[1]

I like a clean house, so I clean my actual house once a week. It always surprises me how much dirt can accumulate in six or seven days. If I've been away for a couple of weeks or so, it's downright shocking what builds up, which makes cleaning it more difficult.

Like any clean house, diligence is the key to keeping it clean. This is also true of the house of your Being. It takes work to keep it dust-free and ready to receive the manifestation of your desires. Ghost energy cannot be allowed in. It will want to creep in just like the dust on your furniture. You can ill afford to shrug your shoulders and say, "Hey, that's life". You must dust every day to keep it clean and clear until the new Map has the same or greater vibrational energy as the old Map and can begin to hold its own.

Being the Master of your ideal weight requires giving your new Map the attention the old Map used to get, but consciously. Remember, the old Map did a lot of running on its own without your conscious energy. Now that you are more aware of it, you can intentionally redirect that energy to the more life-giving place until the new Map can support itself. Don't be fooled, it's work.

Intentionally engage the Law of Perpetual Transmutation of Energy. When the ghost of your old Map starts to knock on or even break down the door, stand your ground. Change the energy. It's your clean house and your new Map. Speak to the old Map... talk to it. Tell it to get off your front porch. Notice when it starts to creep up the steps and tell it to turn around and go away. The Universe will not hand your new manifestations to that old phantom energy unless you let It and It won't hand them to *you* either until you have sent that ghost packing. That can only come from the Mastery of Being the person with the ideal weight in the Present/Now.

TELLING OFF OLD MAPS

There is a very good example of physically telling off your old Maps found in the story of the Temptation of Christ, told in the three Gospels of Matthew, Mark and Luke.[2] We are told Jesus had been fasting for forty days and forty nights in the wilderness. My personal belief is it was during these forty days he was doing the work of cleaning his house in preparation for his new Being; in preparation for his upcoming purpose. In order for this new mission to be successful, just like any of us, he would need to get rid of some old stuff, some old Maps, and put some new ones into place. It was also during this time we are told Jesus was tempted three times by Satan.

I believe Jesus was recognising something about himself during this time in the wilderness. According to some Biblical scholars, Jesus was confirming and defining his messianic mission, which certainly took some effort and some shifting of his thinking. If we may look at the temptation of Jesus in the wilderness as a Master Being making a paradigmatic shift, we can see how a generous shifting of Maps would be required.

The forty-day period was a time to clean up his house, get rid of old Maps and to create new ones to occupy the space. It was a time to define and gain clarity on new desires to be made manifest into those freshly renovated rooms. I can only imagine the amount of Map shifting that would be required in order to embark upon the kind of mission Jesus was about to take. It would naturally necessitate a lot of old, limiting Map removal and with that much activity, it would be of no surprise a significant amount of phantom energy would be stirred up. This was represented by the Devil himself.

I believe the representation of Satan in the Bible is a personalisation of the enemy of all manifestation efforts; of all efforts towards Mastery. If looked at through our manifestation language, Satan is the personification of *doubt*, which involves anything that gets in the way of Being our desires. Doubtful thoughts, emanating from within, will throw roadblocks onto our journey so we must always be mindful and deal with them as the enemy they are.

The temptations Jesus faced were *hedonism* represented by self-gratification and appetites of the flesh, *egoism* demonstrated by Satan tempting him to throw himself off the highest peak of the temple in Jerusalem, and *materialism* represented by Satan offering him all of the kingdoms of the Earth. Of course, Jesus refused to be tempted by the old Maps of hedonism, egoism, and materialism. Or, if he was tempted, he did the work of dissolving the energy and shifting it in the right direction. When it showed up, he refused its entry into the cleared out and cleaned up house he was building for his Being. And, each time he refused, he spoke directly to the doubtful thought.

After forty days and nights, we are told Jesus was very hungry, as one can imagine. Satan, or doubt, comes to tempt him into manifesting loaves of bread out of stones. It is commonly believed Jesus could have manifested some sustenance on his own, but to do so would have been an act of self-indulgence. Sure it would have been nice to chomp down on a loaf of bread after forty days, but that wasn't the point. The point was to affirm Universal truth, not to satisfy hunger.

When this doubtful thought emerged, Jesus spoke directly to it proclaiming a great truth; that man, or our Being, is not comprised solely of the physical body, which is an Effect, but of the energy of the Universe, or God, which is a Cause. As such it is One with God and with *all things*, not just the physical.

> *But he answered and said, "It is written, Man shall not live by bread alone, but by every word that proceedeth out of the mouth of God."*
>
> Matthew 4:4 KJV

Matthew and Luke switch the next two doubt-filled scenes around, but for the sake of ease, let us use the sequence of events recorded in Matthew.

When Satan, or doubt, returned it was a temptation of the ego. As recorded in the book, Satan took Jesus to the highest point on the temple in Jerusalem and tempted him to chuck himself off it. The assumption being a divine rescue would naturally ensue given Jesus' claim to be the embodiment of God's son. Jesus responded directly to the doubtful thought again by rebuking it verbally.

> *Jesus said unto him, "It is written again, Thou shalt not tempt the Lord thy God."*
>
> Matthew 4:7 KJV

The third recorded incident was a temptation of materialism. As told, Satan took Jesus to a very high place to show him all the kingdoms of the Earth. If Jesus would succumb to this temptation by doubting his Being in favour of material wealth, it is told Satan would give him the lot. Jesus again spoke directly to this doubtful thought in this way.

Then saith Jesus unto him, "Get thee hence, Satan: for it is written, Thou shalt worship the Lord thy God, and him only shalt thou serve."

Matthew 4:10 KJV

In Luke it is recorded in this way. Notice the language used here.

And Jesus answered and said unto him, "Get thee behind me, Satan: for it is written, Thou shalt worship the Lord thy God, and him only shalt thou serve."

Luke 4:8 KJV

In versions of the Bible other than the King James, the phrase "Get thee hence", or "Get thee behind me" is translated as "Get away from me", or "Get out of it", or "Get away from here". Regardless of the translation of the phrase, the pattern is one of speaking directly to the doubtful thinking, or the phantom of the old Map trying to pull focus away from the new Map and a clean house.

Jesus spoke directly to the phantom of the old Maps knocking at the door of his Being his true Self, who was about to emerge from the desert. The phantom Maps were trying to throw doubt onto his new Map-making efforts regarding his purpose on Earth; what he had to say. The new Maps Jesus was making were to create a definitive shift in the Universe, one to which we still look for inspiration today. You can see the intensity and diligence engaged when the phantoms began to show up. Not an instant of doubt was to be allowed into his new Being.

There is no low level of diligence involved in a mini-Map shift any more than there is a huge level of diligence necessary for a Map that creates a paradigmatic shift. It's all the same. When you are shifting a Map and the phantom of the old Map appears, get rid of it immediately. Keep watch always. The phantoms will try anything and any way to resurrect themselves.

In the examples above, the rebuke of Jesus' old Maps freed up the energy he needed to support his new Maps in preparation for work. And he had a lot of new Maps emerge, judging from all of the new thought, which was recorded from the Sermon on the Mount, following shortly after his wilderness wanderings.

His teachings were full of new ideas and Maps that people hadn't heard before. They were hearing new ways of thinking and relating to their traditions. They were exposed to new Maps regarding the fulfilment of the Jewish law, murder, adultery, recompense, enemies, the power of thought and even how to pray. He was instructing his followers with new Maps about Heaven, the needy, day-to-day living and the cares thereof (3). This was big stuff and you can imagine the struggle his followers may have had in shifting *their* old Maps to these new ones when their heritage and traditions were so deeply ingrained.

I find captivating the idea of speaking directly to phantom Maps. I have engaged this method frequently and can tell you, it really helps to chase away the ghostly images of old Maps, fast. I also find extraordinarily interesting a connection to another time Jesus spoke directly to phantom Maps much like the examples above. Particularly using the language of "Get thee behind me…".

DO THE PHANTOMS GO AWAY ENTIRELY?

In the sixteenth chapter of Matthew, Jesus is recorded telling his disciples of his pending execution as they approach Jerusalem. After having just commended his disciple Peter for completely understanding Jesus' message of relationship with God, or as the model of Oneness with the Universe, Jesus appears to completely slap Peter down, and hard.

As he is explaining the events about to happen, Peter exclaims to Jesus, "Never, Lord!… This shall never happen to you!" This was doubt personified. It was the Devil himself pushing a phantom Map at Jesus who, as we have seen, spoke directly to the doubt with a dose of a new Map. As well intentioned as Peter's comment may have been, it can have multiple interpretations.

Part of it appears to be speaking words of comfort. Some of it is based in fear. Whether Peter was afraid and cried out "never" as if to say, "I don't want that to happen", or whether he was trying to tell Jesus that he didn't believe him, or whatever other interpretation can be offered, the point of it all is this. Intentionally or not, what Peter was doing was lobbing a doubt ball into the court.

What Jesus did immediately was to tell doubt to take a hike and he called it by what I believe to be doubt's true name, Satan.

> *Jesus turned and said to Peter, "Get behind me, Satan! You are a stumbling block to me; you do not have in mind the concerns of God, but merely human concerns."*
>
> Matthew 16:23 NIV

Here we can see an interesting correlation with the words, "Get behind me, Satan" used here, and the same set of words used in the temptation of Jesus in the wilderness.

> *And Jesus answered and said unto him, "Get thee behind me, Satan: for it is written, Thou shalt worship the Lord thy God, and him only shalt thou serve."*
>
> Luke 4:8 KJV

The major point to understand about these examples is the use of the dynamic tool of speaking directly to doubts, or phantom Maps, as they try knocking on the door of your newly cleaned and freshly

Mapped house. The minor point is the use of the phrase, "Get behind me…" Now, word translations of ancient texts often vary from a little to a lot depending upon who is translating, and the year of translation. However, there is something intriguing about the idea of doubt or old phantom Maps "getting behind" and staying behind the new Map for two reasons.

The first is when you put something behind you, you simply cannot focus 100 per cent of your energy upon it. Out of sight, out of mind, as it were. Doubt always tries to pull focus away from your new Map. Telling the phantom Map to step in line behind you and your new one commands it to take its proper place. It allows you to shift focus back on to the new Map and off the old one.

The second fascination I have with the use of the phrase "Get behind me" is an acknowledgement of what I believe to be a Universal lesson on how It responds to any sort of shift from one structure, paradigm, or Map to another; from one point in Its evolution to the next. I believe it explains how we may be able to forgive someone, but never forget; in spite of the old adage that this may be accomplished. To this end, I believe when an old Map is shifted in favour of a new Map, the old Map never goes away entirely. It is just out of sight and should no longer be given our attention. It is in all likelihood still lurking around, however.

By consistently energising your New Maps and giving them the attention the old Maps used to get, the echoes of the old Maps will eventually grow quieter. Their knocks will grow more faint. Their energy-seeking tactics will fade. Their calls will become almost inaudible and certainly less vibrationally sound until one day they will disappear almost entirely.

I say *almost* because I am fairly convinced they cannot actually disappear completely, without a trace. That doesn't fit how the Universe works, physically. They are just behind you and the new Map. I am still on the fence as to whether this may be a Universal Principle or just one of those things one takes notice of and in which one finds some truth. Let's call it a Universal Noticing.

If you get cut, it bleeds, it heals over and it leaves a scar. If the trunk of a tree is carved into by someone expressing undying love for his mate, the tree trunk will heal. It will scar over eventually, but it will be left with an indelible "D + J –4– ever" for lookers-on to ponder about for years afterwards, concerning who "D" was, who "J" was and if "–4– ever" actually worked out for them.

Emotional wounds are under the same principle. They will leave a scar that experts will tell us will never go away. One just learns how to manage those scars and not let them ruin one's life. Some need the aid of a professional to assist the healing process. Even so, the so-called "cure" does not entirely erase the damage done.

Any addict who has gone through recovery will be the first to tell you they are never cured. They will never be non-addicted. Recovery is not a cure. It is not the complete removal of the addiction. Recovery is a life-long process, the work of which is new Map building and the tearing down of old ones. There will always be a phantom of the addiction present. This is why AA, for example, encourages people in their meetings to begin the conversation with how long they have been sober. Some may have been sober for decades but this practice serves as a reminder of the constant need to focus on the new Map, e.g. *Sobriety*, over the old Map called *Addiction*.

If an asteroid hits a planet, it too causes a lot of damage and leaves a scar in the form of a crater. Eventually it heals over through the process of erosion to the point the crater can hardly be seen anymore. It's still there, however. Our Earth is pocked with barely visible craters like Chicxulub in Mexico, the scar left by the large asteroid that has been dubbed responsible for the mass extinction of the dinosaurs. Or, the Maniitsoq structure in Greenland. It is said to be the remains of a sizeable asteroid that hit the Earth three billion years ago. The power of erosion has worn them both down to practically nothing; it has scarred them over, if you will. Yet, they are still there and can still be seen one way or another, albeit barely.

I sort of chuckle to myself when I hear the phrase "bury the hatchet", a version of "let's stop the squabble and move on". It's a lovely sentiment, but it is simply impossible. Look at it this way. No matter where you bury that hatchet, the hatchet is still there, you know it's there and what's more, *you know where you buried it.* Likewise, the same goes for the idea of "forgive and forget". Also impossible. You may forgive, which I strongly encourage, but you can never forget. The memory will always be with you, however many attempts you make to eradicate it entirely. At best, it can be shoved into the unconscious level and therefore consciously forgotten about but it's still there. The silencing of old Maps is in the same category. They may be forgiven, so to speak, but never be forgotten entirely.

Old Maps never completely disappear. Their phantoms may remain with us forever. Much like what happens at the Haunted Mansion at Disneyland, as you exit the ride. That hitchhiking ghost follows you home. In a similar way, your old Maps have made an impression on the atmosphere of your Being. Even for powerful manifestors like Jesus, the appearance of doubt in the face of his Map about who he was and what he needed to accomplish was met with an immediate response. A rebuke, then an affirmation for his current Map. In the case of Peter's rebuke, he spoke to Satan, or doubt, and told it to get behind him. He then added a confirmation in support of his then current Map.

I say current because his new Map about himself and his paradigmatic thinking by this time wasn't all that new, actually. Several years had passed between Jesus' time in the desert when he was being tempted by doubt and the time he was making his final entrance into Jerusalem for the Passover and, ultimately, his own death. Luke tells us he was about thirty years old at the time he began his work[4] just after exiting the wilderness. It is commonly held he performed his mission for about three and a half years. Assuming he had the vision of what he was to accomplish and knew the consequences at the time in both Roman and Jewish law for having such ideas, his new Map would have been about three years old at the time of Peter's slap-down.

This just shows the diligence and focus necessary, sometimes, for new Maps and ways of Being to become solid. Through Peter, Jesus himself experienced a moment of phantom energy left over from his pre-ministry self, Maps included. And, we can see how quickly he stepped on that doubt; how fast he jumped on it by calling it out and re-affirming his current Map; the concerns of God, or in our language Universal Principles.

With diligence and awareness regarding the new Maps you are forming, sooner or later you will have reached the point at which you will have successfully energised the new Map into being as much a part of you as your old Map was. Your Caretaker will give up the fight and happily busy himself with the constant search for evidence every day and night to support your new Map. The old Map will always have a residual energy, however. Much like a scar. Scars and old Maps fade over time. Yet, once in a while, you will notice them and remember what originally caused them. You will still faintly hear the voice of the old Map whispering in your ear like an echo from the past. Then, hopefully, you will forget about it again. Remember, they are only reminders of what used to be.

When this happens, just notice your old Map and send it away. Speak to it. Tell it where its proper place is. "Get in line behind me. I AM Mastery, mister…" Then re-energise and affirm your new Map and be grateful for the journey on which it takes you. Gratitude has a huge vibrational impact, which the Universe responds to quickly with even more to be grateful for and with a whole basket of new Maps to create on The Masterful Way.

CHAPTER 11

THE MASTERY OF MONSTERS

The mind is very powerful, and never loses its creative force.
It never sleeps. Every instant it is creating... There are no idle
thoughts. All thinking produces form at some level.

A Course in Miracles[1]

All of us are far more powerful and creative than we give ourselves
credit for, frankly. We are in a constant state of creating and
manifesting, day and night and will be forever. Consciously or not,
creation is at our very core; it is our essence. If Oneness is our Godness, creation is our divinity.

If we agree, as do many religions and philosophies, that we are
the so-called children of God and if we further believe that Life, or
the Universe, is the ultimate Creator, it stands to reason the offspring
of the ultimate creator would be powerful creators as well. We are
of the identical nature to God, or the Universe. Therefore, the truth
is we are creating stuff all the time; manifesting through the same
power channels as the Universe itself. By the Law of the Perpetual
Transmutation of Energy, the Universe never stops creating. Likewise,

we never stop creating. The issue for many of us, however, is we do so much of our creating *unconsciously*, which doesn't serve us well.

> *I said, "You are 'gods'; you are all sons of the Most High."*
> Psalm 82:6 NIV

THE MONSTERS WE MAKE

To me, unconscious creation is the biggest mistake ever. And, while we probably won't be able to prevent unconscious creation completely, The Masterful Way is a journey of greater perception and intention. The more unconscious stuff we manifest for ourselves, the more this stuff piles up and gets in our way adding to our personal gravitational pull. Stuff which hinders our intentional manifestations and thwarts our desires – it slows us down. Junk that doesn't go away by itself and which may actually cause some real damage to our efforts of Mastery.

A big chunk of the stuff that gets in our way, which sticks around and isn't got rid of easily, is and are what I refer to as *monsters*. While Maps are deeply engrained patterns of mostly not-thinking and behaving which help us navigate through our individualised expression of the Universe, monsters are things which we create in the moment. Monsters are created piecemeal through irrational thinking and misappropriated pieces of Maps. The monsters we make are scary, fear-based and are definitely not worthy of us. They are things we make up about situations and people, which we replay in our minds and then make real for ourselves.

Monster-making is a skill we developed early on in life and it is a skill we have never lost. From the time we were small, we knew how to create monsters. Almost all of them were created in a dark, scary place. As a child, a bump in the night leads to a creaky floor and footsteps down the hall. Then, otherworldly sounds can be heard in the attic and scratching on the ceiling. Cue the thunderstorm outside.

The shadows on the wall are staring at us. A rap on the door; the rattle of the doorknob. A tap on the window. Then full-blown apparitions appear with red, glowing eyes, trying to devour us in our beds. This is the snowball effect of monster-making. We have a tendency for it; a penchant. We did it then and we do it now.

The movie industry has made a fortune by capitalising upon our tendency to make up monsters. They court our natural propensity. They tease it from us. They do not need to provide much to work with, after all. They are relying upon our innate propensity to scare ourselves. Have you ever noticed? All a scary movie needs to do is create a space, set the tone and leave it to our imagination. We become co-producers right along with them. You may have noticed very often a film doesn't let us see the monster, the stalker, the ghost, demon or alien, until the very end of the picture. This is because nothing the film industry could possibly create for us even half compares to the monster, the stalker, the ghost, demon or alien we create for ourselves in our heads. We are just that good.

Did you ever see the film *When a Stranger Calls* (2006)? At the time, it was a really scary movie mainly due to what we don't know about the "monster" as we watch. It is still a scary movie, actually. As it relates to our innate creative ability and skill at monster making, it has a very profound corollary. Let me offer a quick synopsis…

The lead character is teenage Jill. After she runs up a very exorbitant mobile phone bill, her father decides to take the opportunity to teach Jill a life-lesson in money management. First he grounds her for one month. Then he closes the "Bank of Dad" and insists she pay the bill off herself. To do so, Jill takes a babysitting job. Sounds fairly innocent, doesn't it?

On the night in question, Jill's father drops her off at the stately home of her babysitting employers where she will be sitting for two young children. The house is secluded, of course. It is enormous, filled with well put together living spaces all designed to highlight the peace and serenity of the secluded, natural surroundings. It is clear from what she can see, the family is quite well-to-do and Jill is excited to spend some time in such a grand manner, even if she is only babysitting.

It is the picture-perfect job. Nice digs. Stunning house. No real worries – the kids are already snug in their well-to-do beds. The sub-zero fridge is stocked full of well-to-do food. The well-to-do parents are heading out for dinner and a movie. They won't be home until after midnight – naturally. Jill settles in for a quiet evening. Suddenly, the house phone rings piercing the peaceful darkness. It startles her. Jill picks it up, and on the other end an unfamiliar, creepy and very raspy voice asks, "Have you checked the children?"

Fear and curiosity rise within her as, predictably, a windstorm begins outside. Suddenly, that big, beautiful house she envied only a short time before is now full of the creeps. The phone rings again. It is him. And, again. It is him. The caller's voice begins to create a panic in her. As the calls continue into the night, each becomes more sinister than the one before. The caller begins to reveal details of her activity in the house, which can only mean one thing. He is watching her. He knows what she is doing. As the calls keep coming, it becomes obvious. He is hunting her. Cue storm…

Jill is obviously disturbed and for good reason. Fear catches in her throat with each time the phone rings. Her pulse races; her breathing becomes shallow. She is in fear. Fear for her own safety, and for the safety of the children for whom she's sitting. The fear is tangible and intense. It can be felt in the ethers. Every creak of the house, every moan of the floors underneath her feet, every shadow that passes the window ratchets up that fear factor. The wind from the storm outside only makes things worse as the dark night of terror begins to take over.

The calls continue, becoming more graphic, more disturbing and more menacing. She rings the police to have the calls traced. The police inform her she will need to keep the caller on the line for sixty seconds in order to effectively locate the origin of the call. Then, the phone rings. It's him.

Raging against her own fear, she tries to engage him in some sort of loose conversation to hold him on the line for the required amount of time, but he is not in the mood to have a lovely chat. He remains silent to her questions, leaving only the sound of his breathing and her fear to fill the dreadful void. Reluctantly, she asks him what he wants from her.

His response is graphic and cold, alarming, violent, and majorly distressing – it is designed to shock her… and us, which it does. She quickly hangs up the phone. Immediately the phone rings again, but this time it is the police calling her back. They have successfully traced the call and presumably the caller. They inform her… *The call is coming from inside the house…* The very house she is sheltered within. The usual plotline ensues. The would-be killer is finally revealed. The police come to save the day. Fade-to-black and the credits roll.

This is typical of many scary plotlines. The film-makers leave the actual monster-making to us. All they did was to provide a dark, secluded house, a late night, a windstorm and the unknown. We just took all the ingredients, added a handful of fear and from there we built a monster to be afraid of. This brings up an important truth about all monsters, whether movie monsters or the ones we create for ourselves. They are *all* are made out of some form of fear.

THE FEAR

Fear is a double-whammy, two-fisted sucker punch in the gut. The right-hand punch is to understand fear is instinctual; hard-wired into our very DNA. We can't help it; we can't get away from it. Our ability to create monsters is due to our innate ability to fear. We are extraordinarily good at using fear to create. So much so we are adept at *creating things for ourselves to be afraid of.* But fear for the sake of fear isn't what scares us. We are not afraid of fear. Fear only turns out the lights and surrounds us with the unknown. We are not even afraid of the monsters we make. What we are afraid of is the monster we make *with* a heaping helping of a special sauce; a powerful ingredient known as faith. We have to believe in the monsters we make in order for us to be afraid of them. We have to have a great faith in what we are afraid of or we wouldn't be afraid of it.

Unlike movie monsters, the monsters we create show up more subtly. Our monsters show up as difficult conversations we need to have with others. They appear as unsaid things in a relationship. They dart around the room as the energy we spend making someone wrong for something; then blaming them for that something, which they may not even know they are doing. Then, we make them wrong for not knowing it. And, lastly we make them wrong for not understanding why we are upset.

Monsters show up as frustration, anger, jealously. They show up as the negative stuff we make up about people, things, cultures, strangers, friends, partners, neighbours, sisters, brothers, spouses, the checkout lady, the talking head on the television… Monsters show up as worry, guilt, criticism, boredom, blame, shame, procrastination, laziness and anger. They show up as vices, continued bad habits we allow to have power over us, and negative internal dialogue. They show up as self-righteousness, self-loathing, self-abuse and self-centredness. Some of us make a monster of catching every illness known to man, which turns into a condition known as hypochondria.

Always chasing time? That's a monster. Always too busy? That one is too. Feeling like things just don't seem to go your way? That's a monster. Feeling like, "Why does this always happen to me?" That's a monster, as well. All of these monsters and more are based in fear.

We form our monsters out of fear and in the dark. Then we believe in them. Belief is what gives them their monster-like powers over us, which only serves to make us more afraid of them. So we have to work harder to keep feeding their scariness. Here's the crazy, mixed-up thing though. After all the work we put into them, we justify that work by spending more energy making *them wrong for scaring us*. We further justify all of this energy use by making *ourselves wrong* for being afraid of them. It's a little crazy-party we play with ourselves.

The left-handed sucker punch about fear is that our fears are energised by our own Maps. Fear is only the skeletal structure of the monsters we make. Once the backbone of fear is put into place, we knit together our creation with bits and pieces of old, rotting Maps taken from our Map Room. We then combine them with what is happening in the moment; out there in the dark. It is from this chaos our monsters take form.

We then strengthen them; we give them life through belief. Once they are believable, we proceed to hand them the keys to the kingdom so they may run rampant through the village of our Being. Next, we blame them for having the keys in the first place and then we further foist culpability upon them for having the audacity to go around making us afraid. I know… it's twisted.

Distinction Between Monsters

All monsters are made of fear but not all monsters belong to the same caste. There is a major distinction between movie monsters and the ones we make up ourselves. This distinction uncovers a bigger and more scary facet to our homemade beasts. While movie monsters are designed to *cause* fear, our monsters are designed *from* it and they are attached to us like a parasitic twin.

We all know the jig is up with regard to the monsters of the cinema. We know the secret. Sitting in a dark movie house, we can play a game of make-believe with monsters and have the fun of being freaked out for a while. At the end of the film, however, we know they are fakes; unreal to us and therefore cannot do us harm. When the credits roll, we can leave them behind with the stale popcorn on the cinema floor. The monsters we make are different than those created by others to frighten us. Unlike make-believe monsters, our monsters are even more frightening because they *belong to us so they follow us home*. We can't get away from them in the same way we can the movie ones. We can't lock them out of the house because the truth is, *they live with us* and they have the keys to the front door.

All metaphors aside, from the perspective of the Universal Laws and intentional manifestation, the fear-based monsters we create pose an actual threat to us. They are dangerous. This is because they are made from ingredients that carry very powerful vibrations and emotions which stimulate the Universe to give us more of these unwanted elements; more of which to be afraid. Fear-based Causes produce fear-based Effects and the Law of Attraction will continue to give us more unless we take Action against them.

More to feel insecure about. More to feel needy about. More to feel poor, unwell, frightened, angry… All of these strong emotions breathe life into our monsters, and tend to get very quick responses from the Universe. The Universe responds to these powerful emotions with more of them. It becomes the snowball effect designed to create a necessary response from us. Necessary because it's biological.

Fear always triggers a lizard-brain response within us. Fight or flight. The Universe doesn't know the difference between an actual fight or flight situation, or one that is made from a monster we created in our heads. The snowball effect skips over any lag time between the feeling of fear and receiving more to be afraid of. If what is confronting us were to be an *actual* situation requiring a fight or flight response, if we don't react appropriately, we may lose the game in a very serious way. This is the Universal reason fear has such a strong vibration which gets this kind of immediate response.

When we are fearful, we often become more and more afraid so we may get the hint. We must either fight our way out of whatever is scaring us, or run away. In a real threatening situation, this is certainly appropriate. However, with the monsters we make, the response mechanism is the same; fight or flight. The problem is, until we recognise what is actually going on with the monsters we create, we are not all that invested in either fighting or flighting. This is because, in another crazy-party sort of way, we actually think we need our monsters. We think they serve a vital purpose, albeit an artificial one, and here it is. They are a darn good scapegoat.

Externalising Our Monsters

Once we create a monster, it appears to take a form external to ourselves. Even though our monsters are really in our heads, hearts and in the very fibre of our being, we try to fool ourselves into thinking otherwise. We place them in a position external to ourselves for insane reasons. As long as they remain external to us, kept alive by the constant energy of belief, they remain seemingly out of our control. When things go wrong, we can blame them; we can make them responsible. The object of derision. The trouble with this ill-logic is it's completely false. Since we made the monster from the inside, that's where it hides, in the dark and the dark is scary.

Keeping them in that scary, dark place further widens the separation because we innately do not like to explore dark, scary places. So, we avoid them. As long as we do so, we do not have to take responsibility for making monsters in the first place. We have the privilege of continuing to use them to affirm a lie we tell ourselves… "See? It's not my fault…"

It's their fault things suck. We tell ourselves they have the power to destroy us because they have their own free will *apart from ours*. They can show up at anytime, anywhere and we are helpless against them. So, we keep fearing them and, subsequently, keep avoiding them and their dark hiding places. Additionally, we know deep down that if we ever did confront them, we will have to bear the burden of admitting *we were responsible for them from the get-go.*

Remember fight or flight? Keeping our monsters external to us, refusing to confront them or ignoring them altogether and refusing to take responsibility, puts the most primitive part of our brains in charge – the lizard brain. Taking accountability for them and confronting them is too scary so we go into play-acting mode; pretending to fight them in some way, or we pretend to run away. The problem with running away from them is… we can't. *The call is coming from inside the house,* remember? No matter where we run to get away from them, they are running right along beside us.

Running away can take many forms. In the extreme, running away can show up as alcoholism, food addiction, starvation, drugs, wilful ignorance or a sheer refusal to turn on the lights and look in the closet. We become intentional with our ignorant refusal because we've grown accustomed to our monsters. Fighting against them doesn't work either. Unless we are ready to expose them for what they truly are, our attempts at fighting are actually only play-fighting and play-fighting always backfires. Pretending you are fighting your monsters makes them stronger and makes us fear them even more. And, why wouldn't we? They always win the battle.

In the first place, play-fighting them is always done in the darkness of fear. In this darkness, they have the power; a power which we gave them. In the shadows, we can't see them for what they are. We can't look them in the eye. We make the attempt to slap at them in the dark, half-heartedly, just to say we made the effort; "I tried…" Then we let them win and then blame them for winning.

Did you ever know someone who wanted to stop a bad habit or start a good one but couldn't do it? Everyday they'd start the diet, start quitting smoking, start going to the gym, and every day they would fall off. That's because the monster they made up around whatever it is they want to change is winning. "I don't want to go to the gym because I'm so out of shape, people will laugh at me." Or, "I don't want to quit smoking because I'll gain weight." Or, "Eating healthy sucks." Someone who hasn't turned on the lights and looked their monster in the eyes isn't ready to start the diet and stick with it. Someone who hasn't decided to keep the lights on and start cleaning out ashtrays won't win against smoking. The person who hasn't got clear on *why* they want to start going to the gym, won't go. The light switch is there but it won't flip itself. We need to flip it on to see what's happening around us. Until we do, the monsters will remain in the darkness, happily using up the energy we would otherwise be using to manifest our desires. And, it is this point right here that is the biggest problem with this whole monster-making thing. They are using up our energy resources.

HIDE AND SEEK

Another energy sucker in all of this creating, false fighting or flighting and blaming is this. We all like to play hide and seek. We hide from our monsters and our monsters hide from us. Although we are the creators of our monsters, we also do our level best to hide from them one way or another. Hiding from them is an attempt to avoid the reasons we made them. But, hiding from them or even ignoring them doesn't get rid of them, which is our secret hope. By avoiding, we merely perpetuate them and make them stronger. In the meantime, they are vibrating and attracting more of the stuff they are made from, even if we are ignoring them. They get stronger and more mysterious, so we keep them in the darkness and there, they get scarier and more powerful at taking away our energy.

We get overwhelmed, so we want to crawl under the bed and hide. The strangest thing of all is when we hide from them, they hide with us. *The call is coming from inside the house.* In the closet, under the bed, behind the curtains, outside the window. Always there, ready to rear their ugly heads. They seek energy from us and we give it to them willingly, even to those monsters residing in our unconscious. That's the way it works. So, ask yourself… do you really want more monsters sucking your much-needed energy from The Masterful Way and away from the manifestation of your desires in the Present/Now?

As is the case with most monsters, they also like the game of hide and seek. Their natural inclination is to hide in the dark anyway, and for sinister reasons. Once our monsters are strong enough to stand on their own, they slip still deeper into the shadows. Since we innately do not like to explore darkened corners, our lack of resolve gives them permission to build a *disguise*.

The intention of the camouflage is single-minded. At its core, the monster wants to live. In order to do so, it needs energy to feed upon. The more conscious we are of our monsters, the more potential we have to stop the flow and they know it. So, the costume they don is designed to fool someone into helping them procure a constant stream of energy and evidence to support their existence. Wrapped in a patchwork Map-quilt, the monster surrenders itself to the jurisdiction of our Caretaker. If left unchecked, the trick will work. The monster can then just slip into the Map Room *disguised as a Map*. As such our Caretaker, who is just doing his job, will continue to feed our monster as he looks for evidence to support this false Map. As it slips quietly into our sub-conscious, our monster lives, fat and happy, with a sense of security that it will most likely never be found out. The energy it needs comes from our unintended focus upon it, which gets attention from the appropriate Universal Laws. But, it's not a full-blown Map. It's only a monster in disguise.

Take this example. It's the end of the day and it's Friday! The weekend is about to begin and you have some definite plans for a little R & R. You have a date night with your partner planned, a night out with friends… *and* the weather is supposed to be great. You might even dust off the bike and take it out for a spin. It's nearly five o'clock. As you pack up your workspace in preparation to take your leave of the place, your boss comes by your office and says, "Sometime before you go, could you stop by my office? I would like to talk to you about something… " What is your reaction?

For most of us, the monsters start to show up. "Uh-oh… what does she want? It's Friday at quitting time. Isn't that usually the time one gets the sack? Wonder what I did wrong. Am I being laid off? Where did I muck up? She's always hated me. Now it's time to get rid of me like she's always wanted. I never liked her much to begin with. Fine! If she wants to fire me, let her. See if I care… " And, so on. What you have done is pulled a Map-clad monster to the forefront and are consciously giving it power. The very reason you have all of these monster bits come up is because that particular monster has been hiding in the Map Room in disguise and you are now making it stronger. You are in fear.

Let's continue… As you approach her office, you are already packing up yours in your head. Another Action in support of that monster. You may be running over the argument in your own defence, picturing yourself sitting on the opposite side of her desk. As you knock sheepishly, you ask, "You wanted to see me?"

"Yes," she says, pulling out a file from her desk. *That's it*, you say to yourself. *It's my employee file and it contains the axe she's about to wield.* "I just wanted to commend you on the work you did on that last project," she says. "The client hasn't stopped praising your work. He loves you!"

Huh? you think to yourself. *Wait, what'd you say?* you almost say out loud as your brain tries to move itself past the monster you made up and into the conversation at hand. You manage to say, "Uh, thank you."

"Take Monday off. Give yourself a three-day weekend. You deserve it," she says. After exchanging a few pleasantries, you make your escape from her office and head back to yours. You begin mentally unpacking that brown cardboard box you filled with your stuff a few minutes before. You begin to laugh at yourself for all of the self-imposed anxiety. That monster goes back into the Map Room, and you head out the door and into your extended weekend. He's still there, however. You know he is because if a similar situation comes up in a few months, you may find him making another appearance.

Take a moment and think about some of the monsters you make up. What monsters are you creating right now? Are there work monsters? Relationship monsters? Or the most insidious of them all, self-loathing monsters? If you can answer that question off the top with a few of the monsters you are making, know they are just a couple of the conscious ones. You already have monsters in disguise lurking in your sub-conscious, or perhaps even unconscious – from inside the house. Not only can those be the most scary but may be the ones doing us the most harm.

The sub- or unconscious monsters lurking around are even more dangerous because we consciously experience their vibrational energy attracting unwanted results. "Why does this always happen to me," for example, is an in-the-moment recognition of a disguised monster pulling energy in the form of focus. As a focus, the Universe sends more of it, which can be used as evidence in support of whatever it is that "always" happens to you. Then, we can't figure out why we are getting results we don't want.

Another reason our sub- or unconscious monsters are so detrimental is their vibrational energy tends to *get faster and bigger results* of the stuff we don't want or need. This is because we are offering *no resistance to them*. We don't see those monsters for what they are and neither does our Caretaker. We don't really know they are there, so we can't stop them from putting those negative vibrations into the Universe to which we receive negative responses in return. They pass under our radar and it is for this primary reason it is so important to flush them out.

With monsters of which we are at least semi-conscious, we have a weapon to use against them until such time as we choose not to have them around anymore. The weapon is simply to catch a monster in the making. When we start making or feeding a conscious monster, when fear or anger starts to well up inside, for example, we can choose to cut off their supply. We can resist letting the emotion take us over and choose a different path; one that is in alignment with the results we are trying to achieve. We can notice when we are in the early stages of monster-making and then put on the brakes.

Have you ever had to have a difficult conversation with someone and you didn't really want to? You had to but didn't want to. I will place money on the fact that most of us spent precious time making up how the conversation would go, what the reactions would be, how offended or angry the other person might be, what would you say, what would they say? You envisioned a dozen different scenarios; rehearsed them in your head and heart. You worked yourself into quite the carbonated froth. You were making a monster.

After a fitful night of restless sleep the day has come to have that convo. You are still making monsters out of the person and the situation, blaming them, blaming yourself or doubting whether you need to have the conversation at all. You are charging up your monster and giving it the breath of life. Then, you have the conversation.

Most of the time, those big, hairy monsters you made up – that snarling next of vipers with venom glistening from their fangs – just didn't show, or they disappeared shortly into the conversation. In fact, the conversation may even have gone *well* and you breathe a heavy sigh of relief. You may have even laughed at yourself for all the anxiety and time you wasted fretting and worrying; creating those monsters, some of which you probably didn't even consciously know you made. But, you could feel their vibrational pull in the form of unease and worry about the whole situation.

> *How many phantoms we all carry around with us in our imagination! How often we have such morbid and unhappy thoughts that they actually appear as gigantic and menacing figures about to seize us in a deathlike grip. And, how seldom do we face these fears and try to find out exactly what they are and where they come from. What a shock and what a surprise it is when we realise we are the ones having the dream; we are the ones who are creating the phantom, and in a certain sense, running away from the shadow of our own fears.*
>
> Ernest Holmes[2]

Getting rid of your monsters, or not making them in the first place, is like everything else in the magical world of manifesting. The manifesting of one doesn't actually take all that much effort. Manifesting doesn't take work. The actual allowing of, or receiving of, is not the challenge either. The challenge for both the intentional creation of our desires, and the creation of a monster is the same. It is in creating the space for them to manifest into. For our desires, it is the space of love; for our monsters, it is the space of fear. Once you have created the space in either fear or love, the rest just flows. The monster is made or the desire manifests.

UN-MAKING MONSTERS

Monster un-making follows the same 5-Step pattern as manifesting your desires. The steps are the same because, according to the Law of Polarity, both monsters and desires are made of the same stuff, energy, and are subject to the same rules. Both are manifestations. For the manifestation of your desires, we have learned that step one is to turn on the lights. For the un-making of a monster, it's the same light switch. Turn on the lights and see what is or what is not going on. For some monsters, the very act of turning on the lights may be enough to make them go away. For others, in fact for most, the remaining steps of manifestation are required. The next step is always to clean up the space, which often takes some time.

Think back. As with most children, being afraid of the dark is part of being a kid. You go to bed, the lights go off and suddenly there were monsters lurking around in the dark waiting for the right moment to pounce on you the minute an adult's back was turned. You imagined they were in the closet just waiting to grab you by the leg and pull you in there with them.

Most of us had similar experiences. So, what happened? You screamed or cried in the dark until, hopefully, someone came to the rescue. What did most rescuers do? They turned on the lights. Most likely they showed you there was nothing in the closet or behind the curtain that would do you any harm. For most of us, turning on the lights made the monsters disappear, at least momentarily. Turning on the lights effectively made us look the monsters in the eye and face them head on, only to discover they weren't there to begin with.

Did that one experience of turning on the lights make them go away forever? Did you suddenly become no longer afraid of the dark? Most likely not. After the buzz of knowing they were never there in the first place wears thin, you realise the lights have been turned off again. You start to disbelieve in their non-existence. At best they become phantoms of their former selves but no less scary. After a time or two of re-enacting the ritual of crying for help and having the lights turned on, some of us achieved the next step in becoming monster busters. We got a nightlight of some nature. A beacon keeping the monsters at bay until dawn. That little tool served us until we grew up enough to realise there are no monsters. There never were and there never would be. We made them up. And, once that realisation is made and believed in, we retired our nightlight and slept peacefully in the darkness. Not the darkness of fear this time, but the peaceful darkness of slumber.

Ridding ourselves of the mental monsters we make up about the scary conversation, or the bad habits we have works in exactly the same way. The first step is to turn on the lights. Face the monster. Call it what it is. Be truthful. Just shine a light on it. For some monsters you may have to keep the lights on for a while so your eyes can adjust to the light and you can figure a way to rid yourself of them. For those very stubborn ones, use your manifestation tools. They are your nightlight. Keep it on until you realise even those tenacious ones don't really exist. As Ernest Holmes writes in *The Science of Mind*, "wake up" and stop drugging yourself with the sleeping potion of fear.[3]

Step Two is always cleaning out the space. That involves changing your thoughts and/or moving your Maps. You don't want the monster, so what *do* you want? The clean-up job will involve noticing any thought or action that doesn't support the new desire. Those unsupportive thoughts and actions are your monsters trying to move back in. Tell them to take a hike and get off your clean floor.

Proceed to Step Three. Replace the ineffective thought with a positive or neutral one. This is gaining clarity. Ask yourself *why* do you want to rid yourself of the monster and replace it with a new desire? What does it feel like to Be someone with the manifestation of this new desire already? What emotions does it bring up for you? Keep cleaning out your space and keep those monsters at bay until you no longer need to use your tools and that nightlight; until you no longer have that thought monster. Until your space is sparkling clean and your desire is crystal clear. Use the Law of Perpetual Transmutation of Energy to intentionally change the vibration.

An Un-Making Example

Let's say you have been retaining some bitterness against someone. They could be dead or alive; it doesn't matter. You still maintain that ineffective energy clinging to that person. You run a monster in the guise of a Map in your head; one of dislike and making them wrong for whatever they did or didn't do. Your Caretaker is working hard at making you remember, over and over, the scenario or scenarios that informed the creation of that monster, and the piecemeal Maps attached to it; the event or events which put an emotional tarnish on your relationship. You get the picture. Now, you realise you no longer want this energy-sucking monster in your life. What do you do?

Step One – Turn on the lights

Realise what you, your monsters and your Caretaker are doing. Realise where you are putting your energy and what you are telling yourself. For most big, hairy monsters, the thoughts supporting the Maps about them are most often sub- or unconscious. So, shining a light on them and calling them out may take some practice. Keep the lights on and get into Step Two. The conscious thoughts about that monster may be very faint, but the energy attached to it is not. You are in the process of *taking back your power* so be diligent with that light switch and grab that broom.

Step Two – Clean the Space

Forgive. You will *never* forget so don't be tempted to believe that. Don't create a monster about yourself not being able to. The Universe doesn't work that way. But, you have to train yourself to stop the flow of energy towards that ineffective place by forgiving.

Forgive them. Wish them well. Most of all, forgive *yourself* for making this huge monster out of it. Forgive the event and the circumstances. Really hold a positive intention for the person or persons involved. Send them all you are desiring for yourself and those you love. I won't say this is easy. You may have to forgive and forgive a thousand times until you get to the place where you actually mean it. Once you do the monster goes away. Forgiveness and the Actions associated with it are Causes to bring about the Effect of a clean space into which you may manifest something more intentional.

Step Three – Take the Time to Get Clear

Take back your energy and put it into really focusing on what it is you desire. In the second step you are getting somewhat clear on what you desire instead of the monster. You are intentionally countering a monstrous thought with a thought of higher vibration. You've cleaned up the space. Now get very intentional with clarity.

Step 4 – Name It

What do you want the space to be filled with? Be specific about the desire, not necessarily about the item or objects. If you already have a desire in the works, place it there. Just be clear on what you want to manifest and why. Make your ask of the Universe and declare your intention; your I AM.

Step Five – Receive

Be the person with the object of your desire manifested and enjoy it, in the Present/Now and do so monster free. *This exercises your Mastery,* and you are back on track.

THE GREMLINS

Now that we have taken the energy away from creating a monster and replaced it with creating the object or artefact of our desires, watch out for little gremlins in this process because they will slow us down. Some of the things we desire have a little monster attached to them in the form of doubt. "What if it doesn't happen?" "What if it doesn't manifest the way I think it should?" "Why is this taking so long?" I have to say, these glitches will definitely make our progress sluggish. So, let's get off our own backs and realise a couple of truths.

The first is – it's OK. The good news about noticing a little monster attached to your desire is that you *noticed* it. This is why the journey of manifesting your desires is mostly a marathon not a sprint. The Masterful Way allows you to weed out that monster and cut the rusty chain binding us to it. That thing is slowing down your manifestation. The road affords the opportunity to scout out any monstrous attachments and rid yourself of them once and for all. They can be a nag but stick with your purpose. Just when you think they are gone, they may try to come knocking. Keep your resolve.

> *The negative flood of thoughts came to him as often as fifty times in an hour; each time he refused to open the door of his mind to these gangsters, assassins, and thieves which he knew would only rob him of peace, wealth, success, and all good things. Instead he opened his mind to the idea of God's Eternal Life Principle of supply flowing through him…*
>
> Dr Joseph Murphy[4]

Monster Making; A Big Picture

While each one of us creates monsters, and we do it well, I believe the collective "we" does this culturally, too. As a collective society we make up monsters all the time especially when big changes or upheavals affect an entire ethos, which ultimately creates fear. A small example of this phenomenon was Y-2K, the Year 2000. Some of us will remember all the hype attached to what was thought may happen when everything computer related, such as banking information, turned the clock at midnight 1999. All hell was supposed to be unleashed. The company I worked with at the time even sold themselves a few years before the event because they didn't believe their computer system would survive the holocaust and the purchasing company's would. Y-2K was one heck of a collective monster that never really materialised.

Let us take a big, big, global example of fear-creating monsters, most of which we still have around today. One of the biggest paradigmatic shifts the world has ever known occurred during the Victorian Era with the Industrial Age. Up until the early 1800s, Britain had not strayed far from its agrarian roots. Life was limited; horsepower was the rule; your village was your world. The Industrial Revolution changed all of that and FAST – perhaps too fast. Fuelled by the ability to harness steam, the Industrial Revolution produced some of the most amazing monsters in history.

The Victorian era began in 1837 and lasted until 1901. During that time, major and seismic shifts in practically every area of people's lives exploded on to the world stage. Innovations in technology, science and industry were making huge strides in the way people did things and in the way they lived in the world. Steam power, mass production, railways, gas lighting, electric lighting, the telegraph, among so many other major, life-changing inventions dramatically altered the way people did things forever.

The factory system all but replaced agrarian lifestyles at an enormous social cost. The growth of cities produced rampant poverty, pollution, and disease. None of this slowed the migration from farms to cities, however. People needed to work. Whilst people migrated both to and from Great Britain, the net population of the country grew exponentially. At the beginning of the Victorian Era, the population of England was about 14 million. By its end in 1901, the population had more than doubled to almost 33–36 million. A huge growth by any standard.

Painting the picture here, you can see the potential fear pockets that dominated the collective character. The fear of poverty, disease, joblessness, homelessness, social status… all of the "what if"s produced a gaping fear hole that would be filled with some now classic monsters we are all familiar with. The explosive rise of the periodical press spread these monsters far and wide. The growth of photography added to popularising the form our monsters took.

In fact, by 1848, monsters, the macabre, and spiritualism were so in vogue and in demand, the popular culture of the time couldn't get enough. People wanted and desired to have monsters around and wanted to be afraid of them. They needed something external upon which to legitimately place their fears. Monster-making was and is a skewed way of people making sense of the upheaval surrounding them.

While all this change translated into huge possibility for some, and by the way made them very rich, for most it created the fear from which a great many monsters we are so familiar with today were created.

Frankenstein (1817/18), *The Mummy* (1827), *Wuthering Heights* (1847), *In a Glass Darkly* (1872), *Jekyll and Hyde* (1886), *Dorian Grey* (1890), *The Invisible Man* (1897), *Dracula* (1897), *The Turn of the Screw* (1898) and so many more…

Then, there were the real-life monsters roaming the Victorian Streets, committing unspeakable crimes which I believe to be a response to the turmoil. Jack the Ripper. Notorious killer of prostitutes in poorer sections of London whose fame was not due to the murder of prostitutes per se, but in the brutal way in which he hacked his victims to death. There was Amelia Dyer, also known as the "Angel Maker". It is thought she killed over 400 babies over a thirty-year timespan. William Burke and William Hare who cashed in on the exploding medical profession, whose need for cadavers fuelled the murder, and subsequent sale, of seventeen of their victims. Mary Ann Cotton who had a penchant for collecting insurance money out of her dead husbands. She had the dubious distinction of being England's first female serial killer.

The list goes on. All of the real-life monsters gained a level of celebrity in an era in which the macabre was both feared and desired. What is interesting here is that these monsters, real or imaginary, continued to scare us well into the twentieth century.

With the advent and expansion of film, they were born and re-born into our collective psyche for decades, providing us with an outlet upon which to put our fears and justify our loathing of what they represented. At the same time, we began to realise the monsters we made were not going away. In many ways, they were here to stay. Until something happened. Our perspective changed.

> *Throughout the 19th century... there is a progressive internalisation of horror, the idea that the monsters are not out there, but to be found within... With the ghost story there's a sense that instead of being able to lock yourself away in your home, to leave the monster outside, the monster lives with you, and has a kind of intimacy.*
>
> Kira Cochran, *The Guardian*[5]

We began to understand they were not real at all; rather something we made up to scare ourselves. The lights started to come on. The black magic was starting to fade, especially by the middle of the twentieth century. We were no longer afraid of the monsters we made up in previous generations. We turned on the lights and saw that behind the rubber masks and movie make-up there was really nothing to fear but by our own design. We began to clean up the collective mess we'd made with them to a degree. In fact, we grew to normalise them. If we had to live with them intimately, we would make them our neighbours, friends, lovers and partners.

In America, television brought our newly normalised monsters into our homes through series such as *The Munsters*. A family of kooky used-to-be monsters, the members of which covered so many of those we made up in the previous century. A Frankenstein's monster dad whose wife was a vampire. They lived together with her vampire father, a werewolf son and a witch for a grandmother. They also had what we would consider to be a beautiful niece living with them who, to our eyes, was stunning, but to theirs, she was hideous. A poor girl they needed to take special care of because of her deformity; that blonde-haired, blue-eyed, bombshell of abnormality.

Another series much like it was *The Addams Family*. A semi-ghoulish family of the macabre who passed for "almost normal" in popular society, yet different enough to still be considered weirdos. Still, we couldn't help but like them in spite of their quirky ghoulishness, and their pallored good looks.

The popular series *Bewitched* showed us witches were not ugly, toothless old hags creating potions and spells to use against us while eating our children and gutting our cats. Witches and warlocks were beautiful, smart and sophisticated. We could marry them and have half-witch children with powers all their own. Witches were just misunderstood for centuries, that's all.

The late twentieth century gave us *The Twilight Saga*. Vampires living in the Pacific northwest in the United States. The teenage vampire kids go to high school, like everyone else. They get married to humans. They have vampire babies. They are hot, handsome, and beautiful.

In the early 2000s, we came to understand how the Wicked Witch of the West, tormenter of Munchkins and a young girl in ruby slippers, was not wicked at all. She was just misjudged and actually had a good heart. It's true. She was even made into a very popular musical, called *Wicked*, still running on Broadway today.

We also now understand that the evil fairy Maleficent, creator of sleeping beauties, was a deeply tortured soul. She had a large and lovely heart but she was wronged and wounded. Her heart was broken and heavy. It was her own sadness and fear that caused those around her to fear her back. Eventually true love healed her and we grew to understand her. We are no longer afraid of Maleficent.

The monsters we made in the collective past have become non-scary and "normal". It took us a while, but we followed the appropriate Universal steps and we conquered the monsters we created. Oh sure, we still like to play monster-in-the-dark now and again, but we aren't mortally afraid of them like we used to be. True to form, however, we have replaced them with different monsters lurking in the recesses of the unknown. The monsters of outer space and slithery serpents of cyber space. The final frontiers. The great unknowns. The truth is we are still both fascinated and afraid of what's out there beyond our atmosphere and what is lurking in our cybersphere. We are even more concerned with *why it's all watching us*. So, we make monsters and the film industry makes millions.

The problem remains. The exercise of keeping our personal monsters outside of ourselves allows us to skip without paying when it comes to admitting we are making monsters out of our own fears. It allows us to point the finger of blame upon something that somehow absolves us of personal responsibility. I'm not saying our lack of manifesting our desires is *entirely the fault* of the flying bat-zombie from the black lagoon, or of little grey men in flying disks making crop circles in Cornwall. What I am saying is, by understanding our proclivity towards making stuff up, creating monsters then using them as a scapegoat, is unproductive. It slows it all down.

Master manifestors know this. They notice when they start to sew a monster together; when they internally start a fear-based attack on someone or something, including themselves. They notice when they emotionally, or physically try to run away from a person or situation. They realise when they are putting their energies into creating the monster under the bed and they realise beyond any shadow of doubt that *if there is a monster under the bed, they are under there with it*. Until that monster is exposed, it will always be there with us. However, there is also another truth which cannot be overlooked and may, in fact, very well help us in conquering our beasts.

THE TEN WORLDS

Nichiren Buddhist practice teaches the concept of Ten Worlds. These are ten states of being, or ten life conditions. We constantly move in and out of and in between them at any time dependent upon our actions and circumstances in response to our environment. We tend to be at the mercy of these elements, at least the lower-based ones, if not utterly controlled by them and because of this, our lives demonstrate imbalance and unhappiness. The Worlds are as follows.

Hell: The realm of despair and suffering. We perceive a complete lack of freedom and it is characterised by self-destructive behaviour and a desire to destroy everything around us.

Hunger: A state characterised by an insatiable hunger for money, fame, power, etc. In this state, we are at the mercy of our hungers and they cannot be controlled.

Animality: This is a state ruled by instinct without reason or morality. In this state there is no hesitation to take advantage of the weakness of others, and to over-idealise those who are stronger.

Anger: A state where the ego develops, and it is selfish and greedy. Its goal is to win; to beat others at any cost because it is always threatened. Self is the only thing of value and all others are contemptible.

Humanity: In this state we can behave in ways that are considered humane. This state is very fragile, however. Strong external influences may make us vulnerable to lower states of being.

Heaven: Intense joy from the fulfilment of desires, or state of physical well-being. This state is, too, heavily influenced by external forces, and the joy felt may be short-lived.

These are the six lower worlds in which happiness is vulnerable to external forces or circumstances. In these states, our identity and our state of being is based upon these external influences. The next four states of Being are considered the higher realms.

Learning: In this realm, we seek truth by studying the teachings of others.

Realisation: In this state we realise truth from our own perception of the world versus the teachings of others. Everything is understood to be impermanent. Therefore, we are no longer prisoner to our reactions based upon circumstances.

Bodhisattva: Those who are on a journey to achieve enlightenment whilst at the same time desire to help others achieve it as well. Bodhisattvas are committed to helping ease the suffering of others. Deep satisfaction comes through altruism.

Buddhahood: A state of perfect freedom in which we are enlightened to the definitive truth of life. This state is identified with boundless compassion and wisdom, without illusions. Absolute happiness. Buddhahood is attainable in this lifetime, not in some far-distant time or place.

As mentioned, we tend to move in and out of many of these realms many times a day, or even many times an hour depending upon the circumstances in which we find ourselves. The Ten Worlds contain a secret weapon, however. Within each of the Ten Worlds are *all the other worlds*. In other words, each of the ten contains the other nine. No matter which world or realm we may find ourselves situated within, the potential to move out of it into a higher state, if necessary, is always there. With conscious choice, we may move intentionally and remain within realms of higher distinction. I believe this description of the Ten Worlds is the Buddhist version of the Primary Laws of the Universe; the Law of Perpetual Transmutation of Energy, and the Law of Divine Oneness.

We may consciously move through the energies of the Ten Worlds within a moment given whatever internal or external influence may be putting pressure on us. We may experience Heaven in one moment, then something happens that makes us angry or upset and suddenly the happiness is gone, replaced by that which now consumes us. Heaven to Hell, as it were. How we interact with our environment and/or circumstances causes us to vacillate between the conditions. Consciously, however, we may choose a world of higher distinction.

All of us are dominated by one world or another most of the time. It's like our dominant vibration. If you have a dominant vibration of Anger – which many of us do – we tend to be driven by that vibration. This isn't to say we are angry and upset all of the time. It just defines the world we are prone towards. The good news is that within the realm of Anger are also the higher realms of Learning, Realisation, Bodhisattva and yes, Buddhahood. Therefore, no matter which world is dominant for us personally, the potential to achieve higher, more enlightened states of being is always with us and subject to our conscious direction.

By the Law of Perpetual Transmutation of Energy, shifting our energy causes a shift in our state of Being. The consistent practice of Buddhism allows us to energise, if you will, our highest nature – our Buddha nature – so it becomes our more dominant state of being – Happiness. All of this sets us free from the mercy of external forces. So, if we are in the world of Hell, of suffering and despair, the world of Buddhahood is also there within the state of Hell. Realising this allows us to tap into the Universal Law of the Perpetual Transmutation and change our thinking in, and therefore the vibration of, Hell into the higher states and do so intentionally – lights on.

Look at it this way. When we hide under the covers in the dark, frightened of the monsters under the bed, the first thing we need to do is to turn on the lights. When we do, we will see and understand we are in fact under the bed *with* the monster we made because it is a part of us – we are One. It's there because we haven't cleaned it out. But remember, there is something else under there as well. There is also a Buddha under that bed. Because of the Law of Divine Oneness, that's us too. Our highest state of Being, our true Self on the road of Mastery. The fulfilment of our desires is right there in whatever Hell we have put ourselves into or find ourselves within.

No matter what monsters you make, admit that you have made them. They go where you go. The Master of Being also goes wherever you go too, remember. So act, stand up and clean those monsters out of there. Use your Buddha nature to free yourself from the illusion there was even a need for a monster in the first place. Intentionally cut the supply of energy so you may be free to use it for your intentional manifestations and personal Mastery.

Or, said in another way…

The price of freedom is simply choosing to be.

Buddha

CHAPTER 12

THE MASTERY OF WHAT'S TOO SMALL

All of us have it and pretend we don't. All of us hold on to it and pretend we aren't. All of us are reluctant to do anything about it and none of us knows why.

Let's face it; it takes work to clear it all out. So we keep it, letting it slip quietly into the background; out of sight but not quite out of mind. We will get to it all someday, we tell ourselves, just… not today… maybe later. Tomorrow, perhaps, we will finally get rid of all of those things that are *too small for us;* those things we never quite get around to cleaning out properly.

WHAT IS TOO SMALL

That which is too small for us is made of the stuff we hold on to emotionally, verbally, mentally, behaviourally, or even physically which clutters us up and slows us down. Much like the things in our wardrobe that are too small for us, that no longer fit, are too old and out of style, or that we simply don't care for anymore but we hang on to anyway. Deep down we know that if we ever expect to get anything new for our closet, internal or external, we need to clean out our old stuff to make room.

As it concerns The Masterful Way, it's like having small potholes on an otherwise fine road. If left untreated, those small potholes can quickly turn into fairly big ones. Unlike the work of a full-blown house cleaning; unlike the work of dealing with fully matured Maps or monsters, those things that are too small for us are more piecemeal and scrappy. Like space junk in the atmosphere of our lovely planet, they are the smaller bits and pieces of junk-like energy hovering around in our personal atmosphere that need to be given some attention. They may be *attached* to Maps, they may be tethered to the grunts and groans of our monsters and give them voice. But one thing is for sure, those things that are too small for us, in their collective, minuscule way, negatively impact our manifestation efforts. What's too small for us is the plaque we need to brush away; the bits of stuff hanging around taking away our energy, cluttering up our vibrations and muddying our waters.

> *There are many ideas in your mind which you have outgrown, and which, from force of habit, you still permit to dictate the actions of your life. Cease all this; abandon everything you have outgrown. There are many ignoble customs, social and other, which you still follow, although you know they tend to dwarf and belittle you and keep you acting in a small way. Rise above this.*
>
> Wallace Wattles[1]

Discovering the bits that are too small for us is a part of the greater work of cleaning our house and of updating our Maps. It's part of the work under the general heading of "The Big Clean". Cleaning out what's too small for us energetically is very much like cleaning out that forgotten closet in the spare room of our physical house. We know there is stuff in there that needs our attention, but we put it off week after week, month after month, even for years. Mastery calls us forwards and now is the time to air it all out. Like that stuff in that forgotten closet, we can't expect to Be the next evolutionary iteration of ourselves while trying to fit our growing self into clothes which are too small or that no longer serve a purpose.

So what exactly is this plaque; this granular energy-sucking sticky stuff that is too small for us? On a broader scale, and simply put, it's more junk. Junk like self-judgment and negative self-talk. Junk like little patterns of behaviour that do not suit the image of the self you are Being. Junk like making others wrong just to be right about something. Junk like the egoic road chosen over the spiritual one. Junk like apologising for who you are now; apologising for your true Being.

It's guilt. It's negative energy. It's anxiety. It's the people you keep in your life that no longer need to be there. It's bits of unforgiveness. It's pieces of anger. It's taking offence. It's allowing your power to be taken from you or giving it away. It's laziness – that's a big one. It's procrastination. That one is too. It's inefficiency. It's complaining. It's competition. It's arrogance. It's not taking care of yourself. It's junk food and poor diet. It's depression. Boredom. Grumpiness. Limitation. Inaction. False action. Condemnation. Disbelieving, dis-allowing, dis-engaging. Wishing. Wallowing. Whining.

I could go on and on… You get the picture I am sure. A little overwhelming if you think about it and how much support we are giving those things which are too small for us by simply ignoring them, of not noticing them, and the procrastination of not doing anything about them. And, that's just the junk that may be discerned without much effort. Those things with even a modicum of presence could be sifted out of our ether. I am very certain most of us have as much junk, if not more, below the surface. Unconsciously. And it's getting in our own way just as clearly, if not more so, than the junk we can see and hear.

There are several reasons why it is so important to understand and to sift out the stuff that is too small for us as it relates to manifesting who we are Being. The first is we cannot move into *fully* Being the manifestation of our desires in a polluted environment. That will just keep us stuck. For example, let's say, regardless of circumstance, you are Being the physical manifestation of someone who is five kilos lighter, a healthy eater and dutiful exerciser. Some of the things that are too small for that Being could be carrying around a deeply ingrained mental Map or picture of the You who is ten kilos heavier. It could be poor behaviour patterns with food, or not taking the time to understand how the things you are eating are working against you. It could be the behaviour of sleeping in that extra half-hour instead of getting up and going to the gym. Your too-small-stuff could include scarfing down two bags of crisps while fixing what would otherwise be a healthy supper.

Let's try another example. Something general. Let's say the person you are Being is the physical manifestation of a more successful, happier You. What's too small for that person is complaining about your family to your co-workers and complaining about your co-workers to your family. It is keeping alive some resentment you have against a friend. It is holding on to self-deprecating dialogue that wouldn't or couldn't be said about the picture of the person you are Being. It is the competition of being right all the time and not allowing for another person's perspective. It is the non-empowering and uninspired language you use with yourself and others that puts the skids on developing better relationships.

Now let's be clear. I'm not saying that you won't manifest your Being until all of the things that are too small for you are *all* cleared out. What I am saying is to get started on it now with Action. Nothing happens without it. It's all about the action-oriented steps forwards on the road of Mastery. Each step is an Action or a Cause, the Effect of which will propel you forwards. But you don't want your next steps to be trod through the mud. You'll just track muck all over the very house you are trying to clean up. With each step, whom you are Being is being set free. Your atmosphere begins to change. Your biology begins to shift. The load gets lighter. So, what is your junk? What is weighing your down? What are you apologising for? What are you waiting for? What would being rid of it feel like?

A Too Small Exercise

Here's an exercise for you. Like everything else, the 5-Step Process is your tool. Take out your journal or whatever workbook you are using. Begin to examine what is too small for you and write it down. It doesn't matter if you start with a large "too small" to get the ball rolling, or a bunch of smaller ones. The image to keep in mind is the *Master of your Being*. If things, words, thoughts and feelings don't fit into that image, they are too small for you.

Start paying attention to the words that come out of your mouth that are too small. This is Step One; Turn on the Lights. Go deep… try to focus in on your self-talk. What are you telling yourself that is too small for you? What are you thinking about others that is too small for you? What judgments do you pass on others for no apparent reason? Even deeper… *why* do you keep holding on to it? What's some little habit you have that you don't need anymore? Can you see it? Do you know it's there? This is Step Two; Clean up the Space. Go even deeper… ask someone you trust to help point out some of the things that are too small for your Being. It's always interesting to see what other people see about you that you don't see yourself. Or, if you can, get a coach to help you.

I'd suggest finding the magic twenty-five for now. Like some of the other exercises in this book, find twenty-five things that are too small for you. Write them down. If that twenty-five comes easily enough, find twenty-five more. This will unfold over time so *take the time* necessary to go deep. Taking the time to get clear is Step Three.

The question is always asked as to how to get rid of the junk once you have identified it. Most of the time it takes building your noticing muscles to the point of observing when you are doing it, saying it or believing it – or the opposite. It takes Being conscious of it. That's the key. Notice it when it's happening and stop it in its tracks. Draw your own attention to it. Call it what it is… "It's too small". Then replace it with a thought more in line with the Master of your Being.

Step Four – Name It. Ask yourself, "Does this yada-yada behaviour/word/thought fit into the person I am Being?" "Would the person I am Being have this thing or this person in their life?" "How would/does it feel to be rid of this stuff?" Keep asking yourself these questions and others like them until the power and energy attached to that which is too small goes away leaving you with that much more energy to live the life of a Master. You may never be 100 per cent free of those things that are too small, but your steps become lighter and more free with each catch. Your gravitational pull becomes less dense.

TOO SMALL WORDS AND THE ENERGY THEY TAKE

All our words carry energy, whether we are aware of them or not, and the Universal Laws respond. Much of what's too small for us shows up in our language and the word choices we make, and so much of the time we are simply unaware of the actual words we are using all day long. *The Science of Mind* describes our word as being the Word of God itself, or The Law. With this thought in mind we owe it to ourselves and to the Universe to become more consciously aware of our words. Remember, of course, that the words we use verbally are only a small fraction of the words we are using non-verbally, energy-wise. There is a dialogue happening between our ears that carries the same weight as the words that come out of our mouths. And, that dialogue is moving much faster.

Estimates vary, but most agree the average person can speak between 100 to 130 words per minute. The brain processes up to 500 words per minute, however. Basically, our brain "speaks" and "listens" faster than our mouth and that is only on the level of awareness. Just think of the records we are playing in our sub- or unconscious minds.

Putting all of these levels together, it is unimaginable how many words we are "speaking" that may not be serving us very well; words that are too small for us and which are most likely working *against* us and the manifestation of our desires.

Think of all the debilitating words we engage with every single day for most of our lives. Think of one of the very first words we were taught as a child. The word NO. Try noticing how often you use this word with yourself and with others. Try and count them. The word "no" has a big power behind it to which the Universe responds. It's a small word but mighty in its negative manifesting power. The word "no" stops us. It shuts us down. I use the word "no" with my dog. Even she knows what the word means and she always gives me a bit of a rejected look when I tell her "no". The word has power even with animals. Just think of the power the word "no" has with other Co-Creators.

How many times per day do we begin a sentence with the word "no"? How many times per day do we toss it out there into our atmosphere without realising it? By the Law of Vibration, each *no* puts out a movement of *no* which attaches itself to the other *nos* we have put out there, accumulating in our environment. Anything else we desire, then, has to pass through a cloud of *nos*. A small word that packs a big wallop.

Here's another word of which to raise your awareness. It is the word "but". Have you ever noticed someone trying to have a conversation with you on a positive note, then threw the word BUT in there to illustrate a certain contrast? It completely negates the positive side of things and stops your brain from digesting what was said before the word *but,* while it tries to catch up to what was said after. "I hear what you are saying, *but…*" Doesn't really work, does it? What that *but* is communicating is that the person may acknowledge what you are saying, they just don't agree with or care to listen to what you are saying. Try and count the number of times you say the word *but* in a day. Try to notice how many times others say the word. Another small word which is mighty in its vibrational power.

How about the word "can't"? "I can't do this; I can't do that". The fact is, the word *can't* is a lie we tell ourselves and others. For most of us "I can't…" has become an unconscious belief in our own so-called inabilities. Remember your Caretaker. Every time you tell yourself *I can't*, he searches the Map Room for your *I Can't Map*. He will find it. He will locate the evidence of anything you have told yourself pertaining to those things you *can't do, can't say, can't believe, can't Be,* etc. He will sub-consciously affirm *I can't* with evidence. With every *I can't,* you give away a little more of your power. You give away your control and it puts something else in charge. The truth is, for most things that you say you can't do, you actually can. You just *choose* not to.

Another little phrase which takes a chunk of power away from us is "I have to…" Every time we say, "I have to…" we externalise the why of having to. We essentially create a dualism that violates the Law of Oneness. We tell ourselves "we have to…" and therefore, push the reason for doing whatever it may be outside of ourselves, and the responsibility for it and of it. "I have to…" implies we are being forced into something beyond ourselves, beyond our will. "Having to" instils fear. "Having to" implies a punishment if we don't. Who wouldn't be afraid of that? Like the word *can't*, the phrase "I have to…" is much the same. You don't *have to* do anything really. You *choose* to.

I have used the following experiment in some of my seminars. Give it a go.

If it's morning, think of all of the things you *have to* do today. Or, if it's later in the day, think of all of the things you *have to* do tomorrow. Think of everything you have to do and write it all down one at a time. With each one, repeat to yourself or to whomever is with you, "I have to…(fill in the blank)".

"I have to go to the gym."
"I have to pick up the dry cleaning."
"I have to go to work."
"I have to finish that report."

"I have to do the marketing."
"I have to empty the dishwasher."
"I have to fill the dishwasher."
"I have to do the laundry."
"I have to eat breakfast."
"I have to take a shower."

Keep going until you have a complete list of all that you *have to* do.

If you are like most of us, as the list becomes more full of all of the stuff you have to do, you may start to feel a bit anxious. That feeling of being anxious is vibrating as such into the Universe and guess what? The Law of Attraction will give you more to be anxious about. So, before it gets more out of hand, look at that list again and try this.

Replace the "I have to's" with "I choose to's" and go through each one of the items on the list. Really mean it when you say, "I choose to…" By the time you get to the end of the list, I would be willing to bet you feel different than you did before. You should feel more empowered because you have, in fact, taken back some of the power you were giving away to the "I have to" monster. You always have a choice and Mastery is mastering that choice.

This isn't to say you *choosing* not to go to work will not produce consequences. This isn't saying choosing not to shower won't have a definite result that may not be pleasant over time, if not for yourself, for those around you. What we are discussing is vibrational energy. Things like this are too small for those choosing the Mastery of Being to engage with anymore. Being sloppy with our language is not acceptable to Mastery. It's too small.

MORE TOO SMALL WORDS

Let's talk about a few more junky words. How about the word "try"? Most often when we use this little word, we don't mean it. It's another lie we tell ourselves and others. If we tell ourselves or others we will "try", it basically says we won't be giving it our best so, if we fail, it's not really our fault because, after all, we *did* try. Basically, a mantra of Mastery is, "Do it or don't. Try is not an option."

How about this very common word that also should be removed from our powerful manifesting vocabulary? It's a word that is tossed around very casually and very frequently these days. Someone asks how we are, and the answer is "busy". Busy, busy, busy. Everybody's busy. And, that's one of the problems with the word, busy. Everyone is. So what? If everyone is busy busying themselves with the zillions of things they *have* to do, our being busy just isn't all that important, and not a very different experience from anyone else's. Usually when we tell someone we are busy, what we are really asking for is the other person to somehow feel sympathy for us, which most often backfires. Someone who is busy feeling sorry for how busy they themselves are is unwilling to give some power over to our own busy-ness in sympathy. At best, our only hope is to find someone with whom to commiserate as we both wallow in being *so busy*, which basically means nothing and accomplishes nothing. The major problem with the word *busy* is, again, it has a strong vibration, which because of its strength will attract more busy-ness to us and fast.

I used to be extremely good at manifesting "busy", and I can tell you, I didn't like it. The more stuff on my plate, the faster I used to think I had to move to get stuff *off* my plate. The trouble was, I was sending out so much vibrational energy of "I am SO busy", that the Universe gave me what I was Acting like I wanted and, through my behaviours, was asking for more of. It handed me more to be busy with and on a much smaller plate.

There is a Universal Truth to the phrase, "The hurrier I go, the behinder I get." We become slaves to busy-ness and we thrust being busy outside of ourselves. Something outside of us is making us busy so we give our power over to it. When I finally woke up to what I was doing to myself, I stopped manifesting busy and started manifesting "productive".[1] It is my choice and I keep my power. Once in a while, the Busy Map shows up. Now, I can feel when it starts to rear its ugly head and most of the time I can stop the vibrational energy of busy before busy takes over, my plate shrinks and I find myself running in concentric circles. I replace the feeling of "busy" with "Being productive". I take back my power and become intentional with where and when I put my energies into a task. Instead of doing twenty-five things at the same time, I try to focus on one or two things at a time productively, and with efficiency. I've found with practice, I get far more efficiently produced in a day than all of the busy-ness could manifest in two.

> *The cause of failure is doing too many things in an inefficient manner and not doing enough things in an efficient manner... Every efficient act is a success in itself, and if every act of your life is an efficient one, your whole life must be a success.*
>
> Wallace Wattles[2]

Being really busy or being in a big hurry is a fear-based space. Being hurried is a manifestation of fear. It implies lack, not-enough of, and a shortage of. It also carries with it an energy of punishment. If you don't manage to get that growing pile of stuff off your shrinking plate, something unpleasant will surely happen. That is simply not a powerful space from which to manifest anything desirable.

It could be argued these words are just that; words. They don't mean anything. It could be argued that it is the feeling behind the words, or the lack thereof, which is the important bit. Well, on paper this may be true. However, my counter argument is this. In spite of how the words are intended, and the actual lack of power we think we give them, we know their real meaning, sub- or unconsciously, and that is the energy we attach to them, willingly or not. Additionally, we are very unconscious of these words and their effect upon our Mastery. Raising our awareness of them is the key to clearing up some negative energy in our otherwise clean house.

Furthermore, our words do not just affect us; they affect others. Others hear, feel or sense our words and they become a part of their atmosphere much like Pig-Pen and his never-ending cloud of dust. These words can literally have a negative effect on *their* journey as well, which further affects our own. As we are all One, we owe it to ourselves and others to be very conscious of the words we are energising.

Finally, the Bible has some very specific things to say about words and their power. One passage in particular really sums it up. It tells us our words proceed from the kind of house we keep; dirty or clean. It tells us our language is born from our personal atmosphere, the world that is of our own creation and which we inhabit. Words are not only powerful tools; they are evidence.

> *...For the mouth speaks what the heart is full of. A good man brings good things out of the good stored up in him, and an evil man brings evil things out of the evil stored up in him. But I tell you that everyone will have to give account on the day of judgment for every empty word they have spoken. For by your words you will be acquitted, and by your words you will be condemned.*
>
> Matthew 12:34–37 NIV

THE POWER OF WORDS

Now, I do not believe for one moment there is some Universal judgment day awaiting us whereby we will stand to account for every single word we have ever spoken or thought, then to be cleared or condemned for them. I am fairly certain most of us would be convicted without question if this were the case. Besides, this way of thinking breaks the Law of Oneness. It would be a Cause of separation and the Universe simply cannot break Its own Laws. I believe instead this verse speaks of something very different. The first is, as mentioned, our words emanate from our thinking, feeling and our inner Selves. They are evidence of how we are keeping our house. Whether our words are "good" or "evil" is simply an indication of how we are occupying our space by virtue of the Law of Correspondence. If we do not necessarily notice, others do, and certainly the Universe does because it must react accordingly, by Law.

Secondly, let's be clear. This "day of judgment" is of our own making. It comes when we realise how powerful we are, how powerful are our thoughts and feelings, and how powerful are our words. Then it is up to us to judge every word, thought and feeling from that point forward; to winnow out our intentional words from the chaff of words that are too small for us.

Think about it this way. If we are to believe the manifestation formula works in a certain way, e.g. ask and we will receive, think of how powerful the words of that "ask" must be. If we believe the ask is powerful enough to be entrusted with bringing about our intentional desires, we must also believe that every so-called "empty" word has tremendous power as well. Once we wrap our thinking around that idea, we will begin to realise how influential *all of our words* are and act accordingly. This includes all of the words of the inner dialogue. Spoken or unspoken, we must take charge of our words. It's Judgment Day.

GUILT, NEED AND WANT

There are many strong emotions that could and should be removed from the Mastery of Being as well. Anger, unworthiness, frustration, worry… to name a few. Of course this isn't to say we shouldn't have these feelings, ever. They will present themselves from time to time and that's OK. The habitual occupancy of these emotional realms is not desirable for many of the reasons already mentioned. The mother-load of undesirable feelings, in my mind, is guilt.

Guilt is way too small for Masters of Being. Guilt is less of an emotion or feeling than it is a *pattern of re-living a fear-based event, or of supporting fear-based Maps.* Guilt preserves a fear-based ego.

It is trapped in the past and, as we know, the past doesn't actually exist. Guilt, however, keeps pulling the past into the present and then makes us wrong over and over again. This perpetuates past thinking and behaviours, which puts fear-based energy into the Universe. Additionally, guilt protects those unproductive Maps and misguides us into believing we can never be rid of them. Guilt is, indeed, a very sinister pattern of belief.

> *Guilt feelings are the preservers of time. They induce fears of retaliation or abandonment, and thus ensure the future will be like the past.*
>
> *A Course in Miracles*[3]

As discussed in the chapter on Desire, two other too-small-words I would go so far as to advise removing from your vocabulary altogether are the words *need* and *want*. The more you want and need, the more often these words come out of your mouth, the more wanting and needing will show up for you. Try taking the words, and their energy, out of your atmosphere altogether. Watch when you think them, speak them, feel them. Then immediately reverse them, replacing them with a Masterful thought and feeling. Using want, for example, "I want better success at work" is a future-based thought. A more powerful thought can be, "Every day I am more successful and happier at work" which is a thought in the Present/Now.

Want is a plea. It's way too small and the consequences are vibrationally frenetic. Replacing wanting better success at work with Being more successful and happy is a very different energy. The latter is much more positive. It doesn't have the resistance of the first. The Universe will start moving better success at work to you every day according to your *feeling of Being* more and more successful. It is a much more productive feeling, creating a much more positive vibration and the Universe will respond by Law.

The word "need" is another tough one. I knew a woman once who used to say very often that she *needed* a new wardrobe; that she needed a whole new closet of clothes. In other words she desired new clothes but wasn't articulating it in such a way. She also wasn't a big fan of all this "manifestation stuff" at the time in spite of the fact that she was a pretty good manifestor without even knowing it.

As she herself said, she *needed* new clothes. What do you suppose she would manifest? The *needing* of new clothes, of course. This need would show up as a stain on her suit that came out of nowhere that she couldn't get out. A tear on a blouse that couldn't really be repaired properly. She even manifested a weight gain so she couldn't fit into many of her old clothes. She *needed* a new wardrobe, so the Universe kept her in need of a new wardrobe. After finally taking some advice, she went from *needing* a new wardrobe to Being someone with a new wardrobe. It didn't manifest overnight, yet she did manifest a new closet of clothes in a relatively short period of time.

> *Receiving cannot happen in a vessel of wanting.*
>
> Tehya Sky[4]

An Example Though The 5-Steps

Using the example above, let's run it through what we now know to be the Universal steps to manifestation. Let's say you are she. You make the switch from someone *needing* a new wardrobe to Being someone with said desired wardrobe. What does this mean and how do we do this? Let's follow the steps as discussed.

1. *Turn on the Lights* – We won't be clear unless we can see what we are doing. The light switch is your desire for a new wardrobe versus the need for one. The desire springs from noticing the old and dull closet of clothes staring us in the face.

2. *Clean up and Clear out the Space* – What is going and what is staying? What do you really still like? What still looks good on you? What are you saving *and why*? Would the Master of your Being wear whatever is that piece of clothing? Would your Being enjoy it? If not, get rid of it.

3. *Take the time.* Get clear. What does a new wardrobe involve? What type of clothing do you want? What are the styles? What makes you feel good? What do you look good in? Can it be altered? (Remember the weight gain.) How much do you want to spend? What charity are you donating your old stuff to? Where is your new stuff sold? Are you having it made?

   If you are not in a position to just rid yourself of all the old clothes and replace them with new ones in one day, go slowly. Actually, I believe this works best anyway. It's really about the journey of manifesting something new versus the *I Dream of Jeannie* approach… one blink or twitch and it's done. Start by identifying what, if anything, you might desire to keep out of your old closet of clothes. More importantly, identify what does not belong. Then get rid of it bit by bit while replacing old pieces with new. This is an important part of the process so let's pause right here…

   What we are talking about is energy so it's important we have it right from the get-go. First, we've become clear. Now we are cleaning out the space; making room; cleaning our house. This is engaging the Law of Action and the Law of Cause and Effect. Now, let's use an extreme example to demonstrate a point.

   If I had told you that in order to clean out the space to make room for the new stuff, it would be absolutely necessary to get rid of *all* of the stuff that didn't fit the new "style" of Being right now. Let's say that was practically everything you owned and, for most of us, it would be. Now check your energy. If there is even a shred of angst about this, the whole thing will backfire on you. If you are looking at this request through the lens of knowing you don't have the resources *right now*, that you are unable to afford to completely overhaul your wardrobe with new stuff, the lack of it will be a stronger vibration than the desire for it according to the Law of Polarity. Remember, it's the feeling we're after and the intentionally desired energy we are putting out into the Universe.

If you are OK with it on the outside but you are still "unable to afford it" on the inside, that's your tap on the shoulder to adjust. Take it slowly. Just identify what will stay and what will go as you enjoy Being your new wardrobe. Then choose one or two things you will purchase straight away that you can *do comfortably* and get rid of its no-longer-desirable counterpart.

4. *Name It* – When you are able, make your "ask" of the Universe. You're clear now, very clear, so ask for it and begin the Actions of making it happen. Be intentional. New shoes, new top, new underpants… it doesn't matter what it is. What *does* matter is that you feel each piece *is your new wardrobe* and that it makes you happy. Enjoy the Process. It's a marathon, not a sprint. And, the Process is what it is all about anyway.

    Even if you start with just a pair of socks, that's OK. Get rid of the old socks then go out and find yourself a pair of socks that you really like which are in alignment with your Being. Make sure you get rid of the old ones first. It's important to the Process. Go get something that makes you feel good. Something that makes you happy. It's a start, and it's a good one.

Enjoy the feeling of those new socks. Enjoy the feeling of purchasing them. Enjoy the feeling of wearing them even if no one else can see them. Just think about this. That one pair of socks *IS your new wardrobe*. It's not simply *a part of* the new wardrobe. With that one pair of socks *you have acquired a new wardrobe* from the Universal perspective. Take the time to enjoy Being someone with that new wardrobe. Keep that feeling high and enjoy it.

Wallace Wattles describes a similar scenario. He tells us if you desire to own a department store and you only have the money for a newsstand, great! Get it into your Being, your believing state, that the newsstand is just one department in the department store you are desiring to manifest. If this is Actual Truth, you are in fact Being someone with the desired manifestation of your department store Now. It is the truth so no resistance. Therefore, assuming the department store is still your burning desire, the Universal Laws will work to bring it about with each Action in support of that desire. This is Step Five.

5. *Receive* – In other words, *Be the person with a new wardrobe*. *Be* grateful for the new purchase and how it makes you look and feel. *Be* happy that you were able to purchase it with joy.

Find joy in unusual ways. Find joy, for example, in that you gave someone a job when you purchased your new bits – the job of ringing you up. Find joy in the way someone opened the door for you at the shop. Find joy in the journey of a fully manifested new wardrobe! It's the feeling we are after. It's also the language we use to get to the feeling we are after. All of our words have energy and a vibration. All of our desires have energy and a vibration as well, and we are intentionally seeking a vibrational match between the two. Our role is to use the Universal Laws intentionally and cleanly to get to that place of alignment.

TWO TECHNIQUES

So we have discussed a handful of words that do not serve us. What do we do instead of using such words? Here are two techniques for you to try on. The first is to completely remove toxic words, which are getting in your way. Notice them creeping into your speech and conversation, then call yourself out for using them. Make it a game and have fun with it. This approach will help change the energy more quickly. Have others help you, too. Have them join the "noticing party" and point out to you when you use words such as "no" and "can't". It will help your awareness grow faster. Just don't make them wrong for telling you, by the way. Then recommit to the alignment you are seeking between the energy of your desires and the energy of your words.

The second is to use a replacement method. With toxic words it really helps to change the energy in the moment. As the toxic word is about to escape out of your mouth, and into the Universe, replace it with a neutral or positive word, much like the example provided with the word "busy". Busy becomes "productive". "But" becomes "And". *"I really enjoyed the performance, AND I couldn't quite hear the lines."* "Try" becomes "Will". "I *will* make this happen," not "I'll *try* to make this happen." "Can't" and "have to" become "choose". This is a good way of noticing how often you use those toxic words and in taking Action to change your vibrational position. Once again, the Universe must respond. Just make sure you mean it.

As in most of our exercises, there is a caution. Don't replace "but" with words like "however". Don't replace "Try" with "I'll do my best". Unless you really mean you'll do your best, it's just the same word or words with different letters because the energy *behind* the new word is the same as the energy behind the old word. If you find it hard to replace a toxic word with a word of higher vibrational energy, just don't say the word at all. It may be a bit challenging at first – (but) – you'll soon get the hang of it.

Discovering and dealing with things that are too small for us in our behaviours, our thinking and our language is the level of control and determination of a Master. Everything is energy. Energy is the language of the Universe. It is *our only true* language as well. Controlling our own energy is giving the Universe the space to flow through us without resistance. Controlling our energy is the proper and powerful use of the will; willpower. Properly using the will is the powerful place that creates the space of receiving the physical manifestation of our desires. As with all other clean-up methods, dealing with *what's too small* is well worth the effort and a necessary step of Mastery.

CHAPTER 13

THE MASTERY OF JUDGMENT

OK, that was misleading. Human beings simply cannot be 100 per cent judgment free about *anything*, particularly when it concerns other human beings. Our brains are simply not wired for such a marvellous state of mind. We can, however, improve the quality of our judgments and become Masters of them.

According to a study published in the *Journal of Neuroscience*, the brain immediately passes judgment on a person based upon that person's face. It does this within one-tenth of a second. That's faster than the blink of an eye! The brain does this even before a face is fully perceived which means we judge a face *before* we actually see it full on; or whether we see it at all.[12] Further implication? We are capable of judging a person we have never met based upon the face *we make up for them.*

THE PROCESS OF JUDGMENT

The judgment process takes place in the oldest, most primitive part of our brain, often referred to as the "lizard brain". Our lizard brain is looking for signs of trustworthiness and signs of danger. It is responsible for figuring out two things. One, whether we need to consider another person a threat, signalling danger, or two, whether they are to be trusted. If the latter is deemed to be the case, we conclude they are able to help the both of us survive. Therefore, we allow them into our inner circle of trust and permit them entry into the pack, so to speak, even if we never see them again. If the person is judged to be a threat, it will trigger the fight-or-flight behaviours most of us are all too familiar with.

While this system may have worked very well in the primitive days of human beings, in modern times it doesn't serve the same purpose; it doesn't serve us well. The problem is, our lizard brain doesn't know that, so it keeps on with the same antediluvian system and, if unaware, we react by following through with the judgment process.

Think about this. For better or worse we all do it ALL the time and, for the most part, we are not even aware of it because it happens so fast and so frequently. It is instinctual, but it's not quite fair, is it? Nor is it fair of those whom we are judging because they are judging us right back. So, to attempt to be judgment free is not feasible. Biologically speaking, it's just the way it is. That said, as Masters, it can be what we make of it. In order to do so, we must become more conscious of what's going on. Using the object of people, let's follow the pathway of the crime, the conviction and the sentencing in the judgment process though a simple example.

JUDGMENT MAPPING

We first make an initial judgment based upon our Maps; our past experiences and interactions with everyone we have ever met or have perceived to have met. Once that decision is made, we escort Person X to our Map Room and pass them into the hands of our Caretaker. He sifts them through our entire archive of Maps. What our Caretaker is looking for is evidence in support of whatever judgment we have made about Person X, positive or not, and he will have no trouble finding it. Let's look at a few examples continuing with Mr X.

You are at a cocktail party and you meet Person X. Conscious and unconscious dialogue ensues… Within the first one-tenth of a second, we have formed a judgment about Person X. Whether good or bad, it doesn't matter. We have already judged him. Once so judged, we pass them through the process of Mapping.

Visually, he seems like a nice enough guy. Good energy about him. He seems to have a good head on his shoulders and a nice sense of humour. He has a lot of different interests, too. He reminds you of your best friend from university. He was a great guy too… You miss him. You wonder how he's doing…

OK, so now you are building towards the handover to our Caretaker who is beginning to sort Person X through your Map archive for evidence in support of your newly forming judgment of "Good Guy Person X". He goes to your *College Best Friend Map* and collects the cool, interesting bits that are similar to what you are making up about Person X; the fun times, the laughter… now you are getting emotions tied onto your *Good Guy Person X* judgment call. Then, Caretaker searches through all the other Maps for other good times you've had with other people similar to Best Friend. As the conversation ensues, he will also, in the moment, collect bits and pieces that are similar enough to Person X to attach to your *Good Guy Person X* judgment.

As the chat goes along, you and Caretaker will continue to mine for evidence to support your growing judgment. The way he talks, moves, what he does for a living. The way he dresses, carries himself. He likes tennis. So do you. He's a dog person. So are you! Instinctively you are looking for signs of trustworthiness and, it appears you have found what you were looking for. You like the guy. He's OK… You may even become friends someday. Let's flip the coin over.

Same cocktail party and you just meet Person Y. Unconscious and Conscious dialogue ensues…

Visually, he triggers something less than positive. It could be the unibrow. It could be the generous nose. It doesn't matter; you have already made the judgment call. So, you pass him along to your Caretaker.

As you hand the poor guy over, the same process as in the previous example begins. The only difference is, you are making a *Bad Guy Person Y* judgment call and Caretaker is sifting through all of your Maps that support the making of it. At the same time, you and Caretaker are mining for in-the-moment evidence. You are making a monster out of Person Y.

What's that smell? Woah, exactly how much cologne are you wearing? My grandfather used to wear that stuff and you could smell him a mile away. My grandfather was not a happy guy. He scared me as a boy. My grandmother always complained of his not-so-secret gambling problem. My biology teacher in middle school had that exact same suit. I really didn't like that teacher… This guy seems kind of dull too… Nothing interesting about him. And, he's a bit of a close-talker – Hey buddy, get out of my space…

The *Smelly-Unhappy-Gambling-Family-Destroying Granddad Map*, the *Ugly Biology Teacher Map*, even your *Close-Talking Next Door Neighbour Map*, if it applies… any and every other Map from which bits may be gleaned in support of judging *Bad Guy Person X* is being sorted through.

As the conversation continues, you and Caretaker will be looking for evidence in support of your growing Map about the guy. What he's drinking and how he's drinking it. He mentions his favourite food, which is your least favourite food. Even if it's not, you can find a reason to not like his favourite food momentarily because it can be used as evidence. He likes football… you like football but not as much as tennis. OK, so now you can make him wrong for liking football more than tennis. What's his favourite team, you wonder? He tells you. It's your least favourite. And, he's a cat-person… A-ha! Strike. Pay dirt. Now you can really justify your dislike for the guy. It's your emotional hook as the game continues…

As with both Persons X and Y, you are updating a couple of existing Maps with supporting evidence. Whereas what you are making up about Person Y could seem like you've made a full-blown monster, it differs in that you have rejected the perceived threat Person Y seems to pose and have, most likely, already made your exit and found someone else to talk to. In other words, the flight behaviour kicked in. The Maps of both Good and Bad Guy are now being stored back in your Map room and the experiences will be used as archival evidence for other times involving future Person's X and Y.

All of this happens in a flash; in a fraction of a second. And, while these are just simple examples to demonstrate a point, we do this all the time to varying degrees of intricacy based upon the varying degrees of importance we perceive the person to be to us and how involved we want to get. Once these decisions or judgments have been passed, they are very hard to reverse. As the old saying goes, "you never get a second chance to make a first impression," even one you made up.

Your Caretaker has evidence in millions of files at his fingertips. You will pass judgment on a person, then seek support for that decision with any evidence Caretaker can find. What he doesn't have in evidence, he forces you to look for in the moment in order to make yourself and himself right about the decision. He does this mainly in an unconscious way, which makes the whole process easier for him and for you, incidentally. And you, the very willing participant in this game of judgment, happily comply. He will have you scouring and scrounging around to look for evidence even in the face of what would otherwise be objective reality.

PASSING JUDGMENT HABITUALLY

We pass judgment all day long. Most of the dialogue we carry on with, however, is quite hard to hear because we have been doing it for so long we have learned to tune it out. Walk down the street sometime and tune into what we have trained ourselves to tune out of; all of that judgment muckiness going on even for a moment. We constantly compare and contrast ourselves against each other, all of which is judgment. "We are better than that person," we tell ourselves. "I believe I'm more handsome than those guys are." "I have better hair than she does." "You have a stain on your tie, buddy. Mine is nicer." "What is she wearing? Was she intentionally going for that look?" "Get your nose out of your phone and have a real life, pal. At least I'm not addicted to *my* phone. Wait, where *is* my phone…?" Try watching television sometime while tuned in to the judgment voice in our heads. It can be very self-enlightening.

Here in England, we actually have a regular television show about everyday people watching television shows. It's a bruiser, sometimes. It's brutal in terms of how people entertain themselves with judgment – and how we are entertained by it. *And*, part of the "fun" is to sit back and judge the judges. We watch them watching television, we watch them commenting on it, and then we entertain ourselves by commenting on their comments. Furthermore, we do it all in that snide, judgment-y way all of us have.

All judgment, of course, is not necessarily negative. As we saw with Person X, we judge on the opposite end of the scale too. "She looks nice… so well put together – classy lady for sure." Or, "They are slowing down and stopping to let me cross this busy street. That's so kind of them." Or, "What a lovely email. Really nice of them to say that about my work on that project." All perfectly positive thoughts and certainly not untrue. Judgments, though, all the same.

In the above, as with all cases, what we are doing is judging the classy lady against others who are not. And that right there is the problem. We are comparing the kind driver to all the other jerks who didn't stop to allow us to cross the street. We are contrasting the polite and kind emailer to the zillions of others on the project who either didn't say anything or, from what you make up about their personality, simply *wouldn't* say anything in the first place. All judgments. Even if the judgment is deemed "good" or "positive", it is only so as compared to those judgments which, in our experience, are "bad" or "negative". This is because of the Law of Relativity.

So, good or bad, happy or sad, we sit in judgment all day, every day. We make people wrong and we make people right. We make people good, bad, and ugly. It never stops. It's not necessarily a bad thing. There is no good or bad, really. As Hamlet said, "…for there is nothing either good or bad, but thinking makes it so."[3] Once again, it's about energy and how we Master it.

In addition to the biological reason we cannot entirely get away from the judgment thing, there is a practical reason as well. So, in some ways, we can give ourselves a break. Not an excuse, just a break. Once we understand what's going on, it becomes another thing we need to work on in support of Mastery. It becomes another untidy corner in the house of our Being which we were, up until recently, only barely aware of. Now that we've turned on the lights, we will undoubtedly see that corner needs a good cleaning.

JUDGMENT THROUGH THE LAWS

Practically speaking, judgment is inextricably attached to a Universal Law or three. In addition to the Law of Relativity, we also engage the Law of Polarity and the Law of Compensation. The Law of Relativity basically states that any meaning you give to someone or something is only as valuable as it is relative to someone or something else. Nothing is happy until it is compared with sadness. Nothing is good until it is compared to evil. We compare others against ourselves and, by that comparison, we determine worth or worthiness, even if we will never meet a person again after passing them on the street.

Here is the real kick in the pants. We are not necessarily comparing them against ourselves to determine their worth to us. Allowing them into the tribe of trustworthiness is a very selfish act. However, it is actually not an act of determining their worth to us for survival; at least not anymore. *It is, rather, an act of determining our worth to ourselves.* From a Universal Laws perspective, the Law of Relativity is working to help us suss out our own relative self-worth. As a result, the mirror is turned upon ourselves and we have become self-judge and the self-jury. This is the Law of Polarity. We are all on the same pole. The Law is the Law regardless of who uses it and how it is being used. So while we are sending self-judging energy towards ourselves in the form of judging others, the Law of Attraction is sending back more to judge ourselves about.

> *Do not judge, or you too will be judged. For in the same way you judge others, you will be judged, and with the measure you use, it will be measured to you.*
>
> Matthew 7:1–2 NIV

This verse is often used as a benchmark measurement for the punishment metrics of God as far as judgment is concerned. I believe it is far more profound than that. It is more than an admonition not to judge someone because God will punish us according to the degree of judgment ascribed. Nor is it about not judging someone because it is the right *name-your-religion* thing not to do. I was taught this way and used to think this way. I used to believe this verse referred to a God ready to pounce on us if we, in any way, passed judgment on a fellow human being. What this verse *is* saying is several things as it relates to the ideas in this book. The reason it is important is because of energy and how it is utilised by the Universal Laws.

When we judge someone else for whatever reason, we are quite literally judging *ourselves.* There is a Primary Universal Law attached to the process called the Law of Divine Oneness. We are all One. We are One Being of God, or the Universe, expressing Itself in an individualised and unique way through us.

Here is a powerful perspective. We are not simply cut from the same Universal-God cloth, as is so often taught; brothers and sisters in some meta-religious, symbolic kind of way. Although allegorically, this implies a sort of blood-line relationship, it's much deeper and far more philosophically sophisticated than that. We are not cut away from the cloth. *We are in fact the cloth itself,* unseparated from each other. We, and everything else, are One complete whole. Therefore, judging others is indeed judging ourselves and it is a violation of the Law of Oneness because judgment causes separation, good or bad. One degree is not better or worse than the other.

A further correlation is found in the form of the volume, measurement, or the level of energy associated with the amount of focus. Whatever amount of focus, i.e. energy, we bring to the judging part, and remember we do a lot of this unconsciously, the Universe will bring back more of it to focus on *in proportion to the amount of energy we are measuring out to judge someone else.* It's the Law of Compensation. We therefore waste our energies on judging what we don't want, like or see in others, which produces more of exactly what we don't want, like or see in ourselves. We have doubled the energy in the wrong direction. This energy-wasting endeavour leaves us with far less energy to focus on what we *do want to manifest,* intentionally. The things we do want become overpowered by the multiplied energy used to support those pesky judgments and Maps.

Thirdly, we know a big part of cleaning our house is not just cleaning, it's clearing. If the rooms in our house are filled up with the noise of making others wrong or right, of judging and passing sentence on them, how are we going to cram any new intentional manifestations in there? We can't. That's the Law of Correspondence. As within, so without. How are we going to slap on a new coat of paint when we can't see the walls through all that judgment? How are we going to even flip on the light if we can't get to the switch?

Here, again, the Devil looms on the horizon and he carries the absolute enemy in his breast; doubt. The more we judge others, the more we judge, and therefore doubt, ourselves. As this process doubles the energy of judgment in general, it is rocket fuel for self-doubt. It feeds a *Self-Doubt Map* that is like a boulder chained around our necks, slowing down our journey of Mastery.

Not Good Enough

Without trying to create an oxymoron, I believe perhaps the biggest thing that is too small for us is self-judgment or self-doubt. Most, if not all of us, run some version of a Map that says, "I'm not good enough". It shows up in a lot of different ways. It can show up in the form of having to constantly "prove" something to ourselves or to others. It can take the form of having to demonstrate "worthiness" to receive the object of our desires. It can be marked bravado, or over-confidence, as well as the obvious lack thereof.

The many forms of self-judgment can show up as issues with our weight, our hair, our size, our shape, our habits, our friends. It can show up in our spouses, our lovers, our choices, our fears, our job, our bank accounts, our grades... and they all come with a script of dialogue that carries a vibrational energy being shot into the Universe. More frequently than anywhere else, self-judgment shows up in our self-talk.

You drop your mobile phone... *you idiot!* you say to yourself. You take the wrong exit off the motorway... *oh, how stupid, you dummy.* You burn the toast... not once but twice... *what a moron.* In addition to being overtly self-deprecating, calling yourself names like this is dangerous.

In the first place, the words you use, this self-talk, is always going on inside and at best you are only *barely* aware of it. Where the danger lies is in what the vibrational message is carrying. Regardless of whether or not you are conscious of it, the words and thoughts you are thinking and feeling carry the same vibrational frequency as those that we actually speak. The Universe is non-differentiating and works with what you focus on, whether it is spoken out of your mouth or not. Calling yourself a moron, internally or externally, will only cause the Universe to put other stuff in your way to make you a bigger moron.

Words like that feed that self-destructive Map you have about yourself. Your Caretaker is always looking for evidence. He will seize upon any of it and store it away with your *I'm Not Good Enough Map*, making it even stronger and, subsequently, harder to clean up and clear out. Remember that your Caretaker doesn't like to have Maps shifted or removed, even if it's about yourself. He will fight like a rabid dog to keep his archives intact. The stronger the Maps, the harder they are to clean up and the tighter his grip upon them. It's up to you, of course, but don't you want to be free of stuff like that?

Additionally, as we discussed, words carry energy. Energy that other people and situations respond to. It's natural. It's the Law. Because we are all in Oneness, when you call yourself an idiot, it sends a vibration to which others respond in kind; the energy it attracts from others is to validate you as an idiot. They will help you in your self-fulfilling prophesy by seeing you as a moron. You and everything you do. People will respond to you in that way, in one form or another.

You may get talked down to by the checkout person at the market. You may put your spouse's socks away in the wrong drawer and, not being able to find them, you can be an idiot to them too. You may not move forwards on a green light fast enough for the person behind you, and you get blessed with a loud, obnoxious honk – "The light's green, you idiot."

POOR LITTLE RICH KID

The story of the prodigal son is a great example of self-judgment, self-doubt and Maps. Many of us know the story but I will provide a synopsis of it anyway.

There once lived a father who had two sons. As is the usual case, there was an older son and a younger son. Evidently the father had quite a bit of wealth, which would naturally have passed down to his two boys upon his death. The older son was obedient. He never questioned his father. He worked very hard for him and the family business. He was the picture-perfect older son. The younger son was, by nature, extravagant, wasteful, a bit lazy and reckless with money... in short, prodigal.

One day, the younger son came to a realisation. He figured out that it may be a very long time before he would see the inheritance promised him and he grew impatient. He proceeded to ask his father for his portion of the inheritance now. His father grants his request and gives him what would only be his in the future.

As prodigal sons are want to do, he took the money and ran with it. He moved to a fancier country and lived a lavish lifestyle. As often happens with extravagant living, the young son soon ran out of money to play with. At the same time, a famine struck the land. The story runs very quickly through time in the following sentence...

After he had spent everything, there was a severe famine in that whole country, and he began to be in need.

Luke 15:14 NIV

You and I both know that process had to take some time, even if it is just a story within a story. And I make up within that time period his self-awareness began to shift from one of the happy-go-lucky rich kid with a large bank roll, to one of self-doubt and self-loathing. Because of the emotional disparity between his actual and his former self, his self-judgment energy would have been put into overdrive. Why I believe this is so is due to what happened next.

The famine left a lot of people out of work and, realising his lack of lunch money and any other resource, the son was forced to take a job, and the lowest of the lowest jobs around. He was the caretaker of pigs which in the Jewish tradition is a big, fat no-no. Pigs are considered unclean. But, he had to do what he had to do in order to survive. He was in need so the Universe brought more need to him in the form of the lowest of the low. This job would have further contributed to his already rocket-fuelled self-doubt and self-loathing energy.

Desperately poor, starving and a swineherd to boot, it didn't take him long to come up with a plan. Realising even his father's servants were living the life, he decided to return home and beg for his father's forgiveness. He even rehearsed what he would say to his father when he got back there.

> *I will set out and go back to my father and say to him: "Father, I have sinned against heaven and against you. I am no longer worthy to be called your son; make me like one of your hired servants."*
>
> Luke 15:18–19 NIV

You can bet he made up one heck of a monster about his return home. What his father might say. What the servants would think about him. What his older brother would say or do to him. What would the neighbours think? All of this and more would continue to feed a self-doubt Map, laden with dialogue about not being good enough. And, if the story had gone in a different direction, you can bet the Universe would make "not being good enough" happen for him. It's the Law.

As the younger son got close to home, however, his father saw him in the distance. Filled with love and compassion rather than anger, he ran to greet him. They fell into each other's arms, and through tears and kisses his father ordered the servants find the best robe to put on his back. He ordered them to put shoes on his feet and a ring on his finger. Most significantly, the servants were instructed to prepare the fatted calf and to throw the biggest welcome-home party ever seen in those parts.

It's a heart-warming story and in the context of self-judgment, it fits perfectly. Continuing, he delivered the speech he had rehearsed to his father, chest-beating included.

> *The son said to him, "Father, I have sinned against heaven and against you. I am no longer worthy to be called your son."*
>
> Luke 15:21 NIV

What he was really saying when he was reunited with his dad was…

I am a dirty rat and deserve any punishment you can dish out. I am a broken down, starving, weak, swine-herding brat. I am unclean both physically and spiritually from being around those pigs. I am truly fallen from a status of wealth and privilege and am prepared to take my punishment. I'll lower myself to the level of a servant because I don't deserve anything better. From my vantage point, that's a huge step up.

Most of us would agree that on some level, the boy needed to learn a lesson, which I am certain he did. However, that's none of our business so let's move past that point. What is of interest in this conversation is what must have been going on in the younger son's head.

Usually, by the time something like a self-judging statement comes physically out of our mouths, we have thought it a number of times before. By the time we utter one self-deprecating word, the monster has been created and the Map has already formed around it. The mouth speaks what the heart is full of inside.[4] At that point, the language we use, both internally and externally, is supporting that Map. By the time the young man got around to admitting he was wrong and was willing to subject himself to his father in self-pity, I am sure he had a fairly strong dialogue going on. Let's paint a more detailed picture.

The kid was rich. He was the youngest son in a wealthy household. He had servants and, as one can imagine, plenty of the stuff that tends to define a rich kid. He was given a large chunk of money without being prepared on how to properly use such a tool, so he squandered it. He suddenly found himself on the streets, starving and alone. Ringing in his ears was the lavishness of his former party-boy lifestyle. He was forced by circumstance to take a very demeaning job that not even the lowest servant in the land would take – a pig keeper. You can imagine the things he must have been saying to himself, the monsters he created and the Maps he had formed.

Furthermore, it's interesting to ponder the Map-wrapped monster the older brother was probably making up about his younger sibling. It would have been fun to have a peek inside his Map Room into the *My Selfish Little Bro*, and *That Punk Kid* Maps. In fact we do have a tiny glimpse into exactly that as told in the story. Allow a further synopsis...

The fatted calf had been slaughtered and a lavish meal had been prepared. There was music, dancing... generally a big shindig. The older son was out in the field so had no idea any of this was going on. As he approached the house, he began to hear the song and dance, so he called over a servant to ask what all the fuss was about.

> *"Your brother has come," he replied, "and your father has killed the fattened calf because he has him back safe and sound."*
>
> Luke 15:27 NIV

That answer was not anything the older son had expected and it certainly didn't go over very well. He became angry and refused to go into the house to see his long-lost little brother being made a fuss over. So, his father came out to see if he could talk him off the self-imposed ledge upon which he had placed himself, and his huffy pants.

While his father pleaded with him, the older son countered with an extensive list of all the stuff he had done for his father and their estate over the years. In other words, he shared his *I'm the Perfect Son Map* with his dad. His dialogue revealed bits of how much he'd slaved for his father and how obedient he had always been. He even went so far as to complain that in spite of all of this, his father had never even let him party with his mates with a nice goat stew. Then, he shares a bit of the *My Selfish Little Bro* Map.

> *"But when this son of yours who has squandered your property with prostitutes comes home, you kill the fattened calf for him!"*
>
> Luke 15:30 NIV

Of course, this is just a story, a parable, but if you think about it, how exactly could he have known what or upon whom his younger brother had spent all of that money? Taking literary license here, and putting it all in the perspective of our manifesting paradigm, *he made that up*. He formed a Map and made up a monster about his little brother, most likely based upon past experiences he'd had with him, which is true of most Maps but, nevertheless.

Getting back to the younger son, his self-judgment is an example of what *The Science of Mind* calls "… a theological state of introspective morbidity, which might be classed as one of our worst mental diseases".[5] There is a sense of urgency within this statement. This would not be inappropriate given the double-whammy self-doubt and self-judgment carries, energetically. When that energy is shot out into the Universe, you can bet it will come back with a bang. So, it is indeed with a sense of urgency we should approach the work of cleaning out our self-judgment and self-doubt Maps. They have no place in our Being, and we cannot fully express our Mastery unless we do so.

The story continues as a lovely allegory of love and forgiveness. However, in spite of what some may say, the Universe *does not reproach, does not make wrong and does not condemn*. God does not punish. God does not make unworthy. The Universe does not *judge*. It would be breaking Its own Law causing separation; a violation of Oneness. We do it to ourselves.

Self-dislike is in fact a useless endeavour from the Universal Mind perspective because God is love and cannot understand something so contrary to Itself. It cannot register it or even fathom it. But, It will deliver it to you if that's what *you* desire. The Word and the Law together are certainly creative and will produce a rotating cycle of self-fulfilling prophesy because the energy of it will find ways to make your self-loathing true… for YOU. It isn't *the* truth, it's just a made-up version of a truth, one that doesn't serve and continues to perpetuate breaking of the Law of Divine Oneness.

A UNIVERSAL METHOD

Do not judge, and you will not be judged. Do not condemn, and you will not be condemned. Forgive, and you will be forgiven. Give and it will be given to you. A good measure, pressed down, shaken together and running over, will be poured into your lap. For with the measure you use, it will be measured to you.

Luke 6:37–38 NIV

We can see in these verses the pattern revealed, this time in two directions. Regardless of whether or not you believe yourself to be judging or condemning others, the Universe will work to bring those self-destructive energies, judgments and condemnations back to you. It will also bring to you very positive, uplifting helpings of the good stuff. Put into the Universe the good stuff and the good stuff comes back. Put out the bad stuff, and the bad stuff comes back. It is the Law of Cause and Effect. All, by the way, in direct proportion to the degree to which you put it out there in the first place, which is the Law of Correspondence.

There is a formula here. A certain way of Being and doing which, if Mastered, can boost our intentional manifestations into the ultimate physical reality, while minimising our less than desirable ones. Consider the following as an additional support for this formula.

"For I was hungry and you gave me something to eat, I was thirsty and you gave me something to drink, I was a stranger and you invited me in, I needed clothes and you clothed me, I was sick and you looked after me, I was in prison and you came to visit me."

Then the righteous will answer him, "Lord, when did we see you hungry and feed you, or thirsty and give you something to drink? When did we see you a stranger and invite you in, or needing clothes and clothe you? When did we see you sick or in prison and go to visit you?"

The King will reply, "Truly I tell you, whatever you did for one of the least of these brothers and sisters of mine, you did for me."
Matthew 25:35–40 NIV

Further on in this chapter, we see the flip side of the same formula.

They also will answer, "Lord, when did we see you hungry or thirsty or a stranger or needing clothes or sick or in prison, and did not help you?"

He will reply, "Truly I tell you, whatever you did not do for one of the least of these, you did not do for me."
Matthew 25:44–45 NIV

What these verses are beautifully demonstrating is the Law of Oneness. As it relates to judgment, self- or otherwise, is that judging others is *judging yourself*. And, judging yourself is the barometer by which you judge others. A big measure, or a big judgment, in a positive or negative way, produces a like measure of more of it back. A big measure of blessing people with increase and opulence instead of judgment produces a big measure of the same.

While we cannot get away from judgment entirely, we can do something about it. We can reverse the judgment by energising its opposite. We can use the same formula *for us rather than against us*. We can only do this, however, if we become aware of what's going on. Remember, whether we are conscious of it or not, the energy is being put into the Universe with predictable results.

Exercise daily awareness of your judgment dialogue. When you walk down the street, or when you drive to work; when you wait in a queue for some event, or when you are watching television. That judgment dialogue is huge for most of us and we are only barely aware of it going on. Once you are aware of it, reverse the negative energy and bless what or whomever you are negatively bombarding with less-than-positive judgment. Bless them with what you are intentionally manifesting for yourself. By so doing, you are in fact doubling the energy of your intentional manifestations – the good ones.

This is the meaning of the ideas Jesus proposed in the concept of turning the other cheek.

> *You have heard that it was said, "Eye for eye, and tooth for tooth." But I tell you, do not resist an evil person. If anyone slaps you on the right cheek, turn to them the other cheek also. And if anyone wants to sue you and take your shirt, hand over your coat as well.*
>
> Matthew 5:38–49 NIV

Turning the other cheek is not just a pithy Christian thing to do. To offer someone your left cheek after they just sucker-punched your right one isn't about some non-confrontational, non-violent demonstration of passive-aggressive superiority. It would be very easy to pass a judgment on someone who slugged you for no reason. This is why I do not believe this verse is even referring to a literal cheek-offering, or a literal giving away of your coat after your shirt has been taken off your back. What I believe it is saying is literally and simply don't judge. I believe it is demonstrating for us, and encouraging us to work *with*, Universal Laws that, if used correctly, will serve you and us all to greater levels of manifestational achievement.

As you achieve we all reap the benefits, at least vibrationally. When one manifests their desires, it expands and evolves the entire Universe, thereby increasing the vibrational level of the whole. This is the entire point of Life, of evolution, of God and of the Universe. When you judge something or someone, your perception is breaking the Law of Oneness and slows the progress of Mastery.

One of the best examples of non-judgment comes again from the Bible. As Jesus was teaching a group of people in the temple courtyard in Jerusalem, the temple leaders brought before him a woman caught in an act of infidelity. By Jewish law, this would have been a capital offence. Using her as a way to hopefully trap Jesus into breaking a rule punishable by similar means, they asked him what should be done with her.

As the story goes Jesus simply did nothing. He stooped down and wrote in the dirt. I believe he was actually working at disarming his own judgment cycle while seemingly disregarding the woman's accusers. After ignoring them and their incessant requests to provide an answer, Jesus finally gave them one of the most iconic phrases in the Bible itself.

Let any one of you who is without sin be the first to throw a stone at her.

John 8:7 NIV

How is it possible to judge someone else without actually passing judgment on yourself? Unless you have never made a mistake, you are certainly in no position to condemn those who have. Brilliant! It's a perfect demonstration of Being Judgment Free.

The story continues with the woman's accusers slowly leaving the scene without further fuss. When they had all gone, Jesus asked her where they'd disappeared to.

"Woman, where are they? Has no one condemned you?"
"No one, sir," she said.
"Then neither do I condemn you," Jesus declared. "Go now and leave your life of sin."

Luke 8:10–11 NIV

In other words stop making mistakes by creating Actions beneath who you are Being. Don't put forth Causes that will produce poor results. And, more importantly, don't make the same mistakes as those who came to judge you. Don't fall into the trap of judging them for what they proposed to do to you. Instead, raise the level of your Being to a higher plane of Mastery and help us all in the Being thereof.

*Why do you look at the speck of sawdust in your brother's eye
and pay no attention to the plank in your own eye? How can you
say to your brother, "Let me take the speck out of your eye," when
all the time there is a plank in your own eye? You hypocrite, first
take the plank out of your own eye, and then you will see clearly
to remove the speck from your brother's eye.*

Matthew 7:3–5 NIV

Besides the obvious statement this and the previous story are making,
what is interesting here is the timing of the sequence of events.
For this story and these statements come immediately before the
manifestation formula we are all working with was revealed.

*Ask and it will be given to you; seek and you will find; knock and
the door will be opened to you. For everyone who asks receives;
the one who seeks finds; and to the one who knocks, the door will
be opened.*

Matthew 7:7–8 NIV

I simply cannot ignore the correlation, the intention and the necessity
of non-judgment as it concerns our intentional manifestations. There
is an obvious reason the idea of non-judgment is placed just ahead
of the manifestation formula revealed as it is. Clearly, judgment is a
manifestation killer. The energy of judgment will stop the flow.

Grippingly enough, the manifestation formula itself comes just
before one of the most famous lines from the Bible. It has been called
"The Golden Rule".

*So in everything, do to others what you would have them do to
you, for this sums up the Law and the Prophets.*

Matthew 7:12 NIV

This is a direct statement about the Law of Divine Oneness. The
reference to the summation of the Law and the Prophets is stating a

Universal truth. Doing unto others what you would have them do to you is the Primary Law of the Universe. The so-called "Golden Rule" is the Law of Divine Oneness, which is really all there is, ever was and ever will be.

Whatever energy you are putting into the Universe will come back, good or bad, in direct proportion to the percentage of output. In spite of the fact we all do it all the time, judgment has a potential for some very toxic stuff being your output. While we can't get away from it entirely, our awareness that we are doing it and doing something about it will minimise the percentage of output in the negative direction. Then turning it around with a positive intention maximises the positive output and sets you up to receive exponentially more positive stuff back. Once again, The Masterful Way is an intentional one. It is intentionally working with the Universal Laws and doing so in our favour. Which, as we know, raises the vibrational level of us all.

CHAPTER 14

THE MASTERY OF FORGIVENESS

Therefore, I tell you, whatever you ask for in prayer, believe that you have received it, and it will be yours.
Mark 11:25 NIV

This passage is an oft-quoted manifestation mantra. Ask for it, believe it and receive. However, it is very rare that anyone mentions the second part of this formula beginning with the word "And". Given that it is definitely supposed to be a continuation of the preceding sentence, it logically must be an important piece of the whole manifestation method.

And when you stand praying, if you hold anything against anyone, forgive them, so that your Father in heaven may forgive you…

The first half speaks of the most vital component in the Process of manifesting the object of our desires; belief. Belief and faith are affirmations in agreement with the Law of Cause and Effect. Belief and faith in the reality of what we are manifesting are Causes, the Effect of which is Being the one with the physical manifestation of our desires in the Present/Now. "Believe that you have received it, and it will be yours." The belief comes first, in the Present. The rest follows.

Those of us on the road of Mastery are familiar with the first part. What isn't often spoken of in manifestation circles is the second part of this formula which, when left out of the mix, renders the first part of the effort weak, if not entirely powerless. I believe it is for this reason many manifestors fail in achieving their desired results. It is the *forgiveness* part.

SIN, TRANSGRESSION AND MISTAKES

Before going further, let us gain some clarity on several terms which usually get people very spun out regarding anything which smacks of religion with which these words have come to be associated. With what is to follow, I am in no way being anti-religion, anti-Christian, anti-God, anti-the Bible or anti-anything for that matter. I am merely running some very emotionally sensitive words through our manifestation language. These terms are *sin, forgiveness, transgression* and *atonement*. Let's start with the word sin.

Over the centuries, millennia even, the word *sin* has been used somewhat diabolically, both in and out of religious circles. It conjures up images of a wrathful God who takes offence at some "immoral" act one did or did not do, which, as a result, sentences one to severe punishment. For such a small word, it packs a powerful emotional punch. So, let us take the Devil and the emotion out of the word and look at it from a new perspective.

In broad strokes there are two meanings to the term *sin*. The first is *transgression,* which basically means stepping outside of a given boundary. It is part of a family of words all of which have to do with movement; to step. Transgress, progress, egress, for example, are varying degrees of movement. The prefix, "trans", simply means across, beyond, or over.[1] Therefore, to transgress is to step over the line; to go beyond a boundary. To *sin* is to transgress.

But, let us take a hard look at the actual word sin. For such a little word it has been behind the cause of great unhappiness and hurt. The idea of sin carries with it the idea of wrath, deep guilt, and fear. If one has sinned, he is a *sinner* and, according to some interpretations of Christian texts, for example, is therefore only fit for fuelling the fires of Hades. However, the more correct meaning of sin, and its more direct meaning, is to "have missed the mark". You aim for a target, you miss it, and therefore you have sinned. You have simply made a mistake.

Now, let's pull apart the word *mistake*. According the Cambridge Dictionary, the word *mistake* means an action, decision or judgment that produces an unwanted or unintentional result.[2] Fair enough. We have a missing of the mark; an action that produces an unwanted result, or a Cause that produces an unwanted Effect. Now, let's begin to filter these terms through the language of manifestation and the 12 Universal Laws.

To sin means a mistake has been made. If someone sins against you, or has made a mistake, the action of it creates a disruption of the Law of Divine Oneness. Let me say this again. If someone sins or makes a mistake with you, the action thereof breaks Oneness. In our manifestation language, a sin is to have misplaced focus on the Oneness of all things. It is something someone has done, has said or has been which Caused a mistake creating separation. A breaking of Universal Law. It takes Wholeness away from Oneness. The Law is therefore broken.

A sin has *taken something from you in error*. A *mis*-take. The sin may have taken away trust, faith, hope, belief, friendship, favour, whatever it is, something is now *miss*-ing and therefore the Whole is broken. When that happens to us, and we feel we have been sinned against or wronged, we intrinsically know something is missing and is in need of repair.

We are not Whole anymore. We may understand this consciously or, most often, unconsciously. Regardless, we work to immediately fill the hole in the Whole, even if temporarily. Much like a pothole on the road, the hole needs to be repaired before it causes more damage. Initially what we tend to fill the hole with, however, are reactions of fear and anger, hurt, sadness, tears, etc., all of which are at best temporary fillings. These temporary fixes only go so far. The Whole is still incomplete.

ATONEMENT

As the Oneness is now broken within one's self, It seeks a permanent repair. It seeks Its true and highest state of Being Whole and It seeks it *quickly*. It seeks atonement, or *at-One-ment*. This is the actual meaning of the word. Atonement is to regain Oneness. To Be at Oneness or Wholeness.

After the initial, temporary filling of fear, anger, etc., we quickly proceed to semi-permanently fill the hole left by the mis-take and what we usually fill it with is a monster around which we build a Map. We replay the situation, event or moment, both pre- and post-mistake as we perceive it, in our Map room. Our Caretaker is sifting through similar bits of all the other Maps related to similar mistakes which have happened to us looking for evidence. Each replay of the situation becomes further support. The monster-Map begins to fill the hole in Oneness, which leaves us with the *mistaken* impression Oneness has been restored. The trouble is, as we have learned, this Map does not serve us. It is simply another version of a temporary fix. It, too, is a mistake because the energy of the monstrous Map is drawing more negative energy to us, thereby perpetuating separation.

Further compounding this issue is what often ensues. Most likely, the person who sinned against us is doing the same thing. They often feel the hole in their own Whole and that of the greater Oneness. If this is the case, they would be going through the same fixing process in the same way. What you are both doing is exercising your Maps in order to make the other person wrong and yourself right, creating unforgiveness.

As with all Maps, your Caretaker plods along, continually seeking evidence to keep alive the wrongdoing that caused it to be created in the first place. He replays what was said, done, unsaid, undone. You assist by replaying the mistake over and over to anyone who will listen; telling the story to friends, family, etc. This perpetuates the making of the other person as wrong and the making of yourself as right in the situation, which takes up a lot of energy *even if we are unaware we are doing* it. We create unforgiveness as a by-product.

Anger, fear, loss, regret, accusation, blame, even mild irritation are all powerful energies usually directed at the wrongdoer, or the sinner. These emotions and feelings are being put into the Universe, which will respond with more for which to make the other person wrong. While the hole is theoretically filled with all of that stuff it does not restore Oneness. The Law is still broken and is being further damaged due to the continued acts of separation unforgiveness causes. The pothole on the road cannot be filled with sticks and stones and be expected to restore the road to wholeness. It will continue to grow in size and depth causing further damage along the way. It must be filled with the same stuff, or better, as the road itself in order to restore it to its proper function. It must be made One again; At-One-ment.

FORGIVENESS

Now, let's unpack the term *forgive*. The meaning of the word forgive is to "cease to blame". It means to stop being angry with someone for something that person has done, or to give up the desire to punish them for that thing.[3] Here is the important note regarding forgiveness. Notice the wordsmithing. Forgiveness is the giving up of a *desire* to penalise or to make wrong. The focus here is the word desire. A *desire* to punish or make wrong, which is a *desire* to not forgive, is a *mistaken* use of the Process that is desire. This makes it a sin in itself. It is a mistake. The desire not to forgive takes the Process of desire and turns it upside down.

All desires are the Universe, or God, positioning Itself to expand, grow and evolve through the individualised expression of Itself that is You. Together, then, you Co-Create the manifestation of that desire. The only true reason for the manifestation and the journey of it is happiness. The desire to punish or to make wrong cannot achieve that goal because it is based in anger, and most likely fear, which stamps out happiness and joy. Therefore, the desire to not forgive *is a counterfeit desire.* It cheats the whole Process of Co-Creation because it takes the Process that is God, expanding and expressing Itself through you, out of the equation and puts you in the driver's seat of creating a false desire.

It is a process in reverse, which makes it a mistake. Instead of the Universe initiating the desire through you, you are initiating a *false desire and trying to force it back into the Universe to create and to validate unforgiveness and punishment.* This creates an additional breech of the Law of Divine Oneness. Any form of punishment or of making wrong *takes away* Oneness through separation. It does not give more Oneness through reparation. Unforgiveness is a mis-take on *your* part; a missing of the mark.

MAKING WRONG

> *For every minute you are angry, you lose sixty seconds of happiness.*
>
> Ralph Waldo Emerson

The Universe does not punish or make wrong. It can't. Punishment would be a Cause, the Effect of which would be separation. To make wrong assumes a right. This is by the Law of Polarity. Furthermore, this act of separation defies and breaks the Law of Oneness. The Universe does not recognise either wrong or right. To do so would be God breaking Its own Laws, especially the Primary Law of the Universe. Therefore to believe the Universe punishes is inconceivable by Law.

The Universe does not show favouritism in any way.[4] The sun shines on everyone alike. The rain falls on everybody equally.[5] Gravity does not work on one person differently than another. Similarly, the Universal Laws work for everyone identically. Therefore, it is impossible for It to punish or make the person who sinned against you wrong, which is what the desire to punish is actually hoping to accomplish.

The second reason the desire to punish or to make wrong is a mistake is that unforgiveness is perpetuating a stronger belief in the past and the future than that of the Present/Now, which is the only reality. It is the opposite of The Masterful Way. It is against everything we are accomplishing otherwise. Being is only in the Present/Now state. You cannot expect to Be in the Present manifesting the object of your desires, when you are energising an event or events that have happened in the so-called past. Furthermore, the desire to punish or make wrong is a *future-centric event.* An event that assumes and hopes that someday, somehow whomever wronged you would pay for their mistake, and pay dearly for their sin.

> *If you act in the present with your mind on the future, your present action will be with a divided mind, and will not be effective. Put your whole mind into present action.*
>
> Wallace Wattles[6]

By not forgiving, therefore, you are of two minds, two energy levels, and this causes muddy energy to be shot out into the Universal Laws. This slows down or stops the flow of energy to the manifestation of any of your true desires, regardless of whether or not any of these desires are related to the incident itself.

Forgiveness, then, is simply the giving up of a violation of the Law of Divine Oneness you yourself are perpetuating by unforgiveness. Now hear this. Forgiving is an act of *giving* that bends time and space to the pre-event, or that which was be-*for* the incident or incidents. *For-Giving.* Forgiveness gives back whatever was taken away by the mistake or sin against you, as it was in the state before the event occurred. It is a *for*-giving. By forgiving, the Oneness is restored as it places everything in the space of Now because it repairs Oneness as it was before it all happened, as long as you keep it in that space intentionally.

CONTRIBUTING TO ONENESS

Why is all of this important? There are several reasons. The first and foremost reason is that forgiveness is absolutely necessary to the equation of manifesting our desires. The manifestation of our desires is not a selfish act. Manifesting our desires is contributing to the Oneness of us all. Intentionally manifesting these desires profits everyone because in truth, everyone benefits. As you have a desire manifest, you raise your own vibrational frequency, which raises the vibrational frequencies of all of us. We are all One, so when one person achieves, we all do. Manifesting for yourself is manifesting for others as well. It is an act of Divine Oneness.

> *My profession is the Activity of the Great Mind working through me. As such It is a Divine Activity and is constantly in touch with Reality.*
>
> Ernest Holmes[7]

While the quote above refers specifically to a *profession*, it is the same truth as it applies to everything we are Being and, by implication, everything we do. Synonyms for "profession" include *living, pursuit, walk of life, engagement, calling, lifework*. In other words, our Being. Therefore, substitute the word Being for *profession* and we have the following.

> *My Being is the Activity of the Great Mind working through me. As such It is a Divine Activity and is constantly in touch with the Reality of the Present/Now.*

Therefore, everything you are Intentionally Being in Mastery is the Divine Activity of the Process that is God growing, expanding and evolving through you as the individualised and indivisible expression of the Great Mind of which we all are a part. That is Joy or Heaven, which is true Reality! Joy or Heaven IS The Masterful Way. Unforgiveness robs us of our Being which is, in fact, the opposite of Heaven; Hell.

EXAMPLES OF THE NEED TO FORGIVE

Further examples from the Bible concerning the necessity of forgiveness show up in what has been called The Lord's Prayer and its subsequent explanation offered by Jesus himself. The parenthetical is mine.

> *... and forgive us our debts (sins) as we also have forgiven our debtors... for if you forgive other people when they sin against you, your heavenly Father will also forgive you. But if you do not forgive others their sins, your Father will not forgive your sins.*
>
> Matthew 6:12, 14–15 NIV

Let's look at this very famous reference through our lens. "Forgive us our debts" is not a request of the Divine, as it is most often taught. It isn't asking God or the Universe for forgiveness. *It is, rather, a statement of the Universal Truth as it relates to forgiveness.* The explanation that follows further clarifies this Truth.

> *... for if you forgive other people when they sin against you, your heavenly Father will also forgive you. But if you do not forgive others their sins, your Father will not forgive your sins.*

"Forgive our debts" or sins is not some Universal transaction whereby if you forgive someone a sin, God ticks a sin off your list of transgressions which is the traditional understanding of this passage.

I believe it is this point whereby this "prayer" has been distorted. It is merely stating that forgiveness is a restoration of the Law of Divine Oneness of all things. If you forgive, the Oneness is returned. If you do not, it remains un-Whole. And, it is so in direct proportion to how much Wholeness you are putting forth. *Forgive our debts as we have forgiven others* is testament to this fact. Forgiving 90 per cent is only 90 per cent of Wholeness. True forgiveness completely saves Oneness from being damaged or destroyed. Forgiveness is the meaning of *salvation.*

Holding grievances is the opposite of God's plan for salvation. And only His plan will work.

A Course in Miracles[8]

This being true by Law, it is also true that holding grudges, or not forgiving someone, is a failure to recognise the Oneness of us all. This is why when you forgive someone their "sins", *"your Father in heaven may forgive you your sins",* because we are One and the same thing. You are forgiving a part of *yourself.* You are, and therefore *we* are, in effect "saved" and made whole. This is the meaning of "love your neighbour as you love yourself".[9] Loving or forgiving "your neighbour" is loving and forgiving yourself because your neighbour is in fact a part of "yourself".

This method is the same for judgment, condemnation, or any other negative act. It is also the same formula for giving and receiving, and everything else as well, because it is Universal Law. The method is the Law of Compensation, the Law of Cause and Effect, the Law of Action, The Law of Vibration, among others. It is especially the Law of Oneness.

Do not judge, and you will not be judged. Do not condemn, and you will not be condemned. Forgive, and you will be forgiven. Give, and it will be given to you. A good measure, pressed down, shaken together and running over, will be poured into your lap. For with the measure you use, it will be measured to you.

Luke 6:37–38 NIV

This is how and why manifesting your desires lifts us all. If, however, you are holding back through unforgiveness, the manifestation of your desires is held back as well. This is the way the manifesting formula works which is why it is vitally important to understand and exercise the *entire formula*, not just the first part of it.

Forgiveness is another activity involved in the cleaning of your house. You cannot pronounce your house is clean when a couple of rooms in it are full of unforgiveness junking up the whole place. When our vibrational energy is muddied up with the energy of a grudge, with bitterness, with resentment and anger, the Universe responds to the muddy energy we are putting out there with muddiness back. It is just doing what It is supposed to be doing by Law. Our work, then, is to get clear and clean on our vibrational energy level. A clean house must be clean all the way through, not in just the rooms visitors get to see.

Breaking Through

Just before I turned the corner on my own manifestational prowess, just before I got really good with it, I had a powerful breakthrough. As a Buddhist I chant twice a day. Once in the morning, and once in the evening. One morning in front of my altar, a powerful realisation began to enter my conscious awareness. It was like something cracked open in my sub-conscious and through that crack my internal dialogue, the heretofore silent internal dialogue, could be heard. I don't mind saying, what I was beginning to hear actually startled me a little and made me profoundly sad on many levels.

What I heard was a lot of judgment and non-forgiveness against a lot of people in my life that had been locked and sealed away. That crack exposed a couple of well-hidden rooms in the house of my Being. The recordings playing over and over inside those rooms, without being conscious of them, became deafening as the crack widened. Those records playing in constant repetition described varying versions of,

"I was wronged and here's how, when and where, and by whom. How can I ever forgive you?" It honestly felt like I could hear Dante's Inferno coming through and it was going on inside of me, unconsciously until that moment. It was then I became aware of a choice I had to make; to explore or to ignore. In spite of a good deal of fear, I chose the latter; to explore what was in there and get rid of it as fast as possible. I had to open wide that door and clean out those storerooms of toxic energy, frightening though it may turn out to be. I had to turn on the light.

I always keep a pad and pencil next to my altar so I can write down things that come to me while chanting. So, I stopped chanting, grabbed the pad, and began writing. I wrote down names of people for whom I had harboured unforgiveness. I wrote down the situations, the offences, the scenes that played out in my sub-conscious mind. As the names and situations began to flow, more detailed mental pictures followed. I don't recall how long I sat there that first morning, but it was a while.

For days afterwards, as I was chanting, more snippets of detail would pour forth and the list grew. Scene after scene, surrounding the instances and people who had wounded my heart, mind and spirit. They started coming to me while walking my dog or running my errands. They would come to me in the shower, in the market, at the gym, on the phone. It was like the floodgates had opened. It was not easy sometimes, but it was truly a remarkable experience; overwhelming in fact. I just needed to figure out what to do with all of this junk that was piling up in my front yard.

Then, I happened upon a sort of formula from *The Power of Your Subconscious Mind*, by Joseph Murphy. I had read the book years ago and since then it held a place in the bookcase amongst the dozens of others similar to it. Several days before all of this began, I had pulled the book from a bookshelf and placed it in my office at home. I think my original intention was to re-read it. I just hadn't got around to it up to that time. So, it was sitting on one of the stacks of books I am always in the middle of around my desk.

While all of this was going on, I randomly picked it up one morning and turned right to the page containing the following formula on forgiveness. I hadn't remembered this when I read the book before, but there it was, and I began to engage with this forgiveness recipe. I'll share it with you here.

I fully and freely forgive (mention the name of the offender); I release him/her mentally and spiritually. I completely forgive everything connected with the matter in question. I am free, and he/she is free. It is a marvellous feeling.[10]

There is more but you get the general idea. As I often do, I adapted my own version of this formula for myself and spent quite a lot of quality time forgiving everyone and everything on that growing list. As each person came to mind, as each scene appeared in my mind's eye, I would apply my version of the forgiveness formula. There were tears – lots of them. There was anger – lots of it. There was frustration, disbelief, profound sadness. I had even recalled events from when I was a very, very young child; situations and abuse I hadn't consciously remembered and yet was holding on to with unforgiveness and anger. The problem with holding on to all of this, or any other negativity, is it becomes your dominant experience from the perspective of the Ten Worlds.

As previously mentioned, in Buddhist practice there are Ten Worlds, or realms, or states of being ranging from Hell to Buddhahood. In the lower worlds, outward circumstances in our environment may cause us to vacillate between them many times a day, even many times an hour. The secret weapon in these states is to recognise that within each of the Ten Worlds are the Ten Worlds, meaning we can, by conscious choice, choose a higher plane of Being by changing our vibrational energy. This is by Law.

Every person has a dominant state of being and for most of us, it is in one of the lower states – Hell, Hunger, Animality, Anger, Humanity and Heaven. Through Buddhist practice, you may change your dominant lower state(s) of being for the higher states – Learning, Realisation, Bodhisattva and Buddhahood. In my case, holding on to all of that messed-up junk affected my dominant energy inclining me towards the world of Anger and I was only barely aware of it. It's not as if I went around growling at people all the time. It was just the presence of that energy that weighed upon me. Until I broke through and developed an understanding of what was going on in there, how it was affecting me, and an awareness of the contrast achieved by getting rid of it, that my dominant world began to change. Now, more in control and conscious, I am better able to shift energies from those nether regions to higher planes of Being through forgiveness. As each event, each person, each situation, comes up for me, I work on forgiveness and Being of a more profound nature. It is a much more powerful state.

Although that was a while ago, some people and situations were, and continue to be, a challenge for me to this day. Most of these people and situations I have forgiven more than once, twice, even a dozen times. For many, though, positive feelings have replaced the bad. The noxious storerooms have slowly been cleaned out and most unwillingness to forgive has faded.

It actually became a true joy to forgive and to bless all of those who had caused me so much pain because I came to realise that by so doing, I was freeing myself. I had held on to this toxic, unconscious dialogue for so many years, it was and is a tremendous relief to just lay it by the side of the road of my own Masterful journey and joyfully move forwards.

HOW MANY TIMES MUST I FORGIVE?

Now, the truth is that just because I opened the door to a couple of storerooms I didn't even know I had, the images and the pain immediately stopped. That is just not how things operate. Cleaning those storerooms was and is dirty work. Much like a stain on the carpet that won't go away, some things need more than one application of solvent and scrubbing to get them clean.

Then Peter came to Jesus and asked, "Lord, how many times shall I forgive my brother or sister who sins against me? Up to seven times?" Jesus answered, "I tell you, not seven times, but seventy-seven times."

Matthew 18:21–22 NIV

So, here it is revealed; the answer to forgiveness. We began with the manifestation formula of "ask and receive" and we explored the often-missing link of forgiveness in that formula. Now we have the actual mechanics of the Biblical forgiveness method itself. Some versions of this verse say to forgive not just 77 times but "seventy times seven". Either way, it's a lot. But, why so many times?

This forgiveness formula was provided to us a long time ago. I'm not convinced, however, we got it completely right. I have heard it explained that we must forgive someone no matter how many times they ill-treat us. While there may be some truth to that thought, I do not think it is necessarily about forgiving someone who habitually wrongs you or habitually does something considered wrong. That's a whole different thing to talk about and to clean up. I do believe, however, what Jesus was explaining was to forgive until you *feel* it, even if it takes 77 or 490 times to get you to the *feeling place* whereby you have truly forgiven someone. Once you pass that point and you can honestly release them and bless them, forgiveness has been made.

The forgiveness recipe works. However, it only works *if you truly are able to release the people you need to forgive* and consecrate them with all the blessings of life. When you can make that happen, you have truly forgiven them. Just saying the words through gritted teeth may help you get started but you must actually *feel* you have forgiven them. It's just like everything else we are talking about here. You have to *feel it* for the Universe to respond.

The 5-Steps of Forgiveness

Like everything else we are talking about here, the steps of forgiveness are the exact same steps as those of manifesting your desires. The process is the same, and the reason why is because it is the *only* Process. It is the Universal Process of evolving and growing; expanding and expressing. Therefore, it applies to anything being manifested, including the manifestation of forgiveness.

Step 1 – Turn on the Lights

My experience, discovering those hitherto unexplored rooms in my house, forced me to turn on the lights and see what was going on; to work through the 5-Step Process and rid myself of toxic junk. Admittedly, there was an element of fear attached. A big one. After all, the smallest crack in the wall let me see into just what was in there, and it was huge and scary. I sat in a mode of "should I/shouldn't I" for just a little bit as that first step forwards took some courage. Hopefully for the rest of us, turning on the lights won't be so dramatic. Just flip the switch. It doesn't matter where you start. Whether it is the most recent infraction on your unforgiveness Map, or whether it's the biggest one that's been looming for years. Start somewhere.

Take out your journal, or equivalent, and start writing down all whom you are willing to forgive. Start there. Those who you *probably should* be forgiving, but are still holding unforgiveness for, can come later. If you can't recall names, write down situations. Just start somewhere and let it flow. I think you may be surprised by what starts to come forwards when you begin to shed some light on the subject.

Step 2 – Clean Up the Space

As you begin to write down some people and situations, begin to clean it all up. Forgive the petty little things that went on in the office this week. Forgive the wonky way your hairstylist didn't quite get it right at your last visit. Forgive the grumpy way your spouse or partner snapped at you this morning before actually being awake enough to have a conversation. These are minor things to clean out of your space. But if left unattended, much like the dust on the windowsill, it can build up. While you are doing this, start working on Step Three.

Step 3 – Take the Time to Get Clear

All of this work will take some time and effort. You may have some stuff lurking around just below the surface that will take time to work itself to the front of the house. Furthermore, take the time to get clear on whom and what you are forgiving and why it is important. Some of the people in my Garden of Unforgiveness came up slowly. Some are still poking through the surface. For some, it took a while to get to a space of *willingness to forgive* before I could begin the process of it. I had to get clear on *why* it was important to do so before willingness came.

For all of us, the *why* of forgiveness goes beyond just wanting to be better manifestors. The Process of forgiveness is the Process of restoring Oneness to the Universal Whole, as well as to us as individualised points within it. Getting clear on the whys and what-fors are necessary stages. Like being clear on the object or artefacts of our desires, clarity on forgiveness is the secret to the powerful next step.

Step 4 – Name it

This is your "ask". The desire in this case is forgiveness. It is the Cause in the great Law of Cause and Effect. Once you are clear on what, whom and why, state your intention to the Universe. Name it; ask for it. Ask for assistance as well. As mentioned, you may have to forgive 490 times or more before it actually manifests as true forgiveness. For a couple of mine, I'm still in the 300s. Ask for help to hear and to see forgiveness when whatever or whomever appears again, phantom-like, in your Map room.

For me, a really good time to catch a hold of some of these unforgiveness phantoms is in the morning as I begin my day. They often just show up as I am making tea or coffee, or feeding the dog her breakfast, or puttering about the refrigerator. They show up as unfinished conversations that only take place in my head that I keep perpetuating. Conversations with folks I still needed to forgive, one more time. And that is exactly what I got into the habit of doing. One more time, as I became aware of what was going on, I would forgive them – at least I grow my willingness to forgive one step further. The hard part is awareness.

Step 5 – Receive

Be the person who has lightened his or her gravitational load. Be what it feels like to have freedom from the heavy burden of unforgiveness. Most of all, Be happy that all of this is coming out, freeing up your energies to support Being the one with the clear and clean object of your true desires made manifest. All of the energies that were supporting those unforgiveness Maps can now be channelled into all the good stuff the road of Mastery brings. It's a much happier happiness without all of that junk in your trunk.

THREE ELEMENTS IN FORGIVENESS

As with all things tending towards the Universal, there are three elements, or entities, in this whole forgiveness thing. There is the You who needs to forgive, there is the You who needs to be forgiven and, there is the You who needs to forgive *Yourself*. Let's take it one at a time.

First, there is the You who is the wronged party; the one sinned against. If you have made your list, which will most likely keep growing as you work though all of this, use Joseph Murphy's formula above as your guide, or one of your own design, to work out forgiveness for them. As mentioned, it may take some time to get to the feeling point of true forgiveness. Take it. Don't assume it's a done deal until you can actually *feel* you have forgiven them and can *will*, not wish, them well. Then be grateful and move forwards.

There are those who would promote some version of a face-to-face "I forgive you" party such as a letter-writing campaign, or a phone call to inform the wounding party that you have forgiven them. I am not an advocate of this and here is why.

Whether we care to admit it to ourselves or not, in many cases, as the wronged party, there probably remains a little piece of us which hopes the wrong-doer will feel a pang of remorse for having caused us pain. If you approach some face-to-face forgiveness event with any artificial expectation they will crumble with contrition, you're not in it for the right reason. This will backfire on you vibrationally because you are not actually forgiving. You are Causing the fault to revive itself. In the event they don't *"mea culpa"* all over you and themselves, you will unnecessarily make them wrong for that too, which is a worse off place than before.

If you do choose to have some version of a face-to-face, and if they do beat their breast for what they have done, consider it the icing on the forgiveness cake and leave it at that. Avoid the trap of validating how right you were and how wrong they were. That's a powerful energy and the Universe, being what It is, will respond with more for which to make them wrong and more to not forgive. You'll be right back where you started, if not further behind.

My advice is to do your forgiving in your private space, by yourself, in your own time. The work is internal. This is *your* release from the bondage and resistance *you imposed upon yourself* through keeping those Maps of unforgiveness alive. Use whatever means you wish to work through the process, but I would suggest this be a private journey. If, however, you feel it absolutely necessary to throw a clemency party, go for it. Just be *very* clear about the kind of energy you are using to make that happen. If in doubt, don't go there.

The second entity in the forgiveness triangle is the You who needs to be forgiven. We all need to be forgiven for some reason or another. Take out your journal and follow the same five steps for yourself as you performed for those who needed your forgiveness. Turn on the light, clean up the space and get clear on what you need to be forgiven for and make amends. But, with a caveat or two before you head down that road.

There is some very powerful stuff in 12-step programmes. I have never been through one myself, however many of the steps are based upon some very profound Universal principles, so I have used bits and pieces in my practice for years. One of the steps as it pertains to this conversation is as follows. I paraphrase here but I am sure you get the intended gist.

Make a list of all those you have wronged and be willing to make amends.

Similar to the list in your journal you made for those you needed to forgive, do the same for yourself and for those who you may have wronged; those who need to forgive you. I won't kid you; this may not be all that easy. But don't skip over it.

Go through the five steps above for yourself. Be honest. Turn on that light and take a good look in the mirror. If you need an *actual* mirror to do this, get one. Write down who needs to forgive you and why. Then start the process of gaining forgiveness for yourself.

I draw your attention to the exact words used in the sentence above. Be *willing* to make amends. This implies two things. The first is the willingness part. This means the willingness itself is the first step of the process of "ask"-ing for forgiveness, both for your forgiveness and for you being forgiven. A willingness is the first-level Action. It is the Cause. You have to direct your willpower properly or the Process of forgiveness is a waste of energy. Take notice of the next step that follows; again paraphrased.

Make direct amends to those to whom you have made a mistake whenever possible, except when to do so would injure them or others.

Now, here is my interpretation on this method. They do not tell you to make direct amends at any and all costs. If you feel the need to make amends in some personal way, that's great. I would encourage you to do so. *Unless* so doing would injure, or cause further hurt, to the other party. In other words, if you have wronged someone in such a way that to make amends would cause some very deep hurt by informing them about whatever you did or did not do, then asking for forgiveness would open a huge can of worms. In such cases, the proposed Cause would be to live in a revised way, or to Be different, changing the behaviour surrounding whatever it may be.

Moreover, within the context of "to do so would injure them or others", one has to include one's self in the "others" bit. If making amends in some personal, direct way would cause damage and injury to *you*, emotionally or energetically, I would strongly advise against it. There were a couple of folks in the "It's My Bad" file who *I will not* be around. To do so would cause *me* harm. It's an energy thing and that's OK. I accept what is, I have made amends in my own way, and I am moving forwards sans guilt for my participation in the situation.

The third piece of the triangle is the You who needs to forgive *yourself*. Forgive *you* for making yourself carry the burden of this stuff for so long. Forgive yourself for *your* hand in the situations that caused the mistakes in the first place. Forgive yourself for the monsters you made up, the Maps you kept alive and for straddling the past with the future and squelching the Present/Now. Forgive the self-loathing this has produced, conscious or not, and for not having done it all sooner. In a Journey like this, there is a lot of self-forgiveness to be made. Don't cheat yourself out of this all-important step. Keep this in mind. For whomever you need to forgive, and for the forgiveness of yourself, the energy necessary for this transaction is obviously one-sided. The energy is upon your initiation. This is your opportunity to fix a broken Law; for you to make atonement; *at-One-ment*.

Another piece of the whole forgiveness pie often comes to us through the Process. What sometimes makes people stumble is the idea of seeking forgiveness. It begs a question. Doesn't the other party need to forgive you? The simple answer is, no. It is not necessary for them to forgive you. In some situations, the events requiring forgiveness may have happened a very long time ago. People may have passed this life. Or, as explained above, if seeking forgiveness causes harm, it is absolutely the wrong idea to try and milk forgiveness in order for you to somehow feel better while hurting the other person in the process. Similarly, as in cases requiring your forgiveness, those who need to be forgiven do not need a face-to-face audience and, in some cases, it's not possible.

The reason those both requiring forgiveness and those who need to forgive you do not necessitate this element is due to the two Primary Laws. The Law of Divine Oneness, and the Law of the Perpetual Transmutation of Energy. We all share the same energy. We are all made of one Universal substance. Living or dead, that energy Is. For the living, it is manifested as your Being. For those no longer with us, that energy is evolving into a different form. The energy is not different. Just the form. Therefore, putting the energy of forgiveness out into the Universe for a long-passed away family member is a Cause the same as any for a living family member. The Effect is reparation of Oneness. Since we are all a part of everything and everyone, the Effect is still the same. Similarly, for situations for which we need to be forgiven, the ask of the Universe is the same as asking in person. The energy is the same regardless of the form, regardless of the distance or of the need to be absolved. The ask is the Cause, atonement is the Effect.

Forgiving and asking for forgiveness can be done in many ways. Personally, after I get clear, and in a private space, I put the energy of forgiveness on the person, the situation or the event out into the Universe. I talk directly to the being God took the form of through that person. I apply my version of the forgiveness formula, bless them, then begin Being the person who is released from that particular need to forgive. I use the same pattern with those from whom I need to seek forgiveness. I get clear, get into the communal space with the Universe and sincerely make atonement. Then, I move forwards as Being the one free of the need for forgiveness and the who has made reparation to Oneness.

Use whatever method works best for you. Some write letters. Some act out telephone calls. Some sit down and have an imaginary conversation with whomever. Whatever method works for you, that is the key to it all. It must work for *you*. For me, writing a letter doesn't work. For me, it's the conversation I have with the Universal Substance that does the trick.

This is not to say you get to run into an empty room and ask through the Universe to forgive the transgression you just made this morning with your spouse or significant other, when you grumpily snapped at him or her for asking too many questions before you were quite awake enough to answer them. The methods described above are generally for those situations in which it is not possible or plausible for the other party to be present, or for when undue harm would be caused. For those other minor infractions, take the responsibility to show up as the Master you are and do your repairs.

Remember, too, forgiveness does not mean forgetting. The whole "forgive and forget" thing is impossible as discussed earlier. My unforgiveness storerooms took some time and a great deal of effort to clear out. Once in a while a phantom of unforgiveness appears; a ghost of the past in the pre-forgiveness stage of the incident. I grew to simply notice the ghost in the room and if I had to throw a forgiveness power ball at it I would. Most often now, just noticing when it shows up makes it go away.

What those apparitions of the past are trying to do is the same thing your monsters try to do when you get rid of them. They are seeking energy to revive themselves. If you don't stop the resurrection process, it can quickly take hold of your energy and sap you of your strength. It will steal away your manifestation energy and will cut ties with your desires. So, when you notice one creeping up out of the ethers, tell it to stop in its tracks. Tell it you have already forgiven it and there is no longer a need or a place for it in your clean house. Then, reaffirm the Being you are and move forwards on the road of Mastery.

I absolutely believe the time I spent cleaning out that storeroom caused my manifestation muscles to kick into overdrive. You see, the energy spent sub-consciously keeping all that junk alive was weakening my ability to manifest. With that gone, life just got easier, my dreams and desires grew exponentially and so did the manifestation of them. If you have *anything or anyone* you truly need to forgive, including yourself, please get there. It will take work and you will shed a few tears. Opening old wounds hurts, but I promise you, it's well worth it. You may be surprised at what's actually inside of your hidden storerooms that needed to be binned all along.

The Big IF

While forgiveness is the key that turns the lock of the manifestation formula, and we have now seen why this is, I would like to point out a little something more in the very verse that started this whole chapter.

> And when you stand praying, if you hold anything against anyone, forgive them…
>
> Mark 11:25 NIV

I would like to draw your attention to the smallest word in the sentence above. That word is IF. Now, I make up there is not a person in this world that does not, or has never had to, forgive someone or to be forgiven. That said, there is still the possibility, ergo the "if". In spite of the fact the word *if* used here is very small and seemingly insignificant, I believe behind it is something much more profound. IF, here, would imply the option of never accepting the sin or mistake in the first place.

I have always been intrigued by the idea of "taking offence", or of not taking offence. Offence in this, or any other case, is another word for sin, or mistake, or having wronged or any related word. So, the idea of *taking offence* means you have a choice. It means you can *choose* to take or not to take offence at all. You can choose not to be wronged, or sinned against, or have something mis-taken from you and to keep the Law of Oneness intact, at least from your side of things. This, I believe, is the real meaning of turning the other cheek.

To this end I will conclude this chapter with one of my favourite stories. It is an old story so it has several slightly different versions. I'll give you the one I use often in my practice.

It is said the Buddha was renowned for his ability to respond with good in the face of evil. There was a man who had heard of the Buddha's capacity for this and decided to test it out in public. He travelled for miles over several days and finally reached an area where the Buddha was staying.

Upon his arrival, the man found the Buddha and began hurling insults at him. The man verbally abused him, swore at him and mistreated him terribly. The Buddha was unaffected; nonplussed. After a while, however, the Buddha simply turned and asked the man permission to ask a question of him.

"What do you want…?" the man snootily replied.

The Buddha responded, "If someone offers you a gift and you decline acceptance of the gift, then to whom does the gift belong?"

The man replied, "It belongs to the one who offered it in the first place, of course."

"You are correct," said the Buddha. "So, if I decline to accept all of your abuse, does it all not belong to you?" A bit stunned at this answer, and stunned at the realisation of his own actions, the man turned away and went home.

The best and cleanest way of forgiving is not *to have to forgive in the first place*. If someone tries to sin against you, you actually don't *have* to accept it. If someone tries to mis-take something from you, you have the choice whether or not to allow it. I am absolutely not saying this is an easy thing to do, or not to do. I am also not saying you have to be a doormat. Furthermore, I am not saying if someone does something to you completely against your will, there will not be a wound for a while. But, keeping this story in mind can certainly help alleviate the whole *being wronged* thing and the work it takes to forgive the wrongdoer. Being angry is not a good feeling and can do some very unpleasant things, vibrationally speaking. So, the next time someone offers you a *sin* gift, a present of *missing the mark*, try not to accept it. Remember your Being and the role you have in maintaining the Law of Divine Oneness. And, remember, holding on to any of this stuff only perpetuates separation, which is the opposite of the Universal intention of Oneness. In other words…

> *Holding on to anger is like drinking poison and expecting the other person to die.*
>
> Buddha

PART THREE: THE MINDSET

THE MASTERY OF THE BLOOM

THE MASTERY OF PATIENCE

THE MASTERY OF GRATITUDE

Part Three is about The Masterful Mindset. It is accurately positioning yourself for growth by using your willpower to attain and remain in an attitude of clarity and gratitude through interdependence. This is the language of the Universe.

CHAPTER 15

THE MASTERY OF THE BLOOM

The successful life is the advancing life; and as the advancing life is lived by obedience to the evolutionary principle. The evolutionary principle is that advancement comes by more than filling your present place; and this is true whether you are an employee, or are in business for yourself.

Wallace Wattles[1]

As a Buddhist, one of the practices in which I engage, and wholeheartedly believe in, is the following idea. No matter where you find yourself in life, regardless of circumstance, regardless of how seemingly bad or good things are, do the very best you are absolutely capable of doing every hour, every day. Easier said than done sometimes, I know.

This does not mean doing your best mechanically. It means doing your best with the intentional mindset of the advancement of your Being; the mindset of Mastery. It is the idea of flourishing. It is the idea of "Bloom Where You Are Planted".[2] The phrase has devolved into a bit of a cliché these days; however, it still resonates a Universal truth.

There is a deeper meaning to Bloom Where You Are Planted than what appears on its flowery surface. The only purpose of manifesting anything into your life, and of life in general, is to grow; it is to evolve forwards. The purpose of all life is for God, or the Universe, to continually expand Itself through Itself, and increase Its awareness of Itself, happily.

Let's take a closer look, then, at the idea of blooming. A botanical bloom is the end of one stage of the evolutionary Process; the end of a period of growth. The plant from which the bloom emerges prepares to expand itself exponentially through the seeds contained within the bloom. It is preparing itself to evolve. Without this intention, the bloom would be just a bloom. Lovely to look at, fragrant perhaps, but of little substance or value other than that. The same applies to the idea of blooming where we are planted in the allegorical, but intentional Being sense. By blooming where we are planted, we are intentionally, vibrationally and physically preparing ourselves for growth; a period of evolving to another level.

The bloom is a gateway to desire. The bloom entices fertilisation of the seeds within. In nature, a bloom most often draws to it some form of co-creator in the fertilisation process. Most often an insect or a bird – something like that. When the seeds within the bloom are fertilised, it is time for the bloom to fade in favour of the seeds. The plant puts its energy into preparing the seeds to expand more of itself. This is a wonderful analogy of desire.

Blooming where you are planted may be equated to the birth of our desires. The seeds of desire must come from the bloom and the Co-Creative influences fertilising them. Unfertilised desires produce nothing. Those desires that have been subject to the proper Co-Creative system produce results and that is the key. There is a Universal Process that needs to be taken into consideration. The Action of the bloom must come first, and if properly Co-Creatively fertilised, the seeds follow. In other words, the Actions of Being fully expressed is the bloom. The seeds of desire for more expression follows the blossom.

Bloom With Intention

As with most Universal concepts such as Bloom Where You Are Planted, there is a sequence, a method, or a way of doing things that must go in a specific order to achieve the desired results. These results are achieved through intentional engagement of the Blooming *Process*, regardless of circumstance. Just making up your mind to *bloom* in the midst of an undesirable situation, for example, is a start but will not do much to alleviate the issue you may be having, much like unfertilised seeds. More than likely, it will cause you to reach greater levels of that which is undesirable. Blooming is Actionable. Bloom Where You Are Planted is a Process, as God is a Process. There must be the seeds of intention behind the bloom combined with Action. It requires a clarity of vision and a strong desire to evolve into greater levels of Being through the Co-Creative Process, not just to escape a situation with which you are unhappy. This puts the seeds before the bloom, or unclear desires before fully Being in the Present/Now and desiring to grow forwards.

If you hate your job, for example, and desire a different one, the intention must be one of *Bloom Where You Are Planted* by performing in your current job at the best level at which you are capable. Do your best work with the intention of Being in the new position. Do extra stuff for your boss. Go the extra mile for your co-workers. Do more than you are asked to do. Dress a little nicer, be a little nicer, think a little nicer, all the while keeping the desired intention clearly in mind. In other words, the Mastery of the current reality.

Bloom where you are planted is right in line with the Universal Laws and with manifesting your desires. By exercising the highest potential of which you are capable, you engage several of the Laws and, by implication, all of them. You are raising your vibrational level by aligning yourself to the desired outcome while thriving in your current situation; Blooming. This will stimulate the Law of Polarity which will launch your Journey from the undesired state on one side of the pole, to the desired state on the other, both of which are on the same plane of existence needing only the vibrational lubricant caused by your well-intended Actions to make the shift.

A Blooming Example

Let's continue with the example of the desire for a better paying, more fulfilling job. Let's say your current job is a dead-end dud. You dislike the people with whom you work and they pretty much dislike you back. They complain about everything including each other. Their work is sloppy which affects your work. You don't feel you can trust them.

Your boss seems to always be picking on you. She looks for things for which to make you wrong and she criticises you to make herself *right* for making you wrong. The work itself sucks. It feels mindless, empty and it doesn't seem to contribute to anything very important nor interesting. You are underpaid yet feel like you bend over backwards every day. You come home tired, exhausted, empty and hopeless. There… how's that picture looking?

Quitting outright is certainly an option and, if things are tough in the extreme, it may be time to pull all stakes and head for the hills. However, that might not be the most efficacious nor practical approach, especially from a Universal, manifestation perspective. Besides, we know that if there is any dirt we will be leaving in the house that is the current job, it will follow us into the new position, when we get one. Short of that, then, what else can we do about our situation here?

The first thing would be to recognise it for what it is. While "it sucks" comes to mind, the greater picture here is a huge opportunity to *bloom*. While it does seem that things are pretty grim, this situation, like every other in the Universe, is on a plane within the Law of Polarity.

Let's call this plane the "Satisfaction at Work" pole. I know you may be tempted to call it the "I Hate My Job" pole, but we can see this idea won't get us very far and it is only half the picture. In spite of the fact a situation like this can feel overwhelmingly negative, what you need is perspective. Let's figure out what the pole is and what's on the other end.

On your "Satisfaction at Work" pole, one extreme is the toxic work environment as described above. You might call it the "This Job Bites" extreme in which you are very dissatisfied. On the other extreme is the "I Love My Work" end of the pole. Everything is lopsided because you are pretty well entrenched on the suckie side of the stick. Put in perspective, however, there is a big opportunity here, and a choice.

The opportunity is to *bloom where you are planted*. The choice is either you continue to wallow and complain in that undesired state which, as you know, only attracts more to complain about. Or, you can turn on the lights and see the situation as *nurturing the seeds of a new desire*. The opportunity provided for you by Being on the extreme end of "This Job Bites" is that it creates a desire for "I Love My Work" which is sitting at the opposite end of the "Satisfaction at Work" pole. The two extremes are One and the same. The new desire is your next destination point. It's time to put some intention behind it. It's time to get clear on what your new role will look like, feel like, and Be like. It's time to take Action.

Exercise your intention through several questions to ask yourself. What type of work is it that you desire? How does it make you feel? How much and what type of compensation do you desire? Where will the new position be located? What's your commute like? What kinds of co-workers do you desire to be with? What are the opportunities for advancement? What is the social mission of your new company? What level of satisfaction do you wish to derive? What will your friends and family say about your new role? Can you see yourself waking up excited to get to your work?

The exercise above has to be more than just wishing for something different. The Universe always responds to emotion. What these questions should begin to generate is a state of *elevated emotion*, from negative to very fun and positive to which the Universe responds in a fun and positive way. Keep mapping out your new role until you get as clear as you can and you feel all jazzed up. Then set your intention and make your "ask" of the Universe. Announce the reality of it; I Am… But, that's not where it ends. You have the work of the manifestation steps to perform. You still need to clean up the current space, at least vibrationally, by blooming where you are planted and taking Action. So, let's see what that looks like.

The Law of Perpetual Transmutation of Energy is one of the two Primary Laws of the Universe and, as such, permeates all of the others. It acknowledges your personal ability to act by shifting a lower-based vibrational energy into a higher one. If you are unhappy with your current circumstances, the first thing to change is how you *think* about them which changes your vibrational output, thereby transferring energy in the opposite direction. By finding opportunities to bloom where you are planted, finding elements of your current circumstances you can be grateful for and nurture, you automatically shift into higher vibrational states of Being.

> *If you change the way you look at things, the things you look at change.*
>
> Wayne Dyer

Starting with your co-workers, what is one Map you have about them? Allow me… "*They are crazy, lazy, complaining, nit-wits who are incapable of doing a decent job, and in the process, seem to work overtime at annoying me.*" OK, that's a pretty strong Map. Let's shift it. Let's ask ourselves a few questions.

Are they annoying you on purpose? Or, are you just being annoyed by them in too many ways? Why does what they do affect you so seriously? What are you making up about them? Are you misunderstanding them? Is their work sloppy or is it just not the way you'd do it? Can you work together on some things? Can they teach you something? Maybe they can teach you something that will be of value in your next position. Something you don't do now that will be vital in your next role. Do you start a conversation with them or wait until they start one with you? Could they be avoiding you a bit because your energy about them is too sharp to comfortably be around? *Could some of the problem actually be you?* What are you doing, saying, or being that is contributing to the very thing you are complaining about?

As you start to answer these questions and find alternative ways of thinking about your co-workers, the energy begins to shift and so do your Maps about them; the monsters start to come out of hiding. Now, what would one step forwards look like? What could you do to begin blooming with your co-workers? Can you seek their advice on something? Can you offer your help to them on a project, for example? How about asking how their day is going or how their weekend went? Step-by-step, your whole attitude of resistance will be replaced by the beginnings of a bloom and the desire seeds behind it.

How about your boss? Can you shift your energy about her as well? Maybe she isn't such a pain in the backside after all. Could it be your energy is pulling negative energy from her? Could you be overreacting to the way she treats you? Could she be going through a rough patch herself? Do you know what her expectations are? Does she ask more of you than others? When she tells you to do something, can you do it beyond her expectations? Instead of rushing through whatever it may be, can you spend a little bit more time on it just to make it pop? In what ways can you bloom with your boss?

What about the work itself? What is something about the work that you can find to be happy about? Can you at least be grateful about getting a regular pay cheque from the current job for now? You say it's mindless. Great! Doesn't that provide an opportunity to fill your mind with thoughts in support of your new role in a new job? Doesn't it give you the chance to fill in the blanks of your new Being on your new role? Can you learn something new about the work each day? Can you find out how your function affects the bottom line? Or, how your role contributes to the brand? For a greater perspective, can you find out about a different line of the business and maybe shadow someone so you get a sense of how it all works?

I know this is easier said than done. Believe me, I have been in very similar situations. While on the surface all of this could be poo-pood as a bunch of positive-thinking hogwash, it's actually pretty powerful stuff. These Actions tap into many of the Universal Laws, which is what makes them very powerful indeed. In addition to the Law of Perpetual Transmutation of Energy so obviously demonstrated here, there are many of the Actionable Laws linked to blooming where you are planted. So let's run this situation through our Laws and look at them one at a time.

BLOOMING BY LAW

The Law of Action states we must participate in activities that support a desired state of Being; the fertilisation of your desires. If you don't change your Actions, you are in effect participating in Actions in support of "My Work Sucks". Resistance to the situation itself is an Action in this regard. If another job plunked itself right down in front of you this instant, you would still be behaving like you were at the old job. Can you actually picture yourself with the attitude and vibrational energy of the old job in what you are envisioning to be your new one? Can you see yourself only scraping by, doing what is absolutely necessary to get a job done in your new role? Can you really see yourself in that new role hating your co-workers or boss? Of course that would be impossible. If you could, you wouldn't even have the desire for a new, happier role come up for you in the first place.

By blooming where you are planted, you are engaging in Actions that are in alignment with the person you are Being in the new role. That thought alone should greatly enhance your vibrational energy. That thought alone should slide you further across the pole towards the "I Love My Work" end. It should be motivating enough to get you past the angst you may initially feel about actually having to have the most basic of conversations with your co-workers and to be nice to them, even if they are not nice to you. Bloom where you are planted and Be the Actions of your new role in your current one.

The Actions in support of Being happy and fulfilled at work, regardless of outward appearances in your present situation, are putting Causes into the Universe which will produce favourable Effects, namely those of Being happy and fulfilled at work. Every action has a reaction. By complaining about your undesired states of Being or focusing on the lack of your desired states of Being, you create Causes that will in turn create the Effects of lack. By blooming where you are planted you create higher-based Causes, which in turn create higher-based Effects. Your efforts of getting to know your co-workers better, or of doing better than expected for your boss, are Actions in support of these causes. Simply choosing to see things from a perspective vibrationally higher than the previous one is automatically a better Cause in itself. All of these Actions begin a cycle as each Effect pushes you across the pole towards the desired "I Love My Work" end.

The Law of Correspondence is engaged as well which states your outer world reflects your inner world. There is a correlation between how you feel on the inside and what the outer world shows you in reflection. The world at the polar end of "This Job Bites" is pretty bleak. Your inner world feeds off itself producing more to bite on. The bleaker you feel, the bleaker your outer world appears to be. While being in the thick of it can seem overwhelming, even one thought of blooming where you are planted can begin to change that. *Be* the person in the new role and that will start to reflect back as your outer world.

The Law of Compensation is one of the Action Laws. It is the Law of Cause and Effect as it relates to abundance and blessings in the form of gifts, money, opportunities, etc. Everyone is compensated in direct proportion to what he or she contributes. All of the good Causes you produce by blooming where you are planted will be compensated by Law. The more you contribute, the greater the compensation. *Being* the vibrational energy of your new role and giving more than is asked of you sets you up for lofty return; the visible Effects of your well-intentioned deeds.

And, of course, the Law of Attraction, which involves the rest of the Actionable Laws. Blooming where you are planted creates the energy of Being the manifestation of the "I Love My Work" side of the "Satisfaction at Work" pole. By focusing on blooming, you create the vibrational energy that will attract your desired state of Being one seed at a time. This is in accordance with the Law of Rhythm.

Speaking of desired state, here's another thing to think about. You must remain open to possibilities as they concern the desired state of Being. After doing the work of blooming, of cleaning out the negative vibrational energy, it *may just be* the "I Love My Work" side shows up as your present situation on your present job. It *may just be* you grow to really like your co-workers and really respect your boss. It just *may just be* you begin to find your work so rewarding and to find it making such a contribution, you don't actually want to leave. With your blooming attitude, work ethic, and results you are achieving, your boss promotes you. Or, someone else in the company notices your work and provides a new opportunity for you. Whether you leave the current role, or you stay with it, blooming where you are planted produces the ultimate goal of all things; your happiness. That makes it all worthwhile.

Getting Clear on Blooming

To bloom where you are planted makes a few assumptions. I believe the first assumption is you can be "planted" just anywhere, and you have the ability to grow and to bloom. Well that is basically true. The Universe is full of abundance and provides us with the means to take a hold of it. We know this. So, conceptually, you *do* have the ability to grow just anywhere. It boils down to choice.

A second assumption is that we understand what type of plant we are talking about. Is it a full-grown plant that is about to bloom? Or, is it a seed that needs to be nurtured and to grow into a mature plant ready to bloom? As is the nature of things, I believe blooming where you are planted starts with the basics; being planted. As such, we must start with the basics of this idea. Start with a seed. So many Universal lessons are taught through the reference of seeds and growth, so, let's keep that assumption.

These assumptions dovetail nicely into the story of the farmer as told in the Bible. It's a great metaphor of blooming where you are planted. You can read it yourself if you like, but for convenience's sake here it is…

A FARMER WENT OUT TO SOW

As the story begins, a farmer went out to sow his seed in his field. As he was doing so, some fell on the pathway and birds came and ate them. Some fell among the stones, which didn't have enough soil to grow properly. They sprang up quickly but without proper moisture and no deep roots, they died. Some fell in thorny soil and were choked out. Finally some fell on fertile soil, which had exactly what the seeds needed to flourish. They grew, matured, bloomed and produced various levels of abundant return. They bloomed where they were planted, unlike the others that didn't necessarily get the chance. Of course, they had the proper circumstances, so let's talk about that.

We are given an interpretation of this parable as one relating to faith. However, this explanation falls just shy of something that I believe is the deeper meaning. Let's put this in our manifestational language.

We have to understand the two basic elements involved here; seeds and soil. The seeds represent our desires, whatever they may be. When we have a desire we wish to manifest, we sow a seed. All the seeds have the same potential for manifesting; for multiplying many times over. However, the various soils are not equal. They are representative of our level of commitment or *belief* we have in manifesting our desires.

Or, our ability to Be the physical manifestation of the object of our desires. In this regard, the story does reflect faith and belief.

The first seeds which fell upon the path represent desires, expressed intentionally or not. These weak desires are eaten by thoughts that you can't actually have, or do not deserve to have them. They are consumed by the Devil himself; by doubt. It could also be those desires expressed as wishes or superstitions that actually have no emotion or feeling behind them. They are hollow desires versus things that you are really intending to manifest. They are unfertilised seeds.

The seeds in shallow soil represent those desires for which you have a lot of enthusiasm, initially. Sometimes desires of this nature are often associated with those rather new to the awareness of how all of this Universal-manifestation-Law stuff actually works. Those who are "trying it out". They have a lot of enthusiasm in the beginning. They get all jazzed up. They may even get some pretty amazing results. Usually, however, they have big, audacious desires they are not yet equipped nor prepared to receive. They want to manifest £10 million in 24 hours. The seed of their desires sprouts quickly. However, two or three days go by and nothing shows up at their door. They give it one more day, staring at the doorknob and it still doesn't show. Then the "I told you so's" start flowing instead. They set about making themselves right, everyone else wrong and carrying on with the idea that the whole premise of intentional manifestation is a lot of hooey. With a little setback or lack of focus their desires soon die away.

The seeds in the thorns represent those desires that have real potential… except for those nasty thorns. The thorns are physical and spiritual evidence that the space hadn't been cleaned up properly before planting your desires. The thorny soil is a dirty house! When the seeds sprouted, so did the thorns, which choked them out and all you are left with is thorns, the grime and the dirt that follows you around until you clean it out. Remember, you cannot leave a dirty house. You cannot expect what you are manifesting to show up if your space isn't ready for it. Get rid of those thorns.

The seeds on the good soil are the desires planted in the space in which you did your work. The space is prepared, cleaned up and ready to nurture your Being. The soil is primed and ready to go; ready to receive the seeds of your desired manifestations, and the blooms that will follow; the next level of growth for you. They still need water and care in the form of belief and faith to bloom where they are planted, however. And, it takes a little time in the Present. Notice what happens when all of this works together.

> *... it produced a crop – a hundred, sixty, or thirty times what was sown.*
>
> Matthew 13:8 NIV

Meaning the seeds grew the plants that produced blooms, which further produced exponentially more seeds through the Co-Creative Process. Or, said in another way... the well-intentioned desires produced the physical manifestation of those desires, which further produced more desires with the probability of even greater manifestation potential – expanding and evolving many times over, season after season.

What About the Soil?

Thus far, we can see that blooming where you are planted requires planting in the right way, in the right conditions, in good soil. That soil is our Being. If our Being is unprepared; if our Being is still wishing and asking instead of Being the person with the physical manifestation of our desires in the Present/Now; if our Being is still wallowing around in old Maps with monsters we haven't rid ourselves of, what does that say about our soil?

What about that fella who hated his job? What do you think would happen if he tried to bloom where he was planted without doing the work to prepare those seeds to really take off blooming in his current position? What do you believe would be the result of his attempting to go the extra mile for his boss and co-workers if he was standing in the weeds emotionally and/or mentally with "This Job Bites"? Or, sitting on a bunch of thorns? I can tell you. All his efforts to "bloom" would leave him stuck in the worlds of Hunger, Animality, and Anger, all voraciously feeding off themselves.

Every attempt would most likely go unnoticed, be criticised or be disregarded only fuelling the fire in his belly and his heart. His actions may even come off as insincere, which is a feeling no one likes to be the recipient of. In order for him to bloom where he is planted and produce a bumper crop, he needs to do the work first; the work of cleaning up his mental and emotional house with regard to his suckie job, horrible boss and lame co-workers. He needs to get clear on his intention and turn on the lights. He needs to face his monsters and get them out of his space.

Once he does the work and creates a fertile field, his desires to manifest something better for himself will take root. Once he gets clear on his intention, clears away doubt and shoos out a bunch of monsters, his going the extra mile will be joyful instead of resentful and will be received as such. His doing one extra thing for his boss will feel triumphal instead of miserable. The energy will shift and things will start improving for him. The whole place will be different – at least for him. He may actually want to stay and keep growing in the old position instead of finding a new one. Or, that new position will come along with a bucket full of new opportunities he hadn't even dreamed of.

It could be argued that the seeds which were sown on less favourable ground didn't have the same opportunities as those sown on fertile ground, and that is absolutely true. However, bear this in mind. All seeds or desires in question are equal in that a desire is a desire much like a seed is a seed. While one kind of seed holds one kind of manifestation and another kind of seed a different one, they are still seeds and know what to do. They know their potential within. It is not their responsibility to plant themselves in the most fertile ground. *It is our job to provide the right conditions from which we glean the greatest harvest of our desires manifested.*

The life is in the seed; the bloom is contained within it. The seed represents our desires but where people get tripped up about this has to do with misplaced focus. The story of the farmer is not a story about the seed; it is a story about the soil. The desire has the same life in it regardless of where it may be tossed. I hear so many complaints about desires not manifesting very well, or at all. In my experience, it is nearly always a case of not preparing the soil. The soil needs to be ready to produce; in other words, the soil is the space of Being the bloom already. It is Being a crop yielding 100, 60, or 30 times more of itself. Crappy soil is Being a thorny patch. Crappy soil is Being shallow and dry. Crappy soil is Being a bunch of wishes and doubts, feeding the birds of the air.

As powerful manifestors, our role is to evolve and grow forwards. Our role is to expand the Universe. At least that's how it's supposed to work. We are to continually grow and learn and move. The farmer who went out to sow his seed in the story above is the Universe. It has the desire to expand and grow through us, so we have the desire too. This is what makes us Co-Creators of the evolutionary expansion of It. Once we achieve one desire, we desire to manifest the next crop, which should always propel us forwards. That's the way seeds work. That's the way the Universe works and Master manifestors work with It, not against It.

There is something behind this constant evolutionary growth which is often the forgotten part, but is perhaps the most important piece of the whole "bloom where you are planted" idea. Wallace Wattles said something many years ago that fits perfectly. It has stuck with me because I believe it to be the truth.

If it is true we, the Universe, the whole lot, are on an extraordinary evolutionary journey of expansion; if it is true that the Process of it is the intelligence of the Universe and we are Co-Creators in the Process – or Co-Creators in God – then we have to understand something. Evolution only comes from an excess of life that has reached the *perfection or fulfilment of itself in its current state*. If a form does not continue on the journey of growing and evolving, it stops the process and therefore must pass away. In other words, when a form has completely filled its evolutionary process within its current conditions – and the current conditions have reached capacity – the form must either evolve or die out.

When a certain life form reaches a state whereby it becomes an excess of itself, it has to evolve into something that will propel it to the next evolutionary state or form. It cannot evolve by merely pondering. The evolution of fullness cannot complete itself without Mastering the Present condition which evolves through Action. The form must put energy into Being a creator of a new form, not into competing for existing resources through the old form. By Being the next state or form, it frees up the energy to Be that new form because it has evolved past the need to compete for existence in a space that is overcrowded with the life forms of its former self, all competing for the same resources in a toxic environment.

Every living thing is under this necessity for continuous advancement; where increase of life ceases, dissolution and death set in at once.

Wallace Wattles[3]

Bloom where you are planted until you have reached the full expression of *Being in full bloom in the space you currently occupy.* This, then, compels a new desire to Be the next iteration of your true Self along the Masterful road, Co-Creatively. Blooming and Being at the same time. Blooming where you are planted is Being an excess of the present state, and Being the desired state at the same time.

Many forms of Buddhism and Hinduism use the symbol of the lotus flower to illustrate this very point, among others. Lotus flowers are adaptive; resistant to hot or cold and can adapt to many different environments. Even so they bloom. A lotus flower emerges pure from muddy or murky waters representing less than ideal conditions, and yet it blooms fresh each day in sharp contrast to its surrounding circumstances. Additionally, a lotus flower blooms and seeds at the same time. Both Cause and Effect simultaneously. It is the quintessential symbol of blooming where you are planted; an excess of the present state and the desired state at the same time. Blooming where you are planted is beautifully demonstrated through this symbol. Masterfully blooming and sowing the seeds of Being simultaneously.

Once you get a clear picture of what your next incarnation of Being is *while you are blooming in your current state*, it will compel you forwards. The seeds of desire have been fertilised. Once that picture of your new state of Being is firm, and your "ask" complete, you have begun the Process of creating it; of manifesting it. The balance is to keep your current house clean while building your next one. The rest will take care of itself.

COMPETITION

Besides evolving your Being, the other point to be made here is about competition versus creation. Competition is always, *always* a mindset of fear, lack, and of being in need. It directly supposes there is not enough to go around. One prize, one winner, period. I am certainly not opposed to healthy competition. I consider myself to be somewhat of a competitive person, actually. When I was in school and university, I wanted those As. I competed for those As. I wanted *summa cum laude* and got it, twice. While that's all lovely and what-not, it is, however, a little part of my character that actually gets in the way of manifesting sometimes and here's why.

The true mindset of competition is, from an energy perspective, the energy of the masculine. When we are in a competitive mode or mindset, masculine energy is what is being put out into the Universe. For example, when we have a desire we are manifesting and we *need* the manifestation, that need is competitive. It is based on lack and fear. A lack mentality creates a competitive energy to feed that need; to fill the void. It implies a taking of something from something else to fill the void and fill it fast. Speed is part of the *need*.

As discussed earlier, when we put a desire into the Universe, the giving of the desire into It is the masculine action. The Universe receives it, which is the feminine action. Then there is a role reversal necessary. We must become the feminine energy of receiving in order for the Universe to manifest or to give, through masculine energy, the object of desire. If we are in a competitive mindset, there is a glut of masculine energy both pushing out into the Universe and the Universe pushing back against it as It tries to give you the object of your desire. It's a stalemate.

The feminine energy is that of the creative, always. Once clarity is had and our ask is made via masculine energy, we must switch to the creative energy of the feminine, of receiving which does all the creative work. The creative-feminine looks for opportunities, creates resources, inspires imagination and innovation, and generates new thoughts. The mindset of competition cannot do this.

Another perspective on this is, anytime we move from the space of receiving, which is the feminine energy, to the space of competing, which is masculine, we move from "receiving" to "asking" all over again. This breaks the "ask and receive" rule. It results in doubt and disbelief which does not manifest anything but more of itself. To manifest any desire we must remain in the feminine energy of receiving, once we have given our ask into the Universe and declared its reality. Anytime we shift from creating, to competition, we are moving from Being to asking – from receiving to needing.

The Blooming Mindset

The final point about blooming where you are planted is this. It is a mindset thing. Powerful manifestors have a mindset of blooming always. Not just when the weeds start to appear. Not just when the sun gets too hot and the soil becomes too dry. It's not just for when you wake up one day and discover how miserable your job is and how miserable you are in it. It is an elevated mindset;

a higher vibrational level built on belief, trust and clarity. It is built from alignment with the Universal Laws, a constant state of gratitude, and from Being the Well-Manifested, Well-Intentioned Life. In addition to the obvious emotional state of happiness and joy this places one into, there is a very practical reason behind why Mastering this state is very wise.

Like our person in a lousy job above, being stuck in the weeds is much harder to get out of than not getting stuck at all. The longer you stay in a vibrational match to low-level stuff, the heavier it becomes. By the time you realise how stuck you are and how miserable you have become, the Universe has worn a pretty clear path to provide you with more muck to bring you down. It's not the fault of the Universe, by the way. It's not God picking on you. It's just how the Laws work. They are impartial. They operate through energy and, like it or not, your energy and emotions attract more of the same.

So, I challenge you to be in a constant state of Being fertile soil. The Bloom Where You Are Planted mindset is not just for when times are hard. It should be your approach to everything. Bloom with your family. Bloom with your friends, neighbours, the checkout lady at the till. Bloom on your days off when you are doing those household chores. Constantly be on your guard against energies and emotions that are too small for you. Always be looking for ways to grow and evolve. Be ever vigilant against Maps that no longer serve you, and against monsters knocking at your door. Tend to your soil daily. Keep it in top condition. The better the soil, the better the harvest. And, continually BE a desire-harvest of not just 30 fold, not just 60, but 100 times that of the original seed of desire.

In Buddhist terms, the word Buddha itself is a wonderful acknowledgement of this idea of Blooming Where You Are Planted. While the word Buddha means "One who is awakened", the word also implies "To Bloom".[4] Buddhahood is the highest form of Being. It is to be filled with abundance and the fruits of Heaven, good fortune and Life. This brings us to the reason for blooming no matter where we are, or in whatever world or circumstances in which we find ourselves. There are always the seeds of your highest, juiciest Self present anywhere you find yourself within the Ten Worlds. It is our work to create and to till the fertile soil, and this is done through Mastering the Way.

CHAPTER 16

THE MASTERY OF PATIENCE

When I was a kid, I loved superballs. They were called that for good reason. You know the ones. They were super-dense high-flyers. They came in all sizes and colours but the best ones, my opinion, were the big ones; the ones about the size of a cricket ball, or a smaller baseball.

When you bounced them on the pavement, they would make this deep, rubbery 'thunk' then they would fly amazingly high up in the air, which was and is their only purpose, I suspect. Bounce them hard and they would fly so high you could hardly see them until they began their descent. Upon impact, up they'd go again, almost as high as the first time. Admittedly, they could be a little challenging to catch sometimes because the bouncing action would start to take on a life of its own. And, because they bounced so high for so long, they could end up a fair distance from you, over the fence, or lost in the shrubbery. That's how I lost many of mine. But, with all luck, you'd still have your superball at the end of the day.

Let's try a little imaginary experiment. In your mind's eye, take a handful of superballs, maybe five or six. Give them a good bounce on a hard surface. Naturally, they would do what superballs do best and fly high into the air. However, what goes up must come down. As they come in for a landing, the momentum and spin sends them off into five or six different directions at the same time. The third bounce even more and in directions further afield. While they are bouncing to their rubbery heart's content, in your mind's eye, run and catch them. Depending upon how hard you bounced them, how high they went, and in however many directions, that little task could take some time and energy. You may even lose one or two in the process.

Now, try something different. Again, in your mind's eye, take another handful of superballs and, just as with the first experiment, give them a good solid bounce. As in the first case, they bounce high into the air and come in for a second go, then a third. Unlike the first time, do not go in to try and catch them in the act of bouncing. Simply allow the natural order of things to progress. Your whole role is to allow them to bounce. Do nothing but enjoy. What do you think will happen by just letting them be? Eventually, the balls will stop bouncing, of course. Now, in order to get them back simply go and pick them up wherever they landed. Easier? Certainly it is and here is the lesson. If we just let the Universe do what it's supposed to do, it is a lot easier to get hold of those superballs. As we found out, it's hard to catch a bunch of bouncing balls, but with patience, we can obtain the object of our desire with ease.

SUPERBALLS OF DESIRE

Those superballs are a lot like our desires. Most of us have more than one superball in the air at a time; more than one desire we are manifesting in any given moment. That is perfectly normal. I am certainly not going to suggest you focus on just one desire at a time. But, let's take a look at a few truths as they pertain to bouncing superballs and how they relate to our desires.

When asked to catch the balls in the first scenario, you probably envisioned yourself jumping in frantically, scurrying about trying to catch all the bouncing balls at the same time. Even in your mind's eye you can see how frustrating, if not impossible, that would be. Picture yourself dashing around with one eye on the balls in the air, and the other on the ones on the bounce. Grasping here and there in an attempt to catch even one, while the others bounced further away from you and each other. For a lot of us, that is exactly how we approach manifesting our desires. We send our desires into the Universe then we jump in, frantically grasping at our manifestations and most often miss them. We run from one ill-timed grasp to another. Then, we wonder why our results are sparse and why we are exhausted. We wear ourselves out working against the Universal Laws and principles instead of working with them.

In the second scenario, we operated from a different dynamic. We allowed. We let ourselves and the superballs Be. By allowing we could just have fun watching the many different directions each superball took on their ride through space until such time as they stopped bouncing altogether and we could simply go and pick them up. You see, in this second scenario, the joy is in the journey. In this scenario, there is nothing to be frantic about. It's easy to achieve our manifestations if we just let the Universe alone to do Its work. All we have to do is grab hold of our desires and bounce them in the air; send them off. Then our job is to cooperate with the Co-Creative Process.

In the second scenario, we were operating with the Law of Cause and Effect and Law of Action. Our Causes were agreeing with the process that will manifest the Effects. Then there is the Law of Action to work with. When all our balls stop bouncing, when our desires begin to manifest, we still have a job to do. We still have to go and pick them up. It would be inconceivable, however, to believe we could pick them all up at once. We can really only pick up one or two balls at a time. That's just the way this all works. Our role is to Act by participating in activities in support of our Being the one with a half-dozen superballs in our back pocket. Our desires need Action out of us to support their manifestation. The distinction is our Actions are either inspired Action or frantic action. We can act like a hysterical idiot, running around trying to force-catch a bunch of bouncing balls, or we can allow the Universe to do what It is supposed to in the Action of full belief that our superballs will eventually stop bouncing and land.

By thought you can cause the gold in the heart of the mountains to be impelled toward you, but it will not mine itself, refine itself, coin itself into double eagles, and come rolling along the roads, seeking its way into your pocket.

Wallace Wattles[1]

Why do some of us insist on going against what is so obviously the Universe trying to make things easy for us? We want control. We want it now, that's why. We insist on grabbing and grasping when, with a little patience, the Universe hands our desires to us effortlessly. When the time is right, all we have to do is reach down and pick them up, one at a time.

Remember, it is not in the acquiring of our manifested desires where joy and happiness is located. It is the road of Mastery where happiness is found. Also, remember the Law of Action dictates our part in all of this, together with the other Universal Laws. We understand we don't get to fold our arms, blink our eyes and everything we desire magically appears in front of us. We have Action to complete in its various forms. Again, the intentional manifestation of our desires is a Process, and the Laws need us to participate *with* them, not against them, in order for us to be successful, which often takes something not many of us are good at. Patience.

WORKING WITH THE LAWS

By working with the Law of Action, all of our supportive Actions bring us into greater belief and trust which are absolutely necessary to have in order to manifest anything. Belief and trust don't come in an instant. They come with time and activity. Taking Action brings belief one step at a time. This too takes patience.

The Law of Rhythm states that everything vibrates and moves to a specific beat. These beats produce rhythms and cycles for everything in the Universe. Everything has a season. Spring follows winter, summer follows spring, autumn follows summer, and winter follows autumn. The cycle is stable and cannot be altered. Winter can never follow spring. If it did, nothing would ever grow. So too, your manifestations have a cycle; a season. You can't expect a harvest in the autumn if you are sowing your seeds during the same season. Knowing and accepting the Law of Rhythm also takes patience.

The Law of Cause and Effect states every Action, thought or Cause has a reaction or an Effect. Our intentional and unintentional Causes produce intentional or unintentional Effects. These Effects may take some time to manifest leaving a gap or a lag time between the two points, in the physical realm. The Law is sometimes summarised as, "we reap what we sow". Well, it is a Universal truth that a seed sown takes some time to grow to maturity, producing the fruit of our labour. Things need time to grow. Time to grow takes patience. It allows us to cultivate our soil and get rid of stray weeds.

This does not contradict our Mastery of time. Time is relative and the Universe works a certain way as in the following formula we are all so familiar with by now.

Ask and it will be given to you; seek and you will find; knock and the door will be opened to you. For everyone who asks receives; the one who seeks finds; and to the one who knocks, the door will be opened.

Matthew 7:7–8 NIV

This means the desire and its manifestation are already a done deal from a vibrational perspective. It does not say "ask, sit and wait three years and it will be just handed to you; seek and you will find in six months; knock on the door for a decade and hope the door will be opened." It is immediate as long as we are clear and have done our ask and declared our I AM in full belief. However, there is a 5-Step Process in this Co-Creative business. There is generally a lag time to most manifestations. This is where our part comes in; to work with the Process of turning on the lights, gaining clarity and moving and keeping ourselves on the receiving end of things. The Mastery of time is mastering the relative nature of it and to realise a vibrational manifestation is no different from a physical one. The lag time is subject to our Actions in the state of Being the one with the physical manifestation in the Present/Now space. The rest will follow.

With this in mind there are some manifestation gurus out there who promulgate a Law of Gestation. The Law of Gestation simply states that everything takes time to produce. From inception to finished product, from thought to thing, there is a period of linear time that it takes for whatever it may be to mature enough to present itself to the Universe and to us. This includes the manifestation of our desires.

Our manifestations are subject to the Universal Laws just like everything else. Now, since time and space are relative, we can certainly help speed things up if we want to. By participating in Actions with little or no resistance to the belief in the outcome Being Now, the object of our desires tends to come more quickly. If the belief is strong, so is the energy. The stronger the energy, the quicker the Universe responds. In most cases, however, we cannot avoid some sort of lag time, however short or long it may be.

Now, I believe the Law of Gestation is one of those laws that to me, doesn't work well as a law by itself. I believe the Law of Gestation is part of the Process associated with the seemingly empty space between the two points of Cause and Effect. If the gestation period is isolated from the Law of Cause and Effect, it couldn't stand on its own which explains my resistance to calling it a Law. However, it remains that there is almost always a lag time involved with all of our manifestations, and we have to come to terms with that. And, if it helps to stick a Law of Gestation inside the context of the Law of Cause and Effect, go for it. Besides, and once again, it isn't the manifestation of our desires that brings joy and happiness, which is what we are all seeking in the first place. It is Being happy, Being excited for the evolution of the Universe expanding through us. This is Happiness. The desire is just the conduit.

LETTING GO

Even so, we still just love to speed up the whole Process. We would love to pump our desires up with steroids to get a quicker result. I get it. So, another tool to use to this end is to learn to Be OK with the result, or the manifestation of the object, in whatever way it comes – *even* to the point of Being OK with it *not manifesting*. I know that sounds counterintuitive but let's explore the thought a little further.

When we put our ask into the Universe, when we declare its reality, we must do so with faith, trust, belief, or whatever word you wish to use to describe your conviction and confidence that it is manifested. The bigger the belief, the stronger the faith, the bigger and stronger the manifestation. Jesus tried to teach us this a very long time ago. There were many times he said to whomever he was helping manifest the object of their desire, in most cases a healing of some sort, that in accordance with their faith or belief it was done. This is an affirmation of the Law of Correspondence, which basically says whatever measure you use it is measured back. To say you are letting go of the manifestation itself as an exercise of belief, faith, or trust. It is not to say you believe it will not manifest. Rather it is demonstrating your *trust in the Processes of the Universe*. Believe me, it took me a while to get my own head around this one.

In the meantime, letting completely go to that degree is a powerful exercise in trust. Being OK with how it comes and how long it may take, *and in whatever form it may show up* is trust and belief shooting out into the Universe. And, these – faith, trust, belief, conviction, etc. – are powerful vibrations, which as we know trigger the Law of

Attraction in a big way. These are, in fact, the opposite of fear, doubt, and wanting to control the outcome.

Faith, trust, belief, conviction, etc. are all strong feelings and emotions. Fear, doubt, dis-trust, and manipulation are also very strong feelings and emotions. Both are on the same Pole or plane of energy, just on opposite ends, as explained by the Law of Polarity. Any emotion, feeling or state of Being that vibrates strongly gets a strong vibrational kick-back from the Co-Creative Process, regardless of which end of the Pole it lives on. The journey of Being your desires lives on the side of the Pole where faith, trust, belief and conviction live. This comes from knowing we have already manifested our desires in the Present/Now.

Dr Phineas P. Quimby, known as the founder of New Thought, said man is an incarnation of his beliefs. He said that "man is belief expressed". The fastest way to manifest anything is to trust and believe *in the Process*; to trust and believe no matter what, our manifestations as we envisioned, or something even better, is a done deal because if we can keep in mind it is happiness we are seeking *always*, the specific object itself with every last detail is not really necessary.

Sure five million in cash would be awesome, and that may just be the artefact of your desire but a couple of things to think about. Usually with money, as we discussed earlier, the money itself is not the actual desire. It is what the *tool* of money may facilitate. Therefore, if the manifestation of the tool is the specific desire, could manifesting dozens of other resources that could facilitate the same effect as the tool of money be equal or better manifestations of Being? So, it is the mindset of money or other resources, in other words Being that mindset, which opens up a world of possibilities with which the Universe may work. So, you see, letting go of the specific artefact of desire, i.e. the specific amount of money and that it has to be actual money, demonstrates faith and trust in the Processes of the Universe and releases us to Be a much happier Being in the Present/Now.

Our job in this manifestation game is to get clear, do our ask and then monitor ourselves. It is to clean up resistance. It is to work with our Truth, not against it. It is to keep a clean house and notice when we need to dust in the corners. It is to notice when a doubt and fear monster comes knocking on our door. It is to notice when we begin to go off-road and put ourselves right. It is to notice when we start sliding from Being and receiving into asking again, and then gently and quickly move ourselves back on track. Our role is to Be open-minded to all of these things, not to be dictatorial and controlling the way in which things manifest.

This is keeping your will in check. It is checking your willpower, which is trying to force the Universe to your way of doing things and how they should turn out. All of that mess has nothing to do with your job in the Process, so let it go. Have trust, faith, belief and conviction in the Process. This will allow you to just Be in the Present/Now and to actually embody the Beingness of someone with the objects of their manifestations done.

> *When we do this, just trusting the Spirit, and not laying down the particular details of its action – just telling it what we want without dictating how we are to get it – we shall find that things will open out more and more clearly day by day both on the inner and the outer plane.*
>
> Thomas Troward[2]

A Powerful Exercise in Noticing

One of the ways I started getting pretty good at letting go of the outcome and putting full trust in the Process was through the use of a tool I sort of made up as I went along. It serves three purposes, really. The first purpose is to exercise the knowledge that there is no order of difficulty to manifesting anything, big or small. It is just as easy to manifest a barn as it is a bologna sandwich. The second purpose of this exercise is to work on "letting go of the specifics" and trusting the Process. The third purpose is to grow your ability *to notice things manifesting for you regardless of how they show up.*

So, I will share this with you now. Going back to your journal, find a space to keep a record of your manifestations; those which you have already produced. Title it what you wish, but that is what this section will be for. Mine is my Evidence Journal. Then, decide on something random and silly you would like to manifest. The sillier and more random the better, at least to start. This allows you to be as non-attached to the outcome as possible and allows you to get used to seeing whatever it may be manifest in a multitude of ways. Some of mine have been as follows.

I decided to exercise manifesting a pickle. It's silly, but that's just the point. This took two days. Now while I was thinking of an actual pickle, and imagined it would show up as such, it actually showed up much differently. I was cleaning out a pantry cupboard, and way in the back was a big jar of Branston *pickle*, which is a condiment we have here in England. I didn't even know it was there.

I decided to manifest a metal silver-coloured funnel. Rather like the hat the Tin Man wore in *The Wizard of Oz*. This also took two days. It showed up in a documentary story on commercial cheesemaking I randomly turned to whilst looking for something else. The show was filming the cheese-making factory itself and, there it was. An enormous silver coloured funnel.

I wanted to manifest a US quarter; twenty-five cents. I couldn't imagine where I would come up with one here in England, which made it even more fun. It showed up in a comment to a YouTube video someone sent me which literally said, "I found a quarter". This took one day to manifest. The next day, I found an actual quarter in a suitcase I was cleaning out to give to the charity shops.

I decided to manifest a Coca-Cola sign. This showed up on a random Facebook story on something irrelevant to me about the Coca-Cola company. All over the story were Coca-Cola signs. Two days. A white peacock feather showed up in a week in the form of a pair of white, pewter peacock-shaped candle holders I'd had in a cupboard for years and forgotten all about. I just happened to reach into it for something else and there they were.

I decided to manifest a blue feather next. An actual blue feather showed up on my back-terrace table in one day. A snowflake showed up on a grocery market carry bag. A stack of pancakes dripping with butter and syrup showed up as a picture on an old can of whipped cream I was tossing out when I happened to notice them on the label. Then it showed up on the side of a shipping truck an hour later.

A Cupid? He showed up in October on a rerun of an old television show. A Dalmatian? This showed up in a news story I overheard on TV about an archaeological dig off the Dalmatian coast in Croatia. Mary Poppins? She showed up in a bookstore window the next day. One which, by the way, hadn't changed their window display in months.

I know these are all very random things; trivial as a matter of fact. That's just the point. This is an exercise in manifestation, in noticing, and allowing the Universe to provide you with the object of your desires regardless of the form it takes. In most cases, such as the above examples, the object of my desires, however random, showed up as a form of resource versus the specific thing. For most of these items, it was much preferred.

The silly, random nature of this exercise is what it is all about, fuelled by the emotion of fun. Now, this is not contrary to the emotional attachment to the artefact of your desires as we have discussed thus far. We know the Universal Laws are more powerfully stimulated by the highest level of vibration, which comes from the emotional attachment we can muster by Being the one with the object of our desires Now. Furthermore, I realise it may be difficult to muster a huge amount of emotion to attach to a stack of pancakes. However, where the emotion comes from in this exercise is in the fun and the joy of seeing in what way, shape or form the Universe would manifest a stack of pancakes through me. The randomness of the exercise also stretches the non-resistance muscles profoundly. How much resistance could I muster up by desiring to manifest a pickle? Do you see? Here it is again. It's not the stack of flapjacks or the specific artefact of the desire. It is the road to getting there which is the road of Mastery.

Of course, our desires can actually manifest exactly as you want them to, as well. I manifested exactly the £100 I desired one day, which came from a lottery scratch card that had been sitting around on my desk at home for weeks. I'd forgotten it was there. I randomly chose £100 to manifest into my life one morning just for fun and, a few hours later, there it was.

As an exercise, I wrote out a cheque from the Universe for £65,000, addressed it to myself and popped it into the mail. I didn't really *need* £65,000, it was just a number to play with. When it came in the post, I opened the envelope, got all happy about it, placed the cheque from the Universe near my altar and pretty much forgot all about it. Less than three months later, I received $89,000 – or just £65,000 – from a family lawyer in the US; out of the blue. I didn't know it was due or was coming to me. It just manifested into my life.

We also have to allow the Universe to give us what we desire in random ways; sort of random gifts from the Universe too. For example, I really enjoy fresh flowers in the house and there was a time I had forgotten to pick some up on the way home from doing errands. I silently scolded myself determining to pick some up the next day. However, upon arriving home, there on the front porch was a delivery of fresh flowers placed there while I was gone. Now, they weren't for me, they were for someone else entirely. I tried to do the right thing. I tried to get rid of them by calling the florist who delivered them. For two days I went back and forth with this florist until, on the third day, they finally told me I should just keep them. They lasted over a week and I really enjoyed them.

There was the time I manifested two adult-sized scooters. I was walking my dog to the park one morning and I was suddenly passed by what I took to be a father and his daughter on scooters. He had a dad-sized one and she a child-sized one. I remember thinking two things. One was that it never occurred to me that they even made scooters in adult sizes, and two, that it looked like fun and that maybe I would get scooters for my partner and myself one day. Since something like that was low on my list of priorities, that was the last I'd thought about it until the following week.

Out of the blue, two huge boxes were delivered to my house. Inside were two adult-sized scooters in candy apple red, addressed to me. I hadn't mentioned my thought about scooters to anyone and I didn't order them myself. I questioned everyone I knew and they didn't order them. Why would they? I contacted the supplier and they had no record of them. As a result, I couldn't even return them as I wanted to! I was told to just keep them.

So, play with this exercise. Decide what silly, random thing you want to manifest, write it down in your journal, ask for it, be grateful, and then let it go. Just keep your eyes and ears open to the fun of noticing how it may show up for you, and how long it took to do so. You may find that as you do this more often, the lag time between your ask and your manifestation showing up grows shorter and shorter.

Here is a caution about this exercise; like everything else, a caveat. Don't go around searching for the manifestation. Don't go looking in every shop window or at every TV commercial for that slice of buttered toast you are randomly manifesting. Don't go *trying to make it happen*. That's not how it works. It turns the whole exercise into asking. Just decide what you desire to manifest, get clear, then let the Universe do its job and have fun. Your job is to notice, to receive and to Be the one with a freshly manifested slice of buttered toast.

Another other caveat is to be open-minded. As you can see from some of the examples above, not everything manifests exactly the way you are imagining it would and you have to be OK with that. That's part of the exercise itself and, generally speaking, with pretty much everything you are manifesting. It's about noticing how *resources* are showing up in addition to precise manifestations. The actual stack of pancakes on a plate or the dalmatian did not have to manifest in order to *be* manifested. I mean what would I do with an actual dalmatian anyway? The point is, when you are into higher levels of manifestation, when you start to really get this, you may see that your oft-limited thinking as it relates to the specifics of your desires may not actually be the most efficacious result for you. Remember, our thinking and visualising is based in past experience. The Masterful Way is about creating new experiences, which takes a little bit of releasing what our past thinking conjures up for us.

A Perspective on Resources

Resources are a phenomenal gift. There is a famous story of Solomon in which he asks for something of God. Clearly he had thought about this because after offering 1,000 sacrifices on Gods' altar, God appears to Solomon in a dream and tells him he may ask for whatever he wants. Now, Solomon could have asked for money, wealth, riches, victory over his enemies, etc. I think if most of us were asked, we would probably go that route. However, Solomon asks for wisdom, so he may best rule his people. Of course God grants him that and all the other stuff besides. What Solomon basically did was ask for resources beyond the limited scope of a specific manifestation in any form as mentioned above. He asked for ideas; new ways of thinking and Being. He asked for innovation and finding new ways of doing things. He asked for brain power, not bank power. All of these resources, all of that wisdom, would naturally bring about all of the other stuff, one step at a time. A blank cheque from God would have been awesome, but without wisdom on how to use the tool of money properly, it would have vanished in a short time. He asked for something far more useful than riches or power and what he got was all that and more.[3]

Really think about this as it relates to your manifesting anything into your life. Your specifics may be too small for you. Exactly how you desire something to specifically manifest might be just the tip of the iceberg of what could really be your manifested desire. Trying to limit the Universe, to limit God and how It all wants to work through you, puts a noose around the neck of your manifestations. It is an abuse of your willpower as well. Your willpower is best used upon yourself and monitoring what you say and do and what you are putting into the Universal space of your Being. It is not to be used to bend the Universe to your will and your way of doing things.

While most of the examples above are just fun, silly sorts of manifesting doo-dads, it is no different from those things you are actually desiring in your life. As I said by using the example of money. If you are manifesting ten grand and you have it in your head that it has to be in cash, that's all fine and well. It may be, however, the Universe is Co-Creating 20 grand worth of *resources* that could serve your purposes better. You just can't see them for the money signs in your eyeballs. Resources, I might add, *that may or may not include the cash.* But, if you block yourself off to other ways in which your desires can manifest, you will miss a boat-load of other possibilities.

> *When we advance to the conception of the Spirit as containing in itself the ideal of Form as well as of Power, we shall cease from the effort of trying to force things into a particular shape, whether on the inner or the outer plane, and shall be content to trust the inherent harmoniousness or Beauty of the Spirit to produce combinations far in advance of anything that we could have conceived ourselves.*
>
> Thomas Troward[4]

THE TRUTH ABOUT PATIENCE

The third and final heads-up with this game and any other thing you are manifesting brings us right back to the purpose of this chapter. Be patient. However, the idea of Being patient is somewhat the opposite of how most define patience, in my opinion. According to *The Oxford English Dictionary*, the definition of patience is, "The capacity to accept or tolerate delay, problems, or suffering without becoming annoyed or anxious". Well, easier said than done for most of us and it is precisely this idea which gives patience a bad name.

The difficulty with patience lies with how most of us *demonstrate* patience. From this definition it is evident patience is an Action. It is a Cause. Demonstrating patience is an activity in support of Being the physical manifestation of our desires. This is quite the opposite of how most of us think about patience, however. Most of us think about patience as sitting on our hands, waiting for something to happen. *Nothing will ever manifest this way.* It has no Action to it. Patience is Being. Being is doing. Every step you take, every word you speak from the perspective of Being is an Action in support of that Being. Patience requires activity.

The other tripping point having to do with patience lies in the "without becoming annoyed or anxious" bit. Most of us can do it for a little while, but then impatience soon takes over – "the annoyed and anxious" part. We slip in and out of it like waves on a seashore. Furthermore, we approach patience like we are trying to roll a big rock up a steep hill. We get all sweaty and all self-righteous about it, equating patience with persistence, fortitude, grit, stamina and long-suffering. Patience is none of these things.

Here's the truth. Patience is not all that much work, actually. In my opinion, patience… real and true patience… is nothing more nor less than belief, trust, faith and conviction in how the Universal Laws and Processes work. If I have trust and belief that whatever the object of my desire has manifested in the Present/Now, if I have conviction in the Process of how the Universal Laws make all of that work, all I need do is enjoy the *feeling of having it.* The traditional ideas of patience are no longer necessary because what have I to be patient for, in the traditional sense? What do I have to "tolerate" or "suffer" though? It's already done. From this higher-level vibrational perspective, the Cause I am putting out into the Universe is belief. The Effect is that my desire is manifested and the Universe responds to this higher-level vibration by bringing to me the physical manifestation of said desire.

Therefore I tell you, whatever you ask for in prayer, believe that you have received it, and it will be yours.

Mark 11:24 NIV

This is simply trusting in the vibrational manifestation of our desires more than the lack thereof. It is merely pure acceptance of it as fact. It is truly Being at Oneness with the Universe and letting go of control. It is full acknowledgement that our only role is to keep our houses clean, our energies pure, just to notice, have fun and to Be.

So, stop running around frantically chasing a bunch of bouncing balls. If you just stop, notice and have fun with the bounce as one who has Mastered Being the recipient of your desires in the Present/Now space, eventually all you need to do is just reach down and pick them up. Then head on through to your next desire waiting in the wings.

CHAPTER 17

THE MASTERY OF GRATITUDE

I would maintain that thanks are the highest form of thought,
and that gratitude is happiness doubled by wonder.

G.K. Chesterton

As part of a greater syllabus of Universal Laws, other than the
12 spoken of here, there are some who believe there is a little-
referenced law called the Law of Gratitude. I am not sure I can
quite agree with the idea of gratitude being a *Law* in and of itself,
per se, similar to my thinking on the Law of Gestation. In my
opinion, it lands squarely as an *element* associated with all of the
Universal Laws. Particularly as an integral element within the
Actionable Laws.[1]

Gratitude is something to express and, much like patience, it is
expressed through Action. It is the Action of the *giving of thanks*.
While I am certainly not going to stand in the way of anyone who
believes gratitude to be an actual law, on one point we all agree.
Gratitude is a powerful, *powerful* force and one with which Master
manifestors engage as a part of the regular practice of Being.

You cannot exercise much power without gratitude; for it is gratitude that keeps you connected with Power.

Wallace Wattles[2]

The Power of Gratitude

Gratitude is a deep-in-the-core emotional feeling of connection to the Universe, to God and to the Process of Oneness manifesting through you. It is also the means through which the Process of Co-Creation takes place. As a desire is expressed by God through us and we receive it by Being the physical manifestation of said desire, Being grateful connects us to desire in the Present/Now. Gratitude is an Action of affirmation. It says we have already received the artefact of our Co-Creation and are grateful for it regardless of outward appearance.

Having and expressing true gratitude should feel as deeply emotional as sex and love. Having and expressing gratitude should enhance and increase the desire for more of it, and for good reason. Like sex and love, it is a deeply powerful communication experience between the Universal Presence personified through us, our Being, and within the ether of the Oneness of all things, or of God.

Studies are showing that genuine gratitude stimulates the release of the hormone oxytocin, which is the hormone released during sex and which is associated with love, bonding and trust.[3] Gratitude is also linked to increased levels of dopamine, the hormone secreted in the brain that makes us feel good, which further generates positive emotions and drives prosocial behaviour. Dopamine is linked to intrinsic motivation and the achievement of goals regardless of whether they are personal or professional. Furthermore, studies show a state of gratitude gives us a shot of serotonin, which enhances mood, works as an anti-depressant and increases inspiration and willpower. It is also known as the happiness hormone.[4]

From the Being perspective, the perspective of the Universal Laws and of manifesting our desires, I have to believe there is a purpose for gratitude that goes beyond how it makes us feel. Combining all of the emotions described above, those related to them and their impact on us biologically, it certainly seems the Universe has built gratitude into the manifestation mix on purpose.

If we know the basic formula of manifestation, intentional or otherwise, is "ask then receive", and if we know that Being, remaining in and maintaining the receiving state is vital to our success, then we must conclude Being grateful for the physical manifestation of what we have asked puts us and keeps us in this receiving state. There isn't a more powerful suite of emotions than those associated with sex, love, Oneness, bonding, feeling good, happiness, etc. Maintaining a state of gratitude is the medium through which these emotions bond with us, and how together we bond with the Universe, or with God.

Love and Fear

We know the Universal Laws respond to emotions. The stronger the emotion, the faster the Universe responds. This is so regardless of whether the emotion is good or bad; effective or ineffective. One of the strongest primal emotions is fear, only slightly less powerful than the emotion of love, to which gratitude belongs. Most, if not all, of us have experienced a manifestation based in fear that seemed to materialise so fast it made our heads spin. While other manifestations attached to less volatile emotions took somewhat longer to physically manifest. The same is true with strong positive emotions such as gratitude. The state of gratitude is a super-charged emotion that gets super-fast results.

> *Our gratitude liberates an energy within us that immediately expands into the formless substance, where it is instantly returned to us in kind.*
>
> Wallace Wattles

However, it seems for many of us that unintentional, fear-based manifestations are somehow more easily accomplished than those that are more well-intentioned. So why is it that it appears we are better at fearful emotions, while the loving ones of gratitude are more challenging for us? In looking at these powerful emotions, fear and gratitude or love, I believe there are several reasons behind this. Let us take the emotion of fear first.

Fear is what keeps us from danger. It protects us. While some fears are learned behaviours, basic fears such as those of heights, water, bugs, rats, mice, snakes, and spiders for example are fears that help us survive. We are hardwired for basic fear responses. They are close at hand, ready to help us so we don't get into life-threatening situations in the first place. Or, if we do find ourselves in a less than positive situation – God forbid – fear helps us fight it out, or run from it in reaction to it. The fear response doesn't need to be pondered, or thought out. Stopping to think deeply about being torn apart by a fast-approaching carnivore will in fact get you eaten. Running away because you are afraid of it will, hopefully, keep you alive to see another day.

The second reason I believe fear as an emotion is more easily accessed is because we are so used to it in its many forms, the most common of which these days is stress. *Stress and anxiety are forms of fear* and in our modern cultures, they have become a big health problem. The effects of stress on the brain and body are the same as the effects of fear. While short bursts of stress and fear are a good thing under the appropriate circumstances, we are not built to withstand prolonged stress any more than we are to withstand prolonged states of fear.

Fear and stress shut down non-vital bodily functions, such as digestion and our ability to think rationally. It fills our bodies with chemicals that, over time, can cause major damage. Cardiovascular disease, gastrointestinal issues and lower fertility levels, for example, are all linked to higher levels of stress. This in addition to brain damage, memory loss, impaired decision making and poor mental health, just to name a few of the more lovely results associated with stress.

This puts fear, stress, and anxiety at the top of the list of emotions threatening our overall well-being. Yet, in our collective conscious, it is constantly in our space. Put in simple terms, we are just used to fear hanging around which makes it more accessible. So much so that it taints all of our other emotions, thoughts, and feelings.

Have you ever had, or have you found yourself in, a fear-based conversation with someone? A conversation that is, let's just say, heated. In the moment, you may have discovered it was difficult to formulate rational thoughts or to figure out the best, or worst, thing to say. An hour later, however, all of those juicy bits of great things you could have said come rushing in. All of the, "I wish I'd said that's…"? It's because fear stopped the thinking process and replaced it with the only two thoughts it is designed to muster up; fight or flight. After the chemical fear response dies down, rational thinking mostly returns and all of those things you wish you'd said come to the surface.

The third reason I believe fear-based manifestations are, perhaps, more easily achieved is because a lot of fear is sub- or unconscious. In some ways this is for the better. Think about it. The ever-present, conscious awareness of chronic fear would make our heads explode. Therefore, in order to self-preserve, we push it to a different, less conscious level just for the sake of relief. This, however, becomes the bigger problem. In this way, it does not serve us well.

Fear is a powerful emotion, as we have discussed. And, being so, the Universe responds quickly as a result of its powerful vibration, whether conscious or not, which is the real issue. If a lot of fear is sub- or unconscious, we do not and cannot filter that fear through rational thinking, which would help diminish or alleviate its vibrational impact. Unchecked, then, fear-based thoughts continue to send a powerful signal to the Universe which, by Law, responds powerfully. The Law is always impersonal and neutral, but receptive and reactive. It does not and cannot distinguish between a so-called positive emotion and a negative one. It only responds to the vibrational power of said emotion and responds in kind.

The fourth reason is, I believe, a great many of our Maps are fear-based. They protect us from threats, perceived or otherwise. However, our Maps guide our thinking and our living; our Being. We judge people through our Maps as a way of diminishing our exposure to danger. We have fear-based Maps about traffic signals because if we didn't, driving would be very unsafe; not only for us, but for the other folks on the road. We have fear-based Maps about darkness because, after all, you never know what might be lurking there in the shadows. We have fear-based Maps about playing with fire because many a house has been reduced to an ash heap as a result of messing with a matchbook. We have fear-based Maps about sticking our heads into hot ovens for reasons so obvious they don't need explaining. So Maps, being such a part of us and with so many Maps being fear-based, it stands to reason fear is closer at hand.

At its core state, fear is not conscious. It is a reaction, plain and simple; a reflex. We don't need to colour in the lines. It has no "personality", so to speak. It is merely a physical and emotional response to a threat-based stimulus. When the threat is no longer, fear is released. At least that's the way it should work.

Unlike fear as the unconscious reaction to a stimulus, having and expressing gratitude requires a *conscious* effort on our part. While fear is a reaction, gratitude is a pro-action. They are both Causes, which get very different results or Effects. The Cause of fear achieves the Effect of perceived safety or of winning the fight. The Cause of gratitude achieves the Effect of happiness, feeling good, etc.

Gratitude needs to be actively placed upon something or some situation. For most of our manifestations, it takes the Action of belief in our desires. It takes faith and confidence that we are a powerful channel through which the Universe expresses Itself. It takes knowing what is true and what is not regardless of circumstances, and it takes acting from this mindset. This is Mastery.

Being an Action, gratitude and the giving of thanks is a sacrifice of our energy. For example, Mosaic Law has specific guidelines regarding a host of sacrifices on the altar of God. Burnt offerings, guilt offerings, sin offerings, grain offerings and fellowship offerings, or offerings of thankfulness.[5] I believe this last one in particular is showing us a model of behaviour regarding the sacrifice of gratitude.

Any true sacrifice comes at a cost. In the Old Testament, a sacrifice of food, drink or an animal meant the one offering was giving away something that had a personal cost. A sacrifice of an animal, for example, meant the person offering was taking the animal from the finest of their livestock. Livestock in those times meant wealth, power and status. Therefore, the giving of gratitude or of thanks would be sacrificing something more precious than just one of the herd. It needed to come from the finest of the herd; the most precious, as it were.

The giving of thanks or giving of gratitude also must come from the best of our energies. The energies of love, peace, happiness and joy – the most precious energies we possess. As such, it is costly. It is from this place we consciously energise gratitude and give it back into the Universe. It does come at a cost. However, it is a cost that gives back. According to the Law of Compensation, the level of energy we "sacrifice" for our gratitude, or the measure of it, is given back in the form of greater levels of love, peace, happiness and joy. You cannot be truly grateful without these emotions being generated.

Gratitude is a form of love and love is the grandest, most vibrationally sound emotion in the Universe. *Psychology Today* calls love a "force of nature".[6] Like any true force of nature, it cannot be commanded and bent to our will. Love has a will all of its own and is as unpredictable as a lightning strike. Love cannot be used, borrowed, or stolen. Love cannot be bought or sold. Love is free and without boundaries. Love cannot be contained; *it can only be directed*. A Lao Tzu said, "Love is a decision…" It is the purest of energies, and the most powerful energy in the Universe. It is in the space of love, or the mindset of love, into which our desires manifest. This is why it is said that God is love.

Love is patient, love is kind. It does not envy, it does not boast, it is not proud. It does not dishonour others, it is not self-seeking, it is not easily angered, it keeps no record of wrongs. Love does not delight in evil but rejoices with the truth. It always protects, always trusts, always hopes, always perseveres... And now these three remain: faith, hope and love. But the greatest of these is love.

I Corinthians 13:4–7; 13 NIV

Love is both masculine and feminine energy. Masculine because love is given and feminine because it is also received. Both giving and receiving are necessary in order for love to "work", essentially. Love cannot function without being loved back and gratitude is the communication tool of that mutual lovemaking.

Science Daily describes the emotion of love as residing in a place in the brain called the striatum.[7] This area collects the feel-good chemicals of dopamine and serotonin, which are associated with motor and reward systems. The striatum, and its surrounding area of the ganglia, facilitate voluntary movement or Action particularly as it relates to goals, or in our terms, our desired manifestations. Additionally, these selected movements or Actions help us achieve our goals. At the same time this area of the brain hinders actions that are opposed to their achievement.[8] Therefore, a mindset or a state of gratitude greatly enhances the facilitation or the manifestation of our desires and it does so in the Present/Now. This is powerful stuff.

Concordia University defines love as a *process of conditioning*; a habit formed of sexual desire and the reward of that desire in that part of the brain. Clinically speaking this is fascinating. Looked at through the lens of our manifestation language, through our understanding of God, the Universe and so on, it brings a whole new meaning to the clinical side of things as described above.

Of particular interest is the use of the word "process" to describe love. Love is a process of conditioning, of desire being rewarded. It is rewarded with feeling good, feeling happy, bonding etc., all of the emotions associated with sexual gratification. In chapter two, we discussed God as also Being a Process of evolving, growing, and expressing more of Itself, through Itself and with Itself. It does so through desire within us. Desire is God creating an impulse to express through us and, inasmuch as we and God are made of the same stuff, we Co-Create with the Process of God expanding. It makes sense that if God is love, both love and God would be considered a Process of creation.

THE PROCESS OF LOVE

God is a Process of love and desire expanding and expressing Itself through us. Gratitude for the desire itself is also a process of love directly communicating love back to the Universal Source. Being truly, deeply grateful puts us in an emotional state of Being that is akin to the feel-good state into which love and sex puts us. The result is a chemical release in the brain that produces happiness, Oneness and a deep bonding with God as well as the voluntary Actions in support of our desires. This further shoots a very strong vibrational charge into the Universe, which reacts to it by attracting the object of desire to us. In the meantime, a state of gratitude continually feeds us what we are ultimately seeking through the desire, which is happiness, joy, peace, and all the other feel-good emotions. In other words, the Action of expressing gratitude is a Cause producing a vibrational output to which the Universe responds with the Effect of happiness. This results in more to be grateful for moving towards you in direct proportion to how much gratitude you put out there; the Law of Correspondence. With whatever measure you use, it will be measured to you.

Gratitude can only take place in the Present/Now. You cannot be truly grateful for something manifesting in a future state. Nor can you be truly grateful for where you have already been. The past no longer exists and the future hasn't happened. Yet, the future is where we tend to place the physical manifestation of our desires. This does not work. The future is too abstract a concept for the chemical reaction in the brain to work effectively. Without this reaction, the powerful emotions of which we spoke are not generated and neither are the Actions thereof. Therefore, things slow down or stop drawing themselves to you completely. This is why happiness is found *on the road of Mastery*. It is on the journey where happiness resulting from the manifestation of your desires is found, regardless of its physical appearance, and not with the artefact itself.

Gratitude puts us and keeps us in the feminine state of receiving, allowing the masculine state of delivering the object or artefacts of our manifestations unobstructed. Therefore, the state of gratitude, or the atmosphere of Being is ultimately the thing we are seeking. It is through this atmosphere, the objects of desire are made manifest.

> *"First, you believe that there is one intelligent substance, from which all things proceed. Second, you believe that this substance gives you everything you desire. And third, you relate yourself to it by a feeling of deep and profound gratitude.*
>
> Wallace Wattles[2]

Gratitude builds faith and strengthens belief, which are vital to the success of our Being. Faith and belief are the most necessary tools in our manifestational toolbox. Without faith, it is impossible to work effectively with the Universal Laws.[9] Through faith and belief our perception of what is unseen is seen, and the non-physical becomes "reality" for us regardless of what appears to be physical.

Fear and Doubt

Now, as love and gratitude are interchangeable, so are fear and doubt. In previous chapters I have discussed the enemy of any manifestation effort as being doubt itself. I am convinced doubt is, in fact, the Devil. A doubt is a lie trying to convince you that your Being, the one with all of your desires manifested, is the liar, not the other way around. Doubt is a fast-growing weed in our otherwise fertile soil that is certain to choke out any possibility of producing a desired harvest.

Most of us have had enough experience with doubt and fear to know how fast the smallest spark of doubt can grow into a raging inferno. And, we know the reason behind this is because doubt and fear are vibrationally powerful. So, the Universe brings more of it on a fast track, which gains momentum quickly. This is why it is so vitally important to nip doubt in the bud the very second it starts to appear.

As we have seen from previous chapters, one of the best examples of this bud-nipping appears just after the apostle Peter makes a declaration about the nature of the man Jesus. Jesus begins to explain to all of the disciples what his upcoming final end in Jerusalem would be. Peter had a visceral reaction to this news.

> *Peter took him aside and began to rebuke him. "Never, Lord!" he said. "This shall never happen to you!" Jesus turned and said to Peter, "Get behind me, Satan! You are a stumbling block to me; you do not have in mind the concerns of God, but merely human concerns."*
>
> Matthew 16:22–23 NIV

What Jesus did in the example above was to allow absolutely no time for doubt and fear to fester in any way. He pulled the weed from the garden and pulled it out fast. This is an example we should follow for ourselves. When doubt and fear begin to show up, particularly as it relates to the house of our Being and our manifestations, get rid of it fast.

The best, most effective force against doubt and fear is love and gratitude. In a true state of gratitude and love, doubt cannot creep in. By creating an atmosphere of gratitude and Being in it always, you produce the most fertile ground in the Universe for manifesting your desires and doing so rather quickly. Conversely, in an atmosphere of fear and doubt, desire is lost, love wanes and gratitude fades.

> *There is no fear in love. But perfect love drives out fear, because fear has to do with punishment. The one who fears is not made perfect in love.*
>
> I John 4:18 NIV

In other words, the one who has doubt and fear will be unable to manifest their desires because fear and doubt crowd up the perfect energy space of love. Fear and doubt only succeed in manifesting more fear and doubt. The opposite is also true. Fear cannot take hold in a space filled with love and gratitude. It is in this space where all energies become focused on the manifestation of more desires expanding and expressing the Universe. The more desire, the more avenues for happiness and joy; the more love. Keep your desires always before you and Being grateful for them in the Present/Now.

GRATITUDE AS PART OF THE PROCESS

The Bible records five instances whereby Jesus gave thanks; in other words, when he outwardly pronounced the condition of his inner state of gratitude. I don't believe these instances are the only times he was publicly grateful. Given the circumstances surrounding these incidences, it indicates he had a condition of serial gratitude. However, it is interesting to examine the circumstances surrounding these five references.

The first is recorded both in Luke and Matthew.[10] In Luke, however, we get a more detailed picture of what surrounded the event, so we will use that reference specifically. Jesus had sent seventy-two deputy disciples out to do a little preaching. They came back with some very positive reports for which they and everyone else concerned were very happy. Filled with joy, Jesus burst out with a big helping of gratitude, as well as a little revelation about how the manifestation process works through faith and belief.

> ... I praise you, Father, Lord of heaven and earth, because you have hidden these things from the wise and learned, and revealed them to little children.
>
> Luke 10:21 NIV

While gratitude is certainly evident in this verse, it also drops a hint as to how manifestation works. As a sort of sidebar, he said the wise and learned usually "wise" themselves out of belief. Those who supposedly "know better" are those who often *know too much* to allow for the Process of manifestation, as we know it, to work for them. They lead with doubt instead of faith.

The second reference is recorded in John.[11] As Jesus' popularity grew, so did the crowds of people who followed him around. It is recorded in this reference, 5,000 men – not including women and children – made up this particular mass of people. Knowing they would be hungry, Jesus asked his disciples what they could feed the crowd. One of his disciples found a boy who seemed to be the only one prepared with a boxed lunch; a few loaves of bread and a couple of fish. Jesus took the loaves and fish, I am sure with permission, and before distributing to the crowd he gave thanks for it and, I assume, the boy who donated his lunch to feed them. Incidentally, the story mentions there was a lot of food left over. Twelve baskets full to be precise.

The next recorded incident was when Jesus went to visit his good friends Mary, Martha, and their brother Lazarus.[12] A short time before, Jesus had received word Lazarus had fallen ill. Whether by circumstance or by intention, he was delayed in his visit. When he did finally get to the home of the three siblings, it was too late. Lazarus had passed away and had been buried four days prior.

In perhaps one of the most famous miracles attributed to Jesus, he raised Lazarus from the dead with a loud shout. "Lazarus, come out!" Before he pronounced this command, however, it is recorded that he thanked God for always hearing him no matter what the circumstances. He essentially affirmed his belief in himself though a grateful attitude. He increased his own faith.

The remaining two recordings of gratitude were at the last supper, just before his crucifixion by the Romans. He gave thanks for the bread and the wine, which would become the symbols of communion and unity with God still used to this day in most Christian denominations.[13]

While the first incident reveals a heart full of gratitude expressed as the result of a welling up from deep inside, the remaining four occurrences seem to have come before big, miraculous events. Now, there is no order of difficulty in the miraculous, nor in manifestation. As *A Course in Miracles* aptly positions in the first line of the first chapter...

> *There is no order of difficulty in miracles. One is not "harder" or "bigger" than another. They are all the same. All expressions of love are maximal.*
>
> A Course in Miracles[14]

In other words, it is just as easy to manifest a stick of gum as it is to feed an army on one can of beans. Miracles are miracles; manifestations are manifestations. What is interesting, however, is how gratitude was expressed as a *part of the process* of manifesting Jesus' desires.

I firmly believe Jesus expressed gratitude as a natural state of his Being. I also believe the expressions of gratitude were used as a sort of tool to reaffirm his belief and faith in what was about to happen from a miracles perspective. In his heart and mind the "miracle" had already occurred in the Present/Now. His giving of thanks was an acknowledgement of the fact of its physical manifestation, particularly as recoded in the raising of Lazarus from the dead.

> *Father, I thank you that you have heard me. I knew that you always hear me...*
>
> John 11:41–42 NIV

The way the expression of gratitude is worded clearly indicates that in his mind, in his truth, Lazarus rising from the dead had already manifested and he was expressing his gratitude for it. As a result, this powerful energy caused Lazarus to walk out of his own tomb, wrapped in funerary bandages from head to foot.

So, we can see that gratitude is an important piece of the manifestation pie. Through the examples above, we can understand how much more powerful gratitude, or love, is over fear and doubt. It would seem, then, that we would be better at gratitude than fear, but this is mostly not the case. The simple fact is that gratitude, in our modern culture, is tough to come by.

OBSTACLES TO GRATITUDE

In an article written for *Psychology Today* called "Why Gratitude Is So Hard", the author calls gratitude a "diminishing virtue in modern times".[15] In a society as consumer-driven as ours, our focus has been deeply trained on what we do not have, against what others do have. Then, we strive to get what others have in the vain hope that by acquiring it we will be happier. This is what trips most people up. As has been said many times in this book, it is not the acquiring of the artefact of desire where happiness is found. It is the road of Mastery, of manifesting it, because once desire has been given life, the artefact has already manifested vibrationally and therefore we can find the joy in the Present/Now by Being; by Mastery.

Another obstacle to gratitude is human nature. Some believe that the human characteristics of striving for more and better, the drive for control of one's destiny and the need to compete due to a perceived lack of resources, biologically blocks gratitude from being a natural virtue. While I am not quite certain this is entirely true, I do believe we, the collective "we", are way out of gratitude shape; badly out of practice.

This is evidenced by the use of the word *gratitude* itself. It is a declining word in our collective lexicon. The use of the term gratitude, in both British and American English, in written texts has fallen dramatically within the period between 1800 to around 2008; a drop of about 350 per cent.[16] This means that within a 200-plus year timeframe, the word gratitude has begun an exit from written English and, by implication, from our spoken language as well. That is a telling figure, in my opinion. While there is some hope, as the use of the word has begun to take a slight uptick, it is no wonder deep and true gratitude is difficult to muster up these days in spite of its health and social benefits.

In Buddhism, gratitude is considered a habit to be cultivated as an attitude of mind. This frees us from conditions, good or bad, and keeps us from becoming victim to circumstance. The Buddha said a lack of gratitude is a sure sign of a lack of integrity. According to Buddhist practice, gratitude further teaches patience. Whereas our modern, consumer-focused culture demands instant gratification, the practice of gratitude slows down the need for immediate results, favouring instead what can be had in the Present/Now. Therefore gratitude is the opposite of greed and envy, which are usually born from the space of lack, perceived or otherwise.

Gratitude is deeply linked with the Law of Divine Oneness. A lack of gratitude breaks this Law. It is broken through the ideas and actions related to competition. If everything is seen as separate from everything else, including us, then everyone's need starts a competition with everyone else's. This leads to a "looking out for number one" mindset, which produces actions in violation of the Law. Gratitude is the antidote to separatist thinking. It dismisses competition and reaffirms the unity and Oneness of all things as gratitude appreciates all things as they exist in the Present/Now regardless of physical appearance.

Being grateful keeps us in the space of receiving. The Law of Polarity highlights both what we desire and its opposite. If we find ourselves focusing on what we don't have, or the opposite of gratitude, the Law of Attraction will keep us on the "what we don't have" side of the pole. Gratitude for what we have Now, from the perspective of desire, completely dissolves the "what we don't have" extreme. Furthermore, gratitude for what we desire, and its subsequent manifestation, creates a vibrational fast-track to the opposite side of the pole and the Universe will respond in kind.

Exercising Gratitude

If you do not already have a practice such as Buddhism, or prayer, or meditation through which to exercise gratefulness, I would strongly suggest starting one. I'm not saying you have to take up a religion or join an ashram. There are many ways of practising gratitude and working towards building a *habit* of it, an atmosphere, or a mindset. This is what the Bible means when it tells us to "pray without ceasing". It is the constant state of gratitude and thanks that you not only have the objects of your desires already, but also for the things you already have physically manifested into your life. A constant state of gratitude is a sacrifice of energy, certainly, but it is one that is well spent.

The Universe is an abundant place. This is a statement of what is true and as the truth, then, we have to believe it rewards those who are intentionally, actively and continually grateful for what it provides as we Co-Create and expand It together. I believe an attitude of gratitude is a wonderful thing. I further believe that making a *habit* of gratitude that is so deeply ingrained that it becomes a constant, 24/7 vibrational communication with the Universe, is a force unstoppable. As with any habit, it takes some time to form a neural pathway. Therefore, having several gratitude exercises in our toolbox will help train ourselves towards this end. I would like to share a few that I use regularly. I am not exclusive to just one at a time. I usually engage with several.

A gratitude journal is a very useful tool because it works to grow your awareness of little things to be grateful for on a daily basis. Make it a goal to find *at least* three things per day for which to express gratitude and write them down in your journal. It is best to do this when you are not multitasking yourself to death. Rather take a few quiet moments to be truly grateful for whatever it is you are journaling. Remember it is not the thing itself for which you are expressing gratitude, but the feeling of gratitude the thing elicits within you. Therefore, rushing through this exercise will not serve you well, if at all.

I begin my daily Buddhist practice by spending several minutes with my gratitude journal. Since I usually practise quite early in the morning, I sometimes think about the day before and write down those things that happened to me for which I am grateful. It doesn't have to be the big, boffo things or events either. Of course we should be, and are, grateful for those juicy, big-ticket items. However, I would encourage you to find the more subtle things for this exercise. Training yourself to look for little things really works out your gratitude muscles. It could be gratefulness for your warm bath or shower. Or, that your car started in the cold morning frost. Or, that you found some spare change in the coat you wore last winter. It could even be that you are grateful to be keeping a gratitude journal in the first place.

I would assume that if you are reading this book, you have some sort of list of desires you are manifesting into your Being. It could be a vision board or box of business. It could be a desire journal or other such tool. Take some time each day, fifteen minutes or so at minimum, to go through your desires and express gratitude for their having manifested. These desires are evidence of the Universe requesting expansion through you. That said, your desires have manifested. Give thanks! Let the feelings of gratitude flow through you. This is your love-talk between the Universe and your Being. Give it your undivided attention for that fifteen-minute interval of time, or more.

As always, the only caveat to performing this exercise is to be fully aware of *not* turning it into an exercise in asking. Approaching it with the firm belief in the physical manifestation of the object will keep you in the receiving mode. If you find yourself drifting into asking, call yourself back into gratitude for your desired outcome. If nothing else, be grateful for the desire itself. It is, after all, evidence of God desiring to express and experience having it through you. Think of it as a divine act, then be deeply, truly grateful for it.

Another exercise which I enjoy working with is an adaptation of a mirror technique. Get yourself in front of a mirror, full-length if possible. Look yourself in the eyes and tell your reflection how grateful you are for the Being you see there. Tell your Being how grateful you are for what you have already manifested. Tell your Being how grateful you are for what you are manifesting in the Present/Now. Tell your Being how grateful you are for the experience of Being you, and that you are Co-Creating the desires of the Universe. Be grateful for your success. Be grateful for every wart and freckle and that you alone are a purely unique expression of Divine Oneness. Try doing this at least once per day. I find it helpful to do this when I am dressing in the morning, only because the wardrobe has a full-length mirror on it. In addition to just that practical aspect, practising this exercise at that time of day helps to powerfully set the tone for the rest of it.

An exercise I like to perform is to do a walkabout of gratitude. It may sound silly but in keeping with the theme of building a habit of gratitude, this exercise will help train your noticing muscles to be on full alert for things to be grateful for. Walk around your house and wherever your eyes land, be grateful for whatever it is they landed upon. A picture, a mug, a pencil, a plant, a plate, it doesn't matter. Just exercise gratefulness for whatever it may be. Then extend beyond just the stuff. Be grateful for your home itself; for your neighbours, the postman, the rubbish collectors. Be grateful for your street, your car, your pets. Be grateful for your job and your co-workers and boss, whether or not you particularly like them.

You can take this outside as well. Be grateful for the weather, the sun, the moon, the chill in the air. Be grateful for the seasons, the sounds of the birds, the soft patter of rain. When you drive to work, notice and be grateful for the trees and shrubs that line the roads. Be grateful for the commute itself, for providing the opportunity to see those trees in that exact place on that particular road. Be grateful for the road, too. You can even be grateful for the traffic because it allows you time to sit in it and practise being grateful.

Other activities that will help build a habit of gratitude include making it a point to send a thank-you note to someone once a month. Or, if you have a family, make gratitude a family project and put up a gratitude wall in your home somewhere. Every member of the family puts a note on the wall in gratitude for something that happened to them during the day, or for something another family member did or how they made them feel. Post-it notes work well for this. Have fun with it.

There are all kinds of smartphone apps these days that can help train you to be more grateful. Pull out your phone and give them a try to see which one works best for you. You can even set reminders throughout the day to stop for thirty seconds and be grateful. I have used an app or two for this purpose and it really helped me slow down for a moment to put myself back into a state of gratitude, especially when my day got a little hectic.

Also, remember to be grateful not for just the good stuff but the things that otherwise would be a challenge or a problem for you. When you are met with a bump on the road, be grateful for it if for no other reason than it is exercising your gratitude muscles. A bump or a snag is an opportunity to notice and to manifest living without it. Being grateful for those snags, big or small, is the quickest way towards their resolution, and in so doing you up your gratitude game significantly.

While I am still not convinced that gratitude is an outright Law, it is clear how important the role of gratitude is to our road of Mastery. It is the key to Being. It is the key to unlocking happiness in the Present/Now. It is the fuel that accelerates our desired outcomes. Most importantly, it is packed with health benefits biologically, physiologically, and psychologically. This is not new news, by the way.

Finally... whatever is true, whatever is noble, whatever is right, whatever is pure, whatever is lovely, whatever is admirable – if

anything is excellent or praiseworthy – think about such things…
And the God of Peace will be with you.

Philippians 4:8–9 NIV

In other words, find all kinds of ways and things to be grateful for, for your Being's sake. Be in a constant space of gratitude. Then, the Law of Divine Oneness, or the God of Peace, will be with you, of you and for you. When you speak the language of the Divine Universe through gratitude, you cannot help but notice how differently things start to show up for you and how differently happy you will feel. Which, by the way, is the goal of everything. It is The Masterful Way.

AFTERWORD

In keeping with the tone of the last chapter, I would like to express my gratitude to you for reading this first volume of *The Masterful Way*. I am grateful for your journey of Mastery because the stronger you are, the more Well-Manifested your Being, the more we all benefit. You are the Light of the World. You make the journey much lighter and brighter for the rest of us by the truth of your Being.

As stated in the foreword, my intention for this work is to provide you with insights, tools and exercises to assist you in better understanding how to work with the 12 Universal Laws, the 5-Step Process and, of course, to make it easier to manifest your true desires. Desire is the heartbeat of the Universe. We stand at the borderland of the evolution of the expansion of God. Through us, the Process that is God Co-Creates more of Itself with each experience of manifesting that which is desired. Desire is a divine act and my desire is that you have been able to take something from this book and engage with it to better facilitate your divinity; the deepening of your understanding of what you have to say.

It isn't the easiest job to get out of your own way. We have spent a great deal of time and energy practising how to get in our own way so naturally, it will take some practice to un-learn. It will take exercising the proper use of your willpower over yourself to keep from slipping out of receiving into asking. It will take time and effort to gain clarity on your desires and why you desire them. It will take diligence to clean your house, to work your soil and to ditch that which is too small for your Being. It will take a healthy dose of noticing when a monster or phantom tries to steal the energy away from your Being and to put it in its proper place. Be patient with yourself and fear not.

Those of us who are Being are those who are inspiring and inspired. The more your Being shines through, the more people, situations and opportunities will be drawn to you. Your personal, unique atmosphere will call to them through Actual Truth. Teach them what you know. We are all the Oneness of each other. Let your light shine and teach others how to do so. We all benefit.

Being is a Journey of The Masterful Way. Wisdom is the key. Know this, however. True wisdom of The Masterful Way is operating with the understanding that The Way is never ending. It is the road OF Mastery, not the road TO Mastery. Be a student OF Mastery making each step one of brilliant achievement; a marvellous manifestation of the Universe.

Take Action on every desire. Each desire is the Universe seeking expression through that which is your Being. Each desire is the journey. The goal is to know your Being more than your You; your present more than your past. One important thing to keep in mind. Remember, the journey of Mastery has no destination point. Be a student of your Well-Intended life. Be diligent. Master your Being and you have Mastered the Way.

How may one get to know oneself? Never by contemplation, only, indeed, by action. Seek to do your duty, and you will know at once how it is with you.

Goethe

So, I will end this volume with the same statements and questions with which it began…

Begin the journey of Being a life of intention. Do it for yourself and no one else. Do it through yourself and no one else. Believe me, we will all benefit. We are all One energy. Now get busy, get out of your own way and Master the Co-Creative Process of Being. What are you stumbling over? What is slowing you down and keeping you from Being? More importantly, what do you truly desire? Turn on the lights and ask yourself, "What do I have to say?"

Reading List

Thank you for reading *The Masterful Way* – Volume One. Below is a list of books to further enhance your Journey of Mastery, many of which have influenced this work.

Becoming Supernatural: How Common People Are Doing the Uncommon. By Dr Joe Dispenza.

The Complete Wallace D. Wattles, 9 Books. Timeless Wisdom Collection.

A Course in Miracles, Second Edition. By The Foundation for Inner Peace.

The Edinburgh Lectures and The Dore Lectures. By Thomas Troward.

The Hidden Power: And Other Papers Upon Mental Science. By Thomas Troward

The Holy Bible. By Various Authors and by Various Means.

The Power of Now: A Guide to Spiritual Enlightenment. By Eckhart Tolle.

The Power of Your Subconscious Mind. By Dr Joseph Murphy

The Science of Being Great. By Wallace D. Wattles.

The Science of Getting Rich. By Wallace D. Wattles.

The Science of Mind: A Philosophy, A Faith, A Way of Life. The Definitive Edition. By Ernest Holmes.

ENDNOTES

Chapter 1

1. This idea comes from Craig Beck who is a personal development author.
2. Troward, T. (2012). *The Hidden Power and Other Papers on Mental Science*. Cranston, OH. Angelnook Publishing.

Chapter 2

1. Being – Wickiwand
2. Paulo Coelho (1947–). *The Alchemist.* Paulo Coelho is a Brazilian writer and poet.
3. Matthew 5:45 NIV
4. These two statements are attributed to Phineas Quimby, a nineteenth-century teacher and inventor widely believed to have been the founder of the New Thought Movement.
I5. Thessalonians 5:16–18 NIV

Chapter 3

1. Wattles, W.D. (1910). *The Science of Getting Rich*. Elizabeth Towne Publishing. New York, NY. The original work is now in public domain. For a reference work, please see, *The Complete Wallace D. Wattles, 9 books* (2016). Timeless Wisdom Collection.
2. https://etymonline.com/word/desire.

3. Qahtani, M. 2015 World Champion, Toastmasters International.
4. Oxford Living Dictionary
5. Paulo Coelho (1947–). *The Alchemist*. Paulo Coelho is a Brazilian writer and poet.
6. John 14:10 NLT
7. Murphy, J. (1964). *The Miracle of Mind Dynamics*. New York, NY. Prentice Hall Press. The Penguin Group. Publisher requested to contact Jean. L. Murphy Revocable Trust, and provided address. Request letter returned as "Attempted Not Known".
8. Dandapani is a Hindu priest, speaker and entrepreneur.
9. From the book *Way of the Peaceful Warrior*. Revised Edition Copyright © 2000 by Dan Millman. Reprinted with permission New World Library, Novato, CA. www.newworldlibrary.com.

Chapter 4

1. Hebrews 13:8 NIV
2. There are several references in the Bible whereby Jesus concluded a segment of teaching with this phrase. It is my personal belief he was asking his listeners to let the Universal truths guide their understanding to a greater level of spiritual evolution.
3. Matthew 4:3–9; Luke 4:3–11 NIV
4. John 20:26–29 NIV
5. Holmes, E. (1998). *The Science of Mind*. New York, NY: Jeremy P. Tarcher/Putnam. Used with permission.

Chapter 5

1. Tolle, E. (1999). *The Power of Now; A guide to spiritual enlightenment*. London, England. Hodder & Stoughton Ltd.
2. Troward, T. (2012). *The Hidden Power and Other Papers on Mental Science*. Cranston, OH. Angelnook Publishing.
3. Dispenza, J. (2017). *Becoming Supernatural*. Carlsbad, CA. Hay House.
4. Wattles, W.D. (1910). *The Science of Getting Rich*. Elizabeth Towne Publishing. New York, NY. The original work is now in public domain. For a reference work, please see *The Complete Wallace D. Wattles, 9 books* (2016). Timeless Wisdom Collection.
5. Holmes, E. (1998). *The Science of Mind*. New York, NY: Jeremy P. Tarcher/Putnam. Used with permission.

6. Troward, T. (1904). *Edinburgh Lectures* and (1909) *Dore Lectures at the Dore Gallery, London.* The original works are now in public domain. For a reference work, see *Edinburgh Lectures & Dore Lectures on Mental Science.* Scotts Valley, California.

Chapter 6

1. Hosea 2:16 NIV
2. Troward, T. (1904). *Edinburgh Lectures* and (1909) *Dore Lectures at the Dore Gallery London.* The original works are now in public domain. For a reference work, see *Edinburgh Lectures & Dore Lectures on Mental Science.* Scotts Valley, California.
3. Hill, N. (2003). *Think and Grow Rich.* New York, NY. Jeremy P. Tarcher/ Putnam. Used with permission.
4. The original quote regarding your changing biology is from Dr Joe Dispenza who has done and continues to do great work with how the brain functions in relation to Being. See suggested reading list.
5. Wattles, W.D. (1910). *The Science of Getting Rich.* Elizabeth Towne Publishing. New York, NY. The original work is now in public domain. For a reference work, please see *The Complete Wallace D. Wattles, 9 Books* (2016). Timeless Wisdom Collection.

Chapter 7

1. Bock, J. (Music) & Harnick, S. (Lyrics). (1964). *Fiddler on the Roof.*
2. Davis, G. (2014). *Becoming Magic.*
3. Holmes, E. (1998). *The Science of Mind.* New York, NY: Jeremy P. Tarcher/Putnam. Used with permission.
4. Murphy, J. (2006). *How to Attract Money* (Revised Edition). Milton Keynes, UK. BN Publishing. Used with permission.
5. Troward, T. (1904). *Edinburgh Lectures* and (1909) *Dore Lectures at the Dore Gallery London.* The original works are now in public domain. For a reference work, see *Edinburgh Lectures & Dore Lectures on Mental Science.* Scotts Valley, California.

Chapter 8

1. Wattles, W.D. (1910). *The Science of Getting Rich.* Elizabeth Towne Publishing. New York, NY. The original work is now in public domain.

For a reference work, please see *The Complete Wallace D. Wattles, 9 books* (2016). Timeless Wisdom Collection.

2. Sinek, S. (2006). *Start with Why; How Great Leaders Inspire Everyone to Take Action.* London, England. Penguin Books, Ltd.

3. Davis, G. (2015). *Becoming Rich; A Method for Manifesting Exceptional Wealth.*Chapter 9

4. Holmes, E. (1998). *The Science of Mind.* New York, NY: Jeremy P. Tarcher/Putnam. Used with permission.

5. Wattles, W.D. (1910). *The Science of Being Great.* Elizabeth Towne Publishing. New York, NY. The original work is now in public domain. For a reference work, please see *The Complete Wallace D. Wattles, 9 books* (2016). Timeless Wisdom Collection.

6. Troward, T. (2012). *The Hidden Power and Other Papers on Mental Science.* Cranston, OH. Angelnook Publishing.

7. Dispenza, J. (2017). *Becoming Supernatural.* Carlsbad, CA. Hay House, Inc.

8. Charlie Gorkin.

9. Luke 17:21 NIV

10. Troward, T. (1904). *Edinburgh Lectures* and (1909) *Dore Lectures at the Dore Gallery London.* The original works are now in public domain. For a reference work, see *Edinburgh Lectures & Dore Lectures on Mental Science.* Scotts Valley, California.

11. Murphy, J. (2006). *How to Attract Money* (Revised Edition). Milton Keynes, UK. BN Publishing. Used with permission.

Chapter 10

1. Holmes, E. (1998). *The Science of Mind.* New York, NY: Jeremy P. Tarcher/Putnam. Used with permission.

2. Matthew 4:1–11, Mark 1:12–13, Luke 4:1–13 NIV

3. Matthew Chapters 5–7 NIV

4. Luke 3:23 NIV

Chapter 11

1. Foundation for Inner Peace (1975). *A Course in Miracles.* (T-1.VI.9:5–7, 13–14). New York, NY. The Penguin Group. Used with permission.

2. Reprinted from *Living The Science Of Mind* by Ernest Holmes. DeVorss Publications 9780875166278. Used with permission.

3. Holmes, E. (1998). *The Science of Mind*. New York, NY: Jeremy P. Tarcher/Putnam. Used with permission.

4. Murphy, J. (2006). *How to Attract Money* (Revised Edition). Milton Keynes, UK. BN Publishing. Used with permission.

5. Cochran, K. (2013, 23 December). *Ghost Stories; Why the Victorians Were So Spookily Good at Them*. Retrieved from https://www.theguardian.com/books/2013/dec/23/ghost-stories-victorians-spookily-good

Chapter 12

1. Thank you Sue Lee.

2. Wattles, W.D. (1910). *The Science of Being Great*. Elizabeth Towne Publishing. New York, NY. The original work is now in public domain. For a reference work, please see *The Complete Wallace D. Wattles, 9 books* (2016). Timeless Wisdom Collection.

3. Foundation for Inner Peace (1975). *A Course in Miracles*. (T-5.VI.2:1–2). New York, NY. The Penguin Group. Used with permission.

4. Skye, Tehya (2013, 24 September). 'Why Wanting Doesn't Work and Desire Does'. https://www.ramdass.org/wanting-doesnt-work-desire/

Chapter 13

1. Sifferliln, A. (2014, 6 August). 'Our Brains Immediately Judge People'. *Time Health*. http://time.com/3083667/brain-trustworthiness/

2. Streep, P. (2014, 19 August). '3 more things you didn't realize about how your brain works'. *Psychology Today*. Retrieved from https://www.psychologytoday.com/gb/blog/tech-support/201408/3-more-things-you-didnt-realize-about-how-your-brain-works

3. Shakespeare, W. (1564–1616). *Hamlet*, Act 2, Scene 2.

4. Matthew 12:34 NIV

5. Holmes, E. (1998). *The Science of Mind*. New York, NY: Jeremy P. Tarcher/Putnam. Used with permission.

Chapter 14

1. Dictionary.com

2. Cambridge Online Dictionary

3. *Collins English Dictionary*

4. Acts 10:34 NIV

5. Matthew 5:45 NIV

6. Wattles, W.D. (1910). *The Science of Getting Rich*. Elizabeth Towne Publishing. New York, NY. The original work is now in public domain. For a reference work, please see *The Complete Wallace D. Wattles, 9 books* (2016). Timeless Wisdom Collection.
7. Holmes, E. (1998). *The Science of Mind*. New York, NY: Jeremy P. Tarcher/Putnam. Used with permission.
8. Foundation for Inner Peace (1975). *A Course in Miracles*. (W-71.10:3–4). New York, NY. The Penguin Group. Used with permission.
9. Mark 12:31 NIV
10. Murphy, J. (2008). *The Power of Your Subconscious Mind*. New York, NY. Prentice Hall Press. Used with permission.

Chapter 15

1. Wattles, W.D. (1910). *The Science of Getting Rich*. Elizabeth Towne Publishing. New York, NY. The original work is now in public domain. For a reference work, please see *The complete Wallace D. Wattles, 9 books* (2016). Timeless Wisdom Collection.
2. Bloom where you are planted was popularised by author, artist and illustrator Mary Engelbreit.
3. Wattles, W.D. (1910). *The Science of Getting Rich*. Elizabeth Towne Publishing. New York, NY. The original work is now in public domain. For a reference work, please see *The Complete Wallace D. Wattles, 9 books* (2016). Timeless Wisdom Collection.
4. Daisaku Ikeda

Chapter 16

1. Wattles, W.D. (1910). *The Science of Getting Rich*. Elizabeth Towne Publishing. New York, NY. The original work is now in public domain. For a reference work, please see *The Complete Wallace D. Wattles, 9 books* (2016). Timeless Wisdom Collection.
2. Troward, T. (1909). *Edinburgh Lectures & Dore Lectures on Mental Science*. Scotts Valley, CA.
3. I Chronicles 1:1–12 NIV
4. Troward, T. (1904). *Edinburgh Lectures* and (1909) *Dore Lectures at the Dore Gallery London*. The original works are now in public domain. For a reference work, see *Edinburgh Lectures & Dore Lectures on Mental Science*. Scotts Valley, California.

Chapter 17

1. The Law of Relativity, The Law of Compensation, The Law of Action, The Law of Vibration, The Law of Correspondence.

2. Wattles, W.D. (1910). *The Science of Getting Rich*. Elizabeth Towne Publishing. New York, NY. The original work is now in public domain. For a reference work, please see *The Complete Wallace D. Wattles, 9 books* (2016). Timeless Wisdom Collection.

3. Watson, R. (2014, 13 February). 'Gratitude Sparks Oxytocin and Love'. *Psychology Today*. Retrieved from https://www.psychologytoday.com/gb/blog/love-and-gratitude/201402/gratitude-sparks-oxytocin-and-love-study-points-cd38

4. Burton, L.R. (n.d.). 'The Neuroscience of Gratitude'. Wharton Health Care Management Association. Retrieved from https://www.whartonhealthcare.org/the_neuroscience_of_gratitude W

5. Leviticus Chapters 6–7 NIV

6. Anapol, C. (2011, 25 November). 'What is Love, and What Isn't'. *Psychology Today*. Retrieved from https://www.psychologytoday.com/gb/blog/love-without-limits/201111/what-is-love-and-what-isnt

7. Concordia University (2012, 20 June). 'I Want to Know Where Love Is; First brain map of love and desire'. ScienceDaily. https://www.sciencedaily.com/releases/2012/06/120620101011.htm

8. Neuroscientifically Challenged (2015, 15 February). 'Know Your Brain; Striatum'. Neuroscientifically Challenged. https://neuroscientificallychallenged.com/blog/know-your-brain-striatum

9. Hebrews 11:16 NIV

10. Matthew 11:25 NIV, Luke 10:21 NIV

11. John 6:11 NIV

12. John 11:41 NIV

13. Luke 22:17; 19

14. Foundation for Inner Peace (1975). *A Course in Miracles*. (T-1.I.1:1–4). New York, NY. The Penguin Group. Used with permission.

15. Burton, N. (2016, 24 December). 'Why Gratitude is so Hard'. *Psychology Today*. Retrieved from https://www.psychologytoday.com/gb/blog/hide-and-seek/201612/why-gratitude-is-so-hard

16. Google Ngram: Gratitude

The Author

Daniel Wingate has been developing personal mastery programmes for more than twenty-five years. His work in both public and private organisations, large and small, has been focused on Organisational Development and Organisational Leadership, creating and evolving talent management intelligence through personal achievement. In addition to lectures, seminars and group programmes, Daniel has coached dozens of individuals in private practice. Today, his main role in this genre is as a speaker, presenter, coach and teacher of The Masterful Way.

He is a student of Nichiren Buddhism and its daily practice. He holds a bachelor's degree in Business and a master's degree in Education, and is pursuing his PhD. Daniel currently lives in the United Kingdom, balancing his time between London and his home in Cheshire. While in the United States, he makes his home in Los Angeles, California.

Website: TheMasterfulWay.com
Email: TheMasterfulWay@gmail.com

Soon to come:
The Masterful Way, Day-by-Day
The Masterful Way, Volume Two